Recent Developments in Applied Demand Analysis

Alcohol, Advertising and Global Consumption

Springer
Berlin
Heidelberg
New York
Barcelona
Budapest
Hong Kong
London
Milan
Paris
Tokyo

E. A. Selvanathan
Kenneth W. Clements

Recent Developments in Applied Demand Analysis

Alcohol, Advertising and Global Consumption

With 25 Figures

Springer

E. A. Selvanathan
School of International Business Relations
Griffith University
Nathan Queensland 4111
Australia

Kenneth W. Clements
Economic Research Centre
Department of Economics
University of Western Australia
Nedlands WA 6009
Australia

Library of Congress Cataloging-in-Publication Data

Selvanathan, E. Antony, 1954-
Recent developments in applied demand analysis : alcohol, advertising and global consumption / E. Antony Selvanathan, Kenneth W. Clements.
p. cm.
Includes bibliographical references and index.
ISBN-13:978-3-642-85207-7 (Springer-Verlag Berlin Heidelberg New York : acid-free paper)
1. Alcoholic beverage industry--Econometric models.
2. Advertising--Alcoholic beverages--Econometric models.
3. Consumption (Economics)--Econometric models. 4. Demand functions (Economic theory) I. Clements, Kenneth W., 1950- . II. Title.
HD9350.5.S45 1995
380.1'456631--dc20 95-30838
CIP

ISBN-13: 978-3-642-85207-7 e-ISBN-13: 978-3-642-85205-3
DOI: 10.1007/978-3-642-85205-3

Softcover reprint of the hardcover 1st edition 1995

SPIN 10134209 43/2202 - 5 4 3 2 1 0 – Printed on acid-free paper

Preface

The study of consumer demand is important for a number of reasons. First, as total consumption absorbs more than 70 percent of GDP in most countries, it is the largest of the macroeconomic aggregates, thus having great significance for the state of the economy as a whole and business conditions. Second, the pattern of consumption contains a wealth of useful information regarding economic welfare and living standards. Closely allied to this is that as consumption (both current and future) is the ultimate objective of all economic activity and economic systems (mercantilists notwithstanding), in a fundamental sense consumption patterns are an objective way of measuring and assessing economic performance. Finally, an understanding of the price-responsiveness of consumption is of crucial importance for a host of microeconomic policy issues including public-utility pricing, the measurement of distortions, optimal taxation and the treatment of externalities.

The analysis of consumer demand is one of the major successes of economics as it represents the near perfect marriage of theory and econometrics, a situation almost unparalleled in any other field of economics. This field has attracted a lot of attention since the introduction of the linear expenditure system and its application to British data by Stone (1954), followed by the differential demand system of Barten (1964) and Theil (1965, 1975/76, 1980) and developments thereafter.

This book presents a number of recent developments in demand analysis. These include new simple data-analytic techniques for analysing consumption data; new tests based on computer simulations for hypothesis testing; new methodological results on how to estimate demand equations; innovative applications to alcohol demand; extensions of the system-wide framework to analyse the effects of advertising on consumption; novel approaches to forecasting consumption patterns; and new theoretical results on aggregation of demand systems over consumers. All these innovations are extensively illustrated with the use of data from 18 OECD countries.

The empirical results presented in the book have a number of uses. Application of the above new developments give rise to *reliable* estimates of income and price elasticities of demand for 10 commodity groups in 18 countries, as well as for the alcoholic beverages beer, wine and spirits in the UK and Australia. A feature of these results is that a number of major empirical regularities are identified that seem to hold across different periods and different countries. Some of these empirical regularities include (i) a strong relationship between the income elasticity of food and income; (ii) the similarity of tastes internationally; (iii) beer is always a necessity and spirits a luxury; and (iv) those commodities which are more price elastic also tend to be more luxurious and vice versa. Given that these results seem to hold in a wide variety of circumstances, we can have more than the usual degree of confidence in them. It is not too much of an exaggeration to claim that our research has uncovered a group of "natural constants" regarding consumption patterns.

In many countries, it is argued that advertising of alcohol increases *total* consumption of alcoholic beverages. From the social and health points of view there is thus strong opposition to alcohol advertising. On the other hand, the alcohol industry argues that advertising affects only the choice of brand or beverage, and not total consumption. Accordingly, the industry tends to argue that advertising promotes healthy competition. The results presented in the book regarding the effects of advertising on alcohol consumption have immediate relevance to this important debate.

A Preview

This book emphasizes the unity between theory and applications. Thus we often employ the approach of presenting new analytic developments and then immediately showing their relevance through applications. While each chapter is well integrated with the others, they are also written in a way so as to be largely self-contained.

Chapter 1 lays out the analytical framework for consumer demand. It gives a self-contained exposition of known results and some more recent developments in the theory of consumer demand. This chapter covers demand systems based on specific utility functions (e.g., the linear expenditure system), demand systems based on indirect utility functions (e.g., the translog), those based on cost functions (e.g., the almost ideal demand system) and some others. It then introduces the differential approach to consumption theory, some members of the class of differential demand equations and some new simpler alternatives. This chapter also discusses separable utility functions and demand equations for groups of goods and for goods within a group.

Chapter 2 reviews, distills and systematises some of the major empirical findings on consumption patterns, concentrating in particular on the more recent evidence. This chapter analyses the consumption patterns in OECD countries by presenting a number of Divisia index measures. The chapter then evaluates recent evidence regarding the hypotheses of homogeneity, symmetry and preference independence. It also discusses the issue of constancy of tastes and aspects of functional form of demand equations.

Chapter 3 introduces several new simple data-analytic techniques for analysing consumption data. These techniques are useful to apply before estimating demand equations to obtain a general 'feel' for the data. They provide summary. measures of the data and, under certain assumptions, yield preliminary estimates of key demand parameters. The techniques are illustrated with data pertaining to the demand for beer, wine and spirits in the UK.

Chapter 4 shows how recent advances in the methodology of econometric simulation can be used to test homogeneity, symmetry and preference independence. Full technical details of these techniques are presented and, using a database for 18 OECD countries, this chapter probably presents one of the most extensive and intensive applications in the area of demand analysis. The results show that, in general, consumers satisfy the hypotheses of demand homogeneity, Slutsky symmetry and preference independence. This evidence overturns a large body of previous findings, much of which was based on flawed econometric methodology. This chapter also presents reliable income and price elasticities for 10 commodity groups in the 18 countries.

Demand analysis can be very demanding in terms of data, especially when the number of goods is large. Thus for moderate to large demand systems, samples are not infrequently undersized or nearly so. Chapter 5 investigates alternative ways of estimating demand systems with undersized samples. Using another cross-country database, the chapter analyses the performance of various specifications of the error covariance matrix as solutions to the undersized sample problem.

Chapter 6 presents an extensive analysis of recent consumption patterns of beer, wine and spirits for Australia. This chapter utilizes the data-analytic techniques presented in Chapter 3, the demand equations presented in Chapter 1 and the new econometric techniques introduced in Chapter 4. The analysis shows that beer and wine are necessities and spirits is a strong luxury; and beer and spirits are specific complements. The chapter also presents a comparative analysis of Australian alcohol consumption patterns with those in a number of other countries and investigates to what extent tastes (with respect to alcohol) are similar internationally.

Chapters 7 and 8 give a theoretical and empirical analysis of the effects of advertising on consumption. Chapter 7 obtains demand equations from the theory of the utility-maximising consumer which include advertising variables. This chapter also analyses the intriguing link between the effects of advertising on consumption and the conventional substitution effects. One result is that the products which are more price elastic (due to the availability of good substitutes) will be more sensitive to advertising, something that will be interesting to marketing analysts.

Chapter 8 examines the controversial issue of the influence of advertising on alcohol consumption. This chapter initially extends some of the data-analytic techniques introduced in Chapter 3 to present a preliminary analysis of UK data on advertising and alcohol. This chapter also presents advertising elasticities for beer, wine and spirits and tests the effects of advertising on the consumption of the three beverages individually and alcohol as a whole. Surprisingly, the results indicate that advertising does not increase total consumption -- it just reshuffles it among beer, wine and spirits. Thus, on the basis of this evidence, there is no support for the often-heard claim that alcohol advertising should be prohibited as it increases drinking.

Chapter 9 shows how the demand equations derived in Chapter 1 can be used for the purposes of forecasting market shares and consumption. This chapter also uses Efron's (1979) distribution-free bootstrap techniques to evaluate the quality of the forecasts. The results are illustrated with an application to UK data pertaining to beer, wine and spirits.

The Differential demand systems derived in Chapter 1 are *micro* in nature as they are based on the utility-maximising behaviour of a single consumer. Usually, since the data are available only in some aggregate form (e.g., per capita), it is common practice to use the aggregate form in the micro demand system for estimation. Critics argue that the theoretical properties of the micro system do not carry over to the macro system. Chapter 10, using the convergence approach to aggregation (Barnett, 1979a,1979b,1981; E.A. Selvanathan, 1991; and Theil, 1971,1975/76), establishes the strong result that will silence the critics: *The macro demand equations of the differential approach are completely analogous to the micro equations and all their theoretical properties carry over.* Due to its elegance and power, we believe that this approach to aggregation will receive more attention in the future.

The Uses of the Book

This book communicates in a unified fashion new results combining (i) methodological advances in economic theory and econometrics; and (ii) their empirical applications. Consequently, the book will be of interest to economists who require reliable estimates of income and price elasticities of demand for (a) broad commodity groups such as food, beverages, clothing, housing, durables, medical care, transport, recreation, education and miscellaneous goods in 18 OECD countries; and (b) three alcoholic beverages, beer, wine and spirits in Australia and the UK. Analysts (including marketing researchers) will be interested in our new approaches to measuring the effects of advertising on consumption and to forecasting market shares.

The recently-developed econometric techniques presented in the book and their applications using large databases will be a major attraction to econometricians. The material on simpler demand systems, advertising and aggregation over consumers will be most interesting to theorists as the results are new and sometimes intriguing. The book can also be used for teaching purposes in microeconomics, econometrics and marketing courses at the graduate and advanced undergraduate levels.

References

Barnett, W.A. (1979a). 'Theoretical Foundations for the Rotterdam Model,' *Review of Economic Studies* 46: 109-30.

Barnett, W.A. (1979b). 'The Joint Allocation of Leisure and Goods Expenditure,' *Econometrica* 47: 539-63.

Barnett, W.A. (1981). *Consumer Demand and Labour Supply.* Amsterdam: North-Holland Publishing Company.

Barten, A.P. (1964). 'Consumer Demand Functions Under Conditions of Almost Additive Preferences,' *Econometrica* 32: 1-38.

Efron, B. (1979). 'Bootstrap Methods: Another Look at the Jacknife,' *Annals of Statistics* 7: 1-26.

Selvanathan, E.A. (1991). 'Further Results on Aggregation of Differential Demand Equations,' *Review of Economic Studies* 58: 799-805.

Stone, R. (1954). 'Linear Expenditure Systems and Demand Analysis: An Application to the Pattern of British Demand,' *Economic Journal* 64: 511-27.

Theil, H. (1965). 'The Information Approach to Demand Analysis,' *Econometrica* 33: 67-87.

Theil, H. (1971). *Principles of Econometrics.* New York: John Wiley and Sons.

Theil, H. (1975/76). *Theory and Measurement of Consumer Demand.* 2 vols., Amsterdam: North Holland Publishing Company.

Theil, H. (1980). *The System-wide Approach to Microeconomics.* Chicago: The University of Chicago Press.

Table of Contents

Tables and Figures

List of Tables

List of Figures

Technical Notes

This book contains ten chapters. To aid the reader, each chapter has been written so that it is more or less self-contained.

Each chapter contains a number of sections, subsections, appendices (in some cases) and a list of references. The sections in each chapter are numbered at two levels. The first level refers to the chapter and the second to the order of occurrence of the section within the chapter. For example, Section 2.4 is the fourth section in Chapter 2. Subsections are unnumbered.

Equations are indicated by two numbers, the first refers to the section and the second to the order of occurrence within that section. For example, 'equation (9.3)' of Chapter 3 denotes the third equation in Section 9 of that chapter. This equation is referred to in Chapter 3 as 'equation (9.3)'. If this equation is referred to in another chapter, then we use the terminology 'equation (9.3) of Chapter 3'.

If there is more than one appendix to a chapter, then appendices are numbered at three levels. For example, 'Appendix A4.2' refers to the second appendix of Chapter 4. If there is more than one appendix to a chapter, then the equations of the appendices are numbered at three levels. For example, 'equation (A2.5)' refers to equation 5 of the second appendix of that chapter. If there is only one appendix to a chapter, it is unnumbered. The equations in a single appendix are numbered at two levels, so that equation (A3), for example, refers to the third equation of the appendix.

Tables and figures are indicated by two numbers, the first refers to the chapter and the second to the order of occurrence. For example,

'Table 4.5' refers to the fifth table of Chapter 4 and 'Figure 1.2' refers to the second figure of Chapter 1.

Matrices are indicated by a boldface uppercase symbol (e.g., **A**). Vectors are indicated by a boldface lowercase symbol (e.g., **a**). The notation $[a_{ij}]$ refers to a matrix whose (i,j)-*th* element is a_{ij}, while $[a_i]$ refers to a column vector whose i-*th* element is a_i. Thus, combining this notation, $\mathbf{A} = [a_{ij}]$ and $\mathbf{a} = [a_i]$.

Acknowledgements

The contributors of this book would like to thank R. Bewley, P. de Boer, K. Cole, D. Giles, R. Harkema, D. Johnson, D. MacLaren, R. Ray and D. Treloar for their comments in the writing of various chapters of this book. Clements would also like to thank D. Chenhall and J. Smith for their assistance.

We would also like to thank Dr. Peter Schuster, the Economics Editor of Springer Verlag, for his encouragement and support in completing this project.

1 The Economic Theory of the Consumer

K.W. Clements[1], S. Selvanathan[2] and E.A. Selvanathan[3]

[1] *Economic Research Centre, The University of Western Australia.*
[2] *Faculty of Commerce and Administration, Griffith University, Australia.*
[3] *School of International Business Relations, Griffith University, Australia.*

1.1 Introduction

The demand function for a single commodity explains how changes in income and the prices of all goods affect the quantity consumed of that commodity. The objective of consumption theory is to derive testable hypotheses about the demand functions. These hypotheses take the form of theoretical restrictions on the demand functions, for example, demand homogeneity, Slutsky symmetry, etc. These restrictions come from the utility-maximizing theory of consumer behaviour. Consequently, the objective of this chapter is to set out the theory of the utility-maximizing consumer and the derivation of the demand equations. There are a number of ways of deriving demand equations, including (i) the direct specification of the functional form of the demand equations; (ii) the specification of the direct utility function; (iii) the specification of the indirect utility function; (iv) the specification of the cost function; and (v) the application of the differential approach.

This chapter is structured as follows: Section 1.2 introduces a popular example of directly specified demand equations, the double-log demand system. In Section 1.3 we consider the utility approach to derive the general form of demand equations. Sections 1.4–1.13 deal mainly with two utility–based ways of generating demand equations. The first, discussed in Sections 1.4–1.8, is based on the algebraic specification of some function as an *initial* step, be it the utility function, the indirect utility function or the cost function. The second way of generating demand equations is the differential approach, discussed in

Sections 1.9–1.13. This approach requires no initial algebraic specification of any function. As a result, the demand equations of this approach are completely general, having coefficients which are not necessarily constant. Of course, the estimation of these equations requires some parameterization, but this only comes as the *last* step. Section 1.14 presents a number of examples of the differential demand system. The flexibility of the differential approach is illustrated in Sections 1.15-1.18 which contain four different parameterizations of differential demand equations.

The next two sections (Sections 1.19-1.20) of the chapter present some further income elasticities and clarify some concepts introduced earlier. Sections 1.21-1.25 deals with applications of the differential approach to the demand for groups of goods and to goods within a group.

Major book-length works on the theory and measurement of consumer demand include Barnett (1981), Bewley (1986), Deaton (1975), Deaton and Muellbauer (1980a), Goldberger (1987), Lluch, Powell and Williams (1977), Phlips (1974), Pollak and Wales (1992), Powell (1974), Theil (1975/76), Theil, Chung and Seale (1989), Theil and Clements (1987) and Theil and Suhm (1981). Survey articles of this area are provided by Barten (1977), Blundell (1988), Brown and Deaton (1972) and Deaton (1986).

This chapter draws on Clements(1987a,1987b) and Selvanathan (1987).

1.2 Demand Analysis Without Utility Theory

The major approach to demand analysis emphasized in this book is utility–based, or some variant thereof. This approach, to be explained in detail in later sections of this chapter, derives demand equations by postulating that the consumer behaves as if he chooses the consumption basket to maximize a utility function subject to a budget constraint. This approach gives rise to elegant and intuitive interpretations of the coefficients of the demand equations in terms of the utility function.

This, however, is not the only way of proceeding in demand analysis. There is an older tradition which uses demand equations directly, without any reference to the utility function; according to this approach, the demand equations are directly specified. In this pragmatic approach, the demand for the good is specified as a simple function of income and prices. This procedure, which goes back to Cassel (1932), has been used extensively by Stone (1954a) and others.

A popular example of directly specified demand equations is the *double-log system*,

$$\log q_i = \alpha_i + \eta_i \log M + \sum_{j=1}^{n} \eta_{ij} \log p_j, \qquad i=1,\ldots,n, \tag{2.1}$$

where q_i is the quantity demanded of good i (i=1,...,n); p_j is the price of good j;

$$M = \sum_{i=1}^{n} p_i q_i \tag{2.2}$$

is total expenditure, which we shall refer to as *income* for short; and α_i, η_i and η_{ij} are constant coefficients. (All logarithms in this book are natural logarithms.)

The interpretation of (2.1) is straightforward. The coefficient of income is

$$\eta_i = \frac{\partial(\log q_i)}{\partial(\log M)}. \tag{2.3}$$

This is known as the *income elasticity* of demand for good i and answers the question, if income rises by 1 percent with prices constant, what is the percentage change in consumption of i? Commodities with income elasticities less than unity are called *necessities*, while those with income elasticities greater than unity are known as *luxuries*. If the income elasticity is negative, then the good is said to be *inferior* as its consumption falls with increasing income. Similarly, the coefficient η_{ij} is the percentage change in q_i resulting from a 1 percent change in p_j, income and the other prices remaining constant; η_{ij} is known as the elasticity of demand for i with respect to the price of j.

We define

$$w_i = \frac{p_i q_i}{M} \tag{2.4}$$

as the proportion of income devoted to good i, to be referred to as the *budget share* of this good. The budget shares are positive and, in view of (2.2), have a unit sum. Multiplication of the budget share by the corresponding income elasticity yields

$$w_i \eta_i = \frac{p_i q_i}{M} \frac{\partial(\log q_i)}{\partial(\log M)} = \frac{p_i q_i}{M} \frac{\partial q_i / q_i}{\partial M / M} = \frac{\partial(p_i q_i)}{\partial M} \tag{2.5}$$

where the last step follows from the fact the p_i is held constant. The term on the far right of (2.5) answers the question, if income rises by one dollar how much of this is spent on commodity i? We write this as

$$\theta_i = \frac{\partial(p_i q_i)}{\partial M} \tag{2.6}$$

which shall be referred to as the i-*th marginal share*. As the additional income is entirely spent, the marginal shares have a unit sum; this can be verified by differentiating both sides of (2.2) with respect to income. In contrast to the budget shares, the marginal shares are not always positive; θ_i is negative if i is inferior.

Combining (2.5) and (2.6) shows that the income elasticity can also be expressed as the ratio of the marginal share to the corresponding budget share,

$$\eta_i = \frac{\theta_i}{w_i}. \tag{2.7}$$

As the marginal shares have a unit sum, it follows from (2.7) that a budget–share–weighted average of the income elasticities is equal to unity,

$$\sum_{i=1}^{n} w_i \eta_i = \sum_{i=1}^{n} \theta_i = 1. \tag{2.8}$$

In a household expenditure survey all participating families pay approximately the same price for each good, so that the i-*th* equation of (2.1) reduces to

$$\log q_i = \alpha_i + \eta_i \log M, \tag{2.9}$$

where units are chosen such that the price of each good is unity, so that $\Sigma_j \eta_{ij} \log p_j = 0$.

Although the double–log system is attractive in its simplicity, it does have a serious drawback. As prices are constant, it follows from (2.9) that the logarithmic change in expenditure on good i is a constant multiple η_i of the change in income,

$$d(\log p_i q_i) = \eta_i \, d(\log M).$$

Accordingly, if the income elasticity η_i exceeds unity, then expenditure on i increases at a faster rate than does income. If income rises sufficiently, expenditure on i will eventually exceed income, which violates the adding–up constraint (2.2). Therefore, the weakness of the model is that it does not satisfy the adding–up constraint for all values of income.

Several kinds of price elasticities will be encountered in this book and η_{ij} in (2.1) is one such elasticity. As this equation has money income M on the right–hand side, the income effect of the change in the j-*th* price is included in η_{ij}. This η_{ij} is called the *Cournot price elasticity.*

1.3 The Consumer's Maximization Problem

Perhaps the most straight-forward way of generating demand equations is to derive them by maximizing the utility function subject to the consumer's budget constraint. The utility function takes the form

$$u = u(q_1,...,q_n), \tag{3.1}$$

where, as before, q_i is the quantity consumed of good i. We assume that this function is differentiable and that there is nonsatiation, so that each marginal utility is positive,

$$\frac{\partial u}{\partial q_i} > 0, \qquad i=1,...,n. \tag{3.2}$$

We further assume that there is generalized diminishing marginal utility, so that the Hessian matrix of the utility function is negative definite. As Hessians are symmetric, we have

$$U = \left[\frac{\partial^2 u}{\partial q_i \partial q_j}\right] \tag{3.3}$$

is a symmetric negative definite $n \times n$ matrix.

Writing p_i for the price of good i, the budget constraint is that expenditure on the n goods $p_1q_1 + ... + p_nq_n$ must equal a fixed total M,

$$\sum_{i=1}^{n} p_iq_i = M. \tag{3.4}$$

We shall continue to refer to M as income. Equation (3.4) is identical to (2.2) which we previously referred to as the adding-up constraint.

To maximize (3.1) subject to (3.4) we form the Lagrangian expression

$$u(q_1,...,q_n) - \lambda\left[\sum_{i=1}^{n} p_i q_i - M\right], \tag{3.5}$$

where λ is a Lagrangian multiplier. The first-order conditions for a maximum of (3.5) are (3.4) and

$$\frac{\partial u}{\partial q_i} = \lambda p_i, \qquad i=1,...,n, \tag{3.6}$$

which states that each marginal utility is proportional to the corresponding price. As the prices are positive, it follows from (3.2) and (3.6) that $\lambda > 0$. By dividing both sides of (3.6) by p_i, we obtain $(\partial u/\partial q_i)/p_i = \lambda$, or $\partial u/\partial(p_i q_i) = \lambda$. This shows that a one-dollar increase in income causes utility to rise by λ when this increase is spent on any of the n goods. Accordingly, λ is known as the *marginal utility of income*. The second-order conditions for a maximum are satisfied by (3.3).

The first-order conditions (3.4) and (3.6) constitute (n + 1) equations which can in principle be solved for the (n + 1) unknowns $q_1,...,q_n$ and λ; we assume that the resulting quantities are unique and positive for relevant values of prices and income. The optimal quantities depend on income and the prices, so that we can write

$$q_i = q_i(M, p_1,...,p_n), \qquad i=1,...,n. \tag{3.7}$$

These are the *demand functions*.

Once the utility function is introduced, demand analysis becomes much richer in its implications and applications. The utility framework is the foundation for index number theory, which includes the measurement of real income; the measurement of the effects of distortions such as commodity taxation; and the division of goods into groups which are closely related. In addition, the utility function generates the three major predictions of demand analysis, (i) that the demand equations are homogeneous of degree zero in income and prices; (ii) symmetry of the substitution effects; and (iii) that the substitution matrix is negative semidefinite. These topics are discussed at length in this book.

1.4 Specified Forms of the Utility Function

In this section we shall give various examples of specified forms of the utility function. By this we mean a utility function which takes an algebraically specified form.

A general form of the additive utility function, proposed by Johansen (1969), is

$$u(\mathbf{q}) = \sum_{i=1}^{n} \frac{\beta_i}{\alpha_i} \left[\left(\frac{q_i - \gamma_i}{\beta_i} \right)^{\alpha_i} - 1 \right], \tag{4.1}$$

where $\mathbf{q} = [q_i]$ is the consumption vector; $\alpha_i < 1$; $\beta_i > 0$; and $\gamma_i < q_i$ are constants. Equation (4.1) implies that the marginal utility of good i does not depend on consumption of goods other than the i-*th*,

$$\frac{\partial u}{\partial q_i} = \left[\frac{q_i - \gamma_i}{\beta_i} \right]^{\alpha_i - 1}, \qquad i=1,\dots,n.$$

As the Hessian matrix of the utility function implied by (4.1) is diagonal, (4.1) is said to be of the *preference independent form.*

Substituting the right-hand side of the above equation for $\partial u/\partial q_i$ in (3.6), we obtain the first-order conditions associated with the utility function (4.1),

$$q_i = \gamma_i + \beta_i [\lambda p_i]^{1/(\alpha_i - 1)}, \qquad i=1,\dots,n. \tag{4.2}$$

We shall now consider special cases of (4.1), (4.2) and the implied demand equations.

The Stone-Geary Utility Function

We now consider the special case of (4.1) when $\alpha_i = 0$, i=1,...,n, and $\Sigma_{i=1}^n \beta_i = 1$. Thus when a_i tends to zero, using L'Hospital's rule, we can write utility function (4.1) as

$$u(\mathbf{q}) = \sum_{i=1}^{n} \beta_i \log (q_i - \gamma_i). \tag{4.3}$$

The utility function (4.3) is the well-known *Stone-Geary utility function.* This utility function has also been previously considered by Klein and Rubin (1948).

By substituting $\alpha_i = 0$ in (4.2) and using the budget constraint (3.4) to eliminate λ, we obtain

$$p_i q_i = p_i \gamma_i + \beta_i \left[M - \sum_{j=1}^{n} p_j \gamma_j \right], \qquad i=1,...,n. \tag{4.4}$$

This is the algebraic form of the demand equations (4.3) associated with the Stone-Geary utility function.

As expenditure on good i is a linear function of the n prices and income, (4.4) is known as the *linear expenditure system.* If the γ_i's are all positive, then (4.4) has the following interpretation. The consumer first purchases γ_i units of good i at a cost of $p_i\gamma_i$; this can be termed *subsistence consumption* of that commodity. The total cost of subsistence is $\Sigma_j p_j\gamma_j$, which leaves $M - \Sigma_j p_j\gamma_j$ as *supernumerary income.* A fixed fraction β_i of supernumerary income is then spent on good i. The linear expenditure system was first applied to data by Stone (1954b); for other applications, see, e.g., Deaton (1975) and Lluch and Powell (1975).

It follows from (4.4) that the marginal share θ_i [defined by (2.6)] implied by the linear expenditure system is equal to the constant coefficient β_i. Consequently, the income elasticity of i takes the form

$$\eta_i = \frac{\beta_i}{w_i}. \tag{4.5}$$

A rise in income with prices held constant causes the budget shares of necessities to fall and those of luxuries to rise. It then follows from (4.5) that increasing affluence causes the income elasticities of necessities to rise, while those of luxuries fall; the elasticities of both types of goods become closer to unity. Take the case of food, a necessity. The linear expenditure system implies that as the consumer becomes richer, the η_i for food increases causing food to become less of a necessity or more of a luxury. This behavior of the elasticity is implausible as food should be less of a luxury for a richer consumer.

Recall that the coefficient β_i in the Klein-Rubin must be positive. As this coefficient is interpreted as the marginal share in (4.4), it follows that the linear expenditure system does not admit inferior goods. If we differentiate (4.4) with respect to p_j and multiply both sides by p_j/q_i, we get the uncompensated price elasticities,

$$\eta_{ij} = \frac{(\gamma_i - q_i)}{q_i}\delta_{ij} - \frac{\beta_i\gamma_j p_j}{p_i q_i}, \qquad i,j=1,\ldots,n,$$

where δ_{ij} is the Kronecker delta. Therefore the own-price elasticity of commodity i is

$$\eta_{ii} = -1 + (1 - \beta_i)\frac{\gamma_i}{q_i}. \tag{4.6}$$

Since $\beta_i > 0$ and $\Sigma_{i=1}^{n} \beta_i = 1$, we have $0 < \beta_i < 1$. This together with $0 \leq \gamma_i < q_i$, implies that all own-price elasticities are in the range -1 and 0. Consequently, under the LES all commodities are price-inelastic.

The uncompensated cross-price elasticities are

$$\eta_{ij} = -\frac{\beta_i\gamma_j p_j}{p_i q_i}, \qquad i\neq j. \tag{4.7}$$

If $\gamma_j > 0$, then, as $\beta_i > 0$, all cross-price elasticities are negative, which means that under LES all pairs of commodities are gross complements.

The Constant Elasticity of Substitution Demand System

Substituting $\alpha_i = \alpha$ and $\gamma_i = 0$ in (4.2) and using the budget constraint to eliminate λ, we obtain the *constant elasticity of substitution demand system*

$$q_i = \beta_i \left[\frac{p_i}{P}\right]^{1/(\alpha-1)} \frac{M}{P}, \qquad i=1,...,n, \tag{4.8}$$

where $P^{\alpha/(\alpha-1)} = \Sigma_{k=1}^{n} \beta_k p_k^{\alpha/(\alpha-1)}$. The demand system given by (4.8) is a special case of *direct addilog system* of Houthakker (1960). From equation (4.8) we see that the marginal share is $\theta_i = \beta_i[p_i/P]^{\alpha/(\alpha-1)}$ and the budget share $w_i = \beta_i[p_i/P]^{\alpha/(\alpha-1)}$, which implies that the demand system given by (4.8) results in a unitary income elasticity for each commodity.

The Cobb-Douglas Demand System

Substituting $\alpha_i = 0$ and $\gamma_i = 0$ in (4.2) and using the budget constraint to eliminate λ, we obtain

$$q_i = \left[\frac{\beta_i}{p_i}\right] M, \qquad i=1,...,n. \tag{4.9}$$

Equation (4.9) is known as the *Cobb-Douglas demand system* in which the budget share and the marginal share are both constants and equal to β_i. Under this system, the demand for commodity i does not depend on the prices of other commodities.

If we take the logarithm both sides of equation (4.9) we get

$$\log q_i = \log \beta_i + \log M - \log p_i. \tag{4.10}$$

Equation (4.10) can be considered as a special case of (2.1) with $\alpha_i = \log \beta_i$, $\eta_i = 1$, $\eta_{ii} = -1$ and $\eta_{ij} = 0$, $i \neq j$. This means that under the Cobb-Douglas demand system, the income elasticity is always unity, own-price elasticity is -1 and all cross-price elasticities are zero, so that a commodity cannot be a gross substitute or gross complement with any other commodity.

In Section 1.14 we shall come back to the above demand systems.

1.5 Preference Independence

When the consumer's tastes can be described by a utility function which is the sum of n sub-utility functions, one for each good, the utility function (3.1) takes the form

$$u = \sum_{i=1}^{n} u_i(q_i), \tag{5.1}$$

and the marginal utility of good i is independent of the consumption of j, i≠j. Accordingly, (5.1) is known as *preference independence*. If the commodities are fairly broad groups, such as food, housing, clothing and so on, then (5.1) could be a reasonable working hypothesis as it conveys the idea that total utility is obtained from the utility derived from food *and* utility from housing *and* utility from clothing *and* so on. These broad commodity groups can be interpreted as representing the *basic wants* of the consumer which could be expected to exhibit little interaction in the utility function. The Johansen (1969) utility function (4.1) is a special case of (5.1), with

$$u_i(q_i) = \left(\frac{\beta_i}{\alpha_i}\right)\left[\left(\frac{q_i - \gamma_i}{\beta_i}\right)^{\alpha_i} - 1\right].$$

Weaker versions of preference independence will be analyzed in later sections of this chapter.

As will be described in detail in Section 1.12 below, the number of unknown coefficients in a general system of demand equations is of the order of n^2, where n is the number of commodities. This number of coefficients can only be estimated precisely with data when n is very small; even for moderate-sized systems (n in the vicinity of 6), it is impossible to estimate such a large number of coefficients from the data as they usually are observed. The hypothesis of preference independence comes to the rescue as it serves to simplify the form of the demand equations by greatly reducing the number of unknown coefficients to be estimated. Accordingly, there are two distinct justifications of preference independence: (i) The economic justification, in terms of preference independence being plausible when applied to broad aggregates; and (ii) the statistical justification when n is not small. (A formal account of the implications for the demand equations of preference independence is given in Section 1.13 below.)

In the previous section we noted the incompatibility of the Klein-Rubin with inferior goods. The incompatibility applies to the general case of preference independence: All demand systems derived from a preference independent utility function rule out inferior goods. See Section 1.13 for details.

1.6 Specifying the Form of the Indirect Utility Function

Let $\mathbf{p} = [p_i]$ and $\mathbf{q} = [q_i]$ be vectors of the n prices and quantities and let $\mathbf{q} = \mathbf{q}(M,\mathbf{p})$ be the system of n demand equations (3.7). If we substitute the demand equations into the utility function (3.1), utility becomes a function of income and prices,

$$u = u[\mathbf{q}(M,\mathbf{p})] = u_I(M,\mathbf{p}). \tag{6.1}$$

The function $u_I(\ )$ is called the *indirect utility function*; it gives the maximum utility attainable corresponding to given values of income and prices. For example, it can be readily verified that the indirect utility function associated with the Klein-Rubin (direct) utility function (4.3) is

$$u_I(M,p) = k + \log\left[M - \sum_{i=1}^{n} p_i\gamma_i\right] - \sum_{i=1}^{n} \beta_i \log p_i, \tag{6.2}$$

where $k = \Sigma_i\ \beta_i \log \beta_i$, which is a constant.

It can be shown (see, e.g., Theil, 1980, App B) that (6.1) has the following derivatives

$$\frac{\partial u_I}{\partial M} = \lambda, \qquad \frac{\partial u}{\partial p_i} = -\lambda q_i, \qquad i=1,\ldots,n, \tag{6.3}$$

where λ is the marginal utility of income. Taking the negative of the ratio of the price derivative to the income derivative, we obtain from (6.3)

$$q_i = -\frac{\partial u_I / \partial p_i}{\partial u_I / \partial M}, \qquad i=1,\ldots,n, \tag{6.4}$$

which is known as *Roy's* (1942) *theorem.*

Roy's theorem gives a second way of generating a system of demand equations, viz. specify an algebraic form of the indirect utility function and then apply (6.4). Christensen, Jorgenson and Lau (1975) used this approach and introduced the *translog indirect utility function,*

$$u_I(M,p) = \sum_{i=1}^{n} \beta_i \log \frac{p_i}{M} + \frac{1}{2}\sum_{i=1}^{n}\sum_{j=1}^{n} \beta_{ij} \log \frac{p_i}{M} \log \frac{p_j}{M}, \tag{6.5}$$

where the β_i's and β_{ij}'s are constants. Application of (6.4) to (6.5) yields a result which can be expressed in terms of budget shares,

$$w_i = \frac{\beta_i + \sum_{j=1}^{n} \beta_{ij} \log \frac{p_j}{M}}{\sum_{k=1}^{n} \beta_k + \sum_{k=1}^{n}\sum_{j=1}^{n} \beta_{kj} \log \frac{p_j}{M}}, \qquad i=1,\ldots,n. \tag{6.6}$$

1.7 Specifying the Form of the Cost Function

The consumer's *cost function* is dual to the (direct) utility function in that it gives the minimum expenditure needed to reach a specified level of utility, given the prices. The cost function is also referred to as the expenditure function. We write the cost function as $C(u,\mathbf{p})$, which can be derived by substituting $C(\ )$ for M in the indirect utility function. Doing this for the indirect utility function (6.2), we obtain

$$C(u,\mathbf{p}) = \sum_{i=1}^{n} p_i\gamma_i + e^{u-k} \prod_{i=1}^{n} p_i^{\beta_i}. \tag{7.1}$$

This cost function consists of two parts, the first being the cost of subsistence $\Sigma_i\, p_i\gamma_i$ which is independent of utility. The second part increases with utility and involves a weighted geometric mean of the prices, the weights being the marginal shares β_i .

Cost functions have the property that

$$\frac{\partial C}{\partial p_i} = q_i, \qquad i=1,\dots,n, \tag{7.2}$$

which is referred to as *Shephard's lemma.* Accordingly, a third approach to deriving demand equations is to specify the form of the cost function and then apply (7.2). As an example, Deaton and Muellbauer (1980a,b) suggested

$$C(u,\mathbf{p}) = e^{a(\mathbf{p})+ub(\mathbf{p})}, \tag{7.3}$$

where

$$a(\mathbf{p}) = \sum_{i=1}^{n} \alpha_i \log p_i + \frac{1}{2}\sum_{i=1}^{n}\sum_{j=1}^{n} \gamma_{ij} \log p_i \log p_j, \tag{7.4}$$

$$b(\mathbf{p}) = \beta_0 \prod_{i=1}^{n} p_i^{\beta_i}, \tag{7.5}$$

with the α_i's, γ_{ij}'s and β_i's all constants. Deaton and Muellbauer apply (7.2) to this cost function, which gives a demand system in terms of utility and prices. They then use the indirect utility function to express utility in terms of income and prices, which yields a demand system in terms of income and prices of the form

$$w_i = \alpha_i + \beta_i \log \frac{M}{P} + \sum_{j=1}^{n} \gamma_{ij} \log p_j, \qquad i=1,\ldots,n, \tag{7.6}$$

where

$$\log P = \sum_{i=1}^{n} \alpha_i \log p_i + \frac{1}{2} \sum_{i=1}^{n} \sum_{j=1}^{n} \gamma_{ij} \log p_i \log p_j. \tag{7.7}$$

Deaton and Muellbauer refer to (7.6) as the *almost ideal demand system*, or AIDS for short.

1.8 Working's Model

If prices are constant, as is approximately the case for a household expenditure survey, and if we choose units such that the price of each good is unity, then the AIDS model (7.6) simplifies to

$$w_i = \alpha_i + \beta_i \log M, \qquad i=1,\ldots,n, \tag{8.1}$$

In words, the budget shares are linear functions of the logarithm of income, which was first proposed by Working (1943) to analyse household budget data. As the sum of the budget shares is unity, it follows from (8.1) that $\Sigma_i \alpha_i = 1$ and $\Sigma_i \beta_i = 0$. Choosing the income unit such that $M = 1$ for some household, α_i is then interpreted as the budget share of i for that household. The coefficient β_i gives us 100 times the change in the budget share of i ($\Delta w_i \times 100$) resulting from a 1 percent increase in income.

To derive the marginal shares implied by Working's model we multiply (8.1) by M, which gives $p_i q_i = \alpha_i M + \beta_i M \log M$, and then differentiate with respect to M,

$$\frac{\partial(p_i q_i)}{\partial M} = \alpha_i + \beta_i(1 + \log M)$$

A comparison with (2.6) and (8.1) shows that this can be written as

$$\theta_i = w_i + \beta_i. \tag{8.2}$$

Thus under Working's model the i-*th* marginal share exceeds the corresponding budget share by β_i; as the budget share is not constant with respect to income, neither is this marginal share.

Taking the ratio of the marginal share (8.2) to the corresponding budget share, we obtain for the income elasticity,

$$\eta_i = 1 + \frac{\beta_i}{w_i}. \tag{8.3}$$

This shows that a good with positive (negative) β_i is a luxury (necessity). As the budget share of a luxury increases with income, prices remaining constant, it follows from (8.3) that increasing income causes the η_i of such a good to fall toward 1. The income elasticity of a necessity also declines with increasing income under (8.3). Thus as the consumer becomes more affluent, all goods become less luxurious under Working's model, which is plausible. By contrast, under the linear expenditure system the income elasticities of necessities *increase*, which is implausible, as discussed previously.

1.9 Divisia Indexes

This and the next four sections are concerned with setting out Theil's (1980) differential approach to consumption theory; the exposition in these five sections is based mainly on Theil (1975/76, 1980). We start by introducing the Divisia (1925) indexes which are used in this approach.

The differential of the budget constraint (3.4) is

$$\sum_{i=1}^{n} p_i dq_i + \sum_{i=1}^{n} q_i dp_i = dM$$

Dividing both sides of this by M, using the identity dx/x = d(log x) and $w_i = p_i q_i / M$ we obtain

$$d(\log Q) + d(\log P) = d(\log M), \tag{9.1}$$

where

$$d(\log Q) = \sum_{i=1}^{n} w_i d(\log q_i) \tag{9.2}$$

is the *Divisia volume index*; and

$$d(\log P) = \sum_{i=1}^{n} w_i d(\log p_i) \tag{9.3}$$

is the *Divisia price index*.

Equation (9.1) decomposes the change in income into a volume and price index. The volume index defined in (9.2) is a weighted average of the n logarithmic quantity changes $d(\log q_1)$, ..., $d(\log q_n)$, the weights being the budget shares. Similarly, the price index (9.3) is a weighted average of the price changes.

The Divisia price index d(log P) is defined in (9.3) as a budget-share-weighted-average of the n logarithmic price changes

$d(\log p_1),...,d(\log p_n)$. This can be viewed as a weighted first-order moment of the price changes. The corresponding second-order moment is the *Divisia price variance*

$$\Pi = \sum_{i=1}^{n} w_i \left[d(\log p_i) - d(\log P)\right]^2 = \sum_{i=1}^{n} w_i \left[d\left[\log \frac{p_i}{P}\right]\right]^2. \tag{9.4}$$

This Π vanishes when all prices change proportionately and it increases when the prices change more disproportionately. In other words, Π is a measure of the changes in relative prices.

Similarly, the Divisia volume index $d(\log Q)$, defined in (9.2), is the Divisia (i.e. budget-share-weighted) mean of the quantity changes. There is also the *Divisia quantity variance*

$$K = \sum_{i=1}^{n} w_i \left[d(\log q_i) - d(\log Q)\right]^2 = \sum_{i=1}^{n} w_i \left[d\left[\log \frac{q_i}{Q}\right]\right]^2, \tag{9.5}$$

the *Divisia price-quantity covariance*

$$\Gamma = \sum_{i=1}^{n} w_i d\left[\log \frac{p_i}{P}\right] d\left[\log \frac{q_i}{Q}\right], \tag{9.6}$$

and the corresponding price-quantity correlation is

$$\rho = \frac{\Gamma}{\sqrt{\Pi K}}.$$

This correlation measures the co-movement of prices and quantities. As those commodities having above-average price increases would tend to experience below-average increases in consumption and vice versa, Γ will usually be negative. However, as Γ includes a real-income component, in certain cases it may be positive. See Theil (1975/76, Chapter 11).

1.10 Barten's Fundamental Matrix Equation

In this section and the next we apply the method of comparative statics to obtain information about the demand equations (3.7) in the form of partial derivatives. This involves the use of the first-order conditions (3.4) and (3.6) to ask, how do the values of the endogenous variables $q_1, \ldots, q_n, \lambda$ respond to changes in the exogenous variables $p_1, \ldots, p_n$, M? We proceed in three steps.

We *first* differentiate the budget constraint (3.4) with respect to p_j and M to yield

$$\sum_{i=1}^{n} p_i \frac{\partial q_i}{\partial p_j} = -q_j, \qquad j=1,\ldots,n, \qquad \sum_{i=1}^{n} p_i \frac{\partial q_i}{\partial M} = 1.$$

These can be expressed in matrix form as

$$\mathbf{p}' \frac{\partial \mathbf{q}}{\partial \mathbf{p}'} = -\mathbf{q}' \qquad \mathbf{p}' \frac{\partial \mathbf{q}}{\partial M} = 1, \tag{10.1}$$

where $\partial \mathbf{q}/\partial \mathbf{p}' = [\partial q_i/\partial p_j]$ is the $n \times n$ matrix of price derivatives of the demand functions; and $\partial \mathbf{q}/\partial M = [\partial q_i/\partial M]$ is the vector of n income slopes of the demand functions.

Second, we differentiate the proportionality conditions (3.6) with respect to p_j and M to give

$$\sum_{k=1}^{n} \frac{\partial^2 u}{\partial q_i \partial q_k} \frac{\partial q_k}{\partial p_j} = \lambda \delta_{ij} + p_i \frac{\partial \lambda}{\partial p_j}, \qquad i,j=1,\ldots,n,$$

where δ_{ij} is the Kronecker delta (= 1 if i=j, 0 otherwise), and

$$\sum_{k=1}^{n} \frac{\partial^2 u}{\partial q_i \partial q_k} \frac{\partial q_k}{\partial M} = p_i \frac{\partial \lambda}{\partial M}, \qquad i=1,\ldots,n.$$

We write these in matrix form as

$$\mathbf{U}\frac{\partial \mathbf{q}}{\partial \mathbf{p}'} = \lambda \mathbf{I} + \mathbf{p}\frac{\partial \lambda}{\partial \mathbf{p}'} \qquad \mathbf{U}\frac{\partial \mathbf{q}}{\partial M} = \frac{\partial \lambda}{\partial M}\mathbf{p}, \tag{10.2}$$

where **U** is the Hessian matrix (3.3); I is the n × n identity matrix; and $\partial\lambda/\partial\mathbf{p}' = [\partial\lambda/\partial p_i]$.

Third, we combine (10.1) and (10.2) to give

$$\begin{bmatrix} \mathbf{U} & \mathbf{p} \\ \mathbf{p}' & 0 \end{bmatrix} \begin{bmatrix} \partial \mathbf{q}/\partial M & \partial \mathbf{q}/\partial \mathbf{p}' \\ -\partial\lambda/\partial M & -\partial\lambda/\partial \mathbf{p}' \end{bmatrix} = \begin{bmatrix} \mathbf{0} & \lambda \mathbf{I} \\ 1 & -\mathbf{q}' \end{bmatrix}. \tag{10.3}$$

This is known as *Barten's fundamental matrix equation in consumption theory*, after Barten (1964). The matrix immediately to the left of the equal sign contains the derivatives of all the endogenous variables with respect to all exogenous variables. Our next objective is to solve (10.3) for this matrix.

1.11 Solving the Matrix Equation

The inverse of the matrix on the far left of (10.3) is

$$\begin{bmatrix} \mathbf{U} & \mathbf{p} \\ \mathbf{p}' & 0 \end{bmatrix}^{-1} = \frac{1}{\mathbf{p}'\mathbf{U}^{-1}\mathbf{p}} \begin{bmatrix} (\mathbf{p}'\mathbf{U}^{-1}\mathbf{p})\mathbf{U}^{-1} - \mathbf{U}^{-1}\mathbf{p}(\mathbf{U}^{-1}\mathbf{p})' & \mathbf{U}^{-1}\mathbf{p} \\ (\mathbf{U}^{-1}\mathbf{p})' & -1 \end{bmatrix}.$$

Using this inverse the solution of (10.3) is

$$\begin{bmatrix} \partial \mathbf{q}/\partial M & \partial \mathbf{q}/\partial \mathbf{p}' \\ -\partial\lambda/\partial M & -\partial\lambda/\partial \mathbf{p}' \end{bmatrix}$$

$$= \frac{1}{\mathbf{p}'\mathbf{U}^{-1}\mathbf{p}} \begin{bmatrix} (\mathbf{p}'\mathbf{U}^{-1}\mathbf{p})\mathbf{U}^{-1} - \mathbf{U}^{-1}\mathbf{p}(\mathbf{U}^{-1}\mathbf{p})' & \mathbf{U}^{-1}\mathbf{p} \\ (\mathbf{U}^{-1}\mathbf{p})' & -1 \end{bmatrix} \begin{bmatrix} 0 & \lambda \mathbf{I} \\ 1 & -\mathbf{q}' \end{bmatrix}.$$

Carrying out the matrix multiplication block by block, we obtain

$$\frac{\partial \mathbf{q}}{\partial M} = \frac{1}{\mathbf{p}'\mathbf{U}^{-1}\mathbf{p}} \mathbf{U}^{-1}\mathbf{p} \tag{11.1}$$

$$\frac{\partial \mathbf{q}}{\partial \mathbf{p}'} = \lambda \mathbf{U}^{-1} - \frac{\lambda}{\mathbf{p}'\mathbf{U}^{-1}\mathbf{p}} \mathbf{U}^{-1}\mathbf{p}(\mathbf{U}^{-1}\mathbf{p}') - \frac{1}{\mathbf{p}'\mathbf{U}^{-1}\mathbf{p}} \mathbf{U}^{-1}\mathbf{p}\mathbf{q}' \tag{11.2}$$

$$\frac{\partial \lambda}{\partial M} = \frac{1}{\mathbf{p}'\mathbf{U}^{-1}\mathbf{p}} \tag{11.3}$$

$$\frac{\partial \lambda}{\partial \mathbf{p}} = -\frac{\lambda}{\mathbf{p}'\mathbf{U}^{-1}\mathbf{p}} \mathbf{U}^{-1}\mathbf{p} - \frac{1}{\mathbf{p}'\mathbf{U}^{-1}\mathbf{p}} \mathbf{q}. \tag{11.4}$$

To simplify these expressions we use (11.3) to substitute $\partial\lambda/\partial M$ for the reciprocal of $\mathbf{p}'\mathbf{U}^{-1}\mathbf{p}$ in (11.1), (11.2) and (11.4). Equation (11.1) then becomes

$$\frac{\partial \mathbf{q}}{\partial M} = \frac{\partial \lambda}{\partial M} \mathbf{U}^{-1}\mathbf{p}. \tag{11.5}$$

Next, we replace $\mathbf{U}^{-1}\mathbf{p}$ in (11.2) and (11.4) with $\partial\mathbf{q}/\partial M$ divided by $\partial\lambda/\partial M$, which follows from (11.5). This yields

$$\frac{\partial \mathbf{q}}{\partial \mathbf{p}'} = \lambda \mathbf{U}^{-1} - \frac{\lambda}{\partial\lambda/\partial M} \frac{\partial \mathbf{q}}{\partial M} \frac{\partial \mathbf{q}}{\partial M}' - \frac{\partial \mathbf{q}}{\partial M} \mathbf{q}' \tag{11.6}$$

$$\frac{\partial \lambda}{\partial \mathbf{p}} = -\lambda \frac{\partial \mathbf{q}}{\partial M} - \frac{\partial \lambda}{\partial M} \mathbf{q}. \tag{11.7}$$

Equations (11.5) and (11.6) give the income and price derivatives of the demand functions. We write the latter equation in scalar form as

$$\frac{\partial q_i}{\partial p_j} = \lambda u^{ij} - \frac{\lambda}{\partial\lambda/\partial M} \frac{\partial q_i}{\partial M} \frac{\partial q_j}{\partial M} - \frac{\partial q_i}{\partial M} q_j, \quad i,j=1,\ldots,n, \tag{11.8}$$

where u^{ij} is the (i,j)-*th* element of U^{-1}. This shows that the effect of a change in p_j on q_i, with income and the other prices constant, is made up of three terms. The third term on the right of (11.8), $-q_j(\partial q_i/\partial M)$, is the *income effect* of the price change. The remaining two terms thus represent the *total substitution effect*, the response of q_i to a change in p_j with *real* income (and the other prices) held constant. This total substitution effect comprises the *specific substitution effect*, λu^{ij}, and the *general substitution effect*, $-\frac{\lambda}{\partial\lambda/\partial M}\frac{\partial q_i}{\partial M}\frac{\partial q_j}{\partial M}$, with the terminology from Houthakker (1960). The latter effect is concerned with the competition of all goods for an extra dollar of the consumer's income, while the former deals with the interaction of goods i and j in the utility function.

For future reference, we write (11.5) in scalar terms as

$$\frac{\partial q_i}{\partial M} = \frac{\partial\lambda}{\partial M}\sum_{j=1}^{n} u^{ij}p_j, \qquad i=1,\dots,n. \tag{11.9}$$

1.12 A Differential Demand System

In this section we use the solution to the fundamental matrix equation to derive a general system of differential demand equations. Derivations of the results of this section are given in the next section.

The total differential of (3.7) is

$$dq_i = \frac{\partial q_i}{\partial M}\,dM + \sum_{j=1}^{n}\frac{\partial q_i}{\partial p_j}\,dp_j, \qquad i=1,\dots,n$$

We transform this to logarithmic-differential form by multiplying both sides by p_i/M and using $w_i = p_iq_i/M$,

$$w_i d(\log q_i) = \frac{\partial(p_iq_i)}{\partial M}\,d(\log M) + \sum_{j=1}^{n}\frac{p_ip_j}{M}\frac{\partial q_i}{\partial p_j}\,d(\log p_j). \tag{12.1}$$

We use (11.8) to express the second term on the right of (12.1) as

$$\sum_{j=1}^{n} \frac{p_i p_j}{M} \frac{\partial q_i}{\partial p_j} d(\log p_j) = \sum_{j=1}^{n} \frac{p_i p_j}{M} \left[\lambda u^{ij} - \frac{\lambda}{\partial\lambda/\partial M} \frac{\partial q_i}{\partial M} \frac{\partial q_j}{\partial M} - \frac{\partial q_i}{\partial M} q_j \right] d(\log p_j).$$

Substituting this in (12.1) and rearranging gives

$$w_i d(\log q_i) = \frac{\partial(p_i q_i)}{\partial M} \left[d(\log M) - \sum_{j=1}^{n} w_j d(\log p_j) \right]$$

$$+ \sum_{j=1}^{n} \left[\frac{\lambda p_i p_j u^{ij}}{M} - \frac{\lambda/M}{\partial\lambda/\partial M} \frac{\partial(p_i q_i)}{\partial M} \frac{\partial(p_j q_j)}{\partial M} \right] d(\log p_j). \tag{12.2}$$

In view of (9.1) and (9.3) the term in square brackets on the right of the above is the Divisia volume index d(log Q), which enables us to write

$$\frac{\partial(p_i q_i)}{\partial M} \left[d(\log M) - \sum_{j=1}^{n} w_j d(\log p_j) \right] = \theta_i d(\log Q), \tag{12.3}$$

where we have used (2.6).

To simplify the price substitution term of (12.2), we define

$$\phi = \frac{\lambda/M}{\partial\lambda/\partial M} = \left[\frac{\partial \log \lambda}{\partial \log M} \right]^{-1} < 0 \tag{12.4}$$

as the reciprocal of the income elasticity of the marginal utility of income. For brevity, we shall refer to ϕ as the *income flexibility*. We also define

$$\nu_{ij} = \frac{\lambda}{M} p_i p_j u^{ij}, \qquad i,j=1,\ldots,n, \tag{12.5}$$

which satisfy

$$\sum_{j=1}^{n} \nu_{ij} = \phi\theta_i, \qquad i=1,...,n. \tag{12.6}$$

The substitution term of (12.2) can then be expressed as

$$\sum_{j=1}^{n} \left[\frac{\lambda p_i p_j u^{ij}}{M} - \frac{\lambda / M}{\partial\lambda / \partial M} \frac{\partial(p_i q_i)}{\partial M} \frac{\partial(p_j q_j)}{\partial M} \right] d(\log p_j)$$

$$= \sum_{j=1}^{n} \nu_{ij} [d(\log p_j) - d(\log P')], \tag{12.7}$$

where

$$d(\log P') = \sum_{i=1}^{n} \theta_i \, d(\log p_i) \tag{12.8}$$

is the *Frisch* (1932) *price index.* This index is different from the Divisia price index (9.3) which uses budget shares as weights rather than marginal shares.

Using (12.3) and (12.7) in (12.2) the demand equation for good i becomes

$$w_i d(\log q_i) = \theta_i \, d(\log Q) + \sum_{j=1}^{n} \nu_{ij} \, d\left[\log \frac{p_j}{P'}\right], \tag{12.9}$$

where $d[\log(p_j/P')]$ is interpreted as $d(\log p_j) - d(\log P')$. The variable on the left of (12.9) has two interpretations. First, it is the quantity component of the change in the i-*th* budget share. This interpretation can be verified by taking the differential of $w_i = p_i q_i/M$,

$$dw_i = w_i d(\log p_i) + w_i d(\log q_i) - w_i d(\log M).$$

It is only the quantity component of this change which is endogenous from the consumer's viewpoint. The second interpretation of the left-hand side variable of (12.9) is contribution of good i to the Divisia volume index d(log Q) defined in (9.2).

The first term on the right of (12.9) gives the effect of real income on the demand for good i. This term is a multiple θ_i of the Divisia volume index d(log Q). As this volume index equals d(log M) - d(log P), where d(log P) is the Divisia price index, it follows that the Divisia price index transforms the change in money income into the change in real income. Furthermore, as the Divisia price index is budget-share-weighted, it follows that this index measures the income effect of the n price changes on the demand for the i-*th* good.

The second term on the right of (12.9), $\sum_j \nu_{ij} d[\log(p_j/P')]$, deals with the effects of relative prices. The Frisch price index acts as a deflator of each price change, so that we refer to $d[\log(p_j/P')]$ as the change in the *Frisch-deflated price of j.* It is shown in the next section that the substitution term can be written as the difference between $\sum_j \nu_{ij} d(\log p_j)$, which is the specific substitution effect of the n prices on the demand for good i, and $\phi\theta_i d(\log P')$, which is the general substitution effect. Accordingly, the general substitution effect acts as the deflator of the specific effect by transforming absolute prices into Frisch-deflated prices.

In the substitution term of (12.9), ν_{ij} is the coefficient of the j-*th* relative price, which shall be called the (i,j)-*th* price coefficient. These price coefficients satisfy $\sum_i \sum_j \nu_{ij} = \phi$, which follows from (12.6). If $\nu_{ij} > 0$, then an increase in the Frisch-deflated price of j causes consumption of i to increase. Consequently, we follow Houthakker (1960) and define goods i and j as *specific substitutes (complements)* if $\nu_{ij} > 0$ (< 0). We will have more to say about substitutes and complements in Section 1.20.

In contrast to the other approaches to generating demand equations discussed in this chapter, the differential approach requires no algebraic specification of the utility function, the indirect utility function nor of the cost function. Consequently, the coefficients of the demand equations (12.9) need not be constant; they may be functions of income and prices. The decision how to parameterize differential demand equations comes as the final step, just before estimation. This principle is illustrated later in the chapter.

1.13 Derivations and Extensions

Our first objective is to show that ϕ is negative, as stated in equation (12.4). We use (12.5) and (12.6) to write

$$\sum_{j=1}^{n} \frac{\lambda}{M} p_i p_j u^{ij} = \phi\theta_i, \qquad i=1,...,n.$$

In view of $\Sigma_i\, \theta_i = 1$, summing both sides of the above over i=1,...,n yields

$$\phi = \frac{\lambda}{M} \sum_{i=1}^{n} \sum_{j=1}^{n} p_i p_j u^{ij} \tag{13.1}$$

The right-hand side is proportional to a quadratic form with matrix $\mathbf{U}^{-1}$ and vector $\mathbf{p}$; in view of (3.3) this matrix is negative definite, so that the quadratic form is negative. As the factor of proportionality λ/M on the right of (13.1) is positive, we conclude that $\phi < 0$.

Constraint (12.6) can be verified by multiplying both sides of (11.9) by p_i, which yields

$$\theta_i = \frac{\partial\lambda}{\partial M} \sum_{j=1}^{n} p_i p_j u^{ij}, \qquad i=1,...,n,$$

and then using (12.4) to substitute $\lambda/(\phi M)$ for $\partial\lambda/\partial M$. After using (12.5), we obtain (12.6).

To verify (12.7) we use (2.6), (12.4) and (12.5) to express the substitution term of (12.2) as

$$\sum_{j=1}^{n}\left[\frac{\lambda p_i p_j u^{ij}}{M} - \frac{\lambda/M}{\partial\lambda/\partial M}\frac{\partial(p_i q_i)}{\partial M}\frac{\partial(p_j q_j)}{\partial M}\right] d(\log p_j)$$

$$= \sum_{j=1}^{n} (\nu_{ij} - \phi\theta_i\theta_j) d(\log p_j). \tag{13.2}$$

In view of (12.8), the right-hand side of (13.2) can be written as

$$\sum_{j=1}^{n} (\nu_{ij} - \phi\theta_i\theta_j) d(\log p_j) = \left[\sum_{j=1}^{n} \nu_{ij} d(\log p_j) - \phi\theta_i d(\log P')\right]. \tag{13.3}$$

Substituting $\sum_j \nu_{ij}$ for $\phi\theta_i$ [which follows from (12.6)] on the right-hand side of (13.3) yields the right-hand side of equation (12.7). Therefore (13.2) and (13.3) verify (12.7). Equation (13.3) also shows that the substitution term of (12.9) is the difference between $\sum_j \nu_{ij} d(\log p_j)$ and $\phi\theta_i d(\log P')$.

To further interpret the ν_{ij}'s, we use (12.5) to define the n × n matrix

$$[\nu_{ij}] = \frac{\lambda}{M} \mathbf{P} \mathbf{U}^{-1} \mathbf{P}, \tag{13.4}$$

where $\mathbf{P}$ is the diagonal matrix with $p_1, \dots, p_n$ on the diagonal and $\mathbf{U}^{-1}$ is the inverse of the Hessian of the utility function. On the right of (13.4), λ, M > 0; $\mathbf{P}$ is a symmetric positive definite matrix and $\mathbf{U}^{-1}$ is symmetric negative definite. Therefore

$[\nu_{ij}]$ is a symmetric negative definite n × n matrix. (13.5)

Inverting both sides of (13.4), we obtain

$$\nu^{ij} = \frac{M}{\lambda} \frac{\partial^2 u}{\partial(p_i q_i)\partial(p_j q_j)}, \qquad i,j=1,\dots,n, \tag{13.6}$$

where ν^{ij} is the (i,j)-*th* element of $[\nu_{ij}]^{-1}$. Since $\partial u/\partial(p_i q_i)$ is the marginal utility of a dollar spent on i, $\partial^2 u/\partial(p_i q_i)\partial(p_j q_j)$ on the right of (13.6) is interpreted as the change in this marginal utility when spending on j increases by one dollar. Accordingly, (13.6) shows that $[\nu_{ij}]$ is inversely proportional to the Hessian matrix of the utility function in expenditure terms.

We now return to preference independence (5.1) and analyse the implications of this form of the utility function for the demand equation (12.9). Under (5.1) the Hessian matrix **U** and its inverse are both diagonal. As $u^{ij} = 0$ for i≠j, it follows from (12.5) that $\nu_{ij} = 0$ for i≠j. Equation (12.6) then implies $\nu_{ii} = \phi\theta_i$, so that the demand equation (12.9) takes the simpler form

$$w_i d(\log q_i) = \theta_i d(\log Q) + \phi\theta_i d\left[\log \frac{p_i}{P'}\right]. \tag{13.7}$$

Therefore, preference independence implies that only the own deflated price appears in each demand equation, rather than all n such prices. In other words, preference independence implies that no pair of goods (i,j) can be either a specific substitute or a specific complement. In addition, for $[\nu_{ij}]$ to be a negative definite matrix with diagonal elements $\phi\theta_1,...,\phi\theta_n$ and off-diagonal elements zero, each marginal share θ_i must be positive. Consequently, the hypothesis of preference independence rules out inferior goods.

The substitution term of equation (12.9) is formulated in terms of deflated prices. We use (13.3) to express the substitution term in absolute (or undeflated) prices as

$$\sum_{j=1}^{n} \nu_{ij} d\left[\log \frac{p_j}{P'}\right] = \sum_{j=1}^{n} \pi_{ij} d(\log p_j), \tag{13.8}$$

where

$$\pi_{ij} = (\nu_{ij} - \phi\theta_i\theta_j), \qquad i,j=1,...,n, \tag{13.9}$$

is the (i,j)-*th Slutsky* (1915) *coefficient.* This coefficient gives the total substitution effect on the demand for good i of a change in the j-*th* price. It can be easily verified that

$$[\pi_{ij}] \text{ is a symmetric negative semidefinite } n \times n \text{ matrix with rank n-1.} \tag{13.10}$$

Using (13.8) in (12.9) yields the demand equation for good i in terms of absolute prices,

$$w_i d(\log q_i) = \theta_i d(\log Q) + \sum_{j=1}^{n} \pi_{ij} d(\log p_j). \tag{13.11}$$

Dividing both sides of (13.11) by w_i, we find that the income and compensated price elasticities are

$$\eta_i = \frac{\theta_i}{w_i}, \qquad \eta_{ij}^* = \frac{\pi_{ij}}{w_i}, \qquad i,j=1,\ldots,n. \tag{13.12}$$

These elasticities satisfy demand homogeneity and Slutsky symmetry.

1.14 Examples of Differential Demand Equations

In Sections 1.12 and 1.13 we derived the demand equations (12.9) and (13.11) in relative and absolute prices using the differential approach. These demand equations are *completely* general as their *coefficients* are not necessarily constant. This is in contrast with most other approaches of generating systems of demand equations. These other approaches involve the algebraic specification of either the direct utility function, the indirect utility function or the cost function. Consequently, the coefficients of the resulting demand equations are constants. In this and the next sections we illustrate this characteristic of the differential approach by deriving the algebraic form of the marginal shares, income flexibility, Slutsky and the price coefficients for LES, addilog, CES, Cobb-Douglas, Translog and AIDS demand systems. These coefficients for LES and the addilog system have been previously derived by Deaton (1974) and Theil (1975/76). However, the approach we use here is more general as the coefficients for LES and the addilog system emerge as special cases of a wider family of demand equations.

The Johansen Utility Function Again

From equation (4.2), the first-order conditions corresponding to the Johansen utility function (4.1) can be written as

$$\log\left[\frac{q_i - \gamma_i}{\beta_i}\right] = c_i(\log\lambda + \log p_i), \qquad i=1,\ldots,n, \tag{14.1}$$

where $c_i = [1/(\alpha_i - 1)]$. Since $\alpha_1 < 1$, i=1,...,n, we have $c_i < 0$, i=1,...,n.

Differentiating both sides of (14.1) with respect to log M yields

$$\phi = c_i\left[\frac{q_i - \gamma_i}{q_i\eta_i}\right],$$

where $\eta_i = \partial(\log q_i)/\partial(\log M)$ is the income elasticity of commodity i and $\phi = [\partial(\log\lambda)/\partial(\log M)]^{-1}$ is the income flexibility. Rearrangement of the above equation and using the fact $\Sigma_{i=1}^{n} w_i\eta_i = 1$, we get

$$\phi = \sum_{i=1}^{n} c_i(w_i - v_i). \tag{14.2}$$

where $v_i = p_i\gamma_i/M$. We can show that the marginal shares and income elasticities implied by the Johansen utility function are

$$\theta_i = \frac{c_i}{\phi}(w_i - v_i); \quad \eta_i = \frac{c_i}{\phi}\left[1 - \frac{v_i}{w_i}\right], \qquad i=1,...,n. \tag{14.3}$$

As $\phi < 0$, $c_i < 0$ and $w_i > v_i$ for all i=1,...,n, we can conclude from (14.3) that $\theta_i > 0$ and $\eta_i > 0$ for every commodity. This means that all demand systems obtained from Johansen utility function rule out the possibility of inferior goods.

From (14.1) we have

$$\frac{1}{c_i}\log\left[\frac{q_i - \gamma_i}{\beta_i}\right] - \frac{1}{c_k}\log\left[\frac{q_k - \gamma_k}{\beta_k}\right] = \log p_i - \log p_k, \qquad i,k=1,...,n. \tag{14.4}$$

Differentiation of both sides of (14.4) with respect to $\log p_j$ yields

$$\frac{q_i}{c_i(q_i - \gamma_i)}\eta_{ij} - \frac{q_k}{c_k(q_k - \gamma_k)}\eta_{kj} = \delta_{ij} - \delta_{kj},$$

where we have used $\eta_{ij} = \partial(\log q_i)/\partial(\log p_j)$ and δ_{ij} is the Kronecker delta. Using the results below equation (14.1), the above equation can be simplified to

$$\eta_i\eta_{kj} = \eta_k\eta_{ij} - \phi\eta_i\eta_k(\delta_{ij} - \delta_{kj}), \qquad i,j,k=1,...,n. \tag{14.5}$$

Multiplying both sides of (14.5) by w_k and summing over k=1,...,n, we can write the uncompensated price elasticities as

$$\eta_{ij} = - w_j\eta_i + \phi\eta_i(\delta_{ij} - \theta_j), \qquad i,j=1,...,n. \tag{14.6}$$

where we have used $\Sigma_{k=1}^{n} w_k\eta_{kj} = - w_j$, $\Sigma_{k=1}^{n} w_k\eta_k = 1$ and $w_j\eta_j = \theta_j$.

To obtain the compensated price elasticities, η^*_{ij}, we rearrange (14.6) and use the result $\eta^*_{ij} = \eta_{ij} + w_j\eta_i$ to give

$$\eta^*_{ij} = \phi\eta_i(\delta_{ij} - \theta_j), \qquad i,j=1,\dots,n. \tag{14.7}$$

For i ≠ j, $\eta^*_{ij} = - \phi\theta_j\eta_i > 0$ for every i,j=1,...,n. This indicates that for the demand systems derived from Johansen utility function, all goods are net substitutes.

From equations (13.9), (13.12) and (14.7), we obtain the Slutsky coefficients and the price coefficients

$$\pi_{ij} = \phi\theta_i(\delta_{ij} - \theta_j), \qquad i,j=1,\dots,n, \tag{14.8}$$

and

$$v_{ij} = \phi\theta_i\delta_{ij}, \qquad i,j=1,\dots,n. \tag{14.9}$$

It is easy to verify from (14.8) that $\pi_{ij} = \pi_{ji}$ and $\Sigma_{j=1}^{n} \pi_{ij} = 0$. Now we shall apply (14.2)-(14.3) and (14.6)-(14.9) to the following special cases of the Johansen utility function.

The Linear Expenditure System

The linear expenditure system is derived in Section 1.4 as a special case of the Johansen utility function (4.1) when $\alpha_i = 0$, i=1,...,n. This implies that $c_i = -1$, i=1,...,n. Therefore equations (14.2)-(14.3) and (14.6)-(14.9) corresponding to LES are

$$\phi = -1 + \sum_{j=1}^{n} v_j; \tag{14.10}$$

$$\theta_i = \frac{1}{\phi}(v_i - w_i) = \beta_i; \qquad \eta_i = \frac{\beta_i}{w_i}, \qquad i=1,\dots,n, \tag{14.11}$$

where we have used (14.10) and (4.4) in the form $w_i = v_i + \beta_i\left[1 - \Sigma_{j=1}^{n} v_j\right]$;

$$\eta_{ij} = \frac{\beta_i}{w_i}[- w_j + \phi(\delta_{ij} - \beta_j)], \qquad i,j=1,...,n; \tag{14.12}$$

$$\eta^*_{ij} = \phi \frac{\beta_i}{w_i}(\delta_{ij} - \beta_j), \qquad i,j=1,...,n; \tag{14.13}$$

$$\pi_{ij} = \phi\beta_i(\delta_{ij} - \beta_j), \qquad i,j=1,...,n; \tag{14.14}$$

and

$$\nu_{ij} = \phi\beta_i\delta_{ij}, \qquad i,j=1,...,n. \tag{14.15}$$

The Addilog Demand System

The addilog demand system is a special case of (4.1) with $\gamma_i = 0$, which means that $v_i = 0$, i=1,...,n. Therefore equations (14.2)-(14.3) and (14.6)-(14.9) under the addilog demand system become

$$\phi = \sum_{i=1}^{n} w_i c_i; \tag{14.16}$$

$$\theta_i = \frac{c_i w_i}{\phi}; \qquad \eta_i = \frac{c_i}{\phi}, \qquad i=1,...,n; \tag{14.17}$$

$$\eta_{ij} = - w_j \frac{c_i}{\phi} + c_i\left[\delta_{ij} - \frac{c_j w_j}{\phi}\right], \qquad i,j=1,...,n; \tag{14.18}$$

$$\eta^*_{ij} = \frac{c_i}{\phi}(\phi\delta_{ij} - c_j w_j), \qquad i,j=1,...,n; \tag{14.19}$$

$$\pi_{ij} = \frac{c_i w_i}{\phi}(\phi\delta_{ij} - c_j w_j), \qquad i,j=1,...,n; \tag{14.20}$$

and

$$\nu_{ij} = c_i w_i \delta_{ij}, \qquad i,j=1,...,n. \tag{14.21}$$

The CES Demand System

The CES demand system can be obtained from the Johansen utility function under the condition that $\alpha_i = \alpha$ and $\gamma_i = 0$, i=1,...,n. Therefore $c_i = [1/(\alpha - 1)]$ = a constant and $v_i = 0$ for all i=1,...,n. If we substitute these restrictions in equations (14.2)-(14.3) and (14.6)-(14.9), we obtain

$$\phi = \frac{1}{\alpha - 1}; \tag{14.22}$$

$$\theta_i = w_i; \qquad \eta_i = 1, \qquad i=1,...,n; \tag{14.23}$$

$$\eta_{ij} = - w_j + \phi(\delta_{ij} - w_j), \qquad i,j=1,...,n; \tag{14.24}$$

$$\eta^*_{ij} = \phi(\delta_{ij} - w_j), \qquad i,j=1,...,n; \tag{14.25}$$

$$\pi_{ij} = \phi w_i(\delta_{ij} - w_j), \qquad i,j=1,...,n; \tag{14.26}$$

and

$$\nu_{ij} = \phi w_i \delta_{ij}, \qquad i,j=1,...,n. \tag{14.27}$$

The Cobb-Douglas Demand System

For $\alpha_i = \gamma_i = 0$, i=1,...,n, the Johansen utility function takes the Cobb-Douglas form. Now we have $c_i = -1$ and $v_i = 0$ for all i=1,...,n. With this substitution, equations (14.2)-(14.3) and (14.6)-(14.9) become

$$\phi = -1; \tag{14.28}$$

$$\theta_i = w_i; \qquad \eta_i = 1, \qquad i=1,\ldots,n; \tag{14.29}$$

$$\eta_{ij} = -\delta_{ij}, \qquad i,j=1,\ldots,n; \tag{14.30}$$

$$\eta^*_{ij} = w_j - \delta_{ij}, \qquad i,j=1,\ldots,n; \tag{14.31}$$

$$\pi_{ij} = w_i(w_j - \delta_{ij}), \qquad i,j=1,\ldots,n; \tag{14.32}$$

and

$$\nu_{ij} = -w_i\delta_{ij}, \qquad i,j=1,\ldots,n. \tag{14.33}$$

The Translog Demand System

If we write $w_i = p_iq_i/M$ in (6.6) and rearrange it for q_i and take the logarithm of both sides of equation (6.6), we get

$$\log p_i + \log q_i - \log M = \log\left[\beta_i + \sum_{\ell=1}^{n}\beta_{i\ell}\log\left[\frac{p_\ell}{M}\right]\right]$$
$$- \log\left[\sum_{k=1}^{n}\beta_k + \sum_{k=1}^{n}\sum_{\ell=1}^{n}\beta_{k\ell}\log\left[\frac{p_\ell}{M}\right]\right]. \tag{14.34}$$

We differentiate both sides of (14.34) with respect to log M, to give

$$\eta_i = 1 + \frac{-\sum_{\ell=1}^{n}\beta_{i\ell}}{\left[\beta_i + \sum_{\ell=1}^{n}\beta_{i\ell}\log\left[\frac{p_\ell}{M}\right]\right]} + \frac{\sum_{k=1}^{n}\sum_{\ell=1}^{n}\beta_{k\ell}}{\left[\sum_{k=1}^{n}\beta_k + \sum_{k=1}^{n}\sum_{\ell=1}^{n}\beta_{k\ell}\log\left[\frac{p_\ell}{M}\right]\right]},$$
$$i=1,\ldots,n. \tag{14.35}$$

Using $\theta_i = \eta_i w_i$ and (6.6), we obtain the marginal share

$$\theta_i = w_i + \frac{w_i \sum_{k=1}^{n} \sum_{\ell=1}^{n} \beta_{k\ell} - \sum_{\ell=1}^{n} \beta_{i\ell}}{\left[\sum_{k=1}^{n} \beta_k + \sum_{k=1}^{n} \sum_{\ell=1}^{n} \beta_{k\ell} \log\left[\frac{p_\ell}{M}\right]\right]}, \qquad i=1,\dots,n. \tag{14.36}$$

Application of (6.3) to (6.5), gives

$$\lambda M = -\sum_{i=1}^{n} \beta_i - \frac{1}{2} \sum_{i=1}^{n} \sum_{\ell=1}^{n} \beta_{i\ell}(\log p_i + \log p_\ell) + \left[\sum_{i=1}^{n} \sum_{\ell=1}^{n} \beta_{i\ell}\right] \log M.$$

Taking the logarithm of both sides of this equation and differentiating with respect to log M we obtain

$$1 + \frac{\partial(\log \lambda)}{\partial(\log M)}$$

$$= \frac{\sum_{i=1}^{n} \sum_{\ell=1}^{n} \beta_{i\ell}}{-\sum_{i=1}^{n} \beta_i - \frac{1}{2} \sum_{i=1}^{n} \sum_{\ell=1}^{n} \beta_{i\ell}(\log p_i + \log p_\ell) + \left[\sum_{i=1}^{n} \sum_{\ell=1}^{n} \beta_{i\ell}\right] \log M}$$

Therefore

$$\phi = \frac{-\sum_{i=1}^{n} \beta_i - \frac{1}{2} \sum_{i=1}^{n} \sum_{\ell=1}^{n} \beta_{i\ell}(\log p_i + \log p_\ell) + \left[\sum_{i=1}^{n} \sum_{\ell=1}^{n} \beta_{i\ell}\right] \log M}{\sum_{i=1}^{n} \beta_i + \frac{1}{2} \sum_{i=1}^{n} \sum_{\ell=1}^{n} \beta_{i\ell}(\log p_i + \log p_\ell) + \sum_{i=1}^{n} \sum_{\ell=1}^{n} \beta_{i\ell}(1 - \log M)}$$

(14.37)

If we differentiate both sides of (14.37) with respect to log p_j, we get

$$\delta_{ij} + \eta_{ij} = \frac{\beta_{ij}}{\left[\beta_i + \sum_{\ell=1}^{n} \beta_{i\ell} \log \left[\frac{p_\ell}{M}\right]\right]} - \frac{\sum_{k=1}^{n} \beta_{kj}}{\left[\sum_{k=1}^{n} \beta_k + \sum_{k=1}^{n} \sum_{\ell=1}^{n} \beta_{k\ell} \log \left[\frac{p_\ell}{M}\right]\right]}.$$

Using (6.6), we can simplify this to

$$\eta_{ij} = -\delta_{ij} + \frac{\frac{\beta_{ij}}{w_i} - \sum_{k=1}^{n} \beta_{kj}}{\left[\sum_{k=1}^{n} \beta_k + \sum_{k=1}^{n} \sum_{\ell=1}^{n} \beta_{k\ell} \log \left[\frac{p_\ell}{M}\right]\right]}, \qquad i,j=1,\dots,n. \tag{14.38}$$

In view of $\eta^*_{ij} = \eta_{ij} + w_j \eta_i$, we get

$$\eta^*_{ij} = -\delta_{ij} + \frac{\frac{\beta_{ij}}{w_i} - \sum_{k=1}^{n} \beta_{kj}}{\left[\sum_{k=1}^{n} \beta_k + \sum_{k=1}^{n} \sum_{\ell=1}^{n} \beta_{k\ell} \log \left[\frac{p_\ell}{M}\right]\right]} + \eta_i w_j, \quad i,j=1,\dots,n. \tag{14.39}$$

Therefore the Slutsky coefficients can be written as

$$\pi_{ij} = -w_i \delta_{ij} + \frac{\beta_{ij} - w_i \sum_{k=1}^{n} \beta_{kj}}{\left[\sum_{k=1}^{n} \beta_k + \sum_{k=1}^{n} \sum_{\ell=1}^{n} \beta_{k\ell} \log \left[\frac{p_\ell}{M}\right]\right]} + \theta_i w_j, \qquad i,j=1,\dots,n, \tag{14.40}$$

where $\theta_i = w_i\eta_i$. When $\beta_{ij} = \beta_{ji}$ we can easily verify that the π_{ij}'s given by (14.40) satisfy $\pi_{ij} = \pi_{ji}$ and $\Sigma_{j=1}^{n} \pi_{ij} = 0$. Using equation (13.9), the expression for the ν_{ij}'s is

$$\nu_{ij} = -w_i\delta_{ij} + \frac{\beta_{ij} - w_i \sum_{k=1}^{n} \beta_{kj}}{\sum_{k=1}^{n} \beta_k + \sum_{k=1}^{n} \sum_{\ell=1}^{n} \beta_{k\ell} \log\left[\frac{p_\ell}{M}\right]} + \theta_i(w_j + \phi\theta_j), \qquad i,j=1,\dots,n.$$

(14.41)

The AIDS Model

In Section 1.8 we pointed out that Working's model (8.1) and the AIDS model (7.6) both have the same income term. Thus the income elasticity for the AIDS model is the same as that for Working's model given by (8.3):

$$\eta_i = 1 + \frac{\beta_i}{w_i}, \qquad i=1,\dots,n.$$

Using $\theta_i = w_i\eta_i$, the marginal shares are

$$\theta_i = w_i + \beta_i, \qquad i=1,\dots,n. \tag{14.42}$$

Since $\Sigma_{i=1}^{n} \theta_i = \Sigma_{i=1}^{n} w_i = 1$, the β_i's must satisfy $\Sigma_{i=1}^{n} \beta_i = 0$.

Under the AIDS model the budget share of good i, is given by (7.6), which we reproduce here,

$$w_i = \alpha_i + \beta_i \log\left[\frac{M}{P}\right] + \sum_{\ell=1}^{n} \gamma_{i\ell} \log p_\ell \qquad i=1,\dots,n, \tag{14.43}$$

where

$$\log P = \sum_{k=1}^{n} \alpha_k \log p_k + \frac{1}{2} \sum_{k=1}^{n} \sum_{\ell=1}^{n} \gamma^*_{k\ell} \log p_k \log p_\ell$$

Taking the logarithm of both sides of $w_i = p_i q_i / M$, we get

$$\log p_i + \log q_i - \log M = \log w_i, \qquad i=1,...,n. \tag{14.44}$$

Differentiating both sides of (14.44) with respect to $\log p_j$ and using (14.43), we obtain

$$\delta_{ij} + \eta_{ij} = \frac{1}{w_i} \left[-\beta_i \left[\alpha_j + \sum_{\ell=1}^{n} \gamma_{j\ell} \log p_\ell \right] + \gamma_{ij} \right],$$

where $\gamma_{j\ell} = \frac{1}{2}(\gamma^*_{j\ell} + \gamma^*_{\ell j})$. Therefore, using (14.43), this can be simplified to

$$\eta_{ij} = -\delta_{ij} + \frac{1}{w_i}\left[\gamma_{ij} - \beta_i \left[w_j - \beta_j \log\left[\frac{M}{P}\right]\right]\right], \quad i,j=1,...,n. \tag{14.45}$$

In view of $\eta^*_{ij} = \eta_{ij} + w_j \eta_i$, we have

$$\eta^*_{ij} = -\delta_{ij} + \frac{1}{w_i}\left[\gamma_{ij} + \beta_i \beta_j \log\left[\frac{M}{P}\right]\right] + w_j, \quad i,j=1,...,n, \tag{14.46}$$

where we have used $\eta_i = 1 + \beta_i / w_i$.

Using $\pi_{ij} = \eta^*_{ij} w_i$, the Slutsky coefficients are

$$\pi_{ij} = -w_i(\delta_{ij} - w_j) + \gamma_{ij} + \beta_i \beta_j \log\left[\frac{M}{P}\right], \quad i,j=1,...,n. \tag{14.47}$$

Since $\gamma_{j\ell} = \gamma_{\ell j}$, $\Sigma_{j=1}^{n} \beta_j = 0$ and if $\Sigma_{j=1}^{n} \gamma_{ij} = 0$, it can be easily verified that the Slutsky coefficients given by (14.47) satisfy $\pi_{ij} = \pi_{ji}$ and $\Sigma_{i=1}^{n} \pi_{ij} = 0$.

Table 1.1 contains a convenient tabulation of all the results derived in this and the previous sections.

1.15 The Rotterdam Model

Equation (12.9) is formulated in terms of infinitesimal changes; the Rotterdam model, due to Barten (1964) and Theil (1965), is a finite-change version of (12.9). We write $Dx_t = \log x_t - \log x_{t-1}$ for the finite log-change from period t-1 to t for any positive variable x. The variable $d(\log q_i)$ on the left of (12.9) becomes Dq_{it} and $d[\log(p_j/P')]$ becomes $Dp_{jt} - DP'_t$, where $DP'_t = \Sigma_i \theta_i Dp_{it}$ is a finite-change version of the Frisch price index. As the budget share w_i on the left of (12.9) does not involve a change, we could use $w_{i,t-1}$, w_{it} or a combination thereof which treats t and t-1 symmetrically. The natural choice is to use the arithmetic average of $w_{i,t-1}$ and w_{it}, $\bar{w}_{it} = \frac{1}{2}(w_{i,t-1} + w_{it})$, which is mid-way between the two extremities. The finite-change version of (12.9) is then

$$\bar{w}_{it} Dq_{it} = \theta_i DQ_t + \sum_{j=1}^{n} \nu_{ij}(Dp_{jt} - DP'_t), \tag{15.1}$$

where $DQ_t = \Sigma_i \bar{w}_{it} Dq_{it}$ is a finite-change version of the Divisia volume index.

When the coefficients of (15.1) θ_i and ν_{ij} are treated as constants it is known as the i-*th* demand equation of the *relative price version of the Rotterdam model.* As stated in (13.5), the $n \times n$ matrix of price coefficients $[\nu_{ij}]$ is symmetric negative definite; these coefficients also satisfy (12.6). Constraint (12.6) and the constancy of the coefficients ν_{ij} and θ_i imply that ϕ is also a constant in the model.

TABLE 1.1: PROPERTIES OF SEVEN DEMAND SYSTEMS

Utility function $u(q_1.....q_n)$	Demand equation for commodity i	Income flexibility ϕ	Income elasticity[a] η_i	(i,j)th uncompensated price elasticity η_{ij}	(i,j)th Slutsky coefficient[b] x_{ij}	(i,j)th price coefficient v_{ij}
Johansen:						
$\sum_{i=1}^{n} \frac{\beta_i}{\alpha_i}\left\{\left(\frac{q_i-\gamma_i}{\beta_i}\right)^{\alpha_i}-1\right\}$	$\frac{1}{c_i}\log\left(\frac{q_i-\gamma_i}{\beta_i}\right)-\frac{1}{c_k}\log\left(\frac{q_k-\gamma_k}{\beta_k}\right)$ $=\log p_i-\log p_k$ where $c_i=1/(\alpha_i-1)$	$\sum_{i=1}^{n} c_i(w_i-v_i)$ where $v_i=p_i\gamma_i/M$	$\frac{c_i}{\phi}\left(1-\frac{v_i}{w_i}\right)$	$-w_j\eta_i+\phi\eta_i(\delta_{ij}-\theta_j)$ where $\theta_i=(w_i-v_i)c_i/\phi$	$\phi\theta_i(\delta_{ij}-\theta_j)$	$\phi\theta_i\delta_{ij}$
Stone-Geary:						
$\sum_{i=1}^{n}\beta_i\log\left(\frac{q_i-\gamma_i}{\beta_i}\right)$	$p_iq_i=p_i\gamma_i+\beta_i\left(M-\sum_{j=1}^{n}p_j\gamma_j\right)$	$-1+\sum_{j=1}^{n}v_j$	$\frac{\beta_i}{w_i}$	$\frac{\beta_i}{w_i}\left(-w_j+\phi(\delta_{ij}-\beta_j)\right)$	$\phi\beta_i(\delta_{ij}-\beta_j)$	$\phi\beta_i\delta_{ij}$
Addilog:						
$\sum_{i=1}^{n}\frac{\beta_i}{\alpha_i}\left\{\frac{q_i}{\beta_i}\right\}^{\alpha}$	$\frac{1}{c_i}\log\left(\frac{q_i}{\beta_i}\right)-\frac{1}{c_k}\log\left(\frac{q_k}{\beta_k}\right)$ $=\log p_i-\log p_k$ where $c_i=1/(\alpha_i-1)$	$\sum_{i=1}^{n}w_ic_i$	$\frac{c_i}{\phi}$	$-w_j\frac{c_i}{\phi}+c_i\left(\delta_{ij}-\frac{c_jw_j}{\phi}\right)$	$\frac{c_iw_i}{\phi}(\phi\delta_{ij}-c_jw_j)$	$c_iw_i\delta_{ij}$
CES:						
$\sum_{i=1}^{n}\frac{\beta_i}{\alpha}\left(\frac{q_i}{\beta_i}\right)^{\alpha i}$	$q_i=\beta_i\left(\frac{p_i}{P}\right)^{1/(\alpha-1)}\frac{M}{P}$ where $P^{\alpha/(\alpha-1)}=\sum_{k=1}^{n}\beta_kp_k^{\alpha/(\alpha-1)}$	$\frac{1}{\alpha-1}$	1	$-w_j+\phi(\delta_{ij}-w_j)$	$\phi w_i(\delta_{ij}-w_j)$	$\phi w_i\delta_{ij}$
Cobb-Douglas:						
$\sum_{i=1}^{n}\beta_i\log\left(\frac{q_i}{\beta_i}\right)$	$q_i=\left(\frac{\beta_i}{p_i}\right)M$	-1	1	$-\delta_{ij}$	$w_i(w_j-\delta_{ij})$	$-w_i\delta_{ij}$

continued.....

Utility function $u(q_1, \ldots, q_n)$	Demand equation for commodity i	Income flexibility ϕ	Income elasticity[a] η_i	(i,j)th uncompensated price elasticity η_{ij}	(i,j)th Slutsky coefficient[b] π_{ij}	(i,j)th price coefficient ν_{ij}
Translog:[c]						
$\sum_{i=1}^{n} \beta_i \log\left(\frac{p_i}{M}\right) + 1/2 \sum_{i=1}^{n} \sum_{j=1}^{n} \beta_{ij} \log\left(\frac{p_i}{M}\right) \log\left(\frac{p_j}{M}\right)$	$w_i = \frac{\beta_i + \sum_{j=1}^{n} \beta_{ij} \log\left(\frac{p_j}{M}\right)}{\sum_{k=1}^{n} \beta_k + \sum_{k=1}^{n} \sum_{j=1}^{n} \beta_{kj} \log\left(\frac{p_j}{M}\right)}$	See eq. (14.37)	See eq. (14.35)	See eq. (14.38)	See eq (14.40)	See eq (14.41)
AIDS:[d]						
$e^{a(p)+ub(p)}$, where $b(p) = \beta_0 \prod_{k=1}^{n} p_k^{\beta_k}$ $a(p) = \sum_{k=1}^{n} \alpha_k \log p_k + 1/2 \sum_{k=1}^{n} \sum_{j=1}^{n} \gamma_{kj}^{*} \log p_k \log p_j$	$w_i = \alpha_i + \beta_i \log\left(\frac{M}{P}\right) + \sum_{j=1}^{n} \gamma_{ij} \log p_j$ where $\gamma_{ij} = \left(\gamma_{ij}^{*} + \gamma_{ji}^{*}\right)/2$		$1 + \frac{\beta_i}{w_i}$	$-\delta_{ij} + \frac{1}{w_i}\left\{\gamma_{ij} - \beta_i\left(w_j - \beta_j \log\left(\frac{M}{P}\right)\right)\right\}$	$-w_i\left(\delta_{ij} - w_j\right) + \gamma_{ij} + \beta_i\beta_j \log\left(\frac{M}{P}\right)$	

a ith marginal share can be obtained from $\theta_i = w_i \eta_i$.

b $(i, j)^{th}$ compensated price elasticity can be obtained from $\eta_{ij}^{*} = \pi_{ij} / w_i$.

c Indirect utility function.

d Cost function.

The second version of the Rotterdam model takes as its starting point the differential demand equation in absolute prices (13.11). The finite-change version of that equation is

$$\bar{w}_{it}Dq_{it} = \theta_i DQ_t + \sum_{j=1}^{n} \pi_{ij} Dp_{jt}, \tag{15.2}$$

where π_{ij} is the Slutsky coefficient defined in (13.9). When the coefficients θ_i and π_{ij} are specified as constants, (15.2) is known as the i-*th* equation of the *absolute price version of the Rotterdam model.*

In view of (13.10) the Slutsky coefficients are symmetric in i and j,

$$\pi_{ij} = \pi_{ji}, \qquad i,j=1,\ldots,n, \tag{15.3}$$

which is known as *Slutsky symmetry*. These coefficients also satisfy

$$\sum_{j=1}^{n} \pi_{ij} = 0, \qquad i=1,\ldots,n, \tag{15.4}$$

which follows from (12.6) and (13.9). Constraint (15.4) reflects the homogeneity postulate that a proportionate change in all prices has no effect on the demand for any good under the condition that real income is constant. Accordingly, (15.4) is known as *demand homogeneity*. As stated in (13.10) the Slutsky matrix $[\pi_{ij}]$ is symmetric negative semidefinite with rank n-1; the cause of the singularity is (15.4).

The two versions of the model both have their attractions. The absolute price version and the constraints (15.3) and (15.4) are linear in the parameters, which makes estimation and testing straightforward. However when n becomes larger, the number of π_{ij}'s grows rapidly, making the absolute price version of the model suitable for small systems only. For larger models, it is necessary to use the relative price version of the model (which is nonlinear in the parameters) with suitable constraints on the ν_{ij}'s. These constraints take the form of postulating that certain goods do not interact in the utility function; a special case of this is preference independence when no good interacts with any other. Under preference independence the utility function takes the form (5.1), so that all second-order cross-derivatives vanish. Therefore, in view of (12.5) and (12.6), $\nu_{ij} = 0$ for $i \neq j$ and $\nu_{ii} = \phi\theta_i$. The relative price version of the Rotterdam model (15.1) then takes the form

$$\bar{w}_{it} Dq_{it} = \theta_i DQ_t + \phi\theta_i (Dp_{it} - DP'_t). \qquad (15.5)$$

The number of unconstrained coefficients in (15.5) for i=1,...,n is n, which is made up of n-1 unconstrained θ_i's (1 is constrained by $\sum_i \theta_i = 1$) and ϕ. Note that (15.5) is simply a finite-change version of (13.7).

Remark 1. Barnett (1979) and Selvanathan (1991) analysed the issue of aggregation over consumers in the context of differential demand equations. They started with each individual consumer possessing his own system of demand equations in the form of (12.9) and (13.11) with nonconstant coefficients; tastes are allowed to differ across consumers. Then, using the convergence approach to aggregation over consumers (Theil, 1971 Sec. 11.4), Barnett and Selvanathan obtain the Rotterdam models (15.1) and (15.2) with constant coefficients as a Taylor series approximation to the aggregate (per capita) demand equations. These results are obtained under extremely weak conditions; in particular, the result holds even when there is no individual consumer whose differential demand equations have constant coefficients.

Remark 2. It follows from (13.9) that the constancy of the coefficients θ_i, ν_{ij} and ϕ in the relative price version of the Rotterdam model implies that the Slutsky coefficients π_{ij} are also constant in the absolute price version.

1.16 Simpler Demand Systems

In Section 1.12 we derived a system of differential demand equations and in Section 1.15 we obtained a finite-change version of this demand system, the so called Rotterdam model. In general the number of price coefficients to be estimated in this system is of the order of n^2. When n is anything but small, it is impractical to estimate the number of coefficients with most data sets. The usual resolution to this problem is to impose constraints on the structure of preferences (such as preference independence) to limit the number of free coefficients.

In this section we present a somewhat different approach. Rather than attacking the problem via the utility function, we formulate constraints on the price coefficients directly. Of course, the difference in approaches should not be overemphasized as constraints on the utility function imply constraints on the price coefficients and vice versa. The approach considered in this section was initiated by Keller (1984) and followed by Selvanathan (1985) in the context of differential demand equations.

Now let us consider equations (15.1), (15.2) and (15.5). Dividing both sides of (15.1) by $\bar{w}_{it}$ we obtain $\theta_i/\bar{w}_{it}$ as the income elasticity of demand for good i and $F_{ij} = \nu_{ij}/\bar{w}_{it}$ as the (i,j)-*th Frisch-price elasticity.* This F_{ij} is the elasticity of demand for good i with respect to the Frisch-deflated price of j. It is to be noted that this elasticity involves a relative (or deflated) price. Under preference independence, equation (15.5) implies that $F_{ij} = 0$ for $i \neq j$ and $F_{ii} = \phi\theta_i/\bar{w}_{it}$, which is ϕ times the income elasticity. Using equation (15.2), the conventional compensated (or Slutsky) price elasticity of demand for i with respect to the price of j is $\pi_{ij}/\bar{w}_{it}$. This elasticity involves an absolute (or undeflated) price.

Equation (15.2) for i=1,...,n is the absolute price version of the Rotterdam model. The budget constraint implies that one equation is redundant, so we consider (15.2) for i=1,...,n-1. This model contains n - 1 free marginal shares and (n-1) × n Slutsky coefficients. The homogeneity constraint (15.4) reduces the number of free Slutsky coefficients to

$(n-1) \times n - (n-1) = (n-1)^2$, while symmetry (15.3) further decreases this number to $\frac{1}{2}n(n-1)$. Thus when n is 10, for example, the total number of free parameters to be estimated is $9 + \frac{1}{2}(10 \times 9) = 54$, which is a large number.

The assumption of preference independence reduces the total number of free parameters from $(n-1) + \frac{1}{2}n(n-1)$ to n, comprising n-1 θ_i's and ϕ. Thus for n=10, this number falls from 54 to 10, a substantial economy in parameterization. The cost of this gain is, of course, the preference independence hypothesis is a fairly restrictive assumption. In particular, preference independence implies that the Frisch own-price elasticities F_{ii} are proportional to the corresponding income elasticities.

Consequently, on the one hand, if we use the absolute price version of Rotterdam model there can be too many parameters to estimate, particularly for large systems. On the other hand, if we attempt to solve the problem by invoking the assumption of preference independence, we may impose too rigid a structure in the price responses. Keller (1984) attempts to resolve this conflict by striking a middle ground. He introduces a new simple variant of Rotterdam model which has more parameters than does (15.5), but has no link between income and price elasticities.

Keller considers the following decomposition of π_{ij}:

$$\pi_{ij} = \mu\, \psi_i(\delta_{ij} - \psi_j), \tag{16.1}$$

where μ and ψ_i are constant coefficients with

$$\sum_{i=1}^{n} \psi_i = 1; \tag{16.2}$$

and δ_{ij} is the Kronecker delta. The Slutsky coefficients defined in (16.1) are obviously symmetric in i and j and, in view of (16.2), satisfy homogeneity. Under preference independence the Slutsky coefficients take the form

$$\pi_{ij} = \phi\theta_i(\delta_{ij} - \theta_j), \qquad i,j=1,...,n. \tag{16.3}$$

A comparison of (16.1) with (16.3) shows that Keller's model coincides with preference independence when $\mu = \phi$ and $\psi_i = \theta_i$ for i=1,...,n.

We define the price index

$$DP_{\psi t} = \sum_{j=1}^{n} \psi_j Dp_{jt}. \tag{16.4}$$

Then, if we substitute (16.1) in (15.2) and use (16.4), we obtain

$$\bar{w}_{it}Dq_{it} = \theta_i DQ_t + \mu\psi_i\left[Dp_{it} - DP_{\psi t}\right]. \tag{16.5}$$

This is a simple demand equation with only two variables on the right, real income (DQ) and the own-relative price $\left[Dp_{it} - DP_{\psi t}\right]$. Equation (15.5) also shares this property (although the price deflator in the substitution term is different). Equation (16.5) for i=1,...,n-1 contains (n-1) θ_i's, (n-1) free ψ_i's and μ, a total of 2(n-1) + 1 = 2n-1 parameters. This is (2n-1) - n = n-1 more than the number under preference independence.

Using relative prices, the own-price elasticity implied by (16.5) is $\mu\psi_i/\bar{w}_{it}$, which is independent of the income elasticity $(\theta_i/\bar{w}_{it})$. Using absolute prices, the own-price elasticity is a multiple $(1 - \psi_i)$ of the previous elasticity; again this is independent of the income elasticity. Thus, in (16.5) there is no link between income and price elasticities, in contrast to preference independence. Keller refers to (16.5) for i=1,...,n as the Rotterdam/SI model, where SI stands for substitution independence.

Model (16.5) for i=1,...,n is nonlinear in the parameters. Keller suggests a simple iterative least-squares procedure for estimating the model. From the definition of the price index $DP_{\psi t}$ given in (16.4) it is clear that this is a function of the unknown parameters ψ_i(i=1,...,n). To start the estimation procedure, this index is replaced by the Divisia price index

$DP_t = \Sigma_{i=1}^n \bar{w}_{it} Dp_{it}$. Least squares is then applied to (16.5) on an equation-by-equation basis to obtain the first-round estimates of θ_i and $\mu\psi_i$ (i=1,...,n). Call these estimates $\theta_i^{(0)}$ and $[\mu\psi_i]^{(0)}$.

From (16.2) we have

$$\sum_{i=1}^{n} \mu\psi_i = \mu. \tag{16.6}$$

Using $[\mu\psi_i]^{(0)}$ in (16.6), we obtain the first-round estimate of μ, $\mu^{(0)}$. Next, divide $[\mu\psi_i]^{(0)}$ by $\mu^{(0)}$, to yield the first-round estimates of the coefficients ψ_i, $\psi_i^{(0)}$. The estimates $\psi_i^{(0)}$ are then used to compute $DP_{\psi t}$ according to equation (16.4). This value is then used in the second round of the estimation procedure which is then the same as before. This procedure is repeated until convergence is reached.

Keller also proposed two other simple variants of (16.5), (i) an AIDS-version (AIDS/SI); and (ii) a version which uses Working's model for the marginal shares (CBS/SI). We shall consider CBS/SI model in Section 1.18.

1.17 An Even Simpler Demand System

In this section we present another demand system proposed by Selvanathan (1985), which is even simpler than Keller's. The material in this section is based on Selvanathan (1985).

Selvanathan proposed the simple hypothesis that the larger the budget share of commodity j, the larger is the possibility of the consumer switching from commodity j to another commodity i in response to an increase in the j-*th* price; i.e., the larger is the budget share of j, the higher is the probability that i and j are substitutes. In other words, the compensated price elasticity η^*_{ijt} is proportional to the budget share $\bar{w}_{jt}$,

$$\eta^*_{ijt} = \alpha_i \bar{w}_{jt}, \qquad i \neq j, \tag{17.1}$$

where α_i is an i-subscripted positive constant.

As $\eta^*_{ijt} = \pi_{ijt}/\bar{w}_{it}$, (17.1) implies that

$$\pi_{ijt} = \alpha_i \bar{w}_{it} \bar{w}_{jt}, \qquad i \neq j,$$

It then follows from homogeneity constraint (15.4) and $\sum_{i=1}^{n} \bar{w}_{it} = 1$ that

$$-\pi_{iit} = \sum_{j \neq i} \pi_{ijt} = \sum_{j \neq i} \alpha_i \bar{w}_{it} \bar{w}_{jt} = \alpha_i \bar{w}_{it}(1 - \bar{w}_{it}).$$

Thus,

$$\alpha_i = -\frac{\pi_{iit}}{\bar{w}_{it}(1 - \bar{w}_{it})} = -\frac{\eta^*_{iit}}{1 - \bar{w}_{it}}. \tag{17.2}$$

Equation (15.3) implies that

$$\alpha_i \bar{w}_{it} \bar{w}_{jt} = \alpha_j \bar{w}_{jt} \bar{w}_{it},$$

from which it follows that

$$\alpha_i = \sigma, \tag{17.3}$$

a positive constant independent of i.

It follows from $\eta^*_{ijt} = \pi_{ijt}/\bar{w}_{it}$ and (17.1) – (17.3) that all the Slutsky coefficients can be expressed as

$$\pi_{ijt} = \kappa\bar{w}_{it}(\delta_{ij} - \bar{w}_{jt}), \qquad i,j=1,...,n,$$

where $\kappa = -\sigma$ and δ_{ij} is the Kronecker delta. We write this in matrix form as

$$\boldsymbol{\pi}_t = \kappa(\bar{\mathbf{W}}_t - \bar{\mathbf{w}}_t\bar{\mathbf{w}}_t'), \tag{17.4}$$

where $\boldsymbol{\pi}_t = [\pi_{ijt}]$; $\bar{\mathbf{W}}_t = \mathrm{diag}[\bar{w}_{1t}...\bar{w}_{nt}]$; and $\bar{\mathbf{w}}_t = [\bar{w}_{it}]$. As $\kappa < 0$, we see that

$$\pi_{ijt} = -\kappa\bar{w}_{it}\bar{w}_{jt} > 0, \qquad i\neq j,$$

so that all the goods are substitutes in the Hicksian sense. Using Schwartz's inequality and $\Sigma_{i=1}^{n} \bar{w}_{it} = 1$, it can be easily shown that π_t is negative semidefinite when $\sigma > 0$, which is in agreement with the hypothesis.

As $\pi_{ijt}/\bar{w}_{it}\bar{w}_{jt} = \sigma$ for $i\neq j$, we can interpret σ as the cross-elasticity of substitution. Our hypothesis leads to the conclusion that this elasticity is independent of i and j. This restriction has been previously used in applied work by Leser (1960) for consumer demand systems and by Powell and Gruen (1968) for output supply systems.

Using (17.4) the substitution term of (15.2) can be written as

$$\sum_{j=1}^{n} \pi_{ijt}Dp_{jt} = \kappa\bar{w}_{it} \sum_{j=1}^{n} (\delta_{ij} - \bar{w}_{jt})Dp_{jt} = \kappa\bar{w}_{it}\left[Dp_{it} - DP_t\right],$$

where $DP_t = \Sigma_{j=1}^{n} \bar{w}_{jt}Dp_{jt}$ is the Divisia price index. Therefore, (15.2) simplifies to

$$\bar{w}_{it}Dq_{it} = \theta_i DQ_t + \kappa\bar{w}_{it}\left[Dp_{it} - DP_t\right]. \tag{17.5}$$

As in (16.5), only the own-relative price $\left[Dp_{it} - DP_t\right]$ appears in equation (17.5) (again, with a different price deflator). The Divisia price index DP_t acts as the deflator in (17.5); as this does not depend on unknown parameters the substitution term in (17.5) is even simpler than that in the Rotterdam/SI model (16.5). In addition, model (17.5) is *linear* in the parameters θ_i and κ, by contrast, (16.5) is nonlinear. The number of parameters to be estimated is n [(n-1) marginal shares plus κ], the same as under preference independence. As before, there is no link between income and price elasticities in (17.5). These are highly attractive properties of Selvanathan's model.

Let $y_{it} = \bar{w}_{it}Dq_{it}$ and $Dp^*_{it} = Dp_{it} - DP_t$. We write equation (17.5) for i=1,...,n-1 and t=1,...,T as

$$\begin{bmatrix} y_{11} \\ \vdots \\ y_{1T} \\ \vdots \\ y_{n-1,1} \\ \vdots \\ y_{n-1,T} \end{bmatrix} = \begin{bmatrix} DQ_1 & \cdots 0 \\ \vdots & \vdots \\ DQ_T & \cdots 0 \\ 0 & 0 \\ \vdots & \vdots \\ \vdots & DQ_1 \\ \vdots & \vdots \\ 0 & \cdots DQ_T \end{bmatrix} \begin{bmatrix} \theta_1 \\ \vdots \\ \vdots \\ \vdots \\ \vdots \\ \vdots \\ \theta_{n-1} \end{bmatrix} + \kappa \begin{bmatrix} \bar{w}_{11}Dp^*_{11} \\ \vdots \\ \bar{w}_{1T}Dp^*_{1T} \\ \vdots \\ \bar{w}_{n-1,1}Dp^*_{n-1,1} \\ \vdots \\ \bar{w}_{n-1,T}Dp^*_{n-1,T} \end{bmatrix} + \begin{bmatrix} \varepsilon_{11} \\ \vdots \\ \varepsilon_{1T} \\ \vdots \\ \varepsilon_{n-1,1} \\ \vdots \\ \varepsilon_{n-1,T} \end{bmatrix} \qquad (17.6)$$

We write **z** for the (n-1)T-vector on the left-hand side of (17.6) and z_k for the k-*th* element of this vector. Let **A** denote the (n-1)T × (n-1) matrix immediately to the right of the equals sign in (17.6). Column i of this matrix has $DQ_1,\dots,DQ_t$ as elements T(i-1) + 1 to T × i and zeros elsewhere. That is, $\mathbf{A} = \mathbf{I}_{n-1} \otimes \mathbf{DQ}$, where $\mathbf{I}_{n-1}$ is the identity matrix of order n–1; and $\mathbf{DQ} = [DQ_1 \dots DQ_T]'$. Let a_j be the j-*th* column and a_{kj} be the (k,j)-*th* element of **A**. We also write $\boldsymbol{\theta} = [\theta_1 \dots \theta_{n-1}]'$; **c** for the (n-1)T × 1 column vector associated with κ on the right-hand side of (17.6); and ε for the (n-1)T × 1 error vector. That is,

$$c = [c_k] = \begin{bmatrix} \bar{w}_{11} Dp^*_{11} \\ \cdot \\ \cdot \\ \bar{w}_{1T} Dp^*_{1T} \\ \cdot \\ \bar{w}_{n-1,1} Dp^*_{n-1,1} \\ \cdot \\ \cdot \\ \bar{w}_{n-1,T} Dp^*_{n-1,T} \end{bmatrix}, \qquad \varepsilon = [\varepsilon_k] = \begin{bmatrix} \varepsilon_{11} \\ \cdot \\ \cdot \\ \varepsilon_{1T} \\ \cdot \\ \varepsilon_{n-1,1} \\ \cdot \\ \cdot \\ \varepsilon_{n-1,T} \end{bmatrix}$$

Using the above notation, we can then write (17.6) as

$$\mathbf{z} = \mathbf{A}\boldsymbol{\theta} + \kappa\mathbf{c} + \boldsymbol{\varepsilon}$$

or

$$z_k = \sum_{j=1}^{n-1} \theta_j a_{kj} + \kappa c_k + \varepsilon_k, \qquad k = 1,\ldots,(n-1)T. \tag{17.7}$$

As can be seen, (17.7) is a linear regression model. It can be estimated by LS by regressing **z** on the n explanatory variables $a_1,\ldots,a_{n-1}$ and **c**. Although this is a simple procedure, the estimates are not efficient as the disturbances are non-spherical. Selvanathan (1985) develops the efficient GLS estimator.

1.18 Working's Model Further Considered

The Rotterdam model is a particular parameterization which uses the results of the differential approach. In this section we illustrate the usefulness of the differential approach as a general tool in demand analysis by giving a further parameterization using this approach. This parameterization involves endowing Working's model (8.1) with a substitution term under the assumption of preference independence.

We return to the general differential demand equation under preference independence (13.7) and recall that Working's model implies that the marginal share of good i equals the corresponding budget share plus a constant, $\theta_i = w_i + \beta_i$ [see equation (8.2)]. For a time-series application we write this marginal share as $\bar{w}_{it} + \beta_i$, where $\bar{w}_{it} = \frac{1}{2}(w_{i,t-1} + w_{it})$. To obtain the finite-change version of (13.7) we replace (i) w_i with $\bar{w}_{it}$; (ii) $d(\log q_i)$ with Dq_{it}; (iii) $d(\log Q)$ with $DQ_t = \Sigma_i \bar{w}_{it} Dq_{it}$; (iv) θ_i with $\bar{w}_{it} + \beta_i$; and (v) $d(\log p_i)$ with Dp_{it}. After minor rearrangement, this yields

$$\bar{w}_{it}(Dq_{it} - DQ_t) = \beta_i DQ_t + \phi(\bar{w}_{it} + \beta_i)\left[Dp_{it} - \sum_{j=1}^{n} (\bar{w}_{jt} + \beta_j)Dp_{jt}\right]. \tag{18.1}$$

Here the β_i's and ϕ are constant coefficients. Model (18.1) is the i-*th* demand equation of Working's model with a substitution term added under preference independence with a constant income flexibility. For brevity, we shall refer to (18.1) as *Working's model under preference independence*. Equation (18.1) is also called CBS/SI by Keller (1984).

Equation (18.1) can be compared to the AIDS model (7.6) which reduces to Working's model when prices are constant; see the discussion at the start of Section 1.8. There are two basic differences between (18.1) and AIDS. First, (18.1) is formulated in terms of changes over time, whereas AIDS is in levels; this is the reason for the absence of intercept terms in (18.1). Second, the substitution term of AIDS is much more complicated as it involves double-subscripted parameters; (18.1) has only single-subscripted parameters. Thus, the number of γ_{ij}'s in the AIDS substitution term is of the order n^2, while in Working's model there are only n-1 β_i's (the constraint $\Sigma_i\beta_i = 0$ eliminates one β_i) and ϕ.

1.19 The Behaviour of Implied Income Elasticities

In this chapter we have presented six systems of demand equations: The double-log model (2.1), the linear expenditure system (4.4), the translog model (6.6), AIDS (7.6), the two versions of the Rotterdam model (15.1) and (15.2) and Working's model under preference independence (18.1). As these all describe the demand for the n goods in one form or another, they are competitive specifications. The choice between them is generally made on the basis of statistical criteria such as goodness of fit or likelihood ratios. A different criterion, recommended by Flood et al. (1984), is the economic plausibility of the behaviour of the income elasticities implied by the competing models.

To apply this procedure, Flood et al. (1984) and Finke et al. (1984) used annual Japanese data (1951-1972) to estimate by maximum likelihood the translog model (6.6), as well as Working's model under preference independence (18.1) for $n = 4$ goods: Food (including beverages and tobacco), clothing (including footwear), housing (including furniture) and miscellaneous (everything else). For the estimation of the two models, normal error terms are added to the right-hand sides of (6.6) and (18.1) and we use the ML procedure.

The income elasticity of i is

$$1 + \frac{\sum_{k=1}^{n}\sum_{j=1}^{n}\beta_{kj} - (1/w_{it})\sum_{j=1}^{n}\beta_{ij}}{\sum_{k=1}^{n}\beta_k + \sum_{k=1}^{n}\sum_{j=1}^{n}\beta_{kj}\log\frac{P_j}{M}} \qquad (19.1)$$

under the translog and (8.3) under Working's model. These elasticities are given in Table 1.2. As can be seen, the two models imply substantially different elasticities. The translog elasticity of food *increases* from .42 in the early 1950s to .75 in the early 1970s. By contrast, the food elasticity under Working's model starts off at .72 and gradually *declines* to .54. The increase in this elasticity under the translog model means that the increased affluence of the Japanese over this period caused food to become *more* luxurious, which is implausible. It is much more plausible for food to become *less* of a luxury with increased affluence, as it does under Working's model. Note also that the translog elasticity values for housing in the early years seem too high. Moreover, these values decline by more than 50 percent over the period (from 3.7 to 1.3), while the corresponding values under Working's model are more stable. On the basis of the behaviour of these elasticities, the conclusion is that Working's model is more acceptable than the translog.

1.20 More on Substitutes and Complements

We return to the general differential demand equation (12.9) and recall that the signs of the price coefficients ν_{ij} indicate the pattern of substitutability/complementarity according to the Houthakker definition. Two goods i and j are said to be specific substitutes (complements) if $\nu_{ij} > 0$ (< 0). This definition of substitutability is based on the sign of u^{ij}, the (i,j)-*th* element of the inverse of the Hessian matrix of the utility function, and thus relates to the nature of the interaction of goods in the utility function.

By contrast, Hicks' (1946) definition is based on the sign of the total substitution effect, the sum of the specific and general effects. As the Slutsky coefficients defined in (13.9) combine the latter two effects, their signs reflect substitutability/complementarity in Hicks' sense. If $\pi_{ij} > 0$, then it follows from (13.11) that a rise in the absolute price of j causes consumption of i to increase, real income and other prices remaining

Table 1.2 The behaviour of income elasticities under alternative models: Japan, 1951-1972

	Income elasticities implied by							
	Translog model				Working's model			
Year (1)	Food (2)	Clothing (3)	Housing (4)	Miscellaneous (5)	Food (6)	Clothing (7)	Housing (8)	Miscellaneous (9)
1951	.42	.42	3.74	2.01	-	-	-	-
1952	.46	.47	3.06	1.85	.72	1.02	1.80	1.39
1953	.48	.49	2.71	1.74	.71	1.02	1.72	1.37
1954	.50	.50	2.65	1.69	.71	1.02	1.68	1.35
1955	.51	.51	2.46	1.66	.70	1.02	1.65	1.33
1956	.52	.52	2.27	1.61	.70	1.02	1.61	1.32
1957	.54	.53	2.17	1.56	.69	1.02	1.58	1.32
1958	.55	.54	2.05	1.52	.68	1.02	1.55	1.31
1959	.56	.55	1.94	1.48	.67	1.03	1.50	1.31
1960	.59	.57	1.80	1.42	.65	1.03	1.45	1.30
1961	.61	.59	1.71	1.38	.64	1.02	1.43	1.29
1962	.62	.61	1.62	1.34	.62	1.02	1.42	1.28
1963	.64	.63	1.56	1.30	.61	1.03	1.42	1.26
1964	.66	.65	1.48	1.26	.60	1.02	1.39	1.26
1965	.67	.66	1.47	1.25	.59	1.03	1.38	1.25
1966	.68	.67	1.42	1.23	.59	1.03	1.37	1.25
1967	.70	.68	1.38	1.21	.58	1.03	1.36	1.24
1968	.71	.70	1.35	1.19	.58	1.03	1.35	1.24
1969	.72	.71	1.32	1.18	.57	1.03	1.34	1.24
1970	.73	.72	1.30	1.16	.55	1.03	1.33	1.24
1971	.74	.73	1.28	1.16	.55	1.03	1.32	1.23
1972	.75	.74	1.26	1.15	.54	1.03	1.32	1.23

constant. Accordingly, goods i and j are said to be *Hicksian substitutes (complements)* if $\pi_{ij} > 0$ (< 0).

To clarify this distinction further consider the following example, based on Theil (1980). Let the matrix of price coefficients for n=3 goods be

$$[\nu_{ij}] = \begin{bmatrix} -.25 & -.05 & .05 \\ -.05 & -.20 & .10 \\ .05 & .10 & -.25 \end{bmatrix} \begin{matrix} \text{good 1} \\ \text{good 2} \\ \text{good 3.} \end{matrix} \qquad (20.1)$$
$$\qquad \text{good 1} \quad \text{good 2} \quad \text{good 3}$$

This matrix is symmetric in accordance with (13.5). Its sign pattern indicates that goods 1 and 2 are specific complements; goods 1 and 3 are specific substitutes; and goods 2 and 3 are specific substitutes. Application of (12.6) with $\phi = -.5$ yields the marginal shares as the row sums of (20.1):

$$[\theta_i] = \begin{bmatrix} .5 \\ .3 \\ .2 \end{bmatrix} \begin{matrix} \text{good 1} \\ \text{good 2} \\ \text{good 3.} \end{matrix} \qquad (20.2)$$

Let the three budget shares be

$$[w_i] = \begin{bmatrix} .2 \\ .3 \\ .5 \end{bmatrix} \begin{matrix} \text{good 1} \\ \text{good 2} \\ \text{good 3} \end{matrix} \qquad (20.3)$$

so that, in view of (2.7), the income elasticities are

$$[\eta_i] = [\theta_i/w_i] = \begin{bmatrix} 2.5 \\ 1.0 \\ .4 \end{bmatrix} \begin{matrix} \text{good 1} \\ \text{good 2} \\ \text{good 3.} \end{matrix}$$

Good 1 is a luxury, 3 a necessity, while 2 is a borderline case.

If we divide both sides of (12.9) by w_i we obtain ν_{ij}/w_i as the elasticity of consumption of good i with respect to the Frisch-deflated price of j. This is known as the *Frisch price elasticity*. Using (20.1) and (20.3) yields the following Frisch price elasticity matrix:

$$[\nu_{ij}/w_i] = \begin{bmatrix} -1.25 & -.25 & .25 \\ -.17 & -.67 & .33 \\ .10 & .20 & -.50 \end{bmatrix} \begin{matrix} \text{good 1} \\ \text{good 2} \\ \text{good 3.} \end{matrix}$$
$$\qquad\qquad \text{good 1} \quad \text{good 2} \quad \text{good 3}$$

Thus, a 1 percent increase in the Frisch-deflated price of good 1, other Frisch-deflated prices and income remaining constant, causes consumption of that good to fall by 1.25 percent; consumption of good 2 falls by .17 percent (as 1 and 2 are specific complements) and that of good 3 rises by .10 percent (1 and 3 are specific substitutes).

Using (20.1), (20.2) and $\phi = -.5$ in (13.9) gives the following matrix of Slutsky coefficients:

$$[\pi_{ij}] = [\nu_{ij} - \phi\theta_i\theta_j] = \begin{bmatrix} -.13 & .03 & .10 \\ .03 & -.16 & .13 \\ .10 & .13 & -.23 \end{bmatrix} \begin{matrix} \text{good 1} \\ \text{good 2} \\ \text{good 3.} \end{matrix} \qquad (20.4)$$
$$\qquad\qquad \text{good 1} \quad \text{good 2} \quad \text{good 3}$$

As all the off-diagonal elements are positive, the three goods are pairwise substitutes in Hicks' sense. Dividing both sides of (13.11) by w_i we find that π_{ij}/w_i is the elasticity of demand for i with respect to the j-*th* absolute price, which is known as the *Slutsky price elasticity*. Using (20.3) and (20.4), the Slutsky elasticity matrix is

$$[\pi_{ij}/w_i] = \begin{bmatrix} -.65 & .15 & .50 \\ .10 & -.53 & .43 \\ .20 & .26 & -.46 \end{bmatrix} \begin{matrix} \text{good 1} \\ \text{good 2} \\ \text{good 3.} \end{matrix}$$
$$\qquad\qquad \text{good 1} \quad \text{good 2} \quad \text{good 3}$$

Accordingly, when real income and the other prices are held constant, a 1 percent increase in the absolute price of good 1 leads to a .65 percent fall in consumption of that good and increases in the consumption of the other two goods of .10 and .20 percent, respectively.

1.21 Preference Independence and Block Independence

In Section 1.5 we analyzed the case when preferences can be represented by a utility function that is additive in the n goods,

$$u = \sum_{i=1}^{n} u_i(q_i). \tag{21.1}$$

This form of the utility function is known as preference independence as the marginal utility of good i is independent of the consumption of good j for i ≠ j. Under (21.1) the Hessian matrix of the utility function and its inverse are both diagonal. It then follows from (12.5) and (12.6) that ν_{ij} = 0 for i ≠ j and $\nu_{ii} = \phi\theta_i$, so that the demand equation (12.9) simplifies to

$$w_i d(\log q_i) = \theta_i d(\log Q) + \phi\theta_i d\left[\log \frac{p_i}{P'}\right]. \tag{21.2}$$

Accordingly, under preference independence only the own Frisch-deflated price appears in each demand equation, so that no pair of goods is either a specific substitute or complement. Furthermore, preference independence implies that each θ_i is positive, which rules out inferior goods.

As can be seen, the implications of the preference independence assumption are rather drastic. A weaker version of preference independence is *block independence*, whereby the additive specification (21.1) is applied to *groups* of goods rather than to individual goods. Let the n goods be divided into G < n groups, written $S_1,\dots,S_G$, such that each good belongs to only one group. Further, let the consumer's preferences be such that the utility function is the sum of G group utility functions, each involving the quantities of only one group,

$$u = \sum_{g=1}^{G} u_g(q_g), \tag{21.3}$$

where q_g is the vector of the q_i's that fall under S_g. Under (21.3), the marginal utility of a good depends only on the consumption of goods belonging to the same group. When the goods are numbered appropriately, the Hessian of the utility function and its inverse become block-diagonal. Accordingly, specification (21.3) is known as *block-independent preferences.*

In view of (12.5), block independence implies that $[\nu_{ij}]$ is block-diagonal. Therefore, if i belongs to S_g, equations (12.9) and (12.6) can now be written as

$$w_i d(\log q_i) = \theta_i d(\log Q) + \sum_{j \in S_g} \nu_{ij} d\left[\log \frac{p_j}{P'}\right], \tag{21.4}$$

$$\sum_{j \in S_g} \nu_{ij} = \phi\theta_i, \qquad i \in S_g. \tag{21.5}$$

Thus block independence implies that the only deflated prices that appear in the i-*th* demand equation are those of goods belonging to the same group as the commodity in question. As $\nu_{ij} = O$ for i and j in different groups, under block independence no good is a specific substitute or complement of any good that belongs to a different group.

1.22 The Demand for Groups of Goods under Block Independence

We write

$$W_g = \sum_{i \in S_g} w_i, \qquad \Theta_g = \sum_{i \in S_g} \theta_i \tag{22.1}$$

for the budget and marginal shares of group g. The marginal share Θ_g tells us the increase in expenditure on S_g as a result of a one-dollar increase in income. Summing both sides of (21.5) over $i \in S_g$ shows that

$$\sum_{i\in S_g} \sum_{j\in S_g} \nu_{ij} = \phi\Theta_g > 0, \tag{22.2}$$

where the inequality sign is based on the positive definiteness of the matrix $[\nu_{ij}]$. Accordingly, block independence means that no group as a whole can be inferior; members of the group can be inferior, however.

We define the group Divisia volume and Frisch price indexes as

$$d(\log Q_g) = \sum_{i\in S_g} \frac{w_i}{W_g} d(\log q_i), \tag{22.3}$$

$$d(\log P_g') = \sum_{i\in S_g} \frac{\theta_i}{\Theta_g} d(\log p_i). \tag{22.4}$$

These two indexes aggregate consistently since a budget-share- weighted average of $d(\log Q_1),\ldots,d(\log Q_G)$ equals the Divisia volume index of all the n goods $d(\log Q)$; and a marginal-share-weighted average of $d(\log P_1'),\ldots,d(\log P_G')$ equals the overall Frisch price index $d(\log P')$:

$$\sum_{g=1}^{G} W_g d(\log Q_g) = d(\log Q), \qquad \sum_{g=1}^{G} \Theta_g d(\log P_g') = d(\log P').$$

We obtain the demand equation for the group S_g as a whole under block independence by simply adding over $i\in S_g$ both sides of the demand equation for good i under block independence, equation (21.4). In view of (22.1) and (22.3) this yields

$$W_g d(\log Q_g) = \Theta_g d(\log Q) + \sum_{i\in S_g} \sum_{j\in S_g} \nu_{ij} d\left[\log \frac{p_j}{P'}\right]. \tag{22.5}$$

Our objective is to simplify the price substitution term of this equation. As ν_{ij} is symmetric in i and j [see equation (13.5)], (21.5) can be expressed as

$$\sum_{i \in S_g} \nu_{ij} = \phi\theta_j, \qquad j \in S_g,$$

so that

$$\sum_{i \in S_g} \sum_{j \in S_g} \nu_{ij} d\left[\log \frac{p_j}{P'}\right] = \phi \sum_{j \in S_g} \theta_j d\left[\log \frac{p_j}{P'}\right]$$

$$= \phi\Theta_g d\left[\log \frac{P'_g}{P'}\right],$$

where the second step is based on (22.1) and (22.4). Accordingly, (22.5) can be expressed as

$$W_g d(\log Q_g) = \Theta_g d(\log Q) + \phi\Theta_g d\left[\log \frac{P'_g}{P'}\right], \qquad (22.6)$$

This is the *composite demand equation* for S_g as a group.

Equation (22.6) shows that under block independence, the demand for a group of goods as a whole depends on real income and the relative price of the group $d[\log(P'_g/P')]$. This relative price is the Frisch-deflated Frisch price index of the group. It is to be noted that the relative prices of goods outside the group in question play no role in equation (22.6). By dividing both sides of this equation by W_g, we find that Θ_g/W_g is the income elasticity of demand for the group and that $\phi\Theta_g/W_g$ is the own-price elasticity; this latter elasticity is the elasticity of the Divisia volume index of the group with respect to the Frisch-deflated Frisch price index of the group.

It is instructive to compare equation (22.6) with (21.2), the demand equation for an individual good under preference independence. This comparison reveals that both equations have the same general form:

$w_i d(\log q_i)$ on the left side of (21.2) becomes $W_g d(\log Q_g)$ in (22.6), and $\theta_i d(\log Q)$ and $\phi\theta_i d[\log (p_i/P')]$ on the right in (21.2) are replaced with $\Theta_g d(\log Q)$ and $\phi\Theta_g d[\log (P'_g/P')]$ in (22.6). Therefore in going from (21.2) to (22.6), each variable is replaced by the corresponding group concept, making the latter equation an *uppercase* version of the former. The reason for this is that the demand equation for the group (22.6) is based on block independence, while (21.2) holds under preference independence, and the utility function under block independence (21.3) exhibits preference independence with respect to *groups* of goods, rather than the individual commodities. Another way of expressing this is to note that if S_g consists of only one good, let it be the i-*th*, then (22.6) for this group coincides with (21.2)

1.23 Conditional Demand Equations

As there are G groups of goods, there are G composite demand equations, each of the form (22.6). These equations give the allocation of income to each of the G groups. This allocation depends only on income and the G relative prices of the groups. Given the demand for a group, the next question is how expenditure on the group is allocated to the commodities within the group. This question is answered by the conditional demand equations. In this section we analyze the form of the conditional demand equations under the assumption of block independence.

To obtain the conditional demand equations, we first rearrange (22.6):

$$d(\log Q) = \frac{W_g}{\Theta_g} d(\log Q_g) - \phi d\left[\log \frac{P'_g}{P'}\right]. \tag{23.1}$$

We then substitute the right side of this equation for d(log Q) in (21.4). In the next section it is shown that this yields for $i \in S_g$

$$w_i d(\log q_i) = \theta'_i W_g d(\log Q_g) + \sum_{j\in S_g} \nu_{ij} d\left[\log \frac{p_j}{P'_g}\right], \tag{23.2}$$

where

$$\theta'_i = \frac{\theta_i}{\Theta_g}, \qquad i\in S_g, \tag{23.3}$$

is the *conditional marginal share* of good i within the group S_g, with

$$\sum_{j\in S_g} \theta'_i = 1.$$

This share answers the question, If income increases by one dollar, resulting in a certain additional amount spent on the group S_g, what is the proportion of this additional amount that is allocated to commodity i?

Equation (23.2) is the demand equation for $i\in S_g$, given the demand for the group as a whole $W_g d(\log Q_g)$. It is known as the *conditional demand equation* for $i\in S_g$. This equation shows that the allocation of expenditure to goods within the *g-th* group depends on the total consumption of the group, as measured by $W_g d(\log Q_g)$, and the relative prices of goods within the group. The deflator for these relative prices is the Frisch price index of the group $d(\log P'_g)$, defined in (22.4). Consumption of other groups and the prices of goods outside S_g do not appear in (23.2). Consequently, the within-group allocation of expenditure depends only on variables pertaining to the group in question. It follows from (13.5) that the price coefficients are symmetric in i and j for commodities belonging to the same group.

$$\nu_{ij} = \nu_{ji}, \qquad i,j\in S_g. \tag{23.4}$$

The ν_{ij}'s within S_g are also constrained by (21.5) which we repeat here:

$$\sum_{j\in S_g} \nu_{ij} = \phi\theta_i, \qquad i\in S_g. \tag{23.5}$$

The conditional demand equation (23.2) is to be contrasted with (21.4) which can be described as the corresponding *unconditional demand equation*. The variables on the left of these two equations are the same, but the real income term in (21.4), $\theta_i d(\log Q)$, is replaced by $\theta_i' W_g d(\log Q_g)$ in (23.2). Also, the price substitution terms are identical, except that the Frisch price index of all goods acts as the deflator in (21.4), while the corresponding group concept $d(\log P_g')$ plays this role in (23.2).

Block-independent preferences imply that the consumer's problem can be solved in two steps. The first decision involves the allocation of income to the G groups, as described by the G group demand equations (22.6). Each of these demand equations contains real income and the relative price of the group in question but not the prices of the individual goods. Then in the second decision, for each of the groups, expenditure is allocated to the goods within the group. The conditional demand equations (23.2) describe this allocation and they contain total consumption of the group, as determined by the previous decision, and relative prices within the group. Accordingly, there is a decision hierarchy under block independence.

The conditional demand equations (23.2) were obtained under block independence. These results also hold, however, under the weaker condition of blockwise dependence; see, e.g., Theil (1975/76).

1.24 Derivations of Conditional Demand Equations

To derive the conditional demand equation (23.2) we first substitute the right side of (23.1) for d(log Q) in the unconditional equation (21.4). This yields

$$w_i d(\log q_i) = \frac{\theta_i}{\Theta_g} W_g d(\log Q_g) - \phi\theta_i d(\log P_g') + \phi\theta_i d(\log P') + \sum_{j\in S_g} \nu_{ij} d(\log p_j) - \sum_{j\in S_g} \nu_{ij} d(\log P'). \tag{24.1}$$

In view of (23.5), the second term on the right in (24.1) can be expressed as

$$-\phi\theta_i d(\log P'_g) = \sum_{j\in S_g} \nu_{ij} d(\log P'_g),$$

and the third term becomes

$$\phi\theta_i d(\log P') = \sum_{j\in S_g} \nu_{ij} d(\log P'),$$

so that it cancels with the last term. Consequently, (24.1) can be written as

$$\begin{aligned} w_i d(\log q_i) &= \frac{\theta_i}{\Theta_g} W_g d(\log Q_g) + \sum_{j\in S_g} \nu_{ij} d(\log p_j) - \sum_{j\in S_g} \nu_{ij} d(\log P'_g) \\ &= \theta'_i W_g d(\log Q_g) + \sum_{j\in S_g} \nu_{ij} d\left[\log \frac{p_j}{P'_g}\right], \end{aligned}$$

which is the conditional demand equation (23.2).

1.25 The Conditional Version of the Rotterdam Model

Consider equation (23.2) in terms of finite changes:

$$\bar{w}_{it} Dq_{it} = \theta'_i \bar{W}_{gt} DQ_{gt} + \sum_{j\in S_g} \nu_{ij}(Dp_{jt} - DP'_{gt}), \tag{25.1}$$

where $\bar{W}_{gt} DQ_{gt} = \Sigma_{i\in S_g} \bar{w}_{it} Dq_{it}$; $DP'_{gt} = \Sigma_{i\in S_g} \theta'_i Dp_{it}$ is the Frisch price index of the group in terms of finite changes; and the other notation is as before. When the conditional marginal share and price coefficients in (25.1) are treated as constants, it is known as the i-*th* equation of the *conditional version of the Rotterdam model*; it is the conditional demand equation for commodity i belonging to the group S_g; see Theil (1975/76).

Equation (25.1) is analogous to the unconditional Rotterdam model given in (15.1). The price coefficients ν_{ij} in these two equations are identical, and the constraint on the ν_{ij}'s within S_g, similar to (12.6) is

$$\sum_{j \in S_g} \nu_{ij} = \phi \Theta_g \theta'_i, \qquad i \in S_g, \tag{25.2}$$

which follows from (23.3) and (23.5). Constraint (25.2) also follows from (23.3) and (12.6) as $\nu_{ij} = 0$ for i and j belonging to different groups. Furthermore, as $[\nu_{ij}]$ is symmetric, the price coefficients within the group are also symmetric.

The absolute price version of (25.1) is

$$\bar{w}_{it} Dq_{it} = \theta'_i \bar{W}_{gt} DQ_{gt} + \sum_{j \in S_g} \pi^g_{ij} Dp_{jt}, \tag{25.3}$$

where

$$\pi^g_{ij} = \nu_{ij} - \phi \Theta_g \theta'_i \theta'_j, \qquad i,j \in S_g, \tag{25.4}$$

is the (i,j)-*th conditional Slutsky coefficient.* This coefficient measures the effect of a change in the price of good j on the consumption of i ($i,j \in S_g$) under the condition that other prices and total consumption of the group remain constant. The conditional Slutsky coefficients satisfy demand homogeneity,

$$\sum_{j \in S_g} \pi^g_{ij} = 0, \qquad i \in S_g, \tag{25.5}$$

which follows from (25.2), (25.4) and $\sum_{j \in S_g} \theta'_j = 1$; and are symmetric,

$$\pi^g_{ij} = \pi^g_{ji}, \qquad i,j \in S_g, \tag{25.6}$$

which follows from (25.3) and (25.4). Equation (25.3) is a conditional version of (15.2); and similarly (25.4), (25.5) and (25.6) are the conditional counterparts of (13.9), (15.4), and (15.3). It is to be noted that, in contrast to the price coefficients ν_{ij}, which are the same in the unconditional and conditional models, the Slutsky coefficients in (25.3) differ from those in (15.2).

References

Barnett, W.A. (1979). 'Theoretical Foundations for the Rotterdam Model.' *Review of Economic Studies* 46: 109-130.

Barnett, W.A. (1981). *Consumer Demand and Labour Supply: Goods, Monetary Assets and Time.* Amsterdam: North-Holland Publishing Company.

Barten, A.P. (1964). 'Consumer Demand Functions Under Conditions of Almost Additive Preferences.' *Econometrica* 32: 1-38.

Barten, A.P. (1977) 'The Systems of Consumer Demand Functions Approach: A Review.' *Econometrica* 45: 23-51.

Bewley, R.A. (1986). *Allocation Models: Specification, Estimation and Applications.* Cambridge, Mass.: Ballinger Publishing Company.

Blundell, R. (1988). 'Consumer Behaviour: Theory and Empirical Evidence -- A Survey,' *Economic Journal* 98: 16-65.

Brown, A. and A. Deaton (1972). 'Surveys in Applied Economics: Models of Consumer Behaviour,' *Economic Journal* 82: 1145-1236.

Cassel, G. (1932). *The Theory of Social Economy*, rev. ed. trans. from the fifth German edition by S.L. Barrow. New York: Harcourt, Brace.

Christensen, L.R., D.W. Jorgenson, and L.J. Lau. (1975). 'Transcendental Logarithmic Utility Functions.' *American Economic Review* 65: 367-383.

Clements, K.W. (1987a). 'Alternative Approaches to Consumption Theory,' Chapter 1 in H. Theil and K.W. Clements, *Applied Demand Analysis: Results from System-Wide Approaches.* Cambridge, Mass.: Ballinger Publishing Company.

Clements, K.W. (1987b). 'The Demand for Groups of Goods and Conditional Demand,' Chapter 4 in H. Theil and K.W. Clements, *Applied Demand Analysis: Results from System-Wide Approaches.* Cambridge, Mass.: Ballinger Publishing Company.

Deaton, A.S. (1974). 'The Analysis of Consumer Demand in the United Kingdom, 1900-1970,' *Econometrica* 42: 341-367.

Deaton, A.S. (1975). *Models and Projections of Demand in Post-War Britain.* London: Chapman and Hall.

Deaton, A.S. (1986). 'Demand Analysis,' in Z. Griliches and M.D. Intriligator (eds), *Handbook of Econometrics.* Volume III, Amsterdam: North-Holland Publishing Company, pp.1768-1839.

Deaton, A.S., and J. Muellbauer. (1980a). *Economics and Consumer Behaviour.* Cambridge: Cambridge University Press.

Deaton, A.S., and J. Muellbauer. (1980b). 'An Almost Ideal Demand System.' *American Economic Review* 70: 312-326.

Divisia, F. (1925). 'L'Indice Monétaire et la Théorie de la Monnaie.' *Revue d'Economie Politique* 39: 980-1008.

Finke, R., L.R. Flood and H. Theil. (1984). 'Maximum Likelihood and Instrumental Variable Estimation of a Consumer Demand System for Japan and Sweden.' *Economics Letters* 15: 13-19.

Flood, L.R., R. Finke and H. Theil. (1984). 'An Evaluation of Alternative Demand Systems by Means of Implied Income Elasticities.' *Economics Letters* 15: 21-27.

Frisch, R. (1932). *New Methods of Measuring Marginal Utility.* Tübingen: J.C.B. Mohr.

Goldberger, A.S. (1987). *Functional Form and Utility: A Review of Consumer Demand Theory*. Boulder and London: Westview Press.

Hicks, J.R. (1946). *Value and Capital*. Second edition (first edition 1939). Oxford: Oxford University Press.

Houthakker, H.S. (1960). 'Additive Preferences,' *Econometrica* 28: 244-257.

Johansen, L. (1969). 'On the Relationships Between Some Systems of Demand Functions,' *Liiketaloudellinen Aikakauskirga* 1: 30-41; Reprint Series No.47, University of Oslo, Institute of Economics.

Keller, W.J. (1984). 'Some Simple but Flexible Differential Consumer Demand Systems,' *Economics Letters* 16: 77-82.

Klein, L.R., and H. Rubin (1948). 'A Constant-Utility Index of the Cost of Living,' *The Review of Economic Studies* 15: 84-87.

Leser, C.E.V. (1960). 'Demand Functions for Nine Commodity Groups in Australia,' *The Australian Journal of Statistics* 2: 102-113.

Lluch, C. and A.A. Powell (1975). International Comparisons of Expenditure Patterns, *European Economic Review* 5: 275-303.

Lluch, C., A.A. Powell and R.A. Williams (1977). *Patterns in Household Demand and Saving*. Oxford: Oxford University Press.

Phlips, L. (1974). *Applied Consumption Analysis*. Amsterdam: North-Holland Publishing Company. Second edition 1983.

Pollak, A.A. and T.J. Wales (1992). *Demand System Specification and Estimation*. New York and Oxford: Oxford University Press.

Powell, A.A. (1974). *Empirical Analytics of Demand Systems*. Lexington, Mass.: D.C. Heath and Compsny.

Powell, A.A. and F.H.G. Gruen (1968). 'The Constant Elasticity of Transformation Production Frontier and Linear Supply System,' *International Economic Review* 9: 315-328.

Roy, R. (1942). *De l'utilité*. Paris: Hermann et Cie.

Selvanathan, E.A. (1985). 'An Even Simpler Differential Demand System,' *Economics Letters* 19: 343-347.

Selvanathan, E.A. (1987). *Explorations in Consumer Demand*, Ph.D. Thesis, Murdoch University, Western Australia.

Selvanathan, E.A. (1991). 'Further Results on Aggregation of Differential Demand Equations,' *The Review of Economic Studies* 58: 799-805.

Slutsky, E. (1915). 'Sulla Teoria del Bilancio del Consumator,' *Giornale degli Economisti* 51: 1-26; translation, 'On the Theory of the Budget of the Consumer,' in G.J. Stigler and K.E. Boulding (eds.), *Readings in Price Theory*. Chicago: Richard D. Irwin, 1952.

Stone, R. (1954a). *The Measurement of Consumers' Expenditure and Behaviour in the United Kingdom, 1920-1938.* Vol. 1, Cambridge: Cambridge University Press.

Stone, R. (1954b). 'Linear Expenditure Systems and Demand Analysis: An Application to the Pattern of British Demand,' *Economic Journal* 64: 511-527.

Theil, H. (1965). 'The Information Approach to Demand Analysis,' *Econometrica* 33: 67-87.

Theil, H. (1971). *Principles of Econometrics.* New York: John Wiley and Sons.

Theil, H. (1975/76). *Theory and Measurement of Consumer Demand.* Two volumes. Amsterdam: North-Holland Publishing Company.

Theil, H. (1980). *The System-Wide Approach to Microeconomics.* Chicago: The University of Chicago Press.

Theil, H., C-F. Chung and J.L. Seale, Jr. (1989). *International Evidence on Consumption Patterns.* Greenwich, Connecticut: JAI Press, Inc.

Theil, H. and K.W. Clements (1987). *Applied Demand Analysis: Results from System-Wide Approaches.* Cambridge, Mass.: Ballinger Publishing Company.

Theil, H. and F.E. Suhm (1981). *International Consumption Comparisons: A System-Wide Approach.* Amsterdam: North-Holland Publishing Company.

Working, H. (1943). 'Statistical Laws of Family Expenditure,' *Journal of the American Statistical Association* 38: 43-56.

2 Empirical Regularities in Consumption Patterns

K.W. Clements[1] and S. Selvanathan[2]

[1] *Economic Research Centre, The University of Western Australia.*
[2] *Faculty of Commerce and Administration, Griffith University, Australia.*

2.1 Introduction

The objective of this chapter is to review, distill and systematise some of the major empirical findings on consumption patterns, concentrating in particular on the more recent (and, in some cases, more controversial) evidence. We start by using price-quantity data for the OECD to introduce indexes of consumption patterns. Then follows a discussion of Engel's law (and its modern extension) and recent evidence on homogeneity and symmetry. Later parts of the chapter deal with preference independence, the issue of the constancy of tastes and aspects of functional form of demand equations. Most of the discussion deals with results from time-series/cross-country data. This chapter draws on Clements and S. Selvanathan (1994).

2.2 OECD Consumption

In this and the next section, which draw on S. Selvanathan (1988a) and Stening (1985), we introduce some basic concepts by using consumption data from most of the OECD countries. Table 2.1 gives some broad characteristics of the database. There are 18 countries with a bit less than 20 annual observations in most.

Let p_{it} be the price and q_{it} the per capita quantity consumed of good i during year t. Let there be n goods, so that total expenditure

Table 2.1 Characteristics of the OECD Database

Country	Sample period	Sample size	Per capita GDP in 1975		Number of commodity groups
			International dollars	(4) with US = 100	
(1)	(2)	(3)	(4)	(5)	(6)
1. US	1960-1981	21	7132	100	10
2. Canada	1960-1981	21	6788	95	10
3. Sweden	1964-1981	17	6749	95	10
4. Switzerland	1960-1981	21	6082	85	9
5. Denmark	1966-1981	15	5969	84	10
6. Australia	1960-1981	21	5919	83	10
7. France	1964-1981	17	5864	82	10
8. Germany	1960-1981	21	5758	81	8
9. Belgium	1960-1981	21	5554	78	10
10. Norway	1964-1981	17	5419	76	10
11. Netherlands	1952-1977	25	5321	75	10
12. Iceland	1960-1973	13	5201	73	10
13. Finland	1960-1977	17	5192	73	10
14. Austria	1964-1981	17	4994	70	10
15. Japan	1970-1981	11	4905	69	8
16. UK	1964-1981	17	4601	65	10
17. Spain	1964-1977	13	4032	57	10
18. Italy	1964-1981	17	3870	54	10

The GDPs in international dollars are from Summers and Heston (1984) and are computed on the basis of the purchasing powers of national currencies, not prevailing exchange rates. Sample size is after lagging.

is $M_t = \Sigma_{i=1}^{n} p_{it}q_{it}$ and the proportion of total expenditure devoted to commodity i is $w_{it} = p_{it}q_{it}/M_t$. This w_{it} is called the budget share of good i. For brevity, we shall refer to M as *income*. Table 2.2 presents the budget shares at sample means for each commodity in the 18 countries. For example, looking at the sixth row we see that, on average, Australians spend 19 percent of their income on food, 9 percent on beverages, 9 percent on clothing, 16 percent on housing and so on. The last row of

Table 2.2 Budget Shares of 10 Commodities for 18 Countries (Means × 100)

Country (1)	Food (2)	Beverages (3)	Clothing (4)	Housing (5)	Durables (6)	Medical care (7)	Transport (8)	Recreation (9)	Education (10)	Miscellaneous (11)
1. US	14.38	4.24	8.03	19.29	7.28	9.46	15.93	6.25	1.81	13.33
2. Canada	16.42	6.21	8.41	18.85	8.73	3.84	15.02	5.96	2.33	14.22
3. Sweden	20.72	7.96	8.41	22.79	7.66	2.27	13.65	9.18	.18	7.18
4. Switzerland	22.73	9.42	6.77	18.06	7.80	6.52	10.99	9.36		8.35
5. Denmark	19.18	9.09	6.97	20.92	8.98	1.92	15.04	7.88	.83	9.19
6. Australia	19.48	8.96	9.13	15.77	8.19	6.04	15.13	5.71	.69	10.89
7. France	21.20	4.69	8.22	14.41	10.23	10.50	11.99	6.05	.29	12.42
8. Germany	30.38		10.36	15.79	12.04	2.68	13.06	7.44		8.55
9. Belgium	23.11	6.95	7.53	15.72	14.14	6.74	10.67	3.98	.23	10.93
10. Norway	23.45	7.56	9.97	14.54	8.86	4.20	13.31	7.68	.54	9.89
11. Netherlands	26.20	6.38	14.78	10.81	12.48	6.67	6.67	3.41	3.10	9.50
12. Iceland	23.50	7.86	10.66	19.06	10.00	6.07	12.13	5.24	.44	5.05
13. Finland	28.24	8.62	8.26	14.36	7.51	2.54	13.60	5.92	1.44	9.49
14. Austria	22.06	7.29	11.37	11.99	8.89	3.49	13.36	5.67	.35	15.54
15. Japan	27.45		7.76	16.78	6.76	8.92	8.97	9.05		14.32
16. UK	18.92	6.26	8.40	18.20	7.78	.85	13.13	7.88	1.98	16.50
17. Spain	38.53	3.51	10.58	13.99	8.55	4.62	9.50	4.28	2.02	8.87
18. Italy	30.85	5.69	9.41	12.94	6.79	3.73	10.48	7.05	.43	12.62
Mean	23.71	6.92	9.16	16.35	9.04	5.05	12.37	6.56	1.11	10.94

the table presents the budget share of each commodity averaged over the 18 countries. As can be seen, the average OECD consumer spends 24 percent of income on food; and food, housing and transport together occupy about 50 percent of the total in most countries.

The log-change in the price of i is defined as $Dp_{it} = \log p_{it} - \log p_{i,t-1}$. When multiplied by 100, this log-change is approximately the annual percentage change. Columns 2-11 of Table 2.3 contain the mean price log-changes. The last row reveals that, on average, all prices grow between 6 and 9 percent per annum. The Divisia price index is a budget-share-weighted average of the price log-changes,

$$DP_t = \sum_{i=1}^{n} \bar{w}_{it} Dp_{it}, \tag{2.1}$$

where $\bar{w}_{it} = \frac{1}{2}(w_{it} + w_{i,t-1})$ is the arithmetic average of the budget share of commodity i in years t-1 and t. Column 12 of Table 2.3 gives the mean of (2.1) for each country.

Columns 2-11 of Table 2.4 present the means of $Dq_{it} = \log q_{it} - \log q_{i,t-1}$, the log-change in per capita consumption of i. Note from the last row that on average transport and recreation grow the fastest (4.9 and 4.5 percent per annum), while food has the lowest growth rate (1.4 percent). The index (2.1) measures the overall growth in prices. The analogous Divisia volume index is defined as

$$DQ_t = \sum_{i=1}^{n} \bar{w}_{it} Dq_{it}. \tag{2.2}$$

This measures the overall growth in per capita consumption and is given in column 12 of Table 2.4. The last entry in this column indicates that per capita consumption as a whole increases by 3.0 percent per annum on average in the OECD.

Table 2.3 Prices of 10 Commodities and Divisia Price Index for 18 Countries (Mean log-changes × 100)

Country (1)	Food (2)	Beverages (3)	Clothing (4)	Housing (5)	Durables (6)	Medical care (7)	Transport (8)	Recreation (9)	Education (10)	Miscellaneous (11)	Divisia price index (12)
1. US	5.00	4.85	3.29	4.67	4.25	5.81	4.87	3.56	5.91	5.37	4.78
2. Canada	6.15	4.71	3.87	5.18	4.49	4.96	4.72	3.89	8.43	6.73	5.27
3. Sweden	7.17	7.27	4.82	8.50	7.30	6.14	7.66	6.57	9.13	9.10	7.43
4. Switzerland	4.00	4.06	3.39	5.43	3.86	6.49	4.55	4.10		5.47	4.55
5. Denmark	8.69	6.68	6.57	11.43	8.55	8.91	8.79	7.62	9.54	9.30	8.90
6. Australia	6.05	6.58	6.12	7.43	4.33	8.42	6.31	6.97	8.38	7.53	6.58
7. France	7.30	6.47	6.74	8.80	6.76	6.99	8.13	6.13	9.02	8.28	7.48
8. Germany	3.23		3.67	5.57	3.04	5.58	4.13	3.74		4.61	3.96
9. Belgium	4.56	4.61	3.89	5.76	4.36	6.02	5.28	5.00	4.54	6.88	5.13
10. Norway	6.96	6.99	6.74	7.20	7.02	8.25	7.32	5.36	7.85	7.91	7.05
11. Netherlands	3.71	2.91	3.48	5.08	2.29	7.73	3.38	5.51	5.91	4.80	4.07
12. Iceland	13.74	11.25	9.69	11.66	10.13	14.10	11.25	12.66	12.78	11.48	11.79
13. Finland	7.75	6.87	6.09	5.90	6.25	6.22	7.16	6.32	9.44	8.17	7.02
14. Austria	4.57	2.93	3.67	7.49	3.59	8.94	6.12	4.21	4.20	6.53	5.28
15. Japan	7.61		7.99	7.58	6.71	7.36	8.70	7.35		8.88	7.85
16. UK	9.00	8.49	6.88	11.28	8.68	9.36	10.25	8.85	10.73	9.99	9.56
17. Spain	9.79	7.57	11.24	8.58	11.07	11.69	7.89	12.54	12.82	10.87	10.06
18. Italy	9.67	7.07	10.37	10.89	10.37	8.72	10.83	9.25	10.03	11.65	10.13
Mean	6.94	6.21	6.03	7.69	6.28	7.87	7.08	6.64	8.58	7.98	7.05

Table 2.4 Per capita quantities consumed of 10 commodities and Divisia volume index for 18 countries (Mean log-changes × 100)

Country	Food	Beverages	Clothing	Housing	Durables	Medical care	Transport	Recreation	Education	Miscellaneous	Divisia volume index
(1)	(2)	(3)	(4)	(5)	(6)	(7)	(8)	(9)	(10)	(11)	(12)
1. US	.60	1.41	2.33	2.97	1.64	4.49	2.80	4.10	3.33	1.77	2.43
2. Canada	.91	2.57	3.12	3.17	3.02	.22	4.17	6.27	4.20	2.79	2.87
3. Sweden	.50	.80	2.66	2.35	1.18	3.02	2.06	4.53	3.17	-.95	1.71
4. Switzerland	1.72	1.57	.75	2.08	.62	2.85	3.63	2.98		2.79	2.13
5. Denmark	.17	1.43	.59	3.23	-1.01	1.50	1.49	3.34	8.53	.75	1.42
6. Australia	1.35	1.03	.71	3.54	4.45	1.23	3.49	4.33	-2.40	1.95	2.37
7. France	1.62	1.37	1.71	4.89	3.31	6.68	4.65	5.37	2.43	3.20	3.57
8. Germany	2.02		2.36	3.24	3.51	1.45	5.69	3.90		3.77	3.15
9. Belgium	1.53	2.58	2.76	2.80	4.20	5.13	4.52	4.04	1.98	2.98	3.11
10. Norway	1.35	2.08	1.40	3.43	3.21	2.14	4.06	5.56	1.26	2.17	2.68
11. Netherlands	2.22	4.39	3.19	3.93	6.91	5.53	7.52	4.07	5.15	5.20	4.34
12. Iceland	1.64	5.11	5.65	2.54	8.12	7.20	8.58	5.92	4.54	8.56	5.07
13. Finland	1.77	4.89	1.62	3.60	5.41	6.43	6.48	6.18	-1.60	5.58	3.86
14. Austria	1.90	2.34	4.26	4.29	3.61	2.62	5.58	4.35	1.94	1.98	3.27
15. Japan	1.50		1.47	4.93	1.58	6.07	4.10	3.26		3.40	3.13
16. UK	.15	1.48	2.52	1.87	1.58	.90	2.81	3.65	2.10	1.70	1.76
17. Spain	2.82	4.01	3.00	3.79	3.44	9.24	10.66	5.31	4.24	5.72	4.40
18. Italy	2.20	3.15	2.81	2.80	3.90	6.82	5.71	3.98	1.61	3.65	3.33
Mean	1.44	2.51	2.39	3.30	3.26	4.08	4.89	4.51	2.70	3.17	3.04

2.3 Divisia Variances

The Divisia price and volume indexes, defined by equations (2.1) and (2.2), are budget-share-weighted first-order moments of the price and quantity log-changes. The corresponding second-order moments are the Divisia variances,

$$\Pi_t = \sum_{i=1}^{n} \bar{w}_{it}(Dp_{it} - DP_t)^2, \qquad K_t = \sum_{i=1}^{n} \bar{w}_{it}(Dq_{it} - DQ_t)^2.$$

These variances measure the degree to which the prices and quantities of the individual goods change disproportionately. When all the prices and quantities change proportionately, these two variances vanish.

Tables 2.5 and 2.6 present these variances. Comparing these two tables, we see that the quantity variances systematically exceed the corresponding price variances. This pattern agrees with the results of Clements (1982, 1983), Meisner (1979b), E.A. Selvanathan (1987), Theil (1967) and Theil and Suhm (1981), and seems to have the status of an empirical regularity. Another empirical regularity is that higher inflation (i.e., DP) is associated with a larger dispersion of relative prices (Π); for a survey of the literature on inflation and relative price variability, see Marquez and Vining (1984).

The Divisia price-quantity covariance and correlation are

$$\Gamma_t = \sum_{i=1}^{n} \bar{w}_{it}(Dp_{it} - DP_t)(Dq_{it} - DQ_t), \qquad \rho_t = \frac{\Gamma_t}{\sqrt{\Pi_t K_t}}.$$

These measure the co-movement of prices and quantities. As demand curves slope down, we would expect the consumer to move away from those goods which have above-average price increases and vice versa. Thus we expect ρ to be negative. Table 2.7 presents the Divisia correlations for the OECD. Of the 322 correlations, about 75 percent are

Table 2.5 Divisia Price Variances in 18 Countries

Year (1)	US (2)	Canada (3)	Sweden (4)	Switzerland (5)	Denmark (6)	Australia (7)	France (8)	Germany (9)	Belgium (10)	Norway (11)	Netherlands (12)	Iceland (13)	Finland (14)	Austria (15)	Japan (16)	UK (17)	Spain (18)	Italy (19)
1953	-	-	-	-	-	-	-	-	-	-	.34	-	-	-	-	-	-	-
1954	-	-	-	-	-	-	-	-	-	-	1.18	-	-	-	-	-	-	-
1955	-	-	-	-	-	-	-	-	-	-	.21	-	-	-	-	-	-	-
1956	-	-	-	-	-	-	-	-	-	-	.93	-	-	-	-	-	-	-
1957	-	-	-	-	-	-	-	-	-	-	.49	-	-	-	-	-	-	-
1958	-	-	-	-	-	-	-	-	-	-	.84	-	-	-	-	-	-	-
1959	-	-	-	-	-	-	-	-	-	-	.09	-	-	-	-	-	-	-
1960	-	-	-	-	-	-	-	-	-	-	.86	-	-	-	-	-	-	-
1961	.03	.08	-	.25	-	.72	-	.45	1.82	-	.10	1.39	.28	-	-	-	-	-
1962	.07	.07	-	.12	-	.95	-	.17	.59	-	.08	3.56	.38	-	-	-	-	-
1963	.03	.15	-	.24	-	.89	-	.18	.96	-	.18	3.18	.47	-	-	-	-	-
1964	.82	.17	-	.26	-	.27	-	.21	.18	-	.67	2.29	1.39	-	-	-	-	-
1965	.04	.19	.17	.32	-	.47	.17	.18	1.53	.19	.37	1.00	.87	.35	-	.38	.97	.15
1966	.22	.35	.32	.15	-	.13	.18	.23	.65	.20	.64	2.03	.39	.24	-	.13	.20	.08
1967	.26	.34	.32	.50	1.15	.19	.32	.41	.22	.37	.95	.26	.56	.50	-	.11	.72	.18
1968	.11	.31	.15	.46	.64	.22	.38	.90	.15	.12	.45	.92	3.36	.58	-	.20	.91	.19
1969	.12	.22	.51	.29	.38	.63	.15	.29	.14	.16	.57	6.08	.05	.19	-	.08	.72	.05
1970	.07	.40	.19	.25	.62	.52	.11	.09	.49	.32	.79	2.45	.22	3.16	-	.17	.88	.13
1971	.16	.34	.21	.22	.68	.56	.10	.19	.36	.22	.97	2.16	.17	.51	.39	.29	.37	.23
1972	.15	.35	.42	.41	.50	.16	.14	.08	.45	.08	.67	3.79	.33	.34	.41	.47	.84	.34
1973	1.48	1.71	.39	.59	1.25	.96	.28	.04	.51	.09	.49	2.69	.25	.69	1.68	.99	.59	.52
1974	.62	1.07	2.19	.23	1.09	1.54	.74	.43	.76	.45	1.02	-	1.84	1.04	2.82	.46	.88	1.77
1975	.33	.47	.34	.25	.24	1.65	.20	.05	.88	.90	.90	-	1.87	.37	.75	1.01	.54	.91
1976	.44	.95	.27	.72	.79	.66	.25	.06	.54	.07	.55	-	.91	.52	.47	.36	1.11	1.13
1977	.30	.83	.42	.02	.34	.44	.28	.11	.51	.07	.64	-	1.45	.35	.40	.18	1.56	.67
1978	.40	.98	.62	.41	.30	.77	.06	.08	.27	.32	-	-	-	.45	.81	.40	-	.43
1979	.47	.27	.64	.85	1.83	.42	.24	.43	.76	.25	-	-	-	.40	.24	.54	-	.46
1980	.96	.18	.47	.25	.79	.35	1.01	.16	1.76	.55	-	-	-	.51	.42	1.17	-	1.00
1981	.40	.53	.42	.28	.43	.29	.20	.23	3.45	1.10	-	-	-	.69	.03	2.20	-	.16
Mean	.36	.47	.47	.34	.73	.61	.28	.24	.81	.32	.60	2.45	.87	.64	.77	.54	.79	.49

All entries are to be divided by 1000.

Table 2.6 Divisia Quantity Variances in 18 Countries

Year	US	Canada	Sweden	Switzerland	Denmark	Australia	France	Germany	Belgium	Norway	Netherlands	Iceland	Finland	Austria	Japan	UK	Spain	Italy
(1)	(2)	(3)	(4)	(5)	(6)	(7)	(8)	(9)	(10)	(11)	(12)	(13)	(14)	(15)	(16)	(17)	(18)	(19)
1953	-	-	-	-	-	-	-	-	-	-	2.10	-	-	-	-	-	-	-
1954	-	-	-	-	-	-	-	-	-	-	1.94	-	-	-	-	-	-	-
1955	-	-	-	-	-	-	-	-	-	-	2.21	-	-	-	-	-	-	-
1956	-	-	-	-	-	-	-	-	-	-	1.86	-	-	-	-	-	-	-
1957	-	-	-	-	-	-	-	-	-	-	1.16	-	-	-	-	-	-	-
1958	-	-	-	-	-	-	-	-	-	-	2.35	-	-	-	-	-	-	-
1959	-	-	-	-	-	-	-	-	-	-	1.42	-	-	-	-	-	-	-
1960	-	-	-	-	-	-	-	-	-	-	.60	-	-	-	-	-	-	-
1961	.63	8.64	-	.89	-	.55	-	.62	1.45	-	.60	2.69	2.07	-	-	-	-	-
1962	.72	.57	-	.65	-	2.35	-	.81	.25	-	.68	7.51	1.29	-	-	-	-	-
1963	.44	.63	-	.28	-	3.22	-	.51	.52	-	.48	11.38	1.74	-	-	-	-	-
1964	.34	.47	-	.66	-	.48	-	.56	1.23	-	3.35	5.52	3.86	-	-	-	-	-
1965	.30	.63	.83	.30	-	.19	.52	.81	.50	.54	2.18	1.41	4.49	.84	-	.66	1.72	.50
1966	.46	.87	.71	.30	-	.57	.41	.18	.31	.28	1.98	4.23	.76	.90	-	.16	4.23	.52
1967	.15	.50	.49	.21	.42	.65	.33	.34	.42	.52	1.71	2.69	.93	.30	-	.32	.70	1.06
1968	.59	.61	1.31	.15	.54	.85	.29	.64	.78	.52	1.33	8.39	.75	.31	-	.30	1.75	.10
1969	.55	.35	.76	.21	1.19	1.10	.50	1.91	.52	2.32	2.41	3.33	3.80	.56	-	.24	.97	.73
1970	.69	1.82	.53	.11	.94	.28	.57	1.10	.24	2.61	1.88	19.19	.95	1.60	-	.43	.40	.59
1971	.92	2.51	1.38	.22	1.09	.37	.63	.28	.74	1.02	1.06	8.40	1.06	2.36	.66	.98	.88	.40
1972	.65	1.51	.83	.17	.86	.38	.55	.26	.99	.94	2.86	4.32	1.79	2.39	.49	1.94	2.67	.60
1973	1.31	2.35	1.06	.73	1.17	2.52	.75	.95	2.10	.43	1.61	1.80	2.43	.60	1.29	1.02	1.11	1.03
1974	1.55	1.96	1.45	.93	3.82	1.49	1.19	.62	1.81	.51	1.74	-	2.52	1.16	3.31	1.11	.89	.77
1975	.68	.23	.32	1.78	2.08	1.54	.75	1.21	2.04	.73	4.38	-	2.95	.45	1.59	.21	.48	.97
1976	.54	.35	.40	.47	1.64	.58	.99	.69	.75	1.39	.52	-	3.15	.61	1.06	.16	.28	.32
1977	.31	.67	.73	.35	.55	.56	.44	.88	1.07	1.30	1.49	-	2.04	2.32	.63	.44	.39	.56
1978	.54	.61	.58	.46	.88	.99	.69	.18	.57	2.85	-	-	-	2.21	.97	.71	-	.15
1979	.36	.27	.13	.21	.33	.25	.32	.16	.88	.72	-	-	-	.82	.87	.32	-	.66
1980	1.21	.38	.46	.13	1.96	.44	.55	.26	1.75	.68	-	-	-	.50	1.41	.41	-	.31
1981	.26	.23	.61	.34	.44	.16	.41	.43	.75	1.21	-	-	-	.45	1.07	.52	-	.69
Mean	.63	1.25	.74	.45	1.19	.93	.58	.64	.94	1.09	1.78	6.22	2.15	1.08	1.21	.58	1.27	.59

All entries are to be divided by 1000.

Table 2.7 Divisia Price-Quantity Correlations in 18 Countries

Year	US	Canada	Sweden	Switzerland	Denmark	Australia	France	Germany	Belgium	Norway	Netherlands	Iceland	Finland	Austria	Japan	UK	Spain	Italy
(1)	(2)	(3)	(4)	(5)	(6)	(7)	(8)	(9)	(10)	(11)	(12)	(13)	(14)	(15)	(16)	(17)	(18)	(19)
1953	-	-	-	-	-	-	-	-	-	-	-.45	-	-	-	-	-	-	-
1954	-	-	-	-	-	-	-	-	-	-	-.88	-	-	-	-	-	-	-
1955	-	-	-	-	-	-	-	-	-	-	.21	-	-	-	-	-	-	-
1956	-	-	-	-	-	-	-	-	-	-	-.95	-	-	-	-	-	-	-
1957	-	-	-	-	-	-	-	-	-	-	.33	-	-	-	-	-	-	-
1958	-	-	-	-	-	-	-	-	-	-	.13	-	-	-	-	-	-	-
1959	-	-	-	-	-	-	-	-	-	-	-.64	-	-	-	-	-	-	-
1960	-	-	-	-	-	-	-	-	-	-	-.33	-	-	-	-	-	-	-
1961	.45	.01	-	-.32	-	-.11	-	-.40	-.97	-	-.67	-.27	-.57	-	-	-	-	-
1962	.33	-.69	-	-.61	-	.06	-	-.69	-.38	-	-.01	-.65	-.06	-	-	-	-	-
1963	.10	-.69	-	-.55	-	-.22	-	.74	.59	-	-.82	-.70	.30	-	-	-	-	-
1964	-.08	-.45	-	-.39	-	-.87	-	-.71	.31	-	-.57	-.49	-.72	-	-	-	-	-
1965	.10	-.31	-.38	-.59	-	-.01	.42	-.73	-.04	.05	-.38	-.35	-.57	-.78	-	-.21	-.58	.08
1966	-.30	-.57	.15	.13	-	.61	.15	.10	-.31	-.16	-.43	-.62	.22	.54	-	.15	-.58	-.15
1967	-.06	.22	-.23	.19	-.12	-.29	.63	.12	-.21	-.36	-.14	.17	.50	.11	-	.27	-.08	-.13
1968	-.18	-.37	-.19	.61	.69	.05	.20	.11	.29	-.87	-.25	-.46	-.53	.15	-	.41	-.78	.01
1969	-.22	.07	-.47	-.07	-.52	-.74	.44	-.62	-.58	-.67	-.02	-.80	-.25	-.20	-	-.01	.34	-.66
1970	.45	-.06	-.36	-.47	-.10	-.26	.43	-.10	-.25	-.26	-.51	-.16	-.07	-.36	-	-.02	-.30	-.36
1971	.67	.17	-.66	-.06	.19	-.48	-.09	-.07	.27	-.23	-.44	.30	.05	-.42	-.04	.23	.24	.34
1972	-.82	-.65	-.70	-.08	-.71	-.50	-.87	-.89	-.48	-.28	.16	-.61	-.25	-.39	-.27	-.60	-.61	-.60
1973	-.97	-.78	-.64	.37	-.75	-.65	-.77	-.57	-.56	-.45	-.66	-.55	-.43	-.34	-.34	-.90	-.69	-.58
1974	-.59	-.77	-.20	-.26	-.35	-.53	-.62	-.20	-.46	-.08	-.37	-	-.46	-.10	-.75	-.76	-.54	-.63
1975	-.59	-.62	-.56	-.09	-.13	-.67	.04	-.06	.02	-.87	-.49	-	-.32	.38	.34	-.05	-.19	-.52
1976	.08	-.55	-.43	.29	-.59	-.31	-.11	.14	-.38	-.32	-.21	-	-.65	.27	-.74	-.28	.57	.23
1977	.04	-.76	-.61	-.41	-.46	.34	-.58	-.77	.65	.45	-.80	-	-.37	-.55	.29	-.29	-.01	-.31
1978	-.88	-.88	-.16	-.72	-.53	-.58	-.05	-.22	-.11	-.23	-	-	-	.03	-.19	-.36	-	-.30
1979	-.70	-.69	-.44	-.59	.28	.00	-.22	-.10	-.31	-.04	-	-	-	.25	.07	.08	-	-.04
1980	-.70	-.46	-.56	-.42	-.07	-.77	-.48	-.69	-.82	-.49	-	-	-	.00	-.67	-.26	-	.42
1981	-.19	-.67	-.14	-.77	-.28	.04	-.60	-.35	-.70	-.85	-	-	-	-.83	.22	-.26	-	-.03
Mean	-.19	-.45	-.39	-.23	-.23	-.28	-.12	-.28	-.21	-.33	-.37	-.40	-.25	-.13	-.19	-.17	-.25	-.19

negative. The last row of the table shows that, on average, the correlations are negative for each country, as expected.

2.4 Engel's Law

One of the major empirical regularities in consumption economics is *Engel's law*, i.e., the budget share of food falls with increasing income, or, in other words, the income elasticity of demand for food is less than unity. The classic reference in this area is Houthakker (1957) who estimated Engel curves for a large number of household surveys; in each case food was found to be a necessity.

More recently, Theil et al. (1989) have shown that it is now possible to make a more precise statement regarding the dependence on income of the food budget share. Working (1943) observed that the budget share for food seems to be a linear function of the logarithm of income. This observation was generalized by Leser (1963) to a complete set of n commodities to yield

$$w_i = \alpha_i + \beta_i \log M, \qquad i=1,...,n. \tag{4.1}$$

Choosing the income unit such that M = 1 for some household, α_i is then interpreted as the budget share of i for that household. The coefficient β_i is interpreted as 100 times the change in the budget share of i resulting from a 1 percent increase in income. Equation (4.1) is Working's model which was introduced in Section 1.8.

Theil (1987a), using data from Kravis et al. (1982) for 34 countries, plots the budget share of food against the log of real per capita total consumption. Figure 2.1 gives such a plot (with consumption scaled such that M = 1 for the poorest country). The solid line is the LS regression line. As can be seen, the points are all scattered around a downward-sloping line which gives strong visual support for Working's model for food. The slope of the LS line is -.15 (standard error .01),

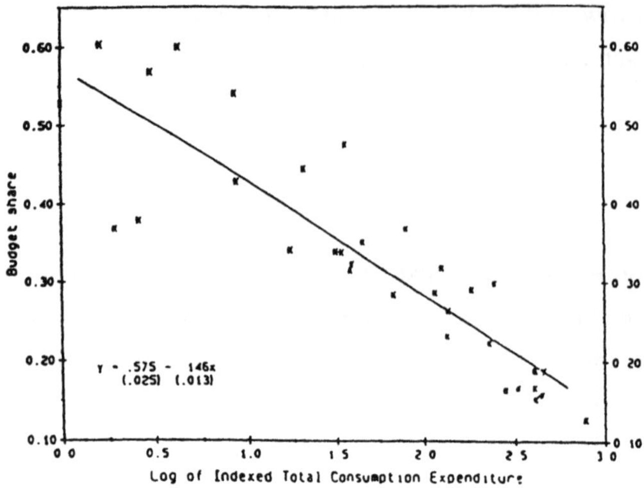

Figure 2.1 Budget Share of Food Against Scaled Total Consumption Expenditure per Capita in 1975 for 34 Countries

which is an estimate of β_i for food. This estimate does not take account of cross-country differences in the relative price of food; however, approximately the same value of β_i emerges when these differences are allowed for (Theil, 1987a). The estimate of β_i of -.15 is in remarkable agreement with other estimates of the food β_i; see Table 2.8. Thus β_i = -.15 seems to be more or less a natural constant.

To analyze the implications of this β_i-estimate, consider moving from one country to another. Assume that the first country's per capita income is M, while that of the second is 2M. Therefore,

$$\Delta(\log M) = \log 2M - \log M = \log 2 = .69.$$

From (4.1) we have

$$\Delta w_i = \beta_i \Delta \log M.$$

Table 2.8 Previous Estimates of Working's Income Coefficient for Food

Author(s)	Country	Estimate
Aasness and Rodseth (1983)	Norway	-.17
Blanciforti and Green (1983)	US	-.13
Chung and Lopez (1988)	Spain	-.18 & -.16
Deaton and Muellbauer (1980b)	Britain	-.16
Finke et al. (1984)	Japan	-.15
Musgrove (1985)	Dominican Replublic	-.14
Theil (1987a)	Cross country	-.14 to -.16
Theil and Finke (1984)	Netherlands	-.13
Theil et al. (1987)	China	-.13

Source: Chung and Lopez (1988, Table 1).

Consequently, when $\beta_i = -.15$ the effect of doubling income on the food budget share is

$$\Delta w_i = -.15 \times .69 = -.10.$$

That is, when income doubles, the budget share declines by 10 percentage points. Theil et al. (1989) refer to this as the *strong version of Engel's law.*

One use of this law is to make real income comparisons across consumers or countries on the basis of the food share. As this share is obviously a pure number, it is directly comparable over time, countries etc., independent of inflation, exchange rates and so on. Consequently, such indirect income comparisons could be an attractive short-cut.

2.5 Homogeneity and Symmetry

The Marshallian demand equation for good i is

$$q_i = q_i(M, p_1,\dots,p_n). \tag{5.1}$$

If income and prices all increase proportionately, then the quantity demanded of each good should remain unchanged. That is, for $\alpha > 0$, $q_i(\alpha M, \alpha p_1,...,\alpha p_n) = q_i(M, p_1,...,p_n)$, or equation (5.1) is homogeneous of zero degree. This is known as the absence of *money illusion* or *demand homogeneity*.

The system of n demand equations given by (5.1) for i = 1,...,n also satisfies *Slutsky symmetry*, viz.

$$\frac{\partial q_i}{\partial p_j} = \frac{\partial q_j}{\partial p_i} \qquad i,j = 1,...,n, \qquad (5.2)$$

where the derivatives hold real income constant. In words, the effect on beer drinking of a \$1-increase in the price of a bottle of wine is exactly equal to the response of wine consumption to the same rise in the price of a bottle of beer.

Homogeneity and symmetry would seem to constitute highly plausible hypotheses, hypotheses that would not be expected to be at great variance with the data. Surprisingly, however, when these restrictions are tested the bulk of the evidence points towards rejection; see Barten (1977) and Keuzenkamp and Barten (1991) for surveys of these tests.

These rejections represented a major puzzle. The response of Theil, and some others, was not to take the evidence too literally. He argued in *Theory and Measurement of Consumer Demand* that these findings reflect

> data imperfections rather than unorthodox consumer behavior. What is needed in such a situation is an explicit recognition on the part of the analyst that his data are imperfect. He should guide these data so that they yield a sensible picture. It is unavoidable that this picture of the real world will be biased toward simplicity, but it is appropriate to realize that this kind of bias is inherent in every model. (Theil, 1975/6, pp. 250-1 of Volume 1)

As a consequence, Theil felt comfortable simply imposing the constraints, especially homogeneity. Others have responded to the rejection puzzle by emphasizing dynamics (Anderson and Blundell, 1983), simultaneity

(Attfield, 1985) and the use of non-stationary variables (Bewley and Elliott, 1989).

Theil's skepticism about the rejections was not shared by everyone. Some took the findings seriously and concluded that consumption theory should be rejected (see, e.g., Christensen et al., 1975). Apparently, this troubled Theil sufficiently to encourage two of his students, Laitinen and Meisner, to study the rejections by means of Monte Carlo experiments. The idea is to simulate data sets under the null, use these data to estimate the demand equations and then test homogeneity and symmetry. As the hypotheses are true by construction, the rejection rates should coincide with the nominal significance levels if the tests are working satisfactorily.

Table 2.9 shows Laitinen's (1978) and Meisner's (1979a) results. As can be seen from columns 2 and 3, the rejections of homogeneity are far too high, with the rejection rate increasing with n, the number of commodities. The results for symmetry (columns 4 and 5) also indicate a substantial bias against the null, but the problems are now not quite so bad for n = 5 or 8. The source of the problem is that these tests involve the replacement of the inverse of the disturbance covariance matrix Σ^{-1} with its estimator S^{-1}, the inverse of the residual moment matrix. This replacement has an asymptotic justification (when the number of observations $T \to \infty$), but this becomes problematic when the number of commodities in the model is large relative to T; in this case, S is near singular and S^{-1} explosive. See Theil (1987b) for further details and Bera et al. (1981) and Bewley (1983, 1986) for related contributions.

If the standard tests are defective, how does one proceed? There are two ways of avoiding the problems associated with asymptotics. First, there is now available an exact finite-sample test for homogeneity (Laitinen, 1978). Second, Monte Carlo testing (Theil, 1987b), which is distribution-free, can be employed. We shall discuss these two approaches in detail in Chapter 4.

In Chapter 4, S. Selvanathan tests homogeneity and symmetry with the Monte Carlo technique for 18 OECD countries. Selvanathan employs a variant of the Rotterdam model (with intercepts to take account of residual

Table 2.9 Percentage Rejections of Homogeneity and Symmetry

Number of commodities, n	Rejections of homogeneity		Rejections of symmetry	
	5 percent	1 percent	5 percent	1 percent
(1)	(2)	(3)	(4)	(5)
5	14	6	9	3
8	30	16	26	8
11	53	35	50	37
14	87	81	96	91

trends). On the basis of these new tests, the conclusion is that, on the whole, homogeneity and symmetry are not grossly incompatible with the data. The previous rejections reported in the literature reflect faulty econometric procedures (the breakdown of asymptotic theory, in particular), rather than a flaw in the theory of the utility-maximizing consumer.

2.6 The Validity of Preference Independence

When the consumer's tastes can be described by means of a utility function which can be written as the sum of n sub-utility functions, each involving one good only, then tastes are said to exhibit *preference independence.* Formally, the utility function is of the preference independent form if

$$u(q_1,...,q_n) = \sum_{i=1}^{n} u_i(q_i), \tag{6.1}$$

so that the marginal utility of good i is independent of the consumption of j, $i \neq j$. The specification (6.1) was previously considered in Section 1.5 and is also known as additive preferences.

If the commodities are fairly broad groups, such as food, housing, clothing and so on, then (6.1) could be a reasonable working hypothesis as it conveys the idea that total utility is obtained from the utility derived from food *and* utility from housing *and* from clothing *and* so on. These broad commodity groups can be interpreted as representing the "basic wants" of the consumer and if these are truly basic wants, they could be expected to exhibit little interaction in the utility function.

In Chapter 1 we argued that the assumption of preference independence leads to an attractive simplification of demand equations. There are two distinct justifications for this assumption: (i) The economic justification in terms of preference independence being plausible when the commodities in question are broad aggregates; and (ii) the statistical justification that the assumption reduces the number of unknown coefficients to be estimated from the order of n^2, which for even moderate-sized systems can be too large for precise estimates, to something much less. However, whether it is truly legitimate to invoke the assumption of preference independence is largely an empirical question. In this section we discuss some empirical evidence on this topic.

We return to equation (15.5) of Chapter 1, the i-*th* demand equation of the Rotterdam model under preference independence. We add a constant term and divide both sides by the budget share to write it in elasticity form:

$$Dq_i = \alpha_i + \eta_i \, DQ + \gamma_i(Dp_i - DP'), \tag{6.2}$$

where η_i is the income elasticity of i;

$$\gamma_i = \phi\eta_i \tag{6.3}$$

is the own-price elasticity of i with ϕ being the income flexibility; and DP' is the Frisch price index.

It is clear from (6.1) that preference independence is the *simplest* possible specification of tastes. The simplicity and transparency of the assumption is also clear from the demand equation (6.2) which focuses exclusively on the role of income and the own-relative price. As a general principle, simplicity is usually to be preferred to complexity in the sense that if the world can be understood with a simple (not to be confused with simplistic!) model, then there is no point to pursuing more complicated alternatives. This is merely a matter of scientific efficiency.

As (6.3) holds for $i=1,...,n$, it is clear that preference independence implies that price elasticities are proportional to income elasticities with ϕ the (negative) factor of proportionality. In other words, luxuries are more price elastic than necessities (Deaton, 1974; Pigou, 1910).

The proportionality between income and price elasticities may, at first, seem counter intuitive. The income elasticity reflects the luxuriousness of the good, while the size of the price elasticity is an indication of the availability of substitutes. As these are different dimensions of the good, one may be tempted to argue that there should be no *a priori* relationship between the elasticities. On the other hand, however, it is common practice to identify as necessities those goods which the consumer cannot easily do without (e.g., food); while luxuries involve discretionary expenditure for which there are many competing uses and thus can be easily foregone or postponed (e.g., durables). This use of language points in the direction of a relationship between the two types of elasticities (Deaton, 1987).

To analyse the evidence on the proportionality relationship (6.3), S. Selvanathan (1988a) estimates (6.2) for 18 OECD countries (with the Frisch price index replaced with its Divisia counterpart). Table 2.10 summarises the results in the form of cross-country frequency distributions of the elasticities. As can be seen, all the income elasticities for food are less than one which supports Engel's law. Also, housing is always a necessity and durables a luxury. Finally, most of the own-price elasticities lie between 0 and -1.

Table 2.10 Frequency Distributions of Income and Price Elasticities of 10 Commodities in 18 Countries (in Percentages)

Range (1)	Food (2)	Beverages (3)	Clothing (4)	Housing (5)	Durables (6)	Medical care (7)	Transport (8)	Recreation (9)	Education (10)	Miscellaneous (11)	All Goods (12)
					Income Elasticity (η_i)						
(− ∞, − 1]	0	0	0	0	0	0	0	0	0	0	0
(− 1, 0]	6	0	0	11	0	6	0	0	13	0	3
(0, 1]	94	75	6	89	0	78	11	28	73	67	52
(1, ∞)	0	25	94	0	100	17	89	72	13	33	45
					Price Elasticity (γ_i)						
(− ∞, − 1]	0	6	28	0	22	0	33	28	13	6	14
(− 1, 0]	100	94	67	72	72	66	62	72	67	83	75
(0, 1]	0	0	5	28	6	28	5	0	20	11	10
(1, ∞)	0	0	0	6	0	6	0	0	0	0	1

The income and price elasticities reported in Table 2.10 are unrestricted in that they are not constrained by (6.3). Table 2.11 gives the joint frequency distribution of the income and price elasticities. As can be seen, 55 percent of commodities are necessities ($\eta_i \leq 1$) and 34/55 = 62 percent of these have own-price elasticities less than one half (in absolute value). Regarding the luxuries, 30/45 = 67 percent possess price elasticities larger than one half. Consequently, there is a distinct tendency for those commodities with lower income elasticities to also have (absolutely) smaller price elasticities and vice versa. This is *prima facie* evidence in favour of (6.3).

Table 2.11 Joint Frequency Distribution of Income and Price Elasticities of 10 Commodities in 18 Countries (Percentages)

Income elasticity η_i	Absolute value of price elasticity $\lvert\gamma_i\rvert$		
	$\leq \frac{1}{2}$	$> \frac{1}{2}$	Total
≤ 1	34	21	55
> 1	15	30	45
Total	49	51	100

Figure 2.2, from S. Selvanathan (1988a), provides another perspective on the relationship between the income and price elasticities. This plots each pair of estimates $\{\gamma_i, \eta_i\}$ averaged over the 18 countries and the solid line is the LS regression line. Here again luxuries tend to be more price elastic. See S. Selvanathan (1988a) for evidence on the proportionality relationship within each of the 18 countries. In a widely-quoted paper, Deaton (1974) carries out a similar analysis of the the elasticities derived from UK data for n = 37 and 8 commodities. He finds no relationship between income and price elasticities and concludes "that *the assumption of additive preferences is almost certain to be invalid in practice and the use of demand models based on such an assumption will lead to severe distortion of measurement.*" (Deaton, 1974, p. 346, his emphasis)

Moreover, Deaton's rejection of preference independence on the basis of indirect evidence (the proportionality of the elasticities) is consistent with a number of more direct tests; see Barten (1977) for a survey. However, these tests have only an asymptotic justification and in light of the poor performance of the asymptotic tests of homogeneity and symmetry (discussed in Section 2.5 above), it is appropriate to exercise caution in taking them at face value.

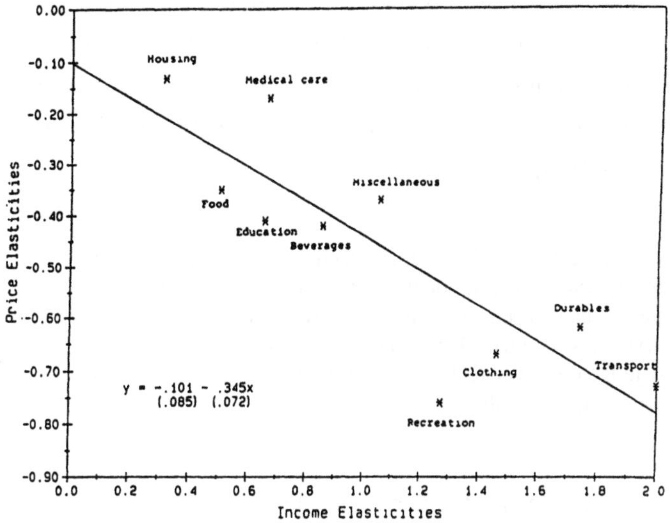

Figure 2.2 Price Elasticities Against Income Elasticities for 10 Commodities

In Chapter 4, S. Selvanathan pursues this matter by developing a Monte Carlo test of preference independence. The results provide at least some tentative indications that the status of the preference independence hypothesis is not as low as was once thought. This conclusion as well as the above results on the proportionality of income and price elasticities indicates that Deaton's rejection on preference independence was premature.

2.7 Are Tastes Constant?

Utility maximization theory usually postulates that tastes are fixed, so that it is only the observable variables income and prices that explain consumption. There is a compelling reason for treating tastes (an unobservable) as constant: As the necessarily *ad hoc* auxiliary assumptions about the evolution of tastes are avoided, utility theory thereby has more applicability, generality and explanatory power. In a highly-influential paper, Stigler and Becker (1977) advocate treating tastes as fixed along these lines. They show that a number of examples of apparently capricious behavior (addiction, custom, tradition, fashion etc.) can in fact be reconciled with the assumption of stable preferences. Stigler and Becker (p. 89) argue that

> no significant behavior has been illuminated by the assumption of differences in tastes. Instead, they, along with the assumption of unstable tastes, have been a convenient crutch to lean on when the analysis has bogged down. They give the appearance of considered judgement, yet really have only been ad hoc arguments that disguise analytical failures.

The hypothesis of stable preferences can be tested by estimating demand equations for different groups of consumers and then analysing the extent to which the parameters (such as the income and price elasticities) differ across consumers. S. Selvanathan (1987c) carries out such a test with the OECD database by estimating (i) country-specific demand equations; and (ii) common demand equations for all countries whereby the data are pooled across countries. The test then involves an analysis of the deterioration in the fit of the demand equations when the data are pooled. In other words, this amounts to investigating the extent to which the *same* demand equations can explain consumption in the different OECD countries. The upper part of Table 2.12 contains the results using the root-mean-squared (RMS) percentage prediction error as the goodness-of-fit criterion. (The 15 OECD countries with 10 commodity groups are used here; see Table 2.1). Although the RMSEs for the country-specific models (given in column 3) are in general a bit lower than those for the pooled model (column 4), the differences are not substantial. In addition, the countries have similar rankings with respect to the two sets of RMSEs.

Looking at the entries in row 17 of columns 3 and 4 of Table 2.12, the weighted means of the RMSEs are 1.87 percent for the individual country models and 1.95 percent for the pooled model. Accordingly, the average "cost" of taking tastes to be identical is 1.95 - 1.87 = .08 percentage

Table 2.12 Quality of Budget Share Predictions in OECD Countries and Australian States

Country/ state	Weight ×100	RMS percentage prediction error	
		Individual country/state model	Pooled country/state model
(1)	(2)	(3)	(4)
		OECD countries	
1. US	51.34	1.65	1.72
2. Canada	5.14	3.16	3.32
3. Sweden	1.84	1.88	1.91
4. Denmark	1.01	2.16	2.16
5. Australia	2.74	2.41	2.46
6. France	10.30	1.39	1.39
7. Belgium	1.81	2.59	2.74
8. Norway	.72	2.07	2.35
9. Netherlands	2.42	3.20	3.58
10. Iceland	.04	4.70	4.99
11. Finland	.82	3.68	3.67
12. Austria	1.25	2.34	2.50
13. UK	8.57	1.77	1.79
14. Spain	4.78	2.33	2.29
15. Italy	7.20	1.88	2.13
16. Unweighted mean		2.48	2.60
17. Weighted mean		1.87	1.95
		Australian states	
18. NSW	38.53	2.16	2.14
19. Victoria	27.31	2.49	2.59
20. Queensland	14.79	3.07	2.97
21. SA	8.29	2.47	2.51
22. WA	8.47	2.54	2.46
23. Tasmania	2.61	3.42	3.56
24. Unweighted mean		2.69	2.70
25. Weighted mean		2.47	2.48

The column 2 weights for the OECD countries are proportional to GDPs in 1975 in international dollars; and the weights for the Australian states are proportional to total consumption expenditures in 1981. The RMS percentage prediction errors in columns 3 and 4 are 100 times the square root of the budget-share-weighted mean of the squared relative prediction errors of the budget shares; as an approximation, these are computed as 100 times the square root of twice the information inaccuracies.

points. This is clearly quite modest and points in the direction that tastes are not too dissimilar across countries. (For a different finding, however, see Pollak and Wales, 1987.)

There are many non-economic differences between some of the OECD countries. For example, language, culture and climate differ substantially in some cases. It may thus come as a surprise to some (not Stigler and Becker!) that tastes in these countries are more or less similar. In an attempt to control for some of the non-economic factors, S. Selvanathan (1988b, Chap. 8) conducts a similar analysis with data from different regions of the same country, the six states of Australia. The lower part of Table 2.12 summarizes the findings and the result is that tastes are even more similar within a country, as expected. However, as the sample size for the states is small, it is appropriate to exercise some caution here.

2.8 The Frisch Conjecture

It can be shown that preference independence implies that the compensated price elasticities η'_{ij} take the form

$$\eta'_{ij} = \phi\eta_i(\delta_{ij} - w_j\eta_j), \tag{8.1}$$

where ϕ is the income flexibility (i.e., the reciprocal of the income elasticity of the marginal utility of income); η_i is the i-*th* income elasticity; δ_{ij} is the Kronecker delta (δ_{ij} = 1 if i = j, = 0 otherwise); and w_j is the budget share of good j.

If we accept the assumption of preference independence, equation (8.1) means that we can then compute the n × n matrix of the price elasticities $[\eta'_{ij}]$ from the value of the scalar ϕ, the n income elasticities and n budget shares. It is the attraction of being able to compute price elasticities in this manner that has lead equation (8.1), or a variant thereof, to be used in at least two types of applications. First, in many developing countries time-series data of sufficient length and quality are not available, so it is impossible to estimate price elasticities. But as income elasticities and budget shares are usually available from household surveys, equation (8.1), together with a ϕ-value, can then be used to generate price elasticities. The second application of this equation is in computable general equilibrium models which have such a large number of commodities that the price elasticities cannot be directly estimated. For example, Dixon et al. (1982, Sec. 29.5) use this approach in a CGE model which distinguishes over 100 consumer goods.

What value of the income flexibility should be used in equation (8.1)? Our starting point for this question is Frisch's famous conjecture that ϕ increases in absolute value as the consumer (or country) becomes more affluent. (Frisch discusses the behavior of $1/\phi$, which he calls the "money flexibility"; for clarity, in what follows we make the necessary translations from $1/\phi$ to ϕ). Frisch (1959, p. 189) provides the following numerical conjectures for the dependence of ϕ on real income:

> We may, perhaps, assume that in most cases the income flexibility has values of the order of magnitude given below.
>
> -.1 for an extremely poor and apathetic part of the population.
>
> -.25 for the slightly better off but still poor part of the population with a fairly pronounced desire to become better off.
>
> -.5 for the middle income bracket, "the median part" of the population.
>
> -1.4 for the better off part of the population.
>
> -10 for the rich part of the population with ambitions towards "conspicuous consumption".
>
> It would be a very promising research project to determine the income flexibility for different countries and for different types of populations. A universal "atlas" should be constructed. It would serve an extremely useful purpose in demand analysis.

Frisch's conjecture has been tested by a number of authors. Brown and Deaton (1972) report estimates of the income flexibility from various studies and conclude that they show no evidence of a dependence on real income. Also, Brown and Deaton suggest that it would be fair to use a value of -.5 for ϕ. DeJanvry et al. (1972) collect estimates of the income flexibility from several studies and find a statistically significant relationship between ϕ and income, which supports Frisch. As noted by Theil (1980), however, the validity of their conclusion is based on the uncritical acceptance of the previous estimates.

Lluch et al. (1977) use time-series data for 14 countries (developed and underdeveloped) at various levels of commodity aggregation to estimate a variant of the linear expenditure system. They find strong evidence in favor of Frisch at the four-commodity level of aggregation, but less support at the two-and one-commodity levels. S. Selvanathan (1987c,d) uses time-series data for the OECD countries and finds that ϕ is unrelated to income. Selvanathan also recommends a value of about -.5 for ϕ.

Using data for 30 countries, Theil (1987a) concludes that the sample cannot support Frisch in spite of the large income variation. Theil and Brooks (1970/71) use a modified version of the Rotterdam model in which the income flexibility is a function of income. They obtain the result that the income flexibility is again unrelated to income.

This brief review indicates a lack of unanimity about the status of Frisch. It seems, however, that the broad thrust of the literature has not been too kind to Frisch's conjecture. This is possibly not unexpected given the nature of the conjecture: The income elasticity of the marginal utility of income relates to a second-order derivative of the (indirect) utility function, so that its dependence on income involves a third derivative. It is not possible for most economic data to reveal much information about such higher-order derivatives. Consequently, it is probably best to treat ϕ as a constant equal to around -.5. It should be noted that the constancy of the income flexibility is not inconsistent with the idea of constant tastes discussed in the previous section.

2.9 Some Further International Consumption Data

In the earlier sections of this chapter we presented consumption data for 18 OECD countries. In this section we use a different database which contains both developed and developing countries. Relative to the OECD, these data exhibit more cross-country variability in income. The material for this and the next two sections is mainly from S. Selvanathan (1988b).

In a pioneering book, Lluch, Powell and Williams (1977, hereafter LPW) use data for 8 commodity groups in 17 countries. Table 2.13 presents an overview of the data for 13 of the 17 countries with countries ordered in terms of declining per capita GNP. (See S. Selvanathan, 1988b, for the reasons for not considering 4 of the LPW countries.) As can be seen, the US has the highest per capita GNP, while Korea has the lowest with only 4 percent of the US value. Table 2.14 presents the budget shares at sample means of the 8 commodities in each country. Note the strong tendency for the food budget share to decline with increasing GNP which is in accordance with Engel's law. The upper half of Table 2.15 presents the average annual price log-changes, while the lower half presents the corresponding per capita quantity log-changes.

Next, we summarize these data with Divisia indexes. Let $\bar{w}_{ic}$ be the budget share of i for country c at sample means (given in Table 2.14); and Dp_{ic} and Dq_{ic} be the mean price and quantity log-changes (Table 2.15). The Divisia price and volume indexes for country c are then

$$DP_c = \sum_{i=1}^{8} \bar{w}_{ic} Dp_{ic}, \qquad DQ_c = \sum_{i=1}^{8} \bar{w}_{ic} Dq_{ic}$$

and are presented in columns 2 and 3 of Table 2.16. As can be seen from the last row of the table, on average, prices in these countries increase by 3.5 percent per annum while per capita consumption grows at a slightly lower rate. Columns 4-6 of the table contain the corresponding second-order moments defined in Section 2.3.

2.10 The Linear Expenditure System

Stone's (1954) linear expenditure system introduced in Section 1.4 is probably the most popular demand system. Notable studies using this

Table 2.13 Characteristics of the LPW Database

Country	Sample period	Per capita GNP at sample midpoint	
		In 1970 US dollars	(3) with US = 100
(1)	(2)	(3)	(4)
1. US	1955-68	3669	100
2. Sweden	1955-68	2962	81
3. Australia	1955-66	2192	60
4. UK	1955-68	1900	52
5. Israel	1959-68	1468	40
6. Italy	1955-68	1207	33
7. Puerto Rico	1955-67	1023	28
8. Ireland	1955-68	1014	28
9. Greece	1958-68	676	18
10. South Africa	1955-68	596	16
11. Panama	1960-68	564	15
12. Thailand	1960-69	148	4
13. Korea	1955-68	142	4

Source: Lluch et al. (1977, Table 3.2).

model include Deaton (1975), Goldberger and Gamaletsos (1970), Kravis et al. (1982), Lluch and Powell (1975), Lluch et al. (1977), Parks (1969), Pollak and Wales (1969, 1992) and Yoshihara (1969). In this section we use the linear expenditure system to present some estimates from LPW.

The LES takes the form

$$p_i q_i = p_i \gamma_i + \theta_i \left[M - \sum_{j=1}^{n} p_j \gamma_j \right], \qquad i=1,\ldots,n. \tag{10.1}$$

The linearity of LES is attractive in its simplicity. When the γ_i's are all positive, the model has the following intuitive interpretation: The

Table 2.14 Budget Shares of 8 Commodities for 13 Countries (Means × 100)

Country (1)	Food (2)	Clothing (3)	Housing (4)	Durables (5)	Personal care (6)	Transport (7)	Recreation (8)	Other services (9)
1. US	26.7	9.5	22.7	7.3	8.1	15.2	5.5	4.9
2. Sweden	36.6	11.5	15.9	7.0	3.7	14.2	8.9	2.4
3. Australia	33.3	11.0	12.7	7.8	5.7	13.1	4.3	12.1
4. UK	39.7	10.7	18.3	6.6	2.3	10.9	7.5	4.0
5. Israel	31.9	9.4	19.2	7.4	6.6	7.3	8.1	10.0
6. Italy	46.3	10.1	16.6	3.2	6.3	8.1	7.5	1.8
7. Puerto Rico	35.6	10.6	15.3	6.9	6.9	12.3	8.8	3.7
8. Ireland	49.2	10.0	12.8	5.7	1.3	8.8	6.3	5.9
9. Greece	46.8	12.2	18.3	3.9	3.6	6.9	6.1	2.3
10. South Africa	36.8	11.8	16.7	7.8	4.8	13.2	4.7	4.1
11. Panama	45.5	7.4	16.7	6.4	4.7	9.4	7.5	2.3
12. Thailand	57.6	8.4	8.0	3.2	5.6	7.9	7.5	1.8
13. Korea	59.9	10.4	11.4	2.8	4.2	4.7	4.4	2.2
14. Mean	42.0	10.2	15.7	5.8	4.9	10.2	6.7	4.4

Source: Lluch et al. (1977, Table 3.3).

consumer first purchases the "subsistence" quantities $\gamma_1,...,\gamma_n$ at a cost of $\Sigma_{j=1}^{n} p_j\gamma_j$. This leaves $M - \Sigma_{j=1}^{n} p_j\gamma_j$ of unspent income which can be called "supernumerary" income. Then, a fraction θ_i of this supernumerary income is spent on good i. Note also that $\theta_i = \partial(p_iq_i)/\partial M$ is the i-*th* marginal share.

Two other aspects of LES should be noted. First, it cannot be used to test the homogeneity and symmetry hypotheses as these are built in or maintained hypotheses in this model. Second, the utility function underlying LES, is of the preference independent form. As discussed in Section 2.6, this imposes certain restrictions on the price elasticities. However, these restrictions may not be at great variance with the data if the model is applied to broad commodity groups.

We return to the LPW database described in the previous section. LPW use time-series data to estimate LES (or a variant thereof, Lluch's, 1973,

Table 2.15 Prices and Per Capita Quantities Consumed of 8 Commodities for 13 Countries (Mean annual log-changes × 100)

Country	Food	Clothing	Housing	Durables	Personal care	Transport	Recreation	Other services
(1)	(2)	(3)	(4)	(5)	(6)	(7)	(8)	(9)
				Prices				
1. US	1.85	1.62	1.70	.55	3.04	1.52	2.35	4.31
2. Sweden	4.00	2.25	3.85	1.79	2.85	3.46	4.22	3.70
3. Australia	2.32	1.39	4.87	.48	3.15	1.96	2.92	3.02
4. UK	2.11	1.70	4.68	1.69	3.09	2.93	4.62	3.80
5. Israel	4.85	4.65	7.81	1.94	6.46	8.06	5.97	7.22
6. Italy	2.52	2.17	3.65	-.16	4.24	2.27	4.07	4.19
7. Puerto Rico	2.62	1.44	1.27	.83	5.76	2.38	3.20	2.46
8. Ireland	3.18	.89	3.98	3.15	1.33	3.13	3.63	4.24
9. Greece	2.57	1.20	1.59	.67	2.48	1.87	.55	.69
10. South Africa	2.27	.20	3.50	.32	3.90	2.40	2.49	3.40
11. Panama	1.95	.59	.54	.11	2.24	.04	.97	.00
12. Thailand	3.24	.19	-2.63	-1.64	1.33	.06	2.43	2.02
13. Korea	13.28	14.75	11.27	12.54	16.70	12.69	13.91	14.80
14. Mean	3.60	2.54	3.54	1.71	4.35	3.29	3.95	4.14
				Quantities				
15. US	.99	2.42	2.79	3.70	3.90	2.78	2.86	3.63
16. Sweden	1.51	1.76	2.77	5.25	5.62	5.32	2.28	4.03
17. Australia	.78	.66	2.34	3.14	4.09	3.12	.10	1.89
18. UK	1.62	2.44	1.98	3.08	3.75	5.53	1.37	6.48
19. Israel	4.62	6.87	5.41	11.67	5.96	9.24	8.58	5.17
20. Italy	4.09	4.62	4.62	8.51	5.96	9.46	4.28	4.47
21. Puerto Rico	-.28	3.91	3.25	4.45	1.40	5.13	4.89	5.89
22. Ireland	1.91	4.88	2.51	5.85	2.71	5.32	3.72	2.47
23. Greece	4.14	7.92	5.99	6.41	5.67	8.94	8.08	6.48
24. South Africa	1.04	2.20	.57	3.21	1.81	3.32	1.22	2.48
25. Panama	2.59	3.23	1.92	5.06	2.55	2.01	4.36	2.84
26. Thailand	2.15	5.30	1.06	10.16	3.70	6.55	5.59	7.16
27. Korea	1.94	2.35	2.27	6.88	4.95	11.55	5.69	3.31
28. Mean	2.08	3.74	2.88	5.95	4.01	6.02	4.08	4.33

Source: Derived from Lluch et al. (1977, Tables 3.4 and 3.5); see S. Selvanathan (1988b, Chap. 1) for details.

Table 2.16 Divisia Moments in 13 Countries

Country	Price index	Volume index	Price variance	Quantity variance	Price-quantity correlation
(1)	(2)	(3)	(4)	(5)	(6)
1. US	1.89	2.47	.57	.97	.20
2. Sweden	3.52	2.83	.56	2.41	-.42
3. Australia	2.51	1.75	1.28	1.32	.09
4. UK	2.88	2.52	1.33	2.15	.05
5. Israel	5.85	6.30	2.89	4.40	-.31
6. Italy	2.82	4.94	.79	2.53	-.30
7. Puerto Rico	2.40	2.49	1.32	5.17	-.30
8. Ireland	3.11	2.97	.73	1.95	-.42
9. Greece	1.93	5.71	.50	2.86	-.80
10. South Africa	2.23	1.67	1.24	.96	-.47
11. Panama	1.21	2.76	.65	.73	-.15
12. Thailand	1.92	3.37	3.63	4.51	-.38
13. Korea	13.36	2.93	1.27	5.11	.05
14. Mean	3.51	3.29	1.29	2.70	-.24

All entries in columns 2 and 3 are to be divided by 100; and those in columns 4 and 5 are to be divided by 10,000.

extended linear expenditure system) for the 13 countries listed in Table 2.13. The model is estimated for each country independently of the others. The upper part of Table 2.17 presents the estimates of the marginal shares θ_{ic} (i=1,...,8 goods; c=1,...,13 countries), while the lower part gives the implied income elasticities,

$$\eta_{ic} = \frac{\theta_{ic}}{\bar{w}_{ic}}, \tag{10.2}$$

with the mean budget shares from Table 2.14. As can be seen from the last row of Table 2.17, on average, food and housing are necessities, clothing is a borderline case, while the remaining five other goods are luxuries.

Table 2.17 First Set of Marginal Shares and Income Elasticities of 8 Commodities for 13 Countries

Country	Food	Clothing	Housing	Durables	Personal care	Transport	Recreation	Other services
(1)	(2)	(3)	(4)	(5)	(6)	(7)	(8)	(9)
				Marginal shares				
1. US	.090	.108	.206	.106	.137	.174	.065	.113
2. Sweden	.278	.071	.145	.079	.052	.253	.097	.024
3. Australia	.143	.050	.220	.082	.133	.224	.009	.138
4. UK	.120	.067	.258	.076	.030	.277	.066	.106
5. Israel	.210	.103	.172	.119	.066	.116	.117	.097
6. Italy	.401	.087	.171	.069	.066	.117	.070	.019
7. Puerto Rico	.177	.112	.144	.068	.114	.176	.137	.072
8. Ireland	.315	.134	.108	.114	.014	.170	.075	.070
9. Greece	.341	.168	.175	.050	.048	.107	.083	.028
10. South Africa	.295	.164	.066	.115	.049	.206	.046	.059
11. Panama	.418	.081	.113	.113	.044	.085	.127	.019
12. Thailand	.482	.101	.013	.052	.052	.123	.150	.028
13. Korea	.434	.069	.085	.077	.074	.146	.078	.038
14. Mean	.285	.101	.144	.086	.068	.167	.086	.062
				Income elasticities				
15. US	.337	1.137	.907	1.452	1.691	1.145	1.182	2.306
16. Sweden	.760	.617	.912	1.129	1.405	1.782	1.090	1.000
17. Australia	.429	.455	1.732	1.051	2.333	1.710	.209	1.140
18. UK	.302	.626	1.410	1.152	1.304	2.541	.880	2.650
19. Israel	.658	1.096	.896	1.608	1.000	1.589	1.444	.970
20. Italy	.866	.861	1.030	2.156	1.048	1.444	.933	1.056
21. Puerto Rico	.497	1.057	.941	.986	1.652	1.431	1.557	1.946
22. Ireland	.640	1.340	.844	2.000	1.077	1.932	1.190	1.186
23. Greece	.729	1.377	.956	1.282	1.333	1.551	1.361	1.217
24. South Africa	.802	1.390	.395	1.474	1.021	1.561	.979	1.439
25. Panama	.919	1.095	.677	1.766	.936	.904	1.693	.826
26. Thailand	.837	1.202	.163	1.625	.929	1.557	2.000	1.556
27. Korea	.725	.663	.746	2.750	1.762	3.106	1.773	1.727
28. Mean	.654	.994	.893	1.572	1.346	1.712	1.253	1.463

Source: The marginal shares are from Lluch et al. (1977, Table 3.6). The income elasticities are derived using equation (10.2).

Notwithstanding its popularity, LES has its drawbacks. Perhaps the most important is the parameterization whereby the marginal shares are treated as constants. It is clear from (10.2) that the constancy of the marginal share implies that the income elasticity is inversely proportional to the corresponding budget share. This can give rise to problems when income is subject to large changes.

Consider the case of food, the dominant commodity in most countries. By Engel's law, food is a necessity (i.e., $\eta_i < 1$ for i=1, representing food, the first commodity). Consequently, if prices remain constant, a rise in income causes consumption of food to increase less than proportionately so that its budget share falls. It then follows from $\eta_1 = \theta_1/w_1$ that as the consumer becomes more affluent, the food income elasticity rises when θ_1 is specified as a constant. That is, food becomes less of a necessity or more of a luxury with increasing income. As discussed in Section 1.4, this behaviour of the elasticity under LES is clearly implausible, a criticism made by Theil (1983).

To illustrate, suppose we take tastes to be the same internationally (following the advice of Section 2.7), pool the LPW data across countries and then apply LES. This model would have the same parameters for each country. From column 2 of Table 2.17, the mean of the individual-country estimates of the food marginal share is .29. It is sufficient for purposes of illustration to use this as the cross-country value of this share. The observed food budget shares are given in Table 2.14: For the US, consumers spend 27 percent of their income on food, while the Koreans spend 60 percent. Thus we have:

	US	Korea
Food marginal share, θ_1	.29	.29
Food budget share, $\bar{w}_{1c}$	.27	.60
Food income elasticity, $\eta_{1c} = \theta_1/\bar{w}_{1c}$	1.07	.48

The above calculation reveals a spectacular disparity in the income elasticity of food. This elasticity for the US (the richest country) is more than twice that for Korea (the poorest). In fact, if we take the results literally, food is a luxury in the US! Note also that these elasticities are nothing like the individual-country estimates given in the lower part of column 2 of Table 2.17. Clearly, LES fails in this cross–country application.

2.11 More on Working's Model

In the previous section we saw that the behaviour of income elasticities implied by LES is unattractive. It should be added that the Rotterdam model (Barten, 1964; Theil, 1965), in which the marginal shares are also specified as constants, suffers from the same defect. In this section we show that Working's (1943) model circumvents the problem.

Working's model is given by equation (4.1) which we reproduce here:

$$w_i = \alpha_i + \beta_i \log M, \qquad i=1,...,n. \tag{11.1}$$

In Section 1.8 we showed that the marginal share and income elasticity of good i implied by Working's model,

$$\theta_i = w_i + \beta_i \tag{11.2}$$

and

$$\eta_i = 1 + \frac{\beta_i}{w_i}. \tag{11.3}$$

In equation (11.2), since the budget share w_i is not constant, neither is the marginal share under Working's model. Equation (11.3) shows that a commodity is a necessity (luxury) if β_i is negative (positive). As the budget share of a necessity falls with increasing income, this expression implies that the income elasticity of such a good falls when income increases. By a similar argument, the income elasticities of luxuries also fall as income rises. That is, as the consumer becomes more affluent, all goods become less luxurious under Working's model, which is plausible. This result is in contrast to the behaviour of the income elasticities from LES and the Rotterdam model, in which the marginal shares are constants. Therefore, Working's model is a plausible alternative to taking the marginal shares as constants.

Like all models, Working's is still not perfect however. Equation (11.1) implies that for sufficiently low or high values of income, the budget share will stray outside the [0, 1] interval. Consequently, the model is only locally valid. It could be argued that as the same local qualification must also apply with equal force to LES, we have been a little too harsh in condemning the constancy of the marginal shares of that model. Although the income elasticities implied by LES always move in the wrong direction, it may be that this is insufficient to cause major problems.

From equation (11.2), in Working's model the marginal share differs from the corresponding budget share by a constant,

$$\beta_i = \theta_i - w_i.$$

Thus, if we have a number of estimates of the marginal share for commodity i, θ_{ic}, c=1,...,N, as well as w_{ic}, c=1,...,N, we can obtain a simple estimate of β_i by averaging,

$$\hat{\beta}_i = \frac{1}{N} \sum_{c=1}^{N} (\theta_{ic} - w_{ic}). \tag{11.4}$$

To implement (11.4) for food, we use the N = 13 countries from LPW, the estimates of the θ_{ic}'s given in Table 2.17 and the corresponding budget shares from Table 2.14. (Note that as the estimates of the marginal shares are obtained country-by-country by LPW, each value is independent of the other.) Table 2.18 contains the results for food (i=1). The standard errors given in the last row indicate that the differences (θ_{1c} - w_{1c}) are less variable than the marginal shares θ_{1c}, which points in the direction of parameterizing on β_1, rather than θ_1. Recall from Section 2.4 that previous estimates of Working's income coefficient for food (β_1) were closely clustered around the value -.15. The new estimate of this coefficient given in row 14 of column 4 of Table 2.18 is -.14 with standard error .02, which is obviously in close agreement with the other estimates. The emergence of more or less the same value of β_i in a wide variety of applications seems to give reassurance that some fundamental behavioural response is being measured here, a response which is more or less constant across consumers, time and countries.

LPW consider the following relation between the food marginal share, θ_1, and GNP per capita, Y :

$$\theta_1 = a + b \log Y, \tag{11.5}$$

where a and b are constants. To interpret this equation, we combine (11.1) and (11.2) for i=1 to yield

$$\theta_1 = \lambda + \beta_1 \log M, \tag{11.6}$$

where $\lambda = \alpha_1 + \beta_1$ is a constant and β_1 is Working's income coefficient for food. A comparison of (11.5) and (11.6) reveals that under the not unreasonable assumption that total expenditure M is proportional to Y, the coefficient b in (11.5) is interpreted as β_1.

LPW (1977, Table 3.11, p. 52) apply (11.5) to their 17 countries and obtain the LS estimate of b of -.179 with standard error .045. Using the 13 countries listed in Table 2.13, GNP of that table and the food marginal shares of Table 2.17, yields a b-estimate of -.103 with standard error .023. Here again, these are insignificantly different from the centre-of-gravity value of -.15.

Table 2.18 Marginal Shares and Budget Shares of Food for 13 Countries

Country (1)	Marginal share (2)	Budget share (3)	Excess of marginal share over budget share (4)
1. US	.090	.267	-.177
2. Sweden	.278	.366	-.088
3. Australia	.143	.333	-.190
4. UK	.120	.397	-.277
5. Israel	.210	.319	-.109
6. Italy	.401	.463	-.062
7. Puerto Rico	.177	.356	-.179
8. Ireland	.315	.492	-.177
9. Greece	.341	.468	-.127
10. South Africa	.295	.368	-.073
11. Panama	.418	.455	-.037
12. Thailand	.482	.576	-.094
13. Korea	.434	.599	-.165
14. Mean	.285	.420	-.135
15. Standard error of the mean	.034	.026	.018

Source: Columns 2 and 3, Lluch et al. (1977, Tables 3.6 and 3.3).

We return to (11.4), the estimator of Working's income coefficient for good i, and use the LPW data to implement it for i=1,...,8 commodities. The procedure is exactly the same as that used for food and Table 2.19 contains the results. The estimates of β_i for food and housing are negative; that for clothing is close to zero; and the remaining ones are positive. This shows that food and housing are necessities, clothing is a borderline case, while the other five goods are luxuries. This is in agreement with the average income elasticities from LPW given in Table 2.17.

Table 2.19 Estimates of Working's Income Coefficients from LPW Data (Standard errors in parentheses)

Commodity (1)	Income coefficient β_i (2)
1. Food	-.135 (.018)
2. Clothing	-.001 (.009)
3. Housing	-.013 (.014)
4. Durables	.028 (.005)
5. Personal care	.019 (.007)
6. Transport	.066 (.012)
7. Recreation	.019 (.008)
8. Other services	.018 (.006)

To explore further the implications of the cross-country β_i-estimates, we compute the implied marginal shares and income elasticities and Table 2.20 contains the results. These are to be compared with the LPW values given in Table 2.17. We can regard the values in Table 2.20 as "fitted" and those in Table 2.17 as "observed". The correlation coefficients between the two sets of marginal shares are:

Food	.86	Personal care	.79
Clothing	.31	Transport	.65
Housing	.64	Recreation	.73
Durables	.61	Other services	.82

As can be seen, except for clothing, the two sets of marginal shares agree well which tends to support the idea that Working's model can be satisfactorily applied to the world as a whole (the "world" being the 13 LPW countries).

Table 2.20 Second Set of Marginal Shares and Income Elasticities of 8 Commodities for 13 Countries

Country	Food	Clothing	Housing	Durables	Personal care	Transport	Recreation	Other services
(1)	(2)	(3)	(4)	(5)	(6)	(7)	(8)	(9)
				Marginal shares				
1. US	.132	.094	.214	.101	.100	.218	.074	.067
2. Sweden	.231	.114	.146	.098	.056	.208	.108	.042
3. Australia	.198	.109	.114	.106	.076	.197	.062	.139
4. UK	.262	.106	.170	.094	.042	.175	.094	.058
5. Israel	.184	.093	.179	.102	.085	.139	.100	.118
6. Italy	.328	.100	.153	.060	.082	.147	.094	.036
7. Puerto Rico	.221	.105	.140	.097	.088	.189	.107	.055
8. Ireland	.357	.099	.115	.085	.032	.154	.082	.077
9. Greece	.333	.121	.170	.067	.055	.135	.080	.041
10. South Africa	.233	.117	.154	.106	.067	.198	.066	.059
11. Panama	.320	.073	.154	.092	.066	.160	.094	.041
12. Thailand	.441	.083	.067	.060	.075	.145	.094	.036
13. Korea	.464	.103	.101	.056	.061	.113	.063	.040
14. Mean	.285	.101	.144	.086	.068	.168	.086	.062
				Income elasticities				
15. US	.494	.989	.943	1.384	1.235	1.434	1.345	1.367
16. Sweden	.631	.991	.918	1.400	1.514	1.465	1.213	1.750
17. Australia	.595	.991	.898	1.359	1.333	1.504	1.442	1.149
18. UK	.660	.991	.929	1.424	1.826	1.606	1.253	1.450
19. Israel	.577	.989	.932	1.378	1.288	1.904	1.235	1.180
20. Italy	.708	.990	.922	1.875	1.302	1.815	1.253	2.000
21. Puerto Rico	.621	.991	.915	1.406	1.275	1.537	1.216	1.486
22. Ireland	.726	.990	.898	1.491	2.462	1.750	1.302	1.305
23. Greece	.712	.992	.929	1.718	1.528	1.957	1.311	1.783
24. South Africa	.633	.992	.922	1.359	1.396	1.500	1.404	1.439
25. Panama	.703	.986	.922	1.438	1.404	1.702	1.253	1.783
26. Thailand	.766	.988	.838	1.875	1.339	1.835	1.253	2.000
27. Korea	.775	.990	.886	2.000	1.452	2.404	1.432	1.818
28. Mean	.662	.990	.912	1.547	1.489	1.724	1.301	1.578

Source: The marginal shares are computed from equation (11.2) with the observed budget shares given in Table 2.14 and the β_i- estimates given in Table 2.19. The income elasticities are computed from (11.3) using the same approach.

2.12 A World Demand System

The results of the previous section are based on income responses of demand which hold constant prices. Those results are sufficiently encouraging to proceed further and extend the approach to deal simultaneously with the effects of income and prices. In this section we ask the question, how much of the cross-country variation in consumption patterns is explained by differences in incomes and prices? To do this we employ a simple extension of Working's model which contains a price substitution term.

Our starting point is a double-log demand equation formulated in terms of changes over time,

$$Dq_{it} = \alpha_i + \eta_i DQ_t + \sum_{j=1}^{n} \eta'_{ij} Dp_{jt} ,$$

where α_i is an intercept; η_i is the income elasticity of i; and DQ_t is the Divisia volume index of the change in real income; and η'_{ij} is the (i,j)-*th* compensated price elasticity. To apply this equation to the LPW cross-country data, we add to the variables and elasticities a country subscript c (c = 1,...,13) and set n = 8 commodities. This yields

$$Dq_{ict} = \eta_{ic} DQ_{ct} + \sum_{j=1}^{8} \eta'_{ijc} Dp_{jct}, \qquad (12.1)$$

Note that as log-changes are unit free, all variables in (12.1) are directly comparable across countries, independent of the different currency units.

The demand system (12.1) for i=1,...,8 contains an 8 × 8 matrix of price elasticities $[\eta'_{ijc}]$ for each of the 13 countries. To reduce the number of unknowns, we shall invoke the assumption of preference independence. As discussed in Section 2.8, the price elasticities for country c then take the form

$$\eta'_{ijc} = \phi\eta_{ic}(\delta_{ij} - \theta_{jc}), \qquad i,j = 1,...,8, \qquad (12.2)$$

where ϕ is the income flexibility (the reciprocal of the income elasticity of the marginal utility of income); δ_{ij} is the Kronecker delta (δ_{ij} = 1 if i = j, = 0 otherwise); and θ_{jc} is the j-*th* marginal share in c. The use of the assumption of preference independence is probably not too bad here as the 8 commodities in the LPW database are broad aggregates. Note that as ϕ in equation (12.2) does not have a country subscript, it as specified as a constant; this is in agreement with the discussion of Section 2.8 above.

Let Dq_{ic} be observed value of the log-change in consumption of i in c; and $\eta_{ic}\, DQ_c + \Sigma_{j=1}^{8}\, \eta'_{ijc}\, Dp_{jc}$ be the corresponding fitted value when numerical values are used for the elasticities. The values of the variables Dq_{ic} and Dp_{ic} are given in Table 2.15, while those of DQ_c are in column 3 of Table 2.16. If e_{ic} is the difference between the observed and fitted values, then one way to measure the quality of the predictions for commodity i is the root-mean-squared error,

$$RMSE_i = \sqrt{\frac{1}{13} \sum_{c=1}^{13} e_{ic}^2}.$$

The performance of the system as a whole can then be measured by the budget-share-weighted average of the $RMSE_i$,

$$RMSE = \sum_{i=1}^{8} \bar{w}_i \, RMSE_i \ ,$$

where $\bar{w}_i$ is the cross-country average of the budget share of i, given in the last row of Table 2.14.

We first use the LPW estimates of the income elasticities given in the lower half of Table 2.17, the marginal shares of the upper half of that table and set the income flexibility ϕ = -.5, the value recommended in Section 2.8. Column 2 of Table 2.21 contains the results. As can be seen, food and housing share the lowest value of the RMSE of about .5 percent; the largest RMSE is 1.9 percent for durables; while the weighted average

Table 2.21 Quality of Predictions of Demand Equations for 8 Commodities in 13 Countries
(Root–mean–squared errors × 100)

Commodity	η_{ic} = LPV ϕ = -.5	η_{ic} = 1 ϕ = -1	η_{ic} = WM ϕ = -.5
(1)	(2)	(3)	(4)
1. Food	.51	1.41	.64
2. Clothing	.61	1.20	1.02
3. Housing	.51	2.30	1.23
4. Durables	1.89	1.63	1.70
5. Personal care	1.15	2.33	2.41
6. Transport	1.01	3.43	1.73
7. Recreation	.62	1.79	1.28
8. Other services	.88	2.42	2.37
9. Weighted mean	.71	1.86	1.15

As the demand equations are formulated in log–changes, the RMSEs×100 are (approximately) RMS percentage prediction errors. The notation η_{ic} = LPV denotes that the income elasticities used for the predictions are the LPV estimates given in the lower part of Table 2.17; and η_{ic} = WM denotes that the income elasticities are from Working's model, given in the lower part of Table 2.20.

is .7 percent. Overall, these RMSEs are very low. However, it should be kept in mind that underlying these predictions are n - 1 = 7 free income elasticities (one is constrained by $\Sigma_{i=1}^{8} w_i\eta_i = 1$) for each of the 13 countries, plus a value of ϕ. Consequently, the column 2 results are based on 7 × 13 + 1 = 92 free parameters. As the income elasticities are unconstrained across countries, in a certain sense tastes are not constant in the demand equations underlying the results of column 2.

Next, we specify that all income elasticities are unity, so that the marginal shares are equal to the corresponding budget shares, and $\phi = -1$. This is a naive extrapolation corresponding to no-change of the budget shares (Theil, 1975/76, p. 219, Volume 1), which serves as a standard of reference. The results in column 3 of Table 2.21 show that most of the $RMSE_i$ increase substantially in relation to those of column 2. The weighted-average RMSE of 1.9 percent in column 3 is about 2.5 times larger than its column 2 counterpart.

Finally, we use the income elasticities and marginal shares implied by Working's model (given in Table 2.20) and $\phi = -.5$. Here tastes are taken to be constant as the income elasticities (and the marginal shares) are based on coefficients from Working's model, $\beta_1,...,\beta_8$, which are the same for all countries. Column 4 of Table 2.21 contains the results. These RMSEs are mostly substantially lower than those of column 3, where all elasticities are unitary. At the same time however, the column 4 values are in general higher than the LPW values given in column 2; the weighted-average RMSE in column 4 of 1.2 percent is about 65 percent higher than its column 2 counterpart. Nevertheless, the average RMSE of 1.2 percent is an excellent result keeping in mind the diversity of countries involved. In addition, the predictions of column 4 are based on only 8 free parameters (7 β_i's, as one is constrained by $\Sigma_{i=1}^{8} \beta_i = 0$, plus ϕ). Consequently, the increase in the average RMSE from .7 percent (in column 2) to 1.2 percent (column 4) is perfectly acceptable given that the number of free parameters falls from 92 to 8.

It is thus fair to make the strong claim that this approach allows world consumption patterns to be adequately described with only 8 parameters. Of course, the qualifications to this claim are obvious: Here we are dealing with broad commodity groups and the "world" is made up of only 13 representative countries. We shall return to the LPW data in Chapter 5. (For a further analysis of these data, see S. Selvanathan, 1988b.)

References

Aasness, J. and A. Rodseth (1983). 'Engel Curves and Systems of Demand Functions,' *European Economic Review* 20: 95-121.

Anderson, G. and R. Blundell (1983). 'Testing Restrictions in a Flexible Dynamic Demand System: An Application to Consumers' Expenditure in Canada,' *Review of Economic Studies* 50: 397-410.

Attfield, C.L.F. (1985). 'Homogeneity and Endogeneity in Systems of Demand Equations,' *Journal of Econometrics* 27: 197-209.

Barten, A.P. (1964). 'Consumer Demand Functions Under Conditions of Almost Additive Preferences,' *Econometrica* 32: 1-38.

Barten, A.P.(1977). 'The Systems of Consumer Demand Functions Approach: A Review,' *Econometrica* 45: 23-51.

Bera, A.K., R.P. Byron and C.M. Jarque (1981). 'Further Evidence on Asymptotic Tests for Homogeneity and Symmetry in Large Demand Systems,' *Economics Letters* 8: 101-5.

Bewley, R.A. (1983). 'Tests of Restrictions in Large Demand Systems,' *European Economic Review* 20: 257-69.

Bewley, R.A. (1986). *Allocation Models: Specification, Estimation and Applications*. Cambridge, Mass.: Ballinger Publishing Co.

Bewley, R.A. and G. Elliott (1989). 'The Rejection of Homogeneity in Demand and Supply Analysis: An Explanation and Solution,' Discussion Paper No. 89/2, School of Economics, The University of New South Wales.

Blanciforti, L. and R. Green (1983). 'An Almost Ideal Demand System Incorporating Habits: An Analysis of Expenditures on Food and Aggregate Commodity Groups,' *Review of Economics and Statistics* 65: 511-15.

Brown, A. and A. Deaton (1972). 'Surveys in Applied Economics: Models of Consumer Behaviour,' *Economic Journal* 82: 1145-236.

Christensen, L.R., D.W. Jorgenson and L.J. Lau (1975). 'Transcendental Logarithmic Utility Functions,' *American Economic Review* 65: 367-83.

Chung, C-F. and E. Lopez (1988). 'A Regional Analysis of Food Consumption in Spain,' *Economics Letters* 26: 209-13.

Clements, K.W. (1982). 'Divisia Moments of Australian Consumption,' *Economics Letters* 9: 43-48.

Clements, K.W. (1983). 'The Demand for Energy Used in Transport,' *Australian Journal of Management* 8: 27-56.

Clements, K.W. and S. Selvanathan (1994). 'Understanding Consumption Patterns,' *Empirical Economics* 19: 69-110.

Deaton, A.S. (1974). 'A Reconsideration of the Empirical Implications of Additive Preferences,' *Economic Journal* 84: 338-48.

Deaton, A.S. (1975). *Models and Projections of Demand in Post War Britain*. London: Chapman and Hall.

Deaton, A.S. (1987). 'Econometric Issues for Tax Design in Developing Countries,' In D. Newbery and N. Stern (eds) *The Theory of Taxation for Developing Countries*. New York: Oxford University Press, pp. 92-113.

Deaton, A.S., and J. Muellbauer (1980). 'An Almost Ideal Demand System,' *American Economic Review* 70: 312-26.

DeJanvry, A., J. Bieri and A. Nunez (1972). 'Estimation of Demand Parameters Under Consumer Budgeting: An Application to Argentina,' *American Journal of Agricultural Economics* 54: 422-30.

Dixon, P.B., B.R. Parmenter, J. Sutton and D.P. Vincent (1982). *ORANI: A Multisectoral Model of the Australian Economy*. Amsterdam: North-Holland Publishing Company.

Finke, R., L.R. Flood and H. Theil (1984). 'Maximum Likelihood and Instrumental Variable Estimation of a Consumer Demand System for Japan and Sweden,' *Economics Letters* 15: 13-19.

Frisch, R. (1959). 'A Complete Scheme for Computing All Direct and Cross Demand Elasticities in a Model with Many Sectors,' *Econometrica* 27: 177-96.

Goldberger, A.S. and T. Gamaletsos (1970). 'A Cross-Country Comparison of Consumer Expenditure Patterns,' *European Economic Review* 1: 357-400.

Houthakker, H.S. (1957). 'An International Comparison of Household Expenditure Patterns, Commemorating the Centenary of Engel's Law,' *Econometrica* 25: 532-51.

Keuzenkamp, H.A. and A.P. Barten (1991). 'Rejection Without Falsification: On the History of Testing the Homogeneity Condition in the Theory of Consumer Demand,' Department of Economics, Tilburg University and Department of Economics, Catholic University Leuven.

Kravis, I.B., A.W. Heston and R. Summers (1982). *World Product and Income: International Comparisons of Real Gross Product.* Baltimore, Md.: The John Hopkins University Press.

Laitinen, K. (1978). 'Why is Demand Homogeneity So Often Rejected?' *Economics Letters* 1: 187-91.

Leser, C.E.V. (1963). 'Forms of Engel Functions,' *Econometrica* 31: 694-703.

Lluch, C. (1973). 'The Extended Linear Expenditure System,' *European Economic Review* 4: 21-32.

Lluch, C. and A.A. Powell (1975). 'International Comparisons of Expenditure Patterns,' *European Economic Review* 5: 275-303.

Lluch, C, A.A. Powell and R.A. Williams (1977). *Patterns in Household Demand and Saving*. Oxford: Oxford University Press.

Marquez, J. and D. Vining (1984). 'Inflation and Relative Price Change: A Survey of the Literature,' In M.Ballabon (ed) *Economic Perspective: An Annual Survey of Economics* 3. New York: Harwood Academic Publishers.

Meisner, J.F. (1979a). 'The Sad Fate of the Asymptotic Slutsky Symmetry Test for Large Systems,' *Economics Letters* 2: 231-33.

Meisner, J.F. (1979b). 'Divisia Moments of U.S. Industry, 1947-1978,' *Economics Letters* 4: 239-42.

Musgrove, P. (1985). 'Household Food Consumption in the Dominican Republic: Effects of Income, Price and Family Size,' *Economic Development and Cultural Change* 34: 83-101.

Parks, R.W. (1969). 'Systems of Demand Equations: An Empirical Comparison of Alternative Functional Forms,' *Econometrica* 37: 629-50.

Pigou, A.C. (1910). 'A Method of Determining the Numerical Values of Elasticities of Demand,' *Economic Journal* 20: 636-40.

Pollak, R.A. and T.J. Wales (1969). 'Estimation of the Linear Expenditure System,' *Econometrica* 37: 611-28.

Pollak, R.A. and T.J. Wales (1987). 'Pooling International Consumption Data,' *Review of Economics and Statistics* 69: 90-99.

Pollak, A.A. and T.J. Wales (1992). *Demand System Specification and Estimation.* New York and Oxford: Oxford University Press.

Selvanathan, E.A. (1987). *Explorations in Consumer Demand.* Ph.D. Thesis, Murdoch University, Western Australia.

Selvanathan, S. (1987a). 'Do OECD Consumers Obey Demand Theory?' Discussion Paper No. 87.04, Department of Economics, The University of Western Australia.

Selvanathan, S. (1987b). 'A Monte Carlo Test of Preference Independence,' *Economics Letters* 25: 259-61.

Selvanathan, S. (1987c). 'How Similar are OECD Consumers?' Discussion Paper No. 87.08, Department of Economics, The University of Western Australia.

Selvanathan, S. (1987d). 'Further Evidence on the Frisch Conjecture,' Discussion Paper No. 87.10, Department of Economics, The University of Western Australia.

Selvanathan, S. (1988a). 'Empirical Regularities in OECD Consumption,' Discussion Paper No. 88.01, Department of Economics, The University of Western Australia.

Selvanathan, S. (1988b). *A System-Wide Analysis of International and Interregional Consumption Patterns.* Ph.D. Thesis, The University of Western Australia.

Stening, K. (1985). 'OECD Consumption: A Database,' Unpublished manuscript, Department of Economics, The University of Western Australia.

Stigler, G.J. and G.S. Becker (1977). 'De Gustibus Non Est Disputandum,' *American Economic Review* 67: 79-90.

Stone, R. (1954). 'Linear Expenditure Systems and Demand Analysis: An Application to the Pattern of British Demand,' *Economic Journal* 64: 511-27.

Summers, R. and A. Heston (1984). 'Improved International Comparisons of Real Product and Its Composition: 1950-1980,' *Review of Income and Wealth* 30: 207-68.

Theil, H. (1965). 'The Information Approach to Demand Analysis,' *Econometrica* 33: 67-87.

Theil, H. (1967). *Economics and Information Theory*. New York: Elsevier/North-Holland, Inc., and Amsterdam: North-Holland Publishing Company.

Theil, H. (1975/76). *Theory and Measurement of Consumer Demand*. Two volumes. Amsterdam: North-Holland Publishing Company.

Theil, H. (1980). *The System-Wide Approach to Microeconomics*. Chicago: The University of Chicago Press.

Theil, H. (1983). 'World Product and Income: A Review Article,' *Journal of Political Economy* 91: 505-17.

Theil, H. (1987a). 'Evidence from International Consumption Comparisons,' Chapter 2 in H. Theil and K.W. Clements *Applied Demand Analysis: Results from System-Wide Approaches*. Cambridge, Mass.: Ballinger Publishing Co., pp. 37-100.

Theil, H. (1987b). 'The Econometrics of Demand Systems,' Chapter 3 in H. Theil and K.W. Clements *Applied Demand Analysis: Results from System-Wide Approaches*. Cambridge, Mass.: Ballinger Publishing Co., pp. 101-62.

Theil, H. and R.B. Brooks (1970/71). 'How Does the Marginal Utility of Income Change when Real Income Changes?' *European Economic Review* 2: 218-40.

Theil, H., C-F. Chung and J.L. Seale, Jr. (1989). *International Evidence on Consumption Patterns*. Greenwich, Connecticut: JAI Press, Inc.

Theil, H. and R. Finke (1984). 'A Time-Series Analysis of a Demand System Based on Cross-Country Coefficient Estimates,' *Economics Letters* 15: 245-50.

Theil, H., J.L. Seale, Jr. and C-F. Chung (1987). 'A Regional Analysis of Food Consumption in China,' *Empirical Economics* 12: 129-35.

Theil, H. and F.E. Suhm (1981). *International Consumption Comparisons: A System-Wide Approach.* Amsterdam: North-Holland Publishing Company.

Working, H. (1943). 'Statistical Laws of Family Expenditure,' *Journal of the American Statistical Association* 38: 43-56.

Yoshihara, K. (1969). 'Demand Functions: An Application to the Japanese Expenditure Pattern,' *Econometrica* 37: 257-74.

3 Data-Analytic Techniques for Consumer Economics

E.A. Selvanathan
School of International Business Relations, Griffith University, Australia

3.1 Introduction

This chapter introduces a number of new data-analytic techniques which can be used in consumption economics. These techniques are useful to apply before estimating demand equations to obtain a general *feel* for the data and provide summary measures of the data and informal estimates of key demand parameters. The Demand Analysis Package DAP (S. Selvanathan et al., 1989) implements many of these techniques in a convenient manner.

We commence by presenting UK alcohol data and their sources and several Divisia index numbers. We then illustrate the new techniques by applying them to the UK alcohol data to obtain preliminary estimates for the marginal shares, income flexibility and income and price elasticities. Finally we compare the preliminary estimates with those reported in E.A. Selvanathan (1987) obtained by estimating the demand equations.

3.2 The Basic Data

Table 3.1 presents UK consumption of beer, wine and spirits, 1955-1985, in litres per capita. The figures for the years 1955-1976 are from the *Brewers' Association of Canada* (1986). This publication gives disaggregated consumption of beer, wine and cider in litres per capita and of spirits in litres of absolute alcohol per capita. By dividing the spirits figures by .4 we convert its consumption into litres per capita. We

Table 3.1 Per Capita Alcohol Consumption and Price Indexes: United Kingdom, 1955-1985

Year	Beer		Wine		Spirits	
	Quantity	Price	Quantity	Price	Quantity	Price
(1)	(2)	(3)	(4)	(5)	(6)	(7)
1955	80.5	54.00	3.35	54.42	1.475	60.10
1956	80.8	55.17	3.35	55.44	1.575	60.17
1957	81.0	57.58	3.58	55.78	1.600	60.22
1958	78.4	58.41	3.52	57.09	1.625	61.28
1959	82.1	54.18	3.87	55.43	1.725	61.59
1960	85.1	52.97	3.98	58.18	1.850	61.50
1961	85.1	57.92	4.09	62.73	1.925	67.26
1962	87.8	61.25	4.03	63.59	1.950	70.42
1963	87.5	63.74	4.37	74.60	2.050	67.52
1964	91.1	67.17	4.66	82.94	2.200	71.64
1965	91.2	74.23	4.66	84.98	2.050	78.81
1966	92.2	78.74	5.01	88.60	2.075	83.53
1967	93.8	82.62	5.74	85.55	2.075	86.35
1968	94.8	85.03	5.85	96.07	2.150	91.41
1969	98.4	91.80	5.86	103.54	2.000	98.01
1970	101.6	100.00	6.54	100.00	2.300	100.00
1971	105.4	108.03	7.05	110.05	2.425	103.32
1972	107.5	115.00	7.84	117.05	2.775	104.39
1973	112.1	119.62	9.54	124.70	3.500	106.70
1974	114.4	134.31	9.26	150.89	3.850	108.66
1975	117.6	168.60	9.38	172.81	3.675	135.81
1976	118.9	202.05	10.51	182.37	4.150	133.64
1977	117.3	230.98	10.27	213.42	3.533	186.34
1978	120.7	244.52	11.41	223.34	4.260	174.67
1979	121.4	279.33	12.20	261.22	4.691	194.52
1980	116.3	338.84	12.06	308.08	4.422	228.37
1981	110.5	399.80	12.91	341.21	4.190	257.37
1982	108.1	441.81	13.86	356.83	3.954	281.87
1983	110.4	478.39	15.28	373.27	4.062	300.28
1984	109.9	519.67	16.20	381.47	4.036	321.06
1985	108.6	570.95	16.52	408.97	4.292	332.62
Mean	100.3	175.70	7.96	158.21	2.853	133.85

Quantities are in litres per capita and the price indexes have base 1970=100.

cross-checked the consumption figures of beer, wine and spirits presented in Table 3.1 with the corresponding figures given in the *Central Statistical Office* (various issues) and found that they are reasonably close. The wine consumption figures presented in Table 3.1 include cider. In 1985, UK per capita consumption of beer is 109 litres, wine is 17 litres and spirits 4 litres.

For the years 1977-1985 we obtained the total consumption figures from the *Central Statistical Office* (1985 and 1986). As the total population figures for the UK are not published after 1981, we use the resident population figures published in the *Central Statistical Office* (1986) to convert the data into per capita values. The current-price expenditure figures for the years 1955-1961 are from McGuinness (1980, App. 2); for 1962-1969 from the *Central Statistical Office* (1973); and for 1970-1985 from the UK *Government Statistical Services* (1979-81 and 1986). As before, we use the resident population figures to convert these total expenditures into per capita values. For the years 1955-1961 we use the per adult expenditures and adult population figures given in McGuinness to calculate the total expenditures and then use the resident population figures to convert the total expenditure figures into per capita values. We then divide these per capita expenditures by the corresponding per capita consumption to obtain the implicit price indexes. Table 3.1 also presents these price indexes.

Figure 3.1 plots alcohol consumption, while Figure 3.2 plots the prices. As can be seen, consumption of all three beverages increase until the late 70's and thereafter beer and spirits decline, while wine consumption continues to grow. All three prices increase throughout the sample period.

In Table 3.2 we give the quantity and price log-changes. The log-change in consumption and the price from year t-1 to t is $Dq_{it} = \log q_{it} - \log q_{i,t-1}$ and $Dp_{it} = \log p_{it} - \log p_{i,t-1}$, where q_{it} and p_{it} represent per capita consumption and the price of i (= beer, wine and spirits) in year t. As can be seen from Table 3.2, the average annual growth in per capita consumption is approximately 1.0, 5.3 and 3.6 percent for beer, wine and spirits, respectively. On average, the prices increased by 7.9, 6.7 and 5.7 percent for beer, wine and spirits. We note that beer has the lowest annual growth in consumption and highest price increase. Figures 3.3 and 3.4 plot the quantity and price log-changes.

Table 3.3 gives the per capita expenditure on beer, wine and spirits. As the expenditure data for wine and cider are available only in an aggregated form, wine expenditure here includes cider. Table 3.4 gives expenditure on each beverage expressed as a fraction of total alcohol expenditure, $w'_{it} = p_{it}q_{it}/M_{gt}$, where $M_{gt} = \Sigma_{i=1}^{3} p_{it}q_{it}$ is total alcohol

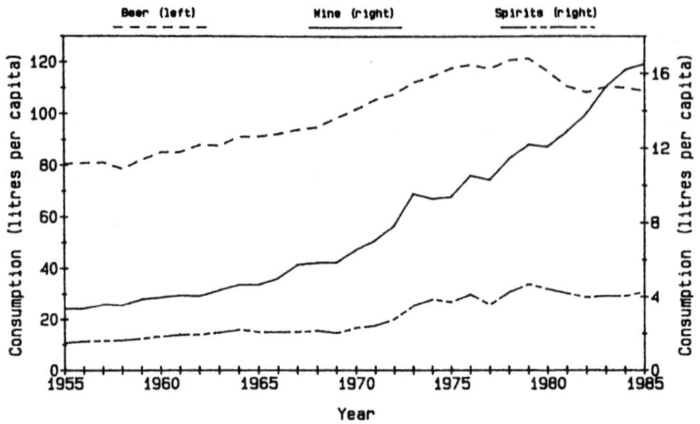

Fig. 3.1 Alcohol Consumption, United Kingdom, 1955-1985

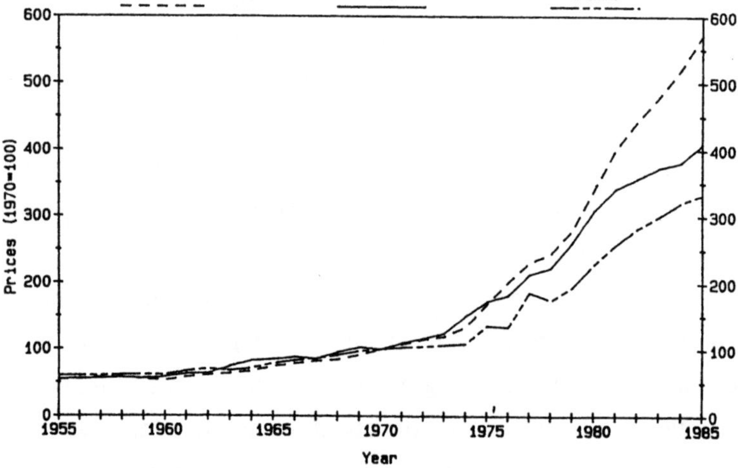

Fig. 3.2 Alcohol Price Indexes, United Kingdom, 1955-1985

Table 3.2 Alcohol Quantity and Price Log-changes: United Kingdom, 1955-1985

Year	Beer		Wine		Spirits	
	Quantity	Price	Quantity	Price	Quantity	Price
(1)	(2)	(3)	(4)	(5)	(6)	(7)
1956	.3720	2.1306	.0000	1.8596	6.5597	.1201
1957	.2472	4.2654	6.6403	.6190	1.5748	.0780
1958	-3.2625	1.4307	-1.6902	2.3177	1.5504	1.7460
1959	4.6114	-7.5177	9.4794	-2.9566	5.9719	.5030
1960	3.5889	-2.2435	2.8027	4.8555	6.9959	-.1393
1961	.0000	8.9285	2.7263	7.5217	3.9740	8.9459
1962	3.1235	5.5807	-1.4779	1.3668	1.2903	4.5927
1963	-.3423	3.9935	8.0997	15.9634	5.0010	-4.2055
1964	4.0319	5.2365	6.4252	10.6045	7.0618	5.9276
1965	.1097	9.9906	.0000	2.4303	-7.0618	9.5432
1966	1.0905	5.9040	7.2421	4.1677	1.2121	5.8140
1967	1.7205	4.8053	13.6023	-3.5079	.0000	3.3200
1968	1.0605	2.8835	1.8983	11.5974	3.5507	5.6910
1969	3.7271	7.6569	.1708	7.4954	-7.2321	6.9782
1970	3.2003	8.5566	10.9788	-3.4823	13.9762	2.0063
1971	3.6719	7.7198	7.5091	9.5772	5.2922	3.2692
1972	1.9728	6.2572	10.6211	6.1639	13.4819	1.0272
1973	4.1901	3.9413	19.6255	6.3286	23.2112	2.1862
1974	2.0310	11.5805	-2.9789	19.0670	9.5310	1.8232
1975	2.7588	22.7368	1.2876	13.5656	-4.6520	22.3058
1976	1.0994	18.0986	11.3747	5.3836	12.1555	-1.6109
1977	-1.3548	13.3835	-2.3100	15.7239	-16.0961	33.2409
1978	2.8573	5.6960	10.5263	4.5418	18.7122	-6.4676
1979	.5783	13.3108	6.6946	15.6656	9.6377	10.7628
1980	-4.2918	19.3113	-1.1542	16.5017	-5.9054	16.0420
1981	-5.1158	16.5445	6.8108	10.2121	-5.3891	11.9572
1982	-2.1959	9.9905	7.1005	4.4769	-5.7973	9.0900
1983	2.1053	7.9554	9.7538	4.5053	2.6948	6.3279
1984	-.4539	8.2766	5.8467	2.1724	-.6421	6.6920
1985	-1.1900	9.4109	1.9561	6.9602	6.1499	3.5374
Mean	.9981	7.8605	5.3187	6.7233	3.5603	5.7035

All entries are to be divided by 100. The quantities are expressed in per capita terms. The year 1956, for example, refers to the transition from 1955 to 1956.

expenditure; these fractions are the *conditional budget shares*. Table 3.4 shows that the share for beer has decreased by about 11 percentage points over this period and is 53.3 percent in 1985. Most of that fall has been offset by the increase in the wine share, which is 10.2 percent in 1955 and 22.2 in 1985. The share for spirits has been much more constant than those of the other two beverages over this period. In Figure 3.5 we plot the conditional budget shares.

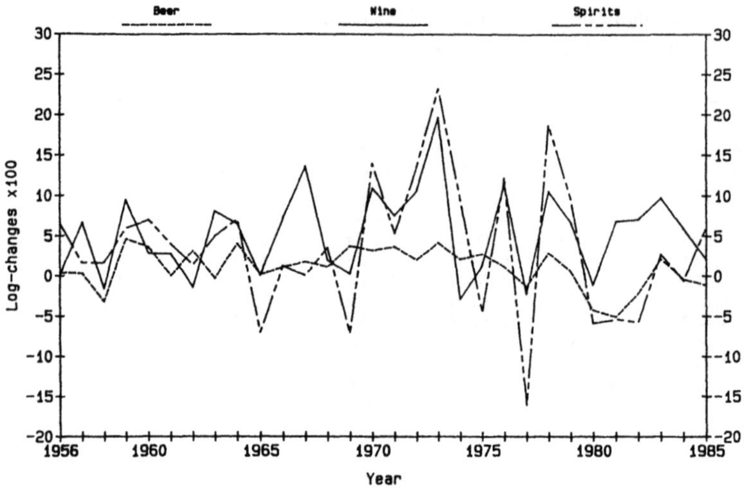

Fig. 3.3 Log-changes in Alcohol Consumption: United Kingdom, 1955-1985

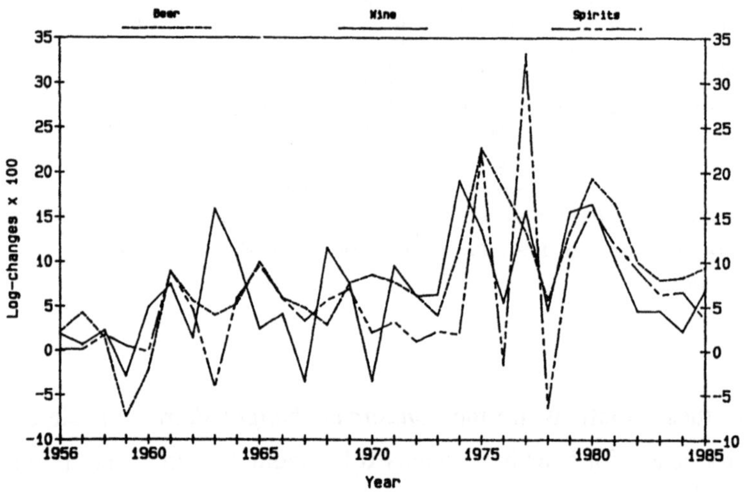

Fig. 3.4 Log-changes in Alcohol Prices: United Kingdom, 1955-1985

Table 3.3 Expenditure on Alcohol: United Kingdom, 1955-1985

Year (1)	Beer (2)	Wine (3)	Spirits (4)	Total (5)
1955	10.42	1.67	4.24	16.33
1956	10.69	1.70	4.53	16.92
1957	11.18	1.83	4.61	17.62
1958	10.98	1.84	4.76	17.58
1959	10.66	1.96	5.08	17.71
1960	10.81	2.12	5.44	18.37
1961	11.82	2.35	6.19	20.36
1962	12.89	2.35	6.57	21.80
1963	13.37	2.98	6.62	22.97
1964	14.67	3.54	7.54	25.75
1965	16.23	3.62	7.73	27.58
1966	17.40	4.06	8.29	29.76
1967	18.58	4.49	8.57	31.64
1968	19.32	5.14	9.40	33.87
1969	21.65	5.55	9.38	36.58
1970	24.36	5.99	11.00	41.34
1971	27.30	7.10	11.98	46.38
1972	29.64	8.40	13.86	51.89
1973	32.15	10.89	17.86	60.90
1974	36.83	12.79	20.01	69.63
1975	47.53	14.84	23.87	86.24
1976	57.59	17.54	26.53	101.66
1977	64.95	20.06	31.49	116.50
1978	70.75	23.32	35.59	129.67
1979	81.30	29.17	43.64	154.11
1980	94.47	34.01	48.30	176.78
1981	105.91	40.32	51.58	197.80
1982	114.49	45.26	53.31	213.06
1983	126.61	52.20	58.34	237.15
1984	136.91	56.56	61.98	255.45
1985	148.65	61.84	68.28	278.76
Mean	45.49	15.66	21.82	82.97

Expenditures are expressed in current pounds per capita.

Table 3.5 gives the consumer price index from *International Monetary Fund* (1981, 1985, 1986); total (current-price) per capita consumption expenditure M_t, for the years 1955-1974 from *Central Statistical Office* (1986) and for 1975-1985 from *UK General Statistical Services* (1986); and the expenditure on each of the three beverages as a proportion of total consumption expenditure, $w_{it} = p_{it}q_{it}/M_t$, which is the *unconditional budget share*. Column 7 of Table 3.5 contains the budget share for total alcohol, defined as $W_{gt} = \Sigma_{i=1}^{3} w_{it}$. These budget shares are plotted in Figure 3.6.

Table 3.4 Conditional Budget Shares for Alcohol: United Kingdom, 1955-1985

Year (1)	Beer (2)	Wine (3)	Spirits (4)
1955	63.82	10.22	25.96
1956	63.16	10.05	26.79
1957	63.47	10.38	26.16
1958	62.45	10.46	27.09
1959	60.22	11.09	28.70
1960	58.84	11.54	29.63
1961	58.05	11.54	30.42
1962	59.12	10.76	30.12
1963	58.20	12.99	28.82
1964	56.98	13.74	29.28
1965	58.84	13.14	28.02
1966	58.49	13.65	27.86
1967	58.71	14.20	27.09
1968	57.06	15.19	27.75
1969	59.19	15.18	25.63
1970	58.91	14.48	26.61
1971	58.85	15.31	25.84
1972	57.11	16.19	26.70
1973	52.79	17.88	29.33
1974	52.90	18.37	28.74
1975	55.12	17.20	27.68
1976	56.65	17.26	26.09
1977	55.75	17.22	27.03
1978	54.57	17.99	27.45
1979	52.75	18.93	28.32
1980	53.44	19.24	27.32
1981	53.54	20.38	26.08
1982	53.74	21.25	25.02
1983	53.39	22.01	24.60
1984	53.60	22.14	24.26
1985	53.32	22.18	24.50
Mean	57.19	15.55	27.25

All entries are to be divided by 100.

Table 3.6 presents the unconditional budget shares, the budget share for total alcohol and the conditional budget shares, all in arithmetic average form. Here, $\bar{w}_{it} = \frac{1}{2}(w_{it} + w_{i,t-1})$, i=1(beer), 2(wine), 3(spirits), is the

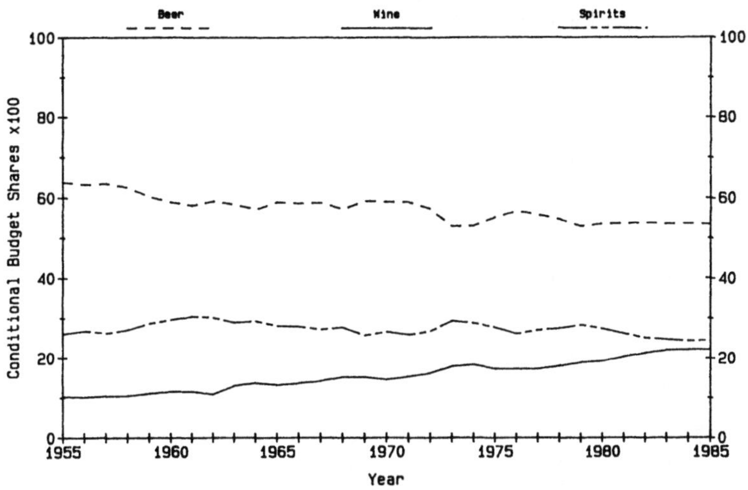

Fig. 3.5 Conditional Budget Shares of Beer, Wine and Spirits: United Kingdom, 1955-1985

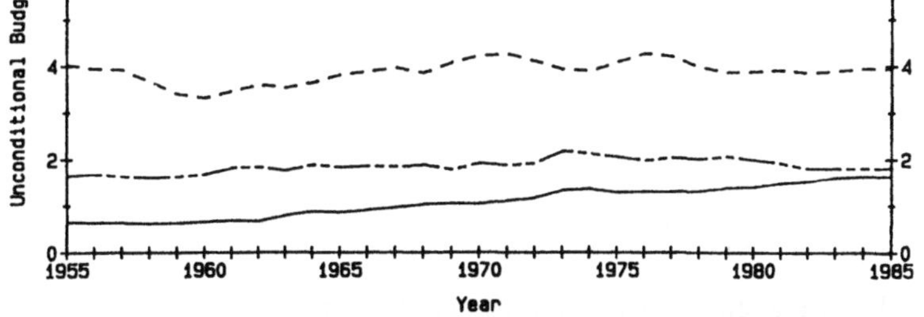

Fig. 3.6 Unconditional Budget Shares of Beer, Wine and Spirits and Total Alcohol: United Kingdom, 1955-1985

Table 3.5 CPI, Total Consumption Expenditure and Unconditional Budget Shares for Alcohol: United Kingdom, 1955-1985

Year	CPI (1970=100)	Total Consumption Expenditure (Pounds/Capita)	Unconditional Budget Shares			
			Beer	Wine	Spirits	Total Alcohol
(1)	(2)	(3)	(4)	(5)	(6)	(7)
1955	60.33	258.5	4.031	.645	1.640	6.316
1956	62.92	271.2	3.940	.627	1.671	6.238
1957	64.94	284.9	3.924	.642	1.618	6.183
1958	66.79	299.4	3.667	.614	1.591	5.872
1959	67.16	313.7	3.400	.626	1.620	5.646
1960	67.90	326.8	3.307	.649	1.665	5.621
1961	69.74	341.0	3.465	.689	1.816	5.970
1962	72.51	358.3	3.597	.655	1.833	6.085
1963	73.99	379.0	3.528	.787	1.747	6.062
1964	76.38	401.9	3.650	.880	1.876	6.406
1965	79.89	425.2	3.816	.852	1.817	6.486
1966	83.03	447.7	3.888	.908	1.852	6.647
1967	85.24	467.7	3.972	.961	1.832	6.766
1968	89.30	501.3	3.855	1.026	1.875	6.756
1969	94.10	529.6	4.089	1.049	1.770	6.907
1970	100.00	574.0	4.243	1.043	1.917	7.203
1971	109.41	639.5	4.268	1.110	1.874	7.253
1972	117.34	720.8	4.112	1.165	1.922	7.199
1973	128.04	818.6	3.927	1.330	2.182	7.439
1974	148.52	943.9	3.902	1.355	2.120	7.377
1975	184.50	1162.3	4.090	1.276	2.054	7.420
1976	215.16	1348.9	4.269	1.300	1.967	7.536
1977	249.10	1542.9	4.210	1.300	2.041	7.551
1978	269.68	1778.1	3.979	1.312	2.002	7.292
1979	306.14	2106.2	3.860	1.385	2.072	7.317
1980	361.01	2436.9	3.877	1.395	1.982	7.254
1981	403.97	2705.7	3.914	1.490	1.906	7.311
1982	438.63	2970.8	3.854	1.524	1.794	7.172
1983	458.84	3243.8	3.903	1.609	1.798	7.311
1984	481.59	3464.6	3.952	1.633	1.789	7.373
1985	510.83	3765.7	3.947	1.642	1.813	7.403
Mean	180.55	1155.8	3.885	1.080	1.853	6.818

All entries in the last four columns are to be divided by 100.

arithmetic average of the unconditional budget share of i;

$$\bar{W}_{gt} = \sum_{i=1}^{3} \bar{w}_{it}$$

is the arithmetic average of the budget share of total alcohol; and

$$\bar{w}'_{it} = \frac{\bar{w}_{it}}{\bar{W}_{gt}}, \qquad i=1,2,3,$$

is the arithmetic average of the conditional budget share of i.

Table 3.6 Arithmetic Average of Unconditional and Conditional Budget Shares: United Kingdom, 1955-1985

Year	Unconditional				Conditional		
	Beer $\bar{w}_1$	Wine $\bar{w}_2$	Spirits $\bar{w}_3$	Total Alcohol $\bar{W}_g$	Beer $\bar{w}'_1$	Wine $\bar{w}'_2$	Spirits $\bar{w}'_3$
(1)	(2)	(3)	(4)	(5)	(6)	(7)	(8)
1956	3.986	.636	1.656	6.277	63.495	10.132	26.373
1957	3.932	.634	1.644	6.211	63.314	10.210	26.476
1958	3.795	.628	1.604	6.028	62.969	10.418	26.614
1959	3.533	.620	1.605	5.759	61.353	10.769	27.878
1960	3.353	.637	1.643	5.633	59.528	11.312	29.160
1961	3.386	.669	1.741	5.795	58.429	11.537	30.034
1962	3.531	.672	1.824	6.027	58.589	11.142	30.268
1963	3.563	.721	1.790	6.074	58.661	11.870	29.469
1964	3.589	.834	1.811	6.234	57.571	13.374	29.054
1965	3.733	.866	1.847	6.446	57.915	13.440	28.646
1966	3.852	.880	1.835	6.567	58.661	13.401	27.938
1967	3.930	.934	1.842	6.707	58.600	13.931	27.469
1968	3.914	.994	1.854	6.761	57.886	14.695	27.419
1969	3.972	1.037	1.823	6.832	58.137	15.183	26.679
1970	4.166	1.046	1.843	7.055	59.049	14.822	26.129
1971	4.256	1.077	1.895	7.228	58.882	14.896	26.222
1972	4.190	1.138	1.898	7.226	57.985	15.746	26.268
1973	4.019	1.248	2.052	7.319	54.916	17.046	28.038
1974	3.915	1.342	2.151	7.408	52.844	18.121	29.035
1975	3.996	1.316	2.087	7.399	54.011	17.782	28.207
1976	4.179	1.288	2.010	7.478	55.889	17.230	26.881
1977	4.240	1.300	2.004	7.544	56.201	17.238	26.561
1978	4.094	1.306	2.021	7.422	55.169	17.596	27.234
1979	3.919	1.348	2.037	7.305	53.657	18.458	27.885
1980	3.868	1.390	2.027	7.285	53.095	19.081	27.824
1981	3.895	1.443	1.944	7.282	53.491	19.812	26.697
1982	3.884	1.507	1.850	7.241	53.638	20.809	25.552
1983	3.879	1.566	1.796	7.241	53.561	21.632	24.807
1984	3.927	1.621	1.794	7.342	53.493	22.077	24.430
1985	3.950	1.637	1.801	7.388	53.460	22.162	24.379
Mean	3.882	1.078	1.858	6.817	57.148	15.531	27.321

The year 1956, for example, refers to the transition from 1955 to 1956. All entries are to be divided by 100.

3.3 Divisia Indexes

In this section we give within group (or conditional) versions of Divisia indexes presented in Section 1.9 in finite-changes and then apply them to the UK alcohol data.

The within-alcohol versions of the Divisia volume and price indexes are

$$DQ_{gt} = \sum_{i=1}^{3} \bar{w}'_{it} Dq_{it}, \qquad DP_{gt} = \sum_{i=1}^{3} \bar{w}'_{it} Dp_{it}, \tag{3.1}$$

and the Divisia variances and covariance are

$$K_{gt} = \sum_{i=1}^{3} \overline{w}'_{it}(Dq_{it} - DQ_{gt})^2, \qquad \Pi_{gt} = \sum_{i=1}^{3} \overline{w}'_{it}(Dp_{it} - DP_{gt})^2, \tag{3.2}$$

$$\Gamma_{gt} = \sum_{i=1}^{3} \overline{w}'_{it}(Dp_{it} - DP_{gt})(Dq_{it} - DQ_{gt}), \tag{3.3}$$

where Dp_{it} and Dq_{it} are the price and quantity log-changes.

The Divisia volume and price indexes defined by (3.1) are given in columns 2 and 3 of Table 3.7. On average, per capita alcohol consumption increased by about 2.4 percent per annum while alcohol prices rose by 7.0 percent. We give the Divisia variances and covariance defined by (3.2) and (3.3) in columns 4, 5 and 6 of the same table. In 19 out of 30 cases, the quantity variance K_g exceeds the price variance Π_g, which agrees with the results of Clements (1982,1983), Meisner (1979), E.A. Selvanathan (1987), Suhm (1979), Theil (1965), Theil and Suhm (1981) and S. Selvanathan (1988). We also present the Divisia price-quantity correlation,

$$\rho_{gt} = \frac{\Gamma_{gt}}{\sqrt{K_{gt}\Pi_{gt}}},$$

in column 7 of Table 3.7. The correlation is negative in 20 cases out of 30 with an average of -.35. This reflects the tendency of the drinker to move away from those beverages having above-average price increases.

The within-alcohol version of the Divisia variance of the logarithmic changes in the budget shares is

$$\Psi_{gt} = \sum_{i=1}^{3} \overline{w}'_{it}\left[Dw'_{it} - \sum_{j=1}^{3} \overline{w}'_{jt}Dw'_{jt}\right]^2,$$

where $Dw'_{it} = \log w'_{it} - \log w'_{i,t-1}$. Column 8 of Table 3.7 gives this

Table 3.7 Divisia Indexes of Alcohol Consumption: United Kingdom, 1955-1985

Year	Volume	Price	Quantity Variance	Price Variance	Price-Quantity Covariance	Price-Quantity Correlation	Budget Share Variance	
	DQ_g ×100	DP_g ×100	K_g ×10000	Π_g ×10000	Γ_g ×10000	ρ_g	Ψ_g ×10000	Γ_g/Π_g
(1)	(2)	(3)	(4)	(5)	(6)	(7)	(8)	(9)
1956	1.97	1.57	7.57	.76	-2.38	-.99	3.57	-3.124
1957	1.25	2.78	3.63	3.81	-2.36	-.64	2.71	-.621
1958	-1.82	1.61	4.34	.08	.29	.51	5.00	3.808
1959	5.51	-4.79	2.25	12.74	2.97	.55	20.93	.233
1960	4.49	-.83	2.64	4.99	.18	.05	7.98	.036
1961	1.51	8.77	3.33	.20	-.18	-.22	3.16	-.907
1962	2.06	4.81	2.24	1.68	1.89	.97	7.70	1.122
1963	2.23	3.00	10.23	35.83	1.65	.09	49.36	.046
1964	5.23	6.16	1.99	3.15	1.22	.49	7.59	.389
1965	-1.96	8.85	10.45	6.43	-1.34	-.16	14.21	-.208
1966	1.95	5.65	4.34	.34	-1.21	-1.00	2.25	-3.570
1967	2.90	3.24	19.08	7.78	-11.21	-.92	4.45	-1.440
1968	1.87	4.93	1.15	9.12	1.34	.41	12.94	.147
1969	.26	7.45	21.97	.08	1.36	1.00	24.77	16.073
1970	7.17	5.06	23.56	20.47	-18.45	-.84	7.13	-.901
1971	4.67	6.83	1.89	4.92	.06	.02	6.92	.012
1972	6.36	4.87	27.34	5.26	-9.85	-.82	12.90	-1.873
1973	12.15	3.86	78.63	1.83	-2.40	-.20	75.65	-1.313
1974	3.30	10.10	19.27	35.62	-26.17	-1.00	2.55	-.735
1975	.41	20.98	10.34	11.94	-.82	-.07	20.64	-.069
1976	5.84	10.61	28.56	76.20	-45.57	-1.00	13.61	-.598
1977	-5.43	19.06	41.23	73.44	-54.97	-1.00	4.73	-.748
1978	8.52	2.18	46.69	28.17	-34.15	-.94	6.55	-1.213
1979	4.23	13.03	16.43	2.76	-2.77	-.41	13.65	-1.004
1980	-4.14	17.87	2.58	2.39	.00	.00	4.97	.001
1981	-2.83	14.07	22.96	7.42	-8.95	-.69	12.47	-1.207
1982	-1.18	8.61	20.27	4.64	-8.44	-.87	8.02	-1.821
1983	3.91	6.81	9.50	1.91	-3.88	-.91	3.66	-2.030
1984	.89	6.54	6.96	5.83	-6.08	-.95	.62	-1.044
1985	1.30	7.44	9.14	5.84	-7.31	-1.00	.37	-1.251
Mean	2.42	7.04	15.35	12.52	-7.92	-.35	12.04	-.127

The year 1956, for example, refers to the transition from 1955 to 1956.

variance. The Divisia variances and covariance satisfy $\Psi_{gt} = K_{gt} + \Pi_{gt} + 2\Gamma_{gt}$. In the last column of Table 3.7, we give the ratio of Γ_g to Π_g. We will come back to this ratio in Section 3.5.

3.4 Scatter Plots

In this section, we use differential demand equations to provide a framework for a preliminary analysis of the UK alcohol data. The Rotterdam parameterization of the group demand equation under block independence [equation (22.6) of Chapter 1] is

$$\bar{W}_{gt} DQ_{gt} = \Theta_g DQ_t + \phi\Theta_g (DP'_{gt} - DP'_t), \tag{4.1}$$

where DQ_{gt} is defined by equation (3.1); Θ_g is the marginal share of the group; DQ_t is the Divisia index of the change in real income; ϕ is the income flexibility; $DP'_{gt} = \Sigma_{i=1}^{3} \theta'_i Dp_{it}$ is the Frisch price index of alcohol; $\theta'_i = \theta_i/\Theta_g$ is the *conditional marginal share* of i; θ_i is the *unconditional marginal share* of i; and $DP'_t = \Sigma_{j=1}^{n} \theta_j Dp_{jt}$ is the overall Frisch price index. Equation (4.1) shows that, under block independence, the demand for a group of goods as a whole depends on the change in real income DQ_t and the change in the relative price of the group, $(DP'_{gt} - DP'_t)$. The relative price is the Frisch-deflated Frisch price index of the group and the relative prices of goods outside the group in question play no role in equation (4.1).

If we replace the marginal shares, θ_i and θ'_i, with the corresponding budget shares, $\bar{w}_{it}$ and $\bar{w}'_{it}$, then the group marginal share Θ_g becomes the group budget share $\bar{W}_g$ and the composite demand equation (4.1) simplifies to

$$DQ_{gt} - DQ_t = \phi(DP_{gt} - DP_t), \tag{4.2}$$

where DP_{gt} is defined by equation (3.1) and

$$DP_t = \sum_{j=1}^{n} \bar{w}_{jt} Dp_{jt}, \tag{4.3}$$

is the overall Divisia price index.

Equation (4.2) shows that growth in consumption of alcohol relative to that of real income, $(DQ_{gt} - DQ_t)$, depends only on the change in the relative price of the group $(DP_{gt} - DP_t)$. Using (4.2), if we plot $(DQ_{gt} - DQ_t)$ against $(DP_{gt} - DP_t)$ for t=1,...,T, the points should be scattered around a straight line with slope ϕ. In order to construct this scatter plot, we give in Table 3.8 the values of DQ_t, which is approximated by $(DM_t - DP_t^*)$, where DM_t is the log-change in income (total expenditure) and DP_t^* is the CPI log-change; DM_t and DP_t^* are also given in that table. We approximate the overall Divisia price index DP_t in (4.3) with DP_t^*.

Figure 3.7 plots $(DQ_g - DQ)$ against $(DP_g - DP^*)$, where the data are from Tables 3.7 and 3.8. This figure also gives the least-squares regression line. As can be seen, the observations fall around a straight line with negative slope, so that alcohol consumption grows less rapidly when its relative price rises. Under (4.2), the slope of this line is interpreted as an estimate of the income flexibility ϕ,

$$\text{Estimate of } \phi \text{ under (4.2)} = -.602\ (.134), \tag{4.4}$$

where the figure in parenthesis is the standard error. This estimate is significantly negative. The intercept (× 100) of regression line is .563 (.400) which is not significant. This value of the intercept can be interpreted as the residual exponential trend rate of growth in per capita alcohol consumption. Thus UK alcohol consumption increases autonomously at .6 percent per annum.

We return to (4.1) with DP_g and DP^* replacing DP_g' and DP', as before. We write this as

$$\bar{W}_{gt} DQ_{gt} = \Theta_g [DQ_t + \phi(DP_{gt} - DP_t^*)]. \tag{4.5}$$

The term in square brackets on the right represents the change in real income adjusted for the change in the relative price of alcohol. Thus if we specify the value of ϕ and plot $\bar{W}_g DQ_g$ against $[DQ + \phi(DP_g - DP^*)]$, the observations should be scattered around a line with slope Θ_g. We take ϕ as -.5 which is consistent with previous econometric findings

Table 3.8 Total Consumption Expenditure, CPI and Real Expenditure Log-changes: United Kingdom, 1955-1985

Year	Total consumption expenditure	CPI	Real total expenditure
	DM	DP^*	$DQ=DM-DP^*$
(1)	(2)	(3)	(4)
1956	4.78	4.20	.58
1957	4.92	3.16	1.76
1958	4.96	2.81	2.15
1959	4.65	.55	4.10
1960	4.10	1.10	3.00
1961	4.27	2.67	1.59
1962	4.96	3.90	1.06
1963	5.59	2.02	3.57
1964	5.87	3.18	2.69
1965	5.66	4.49	1.16
1966	5.14	3.86	1.28
1967	4.38	2.63	1.75
1968	6.94	4.65	2.29
1969	5.50	5.24	.26
1970	8.04	6.08	1.96
1971	10.81	8.99	1.82
1972	11.97	7.00	4.97
1973	12.72	8.73	3.99
1974	14.24	14.84	-.59
1975	20.81	21.69	-.88
1976	14.89	15.37	-.48
1977	13.44	14.65	-1.21
1978	14.19	7.94	6.25
1979	16.93	12.68	4.25
1980	14.59	16.49	-1.90
1981	10.46	11.24	-.78
1982	9.35	8.23	1.12
1983	8.79	4.51	4.29
1984	6.59	4.84	1.75
1985	8.33	5.89	2.44
Mean	8.93	7.12	1.81

All entries are to be divided by 100. Expenditures are expressed in per capita terms. The year 1956, for example, refers to the transition from 1955 to 1956.

(see Section 2.8 of Chapter 2), as well as (4.4). This scatter plot is given in Figure 3.8. The slope of the least-squares line fitted to the points in Figure 3.8 is .078 and has a standard error of .010. Under (4.5), this is interpreted as an estimate of Θ_g:

$$\text{Estimate of } \Theta_g \text{ under (4.5)} = .078\ (.010), \tag{4.6}$$

which is highly significant. This means that a one-dollar increase in income results in a 7.8 cent increase in spending on alcohol. Dividing this estimate by the mean of $\bar{W}_{gt}$ of .068 (see Table 3.6), yields an implied income elasticity of $\Theta_g/\bar{W}_g = .078/.068 = 1.15$ Thus alcohol as a whole has an income elasticity just above unity. Based on these figures, from (4.1) the price elasticity of alcohol is $\phi\Theta_g/\bar{W}_g = -.5 \times 1.15 = -.575$.

The i-*th* equation of the relative price version of the conditional Rotterdam model [again under block independence, see equation (26.1) of Chapter 1] is

$$\bar{w}_{it}Dq_{it} = \theta_i'\bar{W}_{gt}DQ_{gt} + \sum_{j=1}^{3} \nu_{ij}(Dp_{jt} - DP_{gt}'), \tag{4.7}$$

where DP_{gt}' is defined below equation (4.1); and ν_{ij} is the (i,j)-*th* price coefficient satisfying $\Sigma_{j=1}^{3} \nu_{ij} = \phi\theta_i = \phi\Theta_g\theta_i'$, i = 1,2,3. Equation (4.7) is the demand equation for a beverage within the alcoholic beverages group, given the demand for the group as a whole $\bar{W}_{gt}DQ_{gt}$. This equation shows that the allocation of expenditure to each beverage within the alcoholic beverages group depends on the total consumption of the group as measured by $\bar{W}_{gt}DQ_{gt}$, and the relative prices of beverages within the alcoholic beverages group.

Under preference independence within alcohol, we have

$$\nu_{ij} = 0, \qquad i\neq j=1,2,3,$$

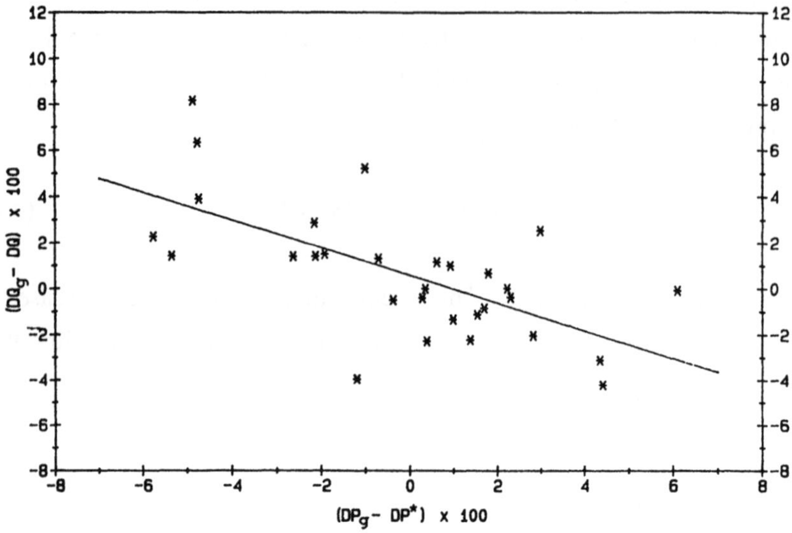

Fig. 3.7 Relative Consumption of Alcohol against Relative Price: United Kingdom, 1955-1985

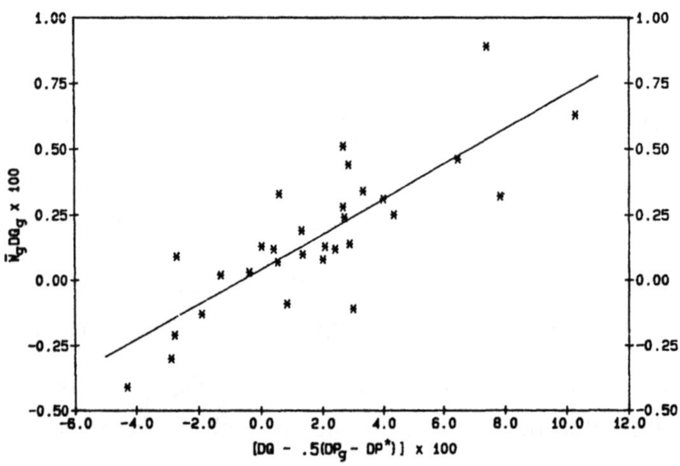

Fig. 3.8 Alcohol Consumption Scattergram, United Kingdom, 1955-1985

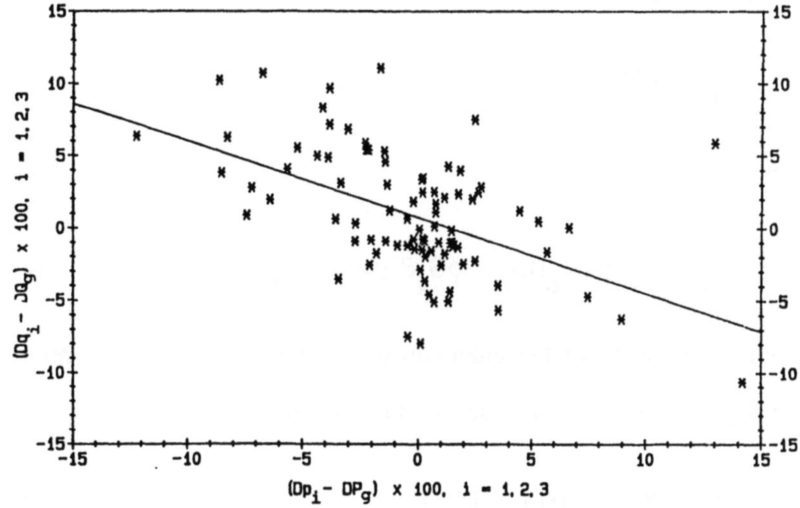

Fig. 3.9 Relative Consumption of Beer, Wine and Spirits against Relative Prices: United Kingdom, 1955-1985

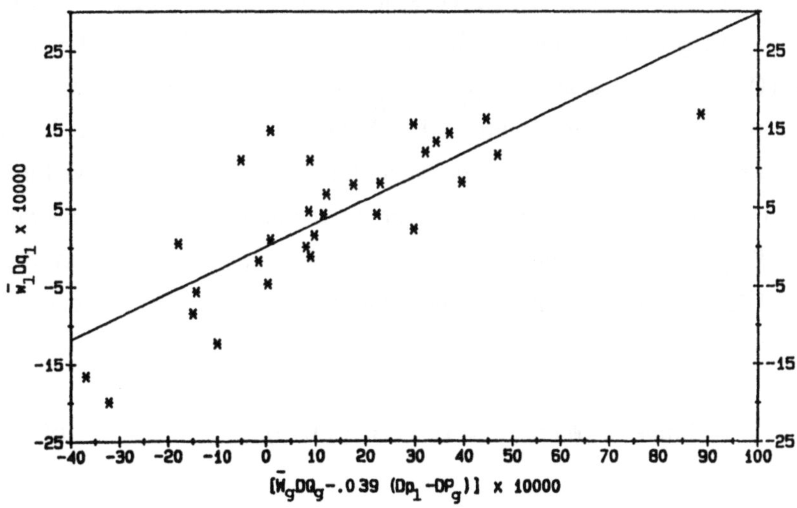

Fig. 3.10 Consumption of Beer against Adjusted Total Alcohol Consumption: United Kingdom, 1955-1985

which implies that

$$\nu_{ii} = \phi\Theta_g\theta_i', \qquad i=1,2,3.$$

Thus (4.7) becomes

$$\bar{w}_{it}Dq_{it} = \theta_i'\bar{W}_{gt}DQ_{gt} + \phi\Theta_g\theta_i'(Dp_{it} - DP_{gt}'). \tag{4.8}$$

To eliminate some of the unknown parameters from (4.8), we replace θ_i' with $\bar{w}_{it}'$ and Θ_g with $\bar{W}_{gt}$, so that the equation becomes

$$Dq_{it} - DQ_{gt} = \phi(Dp_{it} - DP_{gt}). \tag{4.9}$$

Equation (4.9) is a lower-case version of equation (4.2). Using (4.9) for a given i, we can plot the growth in consumption of i relative to the group average $(Dq_{it} - DQ_{gt})$ against the change in its relative price $(Dp_{it} - DP_{gt})$ for t=1,...,T. The points should be scattered around a straight line with slope ϕ. As ϕ is the same for all i=1,2,3, we can also plot on the same graph $(Dq_{it} - DQ_{gt})$ against $(Dp_{it} - DP_{gt})$ for i=1,2,3 and t=1,...,T. This scatter plot is shown in Figure 3.9. Although there is quite a lot of dispersion, most of the observations do fall around a negatively-sloped line. Thus, when the price of a beverage increases more than average $(Dp_i > DP_g)$, its consumption grows at a rate less than average $(Dq_i < DQ_g)$. The slope of the least-squares regression line in Figure 3.9 is

$$\text{Estimate of } \phi \text{ under (4.9)} = -.525\ (.095), \tag{4.10}$$

which is highly significant.

From (4.8), we also have

$$\bar{w}_{it}Dq_{it} = \theta_i'[\bar{W}_{gt}DQ_{gt} + \phi\Theta_g(Dp_{it} - DP_{gt})], \tag{4.11}$$

where DP'_{gt} has been replaced by DP_{gt}, as before. Now, if we plot $\bar{w}_i Dq_i$ against $[\bar{W}_g DQ_g + \phi\Theta_g(Dp_i - DP_g)]$, the observations should be scattered around a straight line with slope θ'_i. Figures 3.10-3.12 give these plots with ϕ = -.5 and Θ_g = .078 [from (4.6)] for beer, wine and spirits, respectively. The slopes of the least-squares regression lines are

$$\text{Estimate of } \theta'_1 \text{ under (4.11)} = .298\ (.044),$$

$$\text{Estimate of } \theta'_2 \text{ under (4.11)} = .167\ (.029)$$

and

$$\text{Estimate of } \theta'_3 \text{ under (4.11)} = .393\ (.029).$$

These estimated conditional marginal shares are all positive and highly significant. It is to be noted that these estimates do not sum to one because we estimate (4.11) for i=1,2,3 separately. Thus we normalize these marginal shares so that they add up to one. This yields

$$\text{Normalized estimate of } \theta'_1 \text{ under (4.11)} = .347,$$

$$\text{Normalized estimate of } \theta'_2 \text{ under (4.11)} = .195,$$

and

$$\text{Normalized estimate of } \theta'_3 \text{ under (4.11)} = .458.$$

These figures indicate that when total expenditure on alcohol increases by one dollar, expenditure on beer, wine and spirits increases by 35, 19 and 46 cents, respectively.

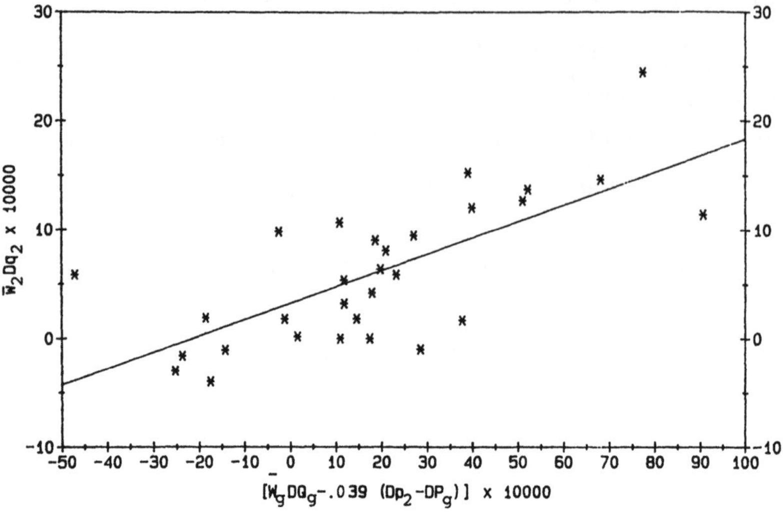

Fig. 3.11 Consumption of Wine against Adjusted Total Alcohol Consumption: United Kingdom, 1955-1985

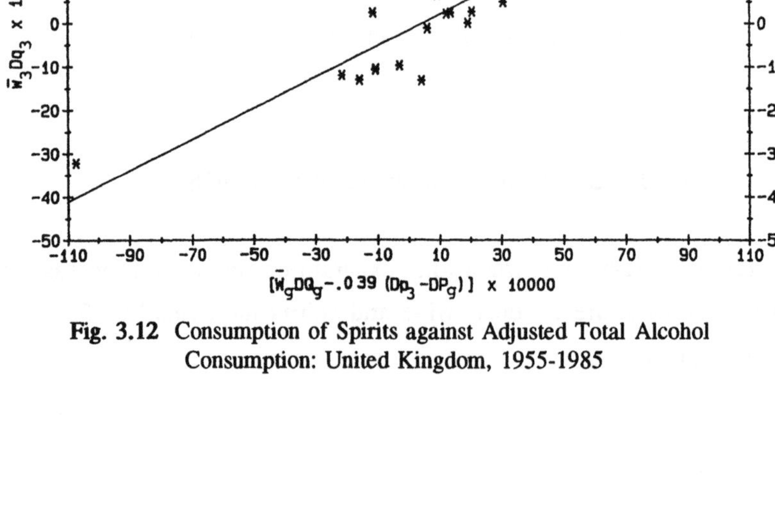

Fig. 3.12 Consumption of Spirits against Adjusted Total Alcohol Consumption: United Kingdom, 1955-1985

3.5. Further Estimates of the Income Flexibility

Now we introduce another procedure to estimate the income flexibility ϕ. Consider again equation (4.8), the conditional demand equation for beverage i under preference independence. We divide both sides of this equation by $\bar{W}_{gt}$ and add a disturbance (ε'_{it}) to give

$$\bar{w}'_{it}Dq_{it} = \theta'_i DQ_{gt} + \phi \frac{\Theta_g}{\bar{W}_{gt}} \theta'_i(Dp_{it} - DP'_{gt}) + \varepsilon'_{it}. \tag{5.1}$$

Again we eliminate the unknown parameters θ'_i and Θ_g by replacing them with $\bar{w}'_{it}$ and $\bar{W}_{gt}$, respectively. Therefore (5.1) becomes

$$\bar{w}'_{it}(Dq_{it} - DQ_{gt}) = \phi\bar{w}'_{it}(Dp_{it} - DP_{gt}) + \varepsilon'_{it}. \tag{5.2}$$

We assume that the disturbances ε'_{it} have zero means and

$$\text{cov}[\varepsilon'_{it}, \varepsilon'_{jt}] = \sigma_t^2\, \bar{w}'_{it}\, \delta_{ij}, \tag{5.3}$$

where δ_{ij} is the Kronecker delta. Specification (5.3) states that the error variance is larger for those goods having a larger conditional budget share, which is plausible. As $\Sigma_{i=1}^{3}\ \varepsilon'_{it} = 0$, the assumption that $\text{cov}[\varepsilon'_{it}, \varepsilon'_{jt}] = 0$ for $i \neq j$ cannot be exactly true. However, as our analysis is designed only to obtain a preliminary feel for the data, we shall use this assumption as an approximation. Accordingly, the transformed disturbances $\varepsilon'_{it}/\sqrt{\bar{w}'_{it}}$ are uncorrelated with zero mean and the same variance σ_t^2. This means that if we divide both sides of (5.2) by $\sqrt{\bar{w}'_{it}}$ and then regress $\sqrt{\bar{w}'_{it}}(Dq_{it} - DQ_{gt})$ on $\sqrt{\bar{w}'_{it}}(Dp_{it} - DP_{gt})$ for i=1,2,3, we obtain for year t the least-squares estimator of ϕ as

$$\hat{\phi}_t = \frac{\sum_{i=1}^{3} \overline{w}'_{it}(Dp_{it} - DP_{gt})(Dq_{it} - DQ_{gt})}{\sum_{i=1}^{3} \overline{w}'_{it}(Dp_{it} - DP_{gt})^2}. \tag{5.4}$$

Using (3.2) and (3.3) we can write (5.4) as

$$\hat{\phi}_t = \frac{\Gamma_{gt}}{\Pi_{gt}}. \tag{5.5}$$

It follows that the sampling variance of this estimator is

$$\text{var}\,\hat{\phi}_t = \frac{\sigma_t^2}{\Pi_{gt}} \tag{5.6}$$

and that σ_t^2 is estimated unbiasedly by

$$\hat{\sigma}_t^2 = \frac{1}{n_g - 1}\left[K_{gt} - \hat{\phi}_t\Gamma_{gt}\right], \tag{5.7}$$

where $n_g = 3$ and K_{gt} is defined in (3.2).

Equation (5.5) shows that, for each t, we can estimate ϕ as the ratio of Γ_{gt} to Π_{gt}. We have tabulated these ratios in the last column of Table 3.7. As is to be expected, these values fluctuate quite a bit. As can be seen, there is an outlier, in 1969. As shown in the last entry of column 9 of the table, with the outlier included, we obtain an average value of these $\hat{\phi}_t$ of -.13, which is much lower (in absolute value) than the previous estimates. When we re-calculate this mean omitting that outlier, we get -.69, which is much closer to the previous findings.

Equation (5.5) provides a one-period estimator of ϕ. Thus if we have T periods we get T estimates of ϕ. If these are independent, an optimal estimator of ϕ for all T periods is given by a weighted average of $\hat{\phi}_1,\ldots,\hat{\phi}_T$ with weights inversely proportional to their variances. This yields

$$\hat{\phi} = \sum_{t=1}^{T} \frac{\Pi_{gt}}{\sum_{\tau=1}^{T} \Pi_{g\tau}} \hat{\phi}_t = \sum_{t=1}^{T} \frac{\Pi_{gt}}{\sum_{\tau=1}^{T} \Pi_{g\tau}} \frac{\Gamma_{gt}}{\Pi_{gt}} = \frac{\sum_{t=1}^{T} \Gamma_{gt}}{\sum_{\tau=1}^{T} \Pi_{g\tau}} = \frac{\bar{\Gamma}_g}{\bar{\Pi}_g}, \tag{5.8}$$

where $\bar{\Gamma}_g = (1/T)\ \Sigma_{t=1}^{T}\ \Gamma_{gt}$; $\bar{\Pi}_g = (1/T)\ \Sigma_{t=1}^{T}\ \Pi_{gt}$; and where we have also assumed that $\sigma_t^2 = \sigma^2$, a constant. In Section 3.6 we show that the sampling variance of $\hat{\phi}$ is

$$\text{var}\ \hat{\phi} = \frac{\sigma^2}{\sum_{t=1}^{T} \Pi_{gt}} = \frac{\sigma^2}{T\ \bar{\Pi}_g} \tag{5.9}$$

and that an unbiased estimator of σ^2 is given by

$$\hat{\sigma}^2 = \frac{1}{[Tn_g - 1]} \sum_{t=1}^{T} (K_{gt} - \hat{\phi}\Gamma_{gt}) = \frac{T}{[Tn_g - 1]} (\bar{K}_g - \hat{\phi}\ \bar{\Gamma}_g), \tag{5.10}$$

where $\bar{K}_g = (1/T)\ \Sigma_{t=1}^{T}\ K_{gt}$. (For a similar approach, see Clements and Theil, 1978.)

Using our data to evaluate (5.8) and (5.9) yields

$$\hat{\phi} = -.633\ (.096), \tag{5.11}$$

which is highly significant and consistent with the previous findings.

3.6. Derivations

In this section we derive equations (5.9) and (5.10).

Under the assumption that the estimates $\hat{\phi}_t$ are independent, it follows from (5.6) and (5.8) that

$$\operatorname{var}\hat{\phi} = \sum_{t=1}^{T} \frac{\Pi_{gt}^2}{\left[\sum_{\tau=1}^{T} \Pi_{g\tau}\right]^2} \operatorname{var}\hat{\phi}_t = \frac{\sigma^2}{\left[\sum_{\tau=1}^{T} \Pi_{g\tau}\right]}, \tag{6.1}$$

where we have used the assumption $\sigma_t^2 = \sigma^2$. Equation (6.1) is equivalent to (5.9).

We now show that $\hat{\sigma}^2$ defined in (5.10) is an unbiased estimator of σ^2 by establishing that

$$E\left[\sum_{t=1}^{T} \left(K_{gt} - \hat{\phi}\Gamma_{gt}\right)\right] = (Tn_g - 1)\sigma^2.$$

We proceed in two steps. In the first step we express K_{gt} and Γ_{gt} in terms of the disturbances ε'_{it}. In the second step we evaluate the above expectation.

Step 1:

From equation (5.2) we have that

$$\sqrt{\overline{w}'_{it}}(Dq_{it} - DQ_{gt}) = \phi\sqrt{\overline{w}'_{it}}(Dp_{it} - DP_{gt}) + \frac{\varepsilon'_{it}}{\sqrt{\overline{w}'_{it}}}.$$

Substituting the right-hand side of the above equation for $\sqrt{\overline{w}'_{it}}(Dq_{it} - DQ_{gt})$ in (3.2) yields

$$K_{gt} = \sum_{i=1}^{3} \left[\phi \sqrt{\overline{w}'_{it}} (Dp_{it} - DP_{gt}) + \frac{\varepsilon'_{it}}{\sqrt{\overline{w}'_{it}}} \right]^2$$

$$= \phi^2 \Pi_{gt} + 2\phi \sum_{i=1}^{3} (Dp_{it} - DP_{gt})\varepsilon'_{it} + \sum_{i=1}^{3} \frac{\varepsilon'^{2}_{it}}{\overline{w}'_{it}}. \qquad (6.2)$$

Substituting in equation (3.3) the right-hand side of (5.2) for $\overline{w}'_{it}(Dq_{it} - DQ_{gt})$ yields

$$\Gamma_{gt} = \sum_{i=1}^{3} (Dp_{it} - DP_{gt})[\phi \overline{w}'_{it}(Dp_{it} - DP_{gt}) + \varepsilon'_{it}]$$

$$= \phi \Pi_{gt} + \sum_{i=1}^{3} (Dp_{it} - DP_{gt})\varepsilon'_{it}. \qquad (6.3)$$

Using equations (6.2) and (6.3), we obtain

$$K_{gt} - \hat{\phi}\Gamma_{gt} = (\phi - \hat{\phi})\phi\Pi_{gt} + 2\phi \sum_{i=1}^{3} (Dp_{it} - DP_{gt})\varepsilon'_{it}$$

$$+ \sum_{i=1}^{3} \frac{\varepsilon'^{2}_{it}}{\overline{w}'_{it}} - \hat{\phi} \sum_{i=1}^{3} (Dp_{it} - DP_{gt})\varepsilon'_{it}. \qquad (6.4)$$

Step 2:

As $\hat{\phi}_t$ is an unbiased estimator of ϕ, it follows from (5.8) that $E[\hat{\phi}] = \phi$. Taking the expectation of both sides of (6.4) yields

$$E\left[K_{gt} - \hat{\phi}\Gamma_{gt}\right] = \sum_{i=1}^{3} \sigma_t^2 - E\left[\hat{\phi} \sum_{i=1}^{3} (Dp_{it} - DP_{gt})\varepsilon'_{it}\right], \qquad (6.5)$$

where we have used $E[\hat{\phi}] = \phi$ and $E[\varepsilon'_{it}] = 0$.

We now simplify the second term on the right of (6.5). Dividing both sides of (6.3) by Π_{gt} and using (5.5), we obtain

$$\hat{\phi}_s = \phi + \frac{1}{\Pi_{gs}} \sum_{i=1}^{3} (Dp_{is} - DP_{gs})\varepsilon'_{is}, \qquad s=1,...,T. \tag{6.6}$$

Multiplying both sides of (6.6) by $\lambda_{gs} = \Pi_{gs}/\Sigma_{\tau=1}^{T}\Pi_{g\tau}$ and then taking the sum over s=1,...,T, we obtain

$$\hat{\phi} = \phi + \sum_{s=1}^{T} \frac{\lambda_{gs}}{\Pi_{gs}} \left[\sum_{i=1}^{3} (Dp_{is} - DP_{gs})\varepsilon'_{is} \right],$$

where we have used (5.8) and $\Sigma_{s=1}^{T} \lambda_{gs} = 1$. Multiplying both sides of the above equation by $\Sigma_{i=1}^{3} (Dp_{it} - DP_{gt})\varepsilon'_{it}$ and taking the expectation gives

$$E\left[\hat{\phi} \sum_{i=1}^{3} (Dp_{it} - DP_{gt})\varepsilon'_{it}\right] = E\left[\sum_{s=1}^{T} \frac{\lambda_{gs}}{\Pi_{gs}} \left[\sum_{i=1}^{3} (Dp_{is} - DP_{gs})\varepsilon'_{is}\right] \times \left[\sum_{i=1}^{3} (Dp_{it} - DP_{gt})\varepsilon'_{it}\right]\right]$$

$$= E\left[\frac{\lambda_{gt}}{\Pi_{gt}} \left[\sum_{i=1}^{3} (Dp_{it} - DP_{gt})\varepsilon'_{it}\right]^2\right],$$

where the second step uses $E[\varepsilon'_{it}, \varepsilon'_{is}] = 0$ for $t \neq s$. As $E[\varepsilon'^2_{it}] = \overline{w}'_{it}\sigma_t^2$,

$$E\left[\hat{\phi} \sum_{i=1}^{3} (Dp_{it} - DP_{gt})\varepsilon'_{it}\right] = \frac{\lambda_{gt}}{\Pi_{gt}} \sum_{i=1}^{3} \overline{w}'_{it}(Dp_{it} - DP_{gt})^2\sigma_t^2$$

$$= \lambda_{gt}\sigma_t^2. \tag{6.7}$$

Substituting (6.7) in (6.5), we obtain

$$E\left[K_{gt} - \hat{\phi}\Gamma_{gt}\right] = \sum_{i=1}^{3} \sigma_t^2 - \lambda_{gt}\sigma_t^2$$

$$= (n_g - \lambda_{gt})\sigma^2,$$

where $n_g = 3$ and we have assumed that $\sigma_t^2 = \sigma^2$. Therefore, we have

$$E\left[\sum_{t=1}^{T} \left[K_{gt} - \hat{\phi}\Gamma_{gt}\right]\right] = \sum_{t=1}^{T} (n_g - \lambda_{gt})\sigma^2$$

$$= (Tn_g - 1)\sigma^2.$$

This shows that $\hat{\sigma}^2$ defined in equation (5.10) is an unbiased estimator of σ^2.

3.7 Comments on Assumptions

We conclude this chapter with a brief recapitulation of the assumptions under which we obtained the preliminary estimates of the income flexibility and the marginal shares. The estimate (4.4) is derived under block-independence with marginal shares replaced by the corresponding budget shares. As the income elasticity is the ratio of the marginal share to budget share, this amounts to assuming unitary income elasticities. The estimate of Θ_g given in (4.6) is also derived under a similar assumption.

The assumptions underlying the estimate of ϕ given in (4.10) are (i) unitary income elasticities and (ii) that the three alcoholic beverages are preference independent in the consumer's utility function. The estimates obtained in Section 3.5 are also based on these two assumptions .

Some of these assumptions are obviously quite strong. Accordingly, the estimates derived in this chapter are only meant to have a preliminary status. E.A. Selvanathan (1987) obtains estimates of demand equations for beer, wine and spirits without any of the above assumptions. However, Table 3.9 reveals that the two sets of estimates are fairly similar. Consequently, the techniques introduced in this chapter seems to provide useful preliminary insights into the properties of consumption data.

Table 3.9 A Comparison of Two sets of Estimates of Key Demand Parameters

Parameter	This chapter	Selvanathan (1987)
Group marginal share, Θ_g	.078	.072
Group income elasticity, $\Theta_g/\bar{W}_g$	1.150	1.093
Conditional marginal shares		
Beer θ'_1	.347	.239
Wine θ'_2	.195	.261
Spirits θ'_3	.458	.501
Income flexibility, ϕ	-.633	-.689
Own-price elasticity of demand for the group, $\phi\Theta_g/\bar{W}_g$	-.575	-.642

References

Brewers' Association of Canada (1986). *International Survey: Alcoholic Beverage Taxation and Control Policies.*

Central Statistical Office (1973, 1985 and 1986). *Annual Abstract of Statistics,* London.

Central Statistical Office (1986). *Economic Trends,* Annual Supplement, London.

Clements, K.W. (1982). 'Divisia Moments of Australian Consumption, *Economics Letters* 9: 43-8.

Clements, K.W. (1983). 'The Demand for Energy used in Transport, *Australian Journal of Management* 8: 27-56.

Clements, K.W. and H. Theil (1978). 'A Simple Method of Estimating Price Elasticities in International Trade,' *Economics Letters* 1: 133-7.

International Monetary Fund (1981, 1985 and 1986). *International Financial Statistics Year Book,* Washington, D.C. 20431.

McGuinness, T. (1980). 'An Econometric Analysis of Total Demand for Alcoholic Beverages in the U.K., 1956-75,' *Journal of Industrial Economics* 29: 85-109. Published with data listing as *Scottish Health Education Unit Report,* 1979.

Meisner, J.F. (1979). 'Divisia Moments of U.S. Industry, 1947-1978,' *Economics Letters* 4: 239-42.

Selvanathan, E.A. (1987). *Explorations in Consumer Demand.* Ph.D. thesis, Department of Economics, Murdoch University.

Selvanathan, S. (1988). *A System-Wide Analysis of International and Interregional Consumption Patterns.* Ph.D. thesis, Department of Economics, The University of Western Australia.

Selvanathan, S., K. W. Clements and E.A. Selvanathan (1989). *Demand Analysis Package DAP.* Economic Research Center, Department of Economics, The University of Western Australia.

Suhm, F.E. (1979). 'A Cross-Country Comparison Based on Divisia Variances and Covariances,' *Economics Letters* 3: 89-96.

Theil, H. (1965). 'The Information Approach to Demand Analysis,' *Econometrica* 33: 67-87.

Theil, H. and K.W. Clements (1987). *Applied Demand Analysis: Results from System-Wide Approaches.* Cambridge, Mass.: Ballinger Publishing Co.

Theil, H. and F.E. Suhm (1981). *International Consumption Comparisons: A System-Wide Approach.* North-Holland Publishing Company.

UK Government Statistical Services (1979-81 and 1986). *U.K. National Accounts, The CSO Blue Book*, London.

4 Hypothesis Testing in Demand Analysis

S. Selvanathan
Faculty of Commerce and Administration, Griffith University, Australia.

4.1 Introduction

In many demand analysis applications *a priori* restrictions such as demand homogeneity, symmetry and strong additivity (or preference independence) are imposed, thus reducing the number of unknown parameters. In a review article on systems of consumer demand functions, Barten (1977) summarizes the results from various empirical applications which test the validity of the hypotheses of homogeneity, symmetry and preference independence. These results show that homogeneity is generally not acceptable; symmetry is a bit more acceptable; while preference independence is not acceptable. Barten concludes that one reason for these negative results is that since the test procedures are usually based on the asymptotic distribution of the test statistic without correction for small-sample bias, the results are biased towards rejection. Simulations by Bera et al. (1981), Bewley (1983), Laitinen (1978) and Meisner (1979) have confirmed this conclusion. In view of these difficulties, Theil (1987) developed alternative testing procedures for homogeneity and symmetry, and Selvanathan, S. (1987) for preference independence based on Barnard's (1963) Monte Carlo simulation procedure. In Section 2.5 we briefly discussed these issues. This chapter presents a detailed account of the conventional tests used for testing the homogeneity and symmetry hypotheses and the new procedure to test the three hypotheses, and illustrate their application with the OECD data.

The organisation of this chapter is as follows. In Section 4.2 we present the demand model. In the following two sections we discuss the conventional tests for the hypotheses homogeneity and symmetry. In most situations, for large demand systems, due to lack of sufficient data, these conventional tests cannot be used. In Sections 4.5-4.8 we introduce the Monte Carlo method and discuss its application to test homogeneity, symmetry and preference independence hypotheses. Section 4.9 proposes a new error covariance matrix structure which can be used when the usual covariance matrix is singular. In Sections 4.10 and 4.11 we present the income and own-price elasticities implied by the demand model for 10 commodities in 18 countries. Through out the chapter, data from 18 OECD countries are used for illustration of the techniques. This chapter draws on S. Selvanathan (1988).

4.2 The Demand Model

Working's (1943) model implies that marginal share of good i equals the corresponding budget share plus a constant, [see equation (8.2) of Chapter 1]. We substitute $\theta_i = \bar{w}_{it} + \beta_i$ in equation (15.2) of Chapter 1 to obtain Working's model with a substitution term added. For commodity i (= 1,...,n, the number of goods) and period t (= 1,...,T, the sample size after lagging), this model takes the form

$$\bar{w}_{it}(Dq_{it} - DQ_t) = \beta_i DQ_t + \sum_{j=1}^{n} \pi_{ij} Dp_{jt} + \varepsilon_{it}, \tag{2.1}$$

where β_i is the income coefficient of commodity i satisfying $\Sigma_{i=1}^{n} \beta_i = 0$; π_{ij} is the (i,j)-*th* Slutsky coefficient with $\Sigma_{i=1}^{n} \pi_{ij} = 0$ [see equation (15.4) of Chapter 1]; and ε_{it} is the disturbance term of the i-*th* equation. The error terms are assumed to be normally distributed with zero mean and are independent over time.

Equation (2.1) for i=1,...,n is a fairly general demand system in the sense that it can be considered as a first-order approximation to the true demand equations. If we sum both sides of (2.1) over i=1,...,n, we get $\Sigma_{i=1}^{n} \varepsilon_{it} = 0$ for t=1,...,T. Therefore, the ε_{it}'s are linearly dependent and one of the equations is redundant and can be deleted (Barten, 1969). We delete the n-*th* equation. It can be shown that the best linear unbiased estimators of the parameters for the system of equations (2.1) for i=1,...,n are the same as those obtained by estimating each equation separately by least squares (LS). See Theil (1971) for details.

Let $\boldsymbol{\Sigma}$ be the (n-1) × (n-1) contemporaneous covariance matrix of the disturbance terms ε_{it} of (2.1) for i=1,...,n-1. In general, $\boldsymbol{\Sigma}$ is unknown. For estimation and hypothesis testing, it is common practice to approximate this matrix by its unbiased estimator **S**, the matrix of mean squares and cross products of the LS residuals.

By denoting $y_{it} = \bar{w}_{it}(Dq_{it} - DQ_t)$, $\gamma_i = [\beta_i\ \pi_{i1} \ldots \pi_{in}]'$ and $\mathbf{x}_t = [DQ_t\ Dp_{1t} \ldots Dp_{nt}]'$ and after deleting the n-*th* equation, (2.1) can be written for t=1,...,T as

$$\mathbf{y}_i = \mathbf{X}\gamma_i + \varepsilon_i, \qquad i=1,\ldots,n-1, \tag{2.2}$$

where $\mathbf{y}_i = [y_{it}]$ is a T-vector; $\mathbf{X}$ is a T × (n+1) matrix whose t-*th* row is $\mathbf{x}_t'$; and $\varepsilon_i = [\varepsilon_{it}]$ is a T-vector. We write (2.2) for i=1,...,n-1 as

$$\mathbf{y} = (\mathbf{I} \otimes \mathbf{X})\boldsymbol{\gamma} + \boldsymbol{\varepsilon}, \tag{2.3}$$

where $\mathbf{I}$ is the identity matrix of order (n-1); and $\mathbf{y} = [\mathbf{y}_i]$, $\boldsymbol{\gamma} = [\gamma_i]$ and $\boldsymbol{\varepsilon} = [\varepsilon_i]$ are vectors consisting of (n-1) subvectors.

4.3 Homogeneity

As discussed in Section 1.15, demand homogeneity postulates that a proportionate change in all prices has no effect on the demand for any good when real income is held constant. In the context of (2.1), homogeneity takes the form

$$\sum_{j=1}^{n} \pi_{ij} = 0, \qquad i=1,...,n. \tag{3.1}$$

Let a = [0 1 ... 1]′. Then (3.1) can be written as

$$a'\gamma_i = 0, \qquad i=1,...,n.$$

For i=1,...,n-1, this can be expressed as

$$R\gamma = 0, \tag{3.2}$$

where $R = I_{n-1} \otimes a'$.

The asymptotic test of homogeneity

The test statistic for the homogeneity restriction (3.2) is

$$\frac{(R\hat{\gamma})'\Sigma^{-1}(R\hat{\gamma})/a'(X'X)^{-1}a}{\mathrm{tr}\ \Sigma^{-1}S}, \tag{3.3}$$

where $\hat{\gamma}$ is the LS estimator of γ; Σ is the error covariance matrix; and S is the LS residual moment matrix, an unbiased estimator of Σ (Theil, 1971). Under the null hypothesis, (3.3) is distributed as F with (n-1) and (n-1)(T-n-1) degrees of freedom. Usually, the error covariance matrix Σ is unknown and is replaced by its estimator S. The test statistic for homogeneity then becomes

$$\Psi_H = \frac{(R\hat{\gamma})'S^{-1}(R\hat{\gamma})}{a'(X'X)^{-1}a}. \tag{3.4}$$

Under the null hypothesis, it can be easily shown that, Ψ_H has an asymptotic χ^2 distribution with (n-1) degrees of freedom. It is worth noting that as (3.4) involves $\mathbf{S}^{-1}$, **S** must be non-singular. The necessary condition for S to be non-singular is that T - 2n - 1 is non-negative (Laitinen, 1978).

We now apply (3.4) to test homogeneity with the OECD data presented in Chapter 2. Among the 18 OECD countries considered in Chapter 2, the matrix **S** is non-singular only for 7 countries. The results for the 7 countries are shown in Table 4.1. The observed value of (3.4) are presented in column 5 of the table. The critical values at the 5 percent level of significance for the asymptotic χ^2-test are presented in column 6. Comparing column 5 with column 6, we see that homogeneity is rejected for 6 out of the 7 countries at the 5 percent level. This agrees with the results from almost all previous studies.

Laitinen's Exact Test for Homogeneity

Laitinen (1978) showed that the exact finite-sample distribution of Ψ_H in (3.4), under the null hypothesis, is distributed as Hotelling's T^2, which itself is distributed as a constant multiple (n-1)(T-n-1)/(T-2n+1) of F(n-1,T-2n+1). The critical values based on finite-sample distributions are presented in the last column of Table 4.1. Comparing the observed values of the test statistic in column 5 with the critical values in column 7, we can see that homogeneity is now acceptable for all countries except Germany. This supports the view of Barten (1977) that the rejection of homogeneity is due to the failure of asymptotic theory.

4.4 Symmetry

We now take homogeneity as given and consider symmetry. The homogeneity-constrained version of model (2.1) is obtained by imposing

Table 4.1 Testing Homogeneity in 7 OECD Countries (Based on **S**)

Country	Number of commodities	Sample size		Test statistic	Asymptotic test critical value	Exact test critical value
	n	T	$T-2n$	Ψ_H	$\chi^2(n-1)$	T^2
(1)	(2)	(3)	(4)	(5)	(6)	(7)
1. U.S.	10	21	1	57.8*	16.9	872.1
2. Canada	10	21	1	19.1*	16.9	872.1
3. Switzerland	9	21	3	101.4*	15.5	132.9
4. Australia	10	21	1	133.4*	16.9	872.1
5. Germany	8	21	5	61.9**	14.1	58.9
6. Belgium	10	21	1	813.4*	16.9	872.1
7. Netherlands	10	25	5	10.7	16.9	86.1

A * denotes that we reject homogeneity at the 5 percent level on the basis of the asymptotic test. A ** denotes that we reject homogeneity at the 5 percent level on the basis of the asymptotic and the exact finite-sample test.

restriction (3.1) on (2.1)

$$y_{it} = \beta_i DQ_t + \sum_{j=1}^{n-1} \pi_{ij}(Dp_{jt} - Dp_{nt}) + \varepsilon_{it}, \qquad i=1,\ldots,n, \quad t=1,\ldots,T. \tag{4.1}$$

Let $\gamma_i^H = [\beta_i \; \pi_{i1} \ldots \pi_{i,n-1}]'$ and $x_t^H = [DQ_t \;\; Dp_{1t}\text{-}Dp_{nt} \ldots Dp_{n-1,t} - Dp_{nt}]'$. Then (4.1) can be written as

$$\mathbf{y}_i = \mathbf{X}^H \gamma_i^H + \varepsilon_i, \qquad i=1,\ldots,n, \tag{4.2}$$

where $\mathbf{X}^H$ is a $T \times n$ matrix whose t-*th* row is $\mathbf{x}_t^{H\prime}$; and $\mathbf{y}_i$ and ε_i are as before. As for the unconstrained case, it can be shown that the best linear unbiased estimators of the γ_i^H's in (4.2) are the single-equation LS estimators (Theil, 1971).

As before, we delete the n-*th* equation and write (4.2) in matrix form as

$$y = (I \otimes X^H)\gamma^H + \varepsilon, \tag{4.3}$$

where $\mathbf{I}$ is the identity matrix of order (n-1); $\gamma^H = [\gamma_i^H]$ is a vector consisting of (n-1) subvectors; and $\mathbf{y}$ and $\boldsymbol{\varepsilon}$ are as before. Let $\hat{\gamma}_i^H$ be the LS estimator of γ_i^H for i=1,...,n; and $\hat{\gamma}^H = [\hat{\gamma}_i^H]$ be the vector consisting of (n-1) subvectors.

When real income is held constant, the effect of an increase in the price of commodity j on the demand for commodity i is equal to the effect of a price increase of i on the demand for j. This is called symmetry of the substitution effects, or Slutsky symmetry. In terms of the parameters of (4.1), Slutsky symmetry takes the form

$$\pi_{ij} = \pi_{ji}, \qquad i,j=1,...,n. \tag{4.4}$$

In vector form for i,j=1,...,n-1, this can be written as

$$R\gamma^H = 0, \tag{4.5}$$

where $\mathbf{R}$ is a $q \times n(n\text{-}1)$ matrix with $q = \frac{1}{2}(n\text{-}1)(n\text{-}2)$ and each row of R consists of zeros except for a 1 and a -1 corresponding to π_{ij} and π_{ji} for some $i \neq j$.

The test statistic for symmetry is

$$\frac{(R\hat{\gamma}^H)'\{R[\Sigma \otimes (X^{H\prime}X^H)^{-1}]R'\}^{-1}(R\hat{\gamma}^H)}{[q/(n-1)]\,\mathrm{tr}\,\Sigma^{-1}S}, \tag{4.6}$$

where $\boldsymbol{\Sigma}$ is the error covariance matrix of model (4.1) for i=1,...,n-1

(Theil, 1971). Under the null, (4.6) is distributed as F with q and (n-1)(T-n) degrees of freedom. As before, we replace $\mathbf{\Sigma}$ by its estimator $\mathbf{S}$ (when $\mathbf{S}$ is non-singular) and the test statistic becomes

$$\Psi_S = (\mathbf{R}\hat{\gamma}^H)'\{\mathbf{R}[\mathbf{S} \otimes (\mathbf{X}^{H\prime}\mathbf{X}^H)^{-1}]\mathbf{R}'\}^{-1}(\mathbf{R}\hat{\gamma}^H), \tag{4.7}$$

which has an asymptotic χ^2 distribution with q degrees of freedom. Using simulation experiments, Meisner (1979) showed that the asymptotic test is biased against symmetry, particularly in large demand systems. Since (4.4) involves cross-equation restrictions, the exact distribution of Ψ_S is complicated and has not yet been derived.

We apply (4.7) to the OECD data and the results are shown in Table 4.2. A comparison of the observed value of (4.7) presented in column 4 with the χ^2-critical values for the asymptotic test presented in column 5 shows that the symmetry is rejected for all countries at the 5 percent level.

4.5 Monte Carlo Testing

It is well accepted in the literature that the negative results of testing the demand homogeneity and Slutsky symmetry are at least in part due to the failure of asymptotic tests which use the moment matrix $\mathbf{S}$ that could be singular (or near singular) for large demand systems with insufficient data sets (for example, see Barten, 1977).

To overcome the previously mentioned problems with the asymptotic tests, distribution-free tests based on Barnard's (1963) Monte Carlo simulation procedure have recently been developed for homogeneity, Slutsky symmetry (see Theil, 1987) and preference independence (S. Selvanathan, 1987). The basic idea behind the Monte Carlo tests is to simulate a large number of values of the test statistic under the null hypothesis to construct its empirical distribution. The observed value of the test statistic is then compared to this distribution, rather than its

Table 4.2 Testing Symmetry in 7 OECD Countries (Based on S)

Country	Number of commodities	Degrees of freedom	Test statistic	Asymptotic test critical value
	n	q	Ψ_S	$\chi^2(q)$
(1)	(2)	(3)	(4)	(5)
1. U.S.	10	36	566.2*	49.8
2. Canada	10	36	172.3*	49.8
3. Switzerland	9	28	103.4*	41.3
4. Australia	10	36	71.4*	49.8
5. Germany	8	21	35.1*	32.7
6. Belgium	10	36	184.3*	49.8
7. Netherlands	10	36	169.9*	49.8

A * denotes that we reject symmetry at the 5 percent level.

asymptotic counterpart. In this section we set out this Monte Carlo procedure and, in the next three sections, then present its application to homogeneity, symmetry and preference independence.

Switching to the standard notation, consider the system of equations $\mathbf{y} = \mathbf{X}\boldsymbol{\beta} + \boldsymbol{\varepsilon}$. Suppose we are interested in testing the null hypothesis $\mathbf{R}\boldsymbol{\beta} = \mathbf{b}$ using a test statistic τ. Obviously τ is a function of the estimate of the parameter vector $\boldsymbol{\beta}$. In general, the Monte Carlo procedure can be summarized as follows:

Step 1: Estimate the unrestricted model and obtain the data-based value τ_1 of τ.

Step 2: Estimate the model under the null hypothesis $\mathbf{R}\boldsymbol{\beta} = \mathbf{b}$ and obtain the estimate $\mathbf{S}$ of the covariance matrix $\boldsymbol{\Sigma}$ of the disturbances.

Step 3: Generate quasi-normal error terms with zero means and covariance matrix **S** and use these errors together with the observed value of **X** and the restricted estimates to generate a new data set for y under the null. Use the generated data to estimate the unrestricted model.

Step 4: Repeat Step 3 a certain number of times, N say, and in each case calculate the simulated value of the test statistic τ.

Step 5: Let $\tau_2,\ldots,\tau_M$ be the values of the test statistic τ obtained from the simulated data sets, where M=N+1. For a one-tailed test, we reject the null hypothesis for the observed sample at the α percent significance level if τ_1 is among the M' largest values of the τ_i's such that $(M'/M)\times 100 = \alpha$.

The number of replications (N) is usually chosen to be sufficiently large to reduce the 'blurring effect', which leads to loss of power (see Marriot, 1979). However, after a certain number of replications, the return for increased computing time diminishes. According to Besag and Diggle (1977), the suggested number of replications to reduce the 'blurring effect' for a 5 percent significance test is 99. If we use the $\alpha = 5$ percent significance level and N = 99 simulations, for a one-tailed test, we reject the null if the rank of τ_1 is 96, 97, 98, 99 or 100. For a two-tailed test, we reject the null when the rank of τ_1 is 1, 2, 3, 98, 99 or 100.

4.6 Homogeneity Revisited

Recall that homogeneity takes the form (3.1). Let $\hat{\pi}_{ij}$ be the LS estimate of π_{ij} in (2.1). Then the test statistic for the homogeneity of the i-*th* equation is

$$\hat{\tau}_i = \sum_{j=1}^{n} \hat{\pi}_{ij} \tag{6.1}$$

and the test statistic for the homogeneity of all n equations jointly is

$$\hat{\tau}_H = \sum_{i=1}^{n} |\hat{\tau}_i|. \tag{6.2}$$

[Since by construction $\Sigma_{i=1}^{n} \hat{\tau}_i = 0$, the sum of the absolute values of the $\hat{\tau}_i$'s are used in (6.2).]

For estimation, we use the Working's model (2.1). To assess the significance of the values of the test statistics (6.1) and (6.2), the Monte Carlo procedure is used. For this purpose, we use the homogeneity-constrained version of (2.1) given by equation (4.1). We estimate (4.1) by single-equation LS to obtain the data-based estimates of the parameters and an unbiased estimate of the contemporaneous covariance matrix of the ε_{it}'s; let this matrix be $\mathbf{S}_H$. Then quasi-normal error terms are generated with zero means and covariance matrix $\mathbf{S}_H$. These errors together with the homogeneity-constrained data-based estimates of the parameters and the observed values of the independent variables are used to generate simulated values for the dependent variables from (4.1). This procedure is repeated 99 times and in each case the unconstrained model (2.1) is estimated by single-equation LS and the simulated values of the test statistics (6.1) and (6.2) are computed. Then the data-based value of the test statistic is ranked among the simulated values.

Table 4.3 presents the results for the 7 countries with non-singular **S**. The upper part of Table 4.3 summarizes the results for model (2.1). Columns 2-11 present the ranks of the data-based values of the test statistics for each equation. Columns 12 and 13 give the percentage which are significant over all equations for each country at the 5 and 1 percent levels. The rank of the data-based test statistic for the homogeneity of the n equations jointly is presented in column 14. The second last and last rows of the upper part of the table present the rejection rate for each good at the 5 and 1 percent levels of significance.

Table 4.3 Rank of the Data-Based Test Statistic for Homogeneity in 99 Simulations for 7 Countries (Based on **S**)

Country	Food	Beverages	Clothing	Housing	Durables	Medical care	Transport	Recreation	Education	Miscellaneous	Percent significant at 5% level	Percent significant at 1% level	All goods
(1)	(2)	(3)	(4)	(5)	(6)	(7)	(8)	(9)	(10)	(11)	(12)	(13)	(14)
							No constant						
1. U.S.	9	67	56	97	4	100	29	6	82	71	10	10	91
2. Canada	66	2	68	76	21	74	15	47	39	39	10	0	45
3. Switzerland	46	19	1	97	1	65	5	100		100	44	44	99
4. Australia	77	2	51	42	75	66	27	29	2	97	20	0	35
5. Germany	12		2	100	13	90	18	95		97	25	10	100
6. Belgium	15	33	68	6	99	97	6	94	65	25	10	0	93
7. Netherlands	42	37	81	91	10	64	71	29	78	58	0	0	44
8. Percent significant at 5% level	0	33	28	14	28	14	0	14	20	14			28
9. Percent significant at 1% level	0	0	14	14	14	14	0	14	0	14			14
							With constant						
10. U.S.	64	97	57	23	2	61	84	8	93	31	10	0	70
11. Canada	73	2	67	78	23	87	10	51	36	33	10	0	59
12. Switzerland	11	45	12	74	16	24	24	100		97	10	10	78
13. Australia	27	11	90	6	96	57	42	14	3	95	10	0	90
14. Germany	17		23	75	55	82	43	87		65	0	0	25
15. Belgium	12	28	75	5	98	93	6	90	67	34	10	0	92
16. Netherlands	42	37	92	95	8	46	48	32	69	37	0	0	52
17. Percent significant at 5% level	0	17	0	0	28	0	0	14	0	0			0
18. Percent significant at 1% level	0	0	0	0	0	0	0	14	0	0			0

Next, we include a constant term in each equation to account for the trend-like changes in tastes etc. The model with the constant terms can be derived from a utility function subject to additive random shocks; see Theil (1967, Section 7.1) for details. Let α_i be the constant term of equation i. When such a constant is included in equation (2.1), the parameter vector γ_i now has (n + 2) elements, $\gamma_i = [\alpha_i\ \beta_i\ \pi_{i1} \dots \pi_{in}]'$; and the **X** matrix is now of order $T \times (n + 2)$ with t-*th* row $\mathbf{x}_t = [1\ DQ_t\ Dp_{1t} \dots Dp_{nt}]'$. Since the constant terms satisfy $\Sigma_{i=1}^{n} \alpha_i = 0$, one of the equations is still redundant. Everything else remains as before. We repeat the Monte Carlo procedure for the 7 countries and the lower part of Table 4.3 gives the results.

Looking at row 8 of Table 4.3, we see that the rejection rate for beverages, clothing and durables are on the high side at the 5 percent level. As can be seen from the lower half of the table, when constant terms are included, homogeneity of the n equations jointly is acceptable at the 5 percent significance level for all 7 countries.

In Section 4.3 we found that homogeneity of the entire model is rejected by the asymptotic test for 6 of the 7 countries in question. Using Laitinen's exact test we found that it is acceptable for all countries except Germany. Since the model used in Section 4.3 is without constants, we compare these results with the Monte Carlo test results given in the upper half of Table 4.3. As can be seen from column 14 of this table, at the 5 percent level homogeneity is acceptable for 5 countries, while it is rejected for Switzerland and Germany. This shows that the Monte Carlo tests of homogeneity are similar to those from the exact test.

4.7 Symmetry Revisited

Given homogeneity (3.1), the demand model (2.1) takes the form (4.1). Let $\hat{\pi}^H_{ij}$ be the LS estimate of the π_{ij} in (4.1). That is, $\hat{\pi}^H_{ij}$ is the homogeneity-constrained LS estimate of π_{ij}. The test statistic for symmetry, given homogeneity, is

$$\hat{\tau}_S = \sum_{i=1}^{n} \sum_{j=1}^{n} |\hat{\pi}^H_{ij} - \hat{\pi}^H_{ji}|. \tag{7.1}$$

To apply the Monte Carlo procedure to assess the significance of this data-based value, the estimates of the symmetry-constrained version of (4.1) are required. In vector form, model (4.1) can be written as (4.3), where $\mathbf{y} = [\mathbf{y}_i]$ with $y_i = [\overline{w}_{it}(Dq_{it} - DQ_t)]$; and $\gamma^H = [\gamma^H_i]$ with

$\gamma_i^H = [\beta_i\ \pi_{i1} \cdots \pi_{i,n-1}]'$. The symmetry constraint (4.4) in vector form is given by (4.5). It can be shown (Theil, 1971) that, under symmetry, the best linear unbiased estimator of γ^H in (4.3) is given by

$$\hat{\gamma}^S = \hat{\gamma}^H - C(\boldsymbol{\Sigma})\mathbf{R}'[\mathbf{R}C(\boldsymbol{\Sigma})\mathbf{R}']^{-1}\mathbf{R}\hat{\gamma}^H, \tag{7.2}$$

where $C(\Sigma) = \Sigma \otimes (\mathbf{X}^{H\prime}\mathbf{X}^H)^{-1}$; $\hat{\gamma}^H$ is the unconstrained LS estimator of γ^H in (4.3); and $\mathbf{R}$ is a $q \times n(n-1)$ matrix defined below (4.5). As before, the unknown Σ matrix is replaced with its homogeneity-constrained unbiased estimate; let this matrix be $\mathbf{S}_H$. In words, $\mathbf{S}_H$ is an estimate of the contemporaneous covariance matrix of the ε_{it}'s in (4.1).

Then, quasi-normal error terms are generated with zero mean and covariance matrix $\mathbf{S}_S$, the unbiased estimate of Σ under symmetry. These errors together with the observed values of the independent variables and the symmetry-constrained parameter estimates are used to obtain simulated values of the dependent variables from equation (4.1). Next, model (4.1) without symmetry is estimated using the simulated data set and the simulated value of the test statistic (7.1) is computed. This procedure is repeated 99 times. Finally, the data-based value of the test statistic $\hat{\tau}_S$ is ranked among the simulated values.

We apply this procedure to the 7 OECD countries with non-singular $\mathbf{S}$. When constant terms are included in model (4.1), obvious adjustments are to be made to the parameter vector γ^H and the matrix $\mathbf{X}^H$ of equation (4.3). Columns 2 and 3 of Table 4.4 give the results. The last two rows give the percentage of countries for which the test statistic is significant at the 5 and 1 percent levels. As can be seen, symmetry is acceptable at the 5 percent level for all 7 countries whether or not there are constant terms in the equations. This is in stark contrast to the results from the asymptotic test discussed in Section 4.4, where symmetry is rejected for all countries. We shall come back to Columns 4 and 5 of Table 4.4 in the next section.

Table 4.4 Rank of the Data-Based Test Statistic for Symmetry in 99 Simulations for 18 Countries

Country	Based on S		Based on Σ^*	
	No constant	With constant	No constant	With constant
(1)	(2)	(3)	(4)	(5)
1. U.S.	29	16	90	71
2. Canada	61	21	72	32
3. Sweden	..	..	51	14
4. Switzerland	54	59	95	96
5. Denmark	..	..	31	41
6. Australia	3	1	18	2
7. France	..	..	42	80
8. Germany	47	72	74	90
9. Belgium	17	5	56	30
10. Norway	..	..	85	11
11. Netherlands	46	20	91	56
12. Iceland	..	..	19	38
13. Finland	..	..	49	42
14. Austria	..	..	6	21
15. Japan	..	..	11	56
16. U.K.	..	..	96	30
17. Spain	..	..	28	87
18. Italy	..	..	47	49
19. Percent significant at 5% level	0	0	6	6
20. Percent significant at 1% level	0	0	0	0

4.8 Preference Independence Revisited

Now we use the Monte Carlo procedure to test the hypothesis of preference independence.

Under preference independence and Working's model specification, the Slutsky coefficients take the form [see, equations (8.2) and (16.3) of

Chapter 1]

$$\pi_{ij} = \phi(\bar{w}_{it} + \beta_i)(\delta_{ij} - \bar{w}_{jt} - \beta_j), \qquad i,j=1,...,n, \tag{8.1}$$

where ϕ is the income flexibility; β_i is the income coefficient of commodity i; and δ_{ij} is the Kronecker delta. Since the income coefficients sum to 0, (8.1) satisfies homogeneity and symmetry.

From equation (18.1) of Chapter 1, the i-*th* demand equation of the Working's model under preference independence is

$$\bar{w}_{it}(Dq_{it} - DQ_t) = \beta_i DQ_t + \phi(\bar{w}_{it} + \beta_i)\left[Dp_{it} - \sum_{j=1}^{n} (\bar{w}_{jt} + \beta_j)Dp_{jt}\right] + \varepsilon_{it}. \tag{8.2}$$

Equation (8.2) can be written as

$$\bar{w}_{it}(Dq_{it} - DQ_t) = \beta_i DQ_t + \phi z_{it} + \varepsilon_{it}, \tag{8.3}$$

where $z_{it} = (\bar{w}_{it} + \beta_i)\left[Dp^*_{it} - \Sigma_{j=1}^{n-1} (\bar{w}_{jt} + \beta_j)Dp^*_{jt}\right]$ and $Dp^*_{it} = Dp_{it} - Dp_{nt}$. Since model (8.3) is nonlinear in the parameters, we estimate it by maximum likelihood (ML). Details of the estimation procedure are presented in Appendix A4.1.

Let $\hat{\pi}^S_{ij}$ be the homogeneity- and symmetry-constrained generalized least squares estimate of π_{ij} (which is the same as the constrained ML estimate of π_{ij}). Let $\hat{\pi}^P_{ij}$ be the ML-estimate under preference independence defined as

$$\hat{\pi}^P_{ij} = \hat{\phi}(\bar{\bar{w}}_i + \hat{\beta}_i)(\delta_{ij} - \bar{\bar{w}}_j - \hat{\beta}_j), \tag{8.4}$$

where $\hat{\phi}$ and the $\hat{\beta}_i$'s are ML-estimates under preference independence; and $\bar{\bar{w}}_i = (1/T)\, \Sigma_{t=1}^{T} \bar{w}_{it}$ is the sample mean of $\bar{w}_{it}$. [Note that in going from (8.1) to (8.4) we have approximated $\overline{w}_{it}$ by $\bar{\bar{w}}_i$; this approximation will be satisfactory as long as there are no large changes in the budget shares during the sample period.] Then the test statistic for preference independence is defined as (see S. Selvanathan, 1987)

$$\hat{\tau}_P = \sum_{i=1}^{n} \sum_{j \leq i} |\hat{\pi}^S_{ij} - \hat{\pi}^P_{ij}|. \tag{8.5}$$

To assess the significance of $\hat{\tau}_P$ we use the Monte Carlo procedure described in Section 4.5. To generate data sets under the null, we first calculate a consistent estimate of the contemporaneous covariance matrix of the ε_{it}'s in (8.3). This matrix is $\mathbf{S}_P = [(1/T)\hat{\varepsilon}_i'\hat{\varepsilon}_j]$, where $\hat{\varepsilon}_i$ is the ML-residual vector for equation i. Then we generate quasi-normal error terms with zero means and covariance matrix $\mathbf{S}_P$. We use these errors together with the observed values of the independent variables and the ML parameter estimates to obtain simulated values of the dependent variables using equation (8.3). This procedure is repeated a certain number of times and in each trial we use the generated data set to estimate the homogeneity- and symmetry-constrained model. We then use these estimates to calculate the simulated value of the test statistic (8.5). This procedure is repeated 99 times. Finally, the data-based value of the test statistic $\hat{\tau}_P$ is ranked among the simulated values.

The results of testing preference independence for the 7 countries with non-singular **S** are presented in columns 2 and 3 of Table 4.5. As can be seen, in both cases, preference independence is rejected at the 5 percent level for 4 of the 7 countries. We shall come back to this topic again in the next section where we discuss the last two columns of Table 4.5.

4.9 Specifying the Covariance Matrix

For 11 out of the 18 OECD countries considered in Chapter 2, T - 2n - 1 (T = sample size after lagging, n = number of commodities) is negative

Table 4.5 Rank of the Data-Based Test Statistic for Preference Independence in 99 Simulations for 18 Countries

Country	Based on **S**		Based on Σ^*	
	No constant	With constant	No constant	With constant
(1)	(2)	(3)	(4)	(5)
1. U.S.	100	100	58	70
2. Canada	98	96	23	15
3. Sweden	..	..	22	89
4. Switzerland	91	86	95	82
5. Denmark	..	..	47	58
6. Australia	86	70	93	92
7. France	..	..	91	86
8. Germany	95	50	84	30
9. Belgium	99	100	43	49
10. Norway	..	..	97	93
11. Netherlands	98	99	39	25
12. Iceland	..	..	7	24
13. Finland	..	..	91	59
14. Austria	..	..	81	79
15. Japan	..	..	50	79
16. U.K.	..	..	43	5
17. Spain	..	..	56	36
18. Italy	..	..	84	77
19. Percent significant at 5% level	57	57	6	0
20. Percent significant at 1% level	14	29	0	0

and therefore, **S** will be singular. Consequently, the usual tests and estimators involving the inverse of the **S** cannot be used. To overcome these problems, following Deaton (1975) and E.A. Selvanathan (1985), S. Selvanathan (1991) used an alternative specification of the covariance matrix,

$$\Sigma^* = \lambda^2 \Omega, \tag{9.1}$$

where $\boldsymbol{\Omega} = \bar{\mathbf{W}} - \bar{\mathbf{w}}\bar{\mathbf{w}}'$; $\bar{\mathbf{W}} = \text{diag}\left[\bar{\bar{w}}_1,\ldots,\bar{\bar{w}}_{n-1}\right]$; $\bar{\mathbf{w}} = \left[\bar{\bar{w}}_1 \; \ldots \; \bar{\bar{w}}_{n-1}\right]'$; $\bar{\bar{w}}_i = (1/T)\,\Sigma_{t=1}^{T}\,\bar{w}_{it}$ is the sample mean of $\bar{w}_{it}$; and the constant parameter λ^2 is to be estimated. It can be easily shown that $\boldsymbol{\Omega}$ is non-singular and that an unbiased LS estimator of λ^2 is

$$\hat{\lambda}^2 = \frac{1}{(T-K)(n-1)} \sum_{i=1}^{n-1} \sum_{j=1}^{n-1} \omega^{ij}\,\hat{\varepsilon}_i'\hat{\varepsilon}_j, \tag{9.2}$$

where K is the number of parameters in each equation; ω^{ij} is the (i,j)-*th* element of $\boldsymbol{\Omega}^{-1}$; and $\hat{\varepsilon}_i$ is the LS residual vector of the i-*th* equation.

Let $\boldsymbol{\Sigma}^* = [\sigma^*_{ij}]$ and $\boldsymbol{\Omega} = [\omega_{ij}]$. Then $\omega_{ii} = \bar{\bar{w}}_i(1 - \bar{\bar{w}}_i)$ and $\sigma^*_{ii} = \lambda^2\omega_{ii}$. It can be easily seen that, for $0 \leq \bar{\bar{w}}_i \leq .5$, σ^*_{ii} increases with $\bar{\bar{w}}_i$. Therefore, since $\bar{\bar{w}}_i$ is less than .5 for all the OECD countries, σ^*_{ii} increases with $\bar{\bar{w}}_i$. Specification (9.1) thus allows for larger error variances for goods which occupy larger shares of the budget, which is plausible. See Barten and Theil (1964) for a multinomial interpretation of (9.1).

S. Selvanathan (1991), using simulation experiments, found that the performance of specification (9.1) is much more reliable than the usual covariance structure for large demand systems. In this section, we use $\boldsymbol{\Sigma}^*$ in the application of testing homogeneity, symmetry and preference independence for the 18 OECD countries.

Homogeneity

To test homogeneity for the 11 countries with singular **S**, we use $\boldsymbol{\Sigma}^*$ instead of **S**. The estimator of the one unknown parameter in Σ^*, λ^2, is given by (9.2). For comparison, we also use $\boldsymbol{\Sigma}^*$ for the other 7 countries. We then follow the same procedure as before. Table 4.6 presents the results. As can be seen from the lower part of column 14 of the table, homogeneity of the entire model (with constant terms) is acceptable for all

Table 4.6 Rank of the Data-Based Test Statistic for Homogeneity in 99 Simulations for 18 Countries (Based on Σ^*)

Country	Food	Beverages	Clothing	Housing	Durables	Medical care	Transport	Recreation	Education	Miscellaneous	Percent significant at 5% level	Percent significant at 1% level	All goods
(1)	(2)	(3)	(4)	(5)	(6)	(7)	(8)	(9)	(10)	(11)	(12)	(13)	(14)
						No constant							
1. U.S.	5	65	56	95	4	100	28	12	59	61	10	10	90
2. Canada	62	19	68	73	37	100	9	50	47	42	10	10	23
3. Sweden	88	57	43	81	31	69	3	90	53	6	10	0	87
4. Switzerland	45	27	1	100	2	59	8	100		97	44	30	100
5. Denmark	78	49	23	99	5	70	7	31	90	77	10	0	92
6. Australia	68	15	56	45	94	69	30	26	6	69	0	0	20
7. France	99	29	5	92	9	95	1	70	67	42	20	10	100
8. Germany	20		2	100	16	78	5	78		83	25	10	100
9. Belgium	10	44	62	3	100	96	23	80	53	13	20	10	100
10. Norway	77	39	23	95	68	79	2	80	41	35	10	0	83
11. Netherlands	45	38	80	82	1	64	68	24	64	66	10	10	25
12. Iceland	41	54	24	90	28	100	2	85	70	52	20	10	92
13. Finland	41	72	43	80	42	39	46	50	25	38	0	0	2
14. Austria	39	2	81	74	40	66	69	34	50	58	10	0	18
15. Japan	8		1	97	14	91	87	9		97	13	10	99
16. U.K.	16	59	39	67	20	32	44	71	50	88	0	0	25
17. Spain	60	55	68	35	54	61	35	69	37	26	0	0	1
18. Italy	12	60	1	77	20	95	99	84	55	77	20	10	99
19. Percent significant at 5% level	6	6	22	22	17	17	28	6	0	0			33
20. Percent significant at 1% level	0	0	17	11	11	17	6	6	0	0			22
						With constant							
21. U.S.	76	89	53	40	1	77	98	3	70	25	30	10	80
22. Canada	65	18	68	68	37	100	8	49	47	39	10	10	29
23. Sweden	91	74	95	24	35	49	2	58	48	37	10	0	75
24. Switzerland	16	45	17	92	29	40	16	96		94	0	0	82
25. Denmark	77	55	14	29	51	23	84	78	13	31	0	0	25
26. Australia	37	35	81	6	100	63	34	9	7	72	10	10	87
27. France	83	60	31	67	95	76	2	58	28	34	10	0	61
28. Germany	23		26	83	52	77	29	72		55	0	0	14
29. Belgium	10	37	70	3	100	93	25	79	55	29	20	10	99
30. Norway	83	1	77	76	61	12	70	63	51	27	10	10	64
31. Netherlands	39	38	92	91	2	55	55	26	59	45	10	0	37
32. Iceland	68	17	48	69	83	57	12	98	44	5	10	0	52
33. Finland	61	48	41	65	66	34	62	70	10	23	0	0	3
34. Austria	40	2	81	72	40	58	78	33	47	58	10	0	18
35. Japan	85		9	50	2	84	81	16		78	13	0	89
36. U.K.	19	81	74	25	85	41	20	64	50	83	0	0	43
37. Spain	63	56	73	35	51	58	37	76	32	25	0	0	2
38. Italy	20	52	41	32	73	95	87	55	32	55	0	0	29
39. Percent significant at 5% level	0	13	0	6	28	6	17	11	0	0			6
40. Percent significant at 1% level	0	6	0	0	17	6	0	0	0	0			0

countries except Belgium at the 5 percent level and is acceptable for all countries at the 1 percent level.

Next, we compare the upper half of Table 4.6 with its lower half. As can be seen, at the 5 percent level, all the commodities except beverages, durables and recreation perform better when constants are added to the equations. Also, looking at the last column of the table we see that the homogeneity of the n equations jointly becomes more acceptable when constants are included. These findings point to the importance of including constants when testing homogeneity.

Tables 4.3 and 4.6 have 7 countries in common. A comparison of the results for all goods (column 14 of both tables) shows that for these countries things do not change much. For example, homogeneity is rejected at the 5 percent level for Switzerland and Germany when there are no constants, while it is accepted for both countries when constants are included irrespective of the choice of $\mathbf{\Sigma}$. Consequently, there is no evidence that the use of $\mathbf{\Sigma}^*$ distorts the results.

Symmetry

To test symmetry, we replace **S** by $\mathbf{\Sigma}^*$ and follow the same procedure as before. Columns 4 and 5 of Table 4.4 present the results. At the 5 percent level, symmetry is acceptable for all countries except the UK when there are no constants; and is acceptable for all countries except Switzerland when constants are included. Symmetry is acceptable for all countries at the 1 percent significance level whether or not there are constants.

To analyse the effects of using $\mathbf{\Sigma}^*$ rather than S, for the relevant countries we compare column 2 with 4 and column 3 with 5 in Table 4.4. This shows that the ranks increase in all cases when we use $\mathbf{\Sigma}^*$. Comparing column 2 with 3 and 4 with 5, we see that, on the whole, adding constant terms to the model does not make any major difference to the results.

Preference Independence

Columns 2 and 3 of Table 4.5 give the ranks in 99 simulations of the data-based values of the test statistics for preference independence for the 7 countries with non-singular **S** matrix, with and without constants. As can be seen, in both cases preference independence is rejected at the 5 percent level for 4 out of 7 countries. Columns 4 and 5 of the table present the results when we use $\boldsymbol{\Sigma}^*$ for all 18 countries. When constants are included, preference independence may not be rejected at the 5 percent level for all countries.

In contrast to homogeneity and symmetry testing, for preference independence, there is notable difference between the results based on **S** and $\boldsymbol{\Sigma}^*$; for Table 4.5 compare column 2 with 4 and column 3 with 5. Consider, for example, the US where preference independence is rejected when we use **S** with and without the constants. However, when $\boldsymbol{\Sigma}^*$ is used the hypothesis becomes acceptable. One reason for this could be that the data-based and simulated values of the test statistics for homogeneity and symmetry do not depend on the covariance matrix; see equations (6.1), (6.2) and (7.1). The covariance matrix is used only to generate the error terms under the null and to obtain the restricted estimates for symmetry from (7.2). However, this is not the case for preference independence as the ML-estimates involve the disturbance covariance matrix, be it **S** or $\boldsymbol{\Sigma}^*$. (For details of the estimation procedure, see Appendices A4.1 and A4.2.) Therefore, the data-based and the simulated values of the test statistics are not the same for different specifications of the covariance matrix.

Selvanathan (1993) explores further the effects of the choice of the covariance matrix estimator on the results for preference independence. In view of the effects of the covariance matrix, it would seem best to be cautious and conclude that the findings of this section give some tentative support to the hypothesis of preference independence.

4.10 The Implied Demand Elasticities

In this section we present the income and own-price elasticities implied by the model under preference independence given by (8.3). We also present the estimates of the income flexibility for each country.

Let $\hat{\phi}$ and $\hat{\beta}_i$, i=1,...,n, be the ML-estimates of the parameters of model (8.3) with covariance matrix specified as Σ^* (see Appendix A4.2 for details of the ML estimation procedure). The income elasticity of good i implied by (8.3) is

$$\eta_{it} = 1 + \frac{\hat{\beta}_i}{\bar{w}_{it}}. \tag{10.1}$$

When the budget shares are fairly stable over time, we can replace $\bar{w}_{it}$ by its sample mean $\bar{\bar{w}}_i = (1/T)\,\Sigma_{t=1}^{T}\,\bar{w}_{it}$ in (10.1) and write

$$\eta_i = 1 + \frac{\hat{\beta}_i}{\bar{\bar{w}}_i}. \tag{10.2}$$

Similarly, the Slutsky (or compensated) own-price elasticity of good i implied by (10.3) at means is

$$\eta_{ii} = \frac{\hat{\phi}(\bar{\bar{w}}_i + \hat{\beta}_i)(1 - \bar{\bar{w}}_i - \hat{\beta}_i)}{\bar{\bar{w}}_i}.$$

Columns 2-11 of Table 4.7 present the income elasticities and their root-mean-square errors obtained from 100 simulations. From the table we see that most of the income elasticities are highly significant and all but five of them are positive. We shall come back to these five in Section 4.11. In all countries food is a necessity. The income elasticities

Table 4.7 Income Elasticities of 10 Commodities and Income Flexibility for 18 Countries

(Root-mean-square-errors are in parentheses)

Country (1)	Food (2)	Beverages (3)	Clothing (4)	Housing (5)	Durables (6)	Medical care (7)	Transport (8)	Recreation (9)	Education (10)	Miscellaneous (11)	Income flexibility φ (12)
1. U.S.	.61 (.14)	.28 (.32)	1.33 (.26)	.41 (.13)	1.74 (.24)	.37 (.24)	2.31 (.14)	1.22 (.29)	.82 (.49)	.70 (.18)	-.38 (.06)
2. Canada	.96 (.22)	.59 (.37)	.82 (.37)	.03 (.20)	1.57 (.35)	2.45 (.53)	1.56 (.21)	1.86 (.46)	1.05 (.67)	.93 (.29)	-.55 (.11)
3. Sweden	.55 (.12)	1.10 (.20)	1.45 (.31)	.16 (.15)	1.87 (.27)	.05 (.23)	2.01 (.19)	1.59 (.23)	.58 (.75)	1.03 (.27)	-.58 (.08)
4. Switzerland	.97 (.09)	1.35 (.17)	1.82 (.24)	.15 (.10)	2.10 (.27)	.30 (.24)	1.58 (.18)	1.01 (.24)		.61 (.26)	-.55 (.08)
5. Denmark	.36 (.16)	.69 (.19)	1.63 (.23)	.38 (.12)	1.59 (.16)	.49 (46)	2.25 (14)	1.24 (.23)	-.14 (.61)	.95 (.20)	-.46 (.08)
6. Australia	.26 (.21)	.83 (.27)	1.29 (.30)	.63 (.19)	2.22 (.35)	.70 (.41)	1.49 (.27)	2.25 (.46)	2.82 (1.66)	.54 (.27)	-.46 (.08)
7. France	.46 (.18)	.48 (.30)	1.29 (.25)	.44 (.16)	1.57 (.22)	.56 (.31)	2.21 (.23)	1.02 (.32)	.78 (1.27)	1.31 (.23)	-.53 (.08)
8. Germany	.62 (.11)		1.50 (.18)	.16 (.13)	1.44 (.20)	.83 (.35)	2.30 (.17)	1.00 (.23)		.71 (.21)	-.60 (.10)
9. Belgium	.49 (.18)	.98 (.37)	1.14 (.36)	.58 (.22)	1.49 (.27)	.58 (.41)	.88 (.28)	.94 (.50)	.06 (2.18)	2.37 (.38)	-.13 (.07)
10. Norway	.23 (.12)	1.14 (.20)	1.21 (.21)	.00 (.17)	1.29 (.22)	.79 (.34)	3.20 (.18)	1.03 (.30)	.52 (1.09)	.84 (.21)	-.48 (.09)
11. Netherlands	.50 (.15)	.62 (.18)	2.06 (.18)	.58 (.15)	1.41 (.27)	.60 (.19)	1.77 (.25)	.95 (.48)	.80 (.37)	.76 (.26)	-.84 (.11)
12. Iceland	.45 (.11)	.74 (.21)	1.34 (.16)	-.04 (.11)	1.89 (.19)	.76 (.28)	2.49 (.18)	1.44 (.35)	-.01 (1.30)	1.72 (.30)	-.69 (.09)
13. Finland	.55 (.14)	1.28 (.28)	1.67 (.32)	.15 (.21)	1.56 (.30)	.65 (.62)	1.80 (.19)	1.89 (.38)	1.16 (.64)	.71 (.32)	-.38 (.09)
14. Austria	.21 (.21)	.50 (.32)	1.79 (.25)	.18 (.24)	1.95 (.34)	-.73 (.53)	3.11 (.29)	.80 (.41)	-.40 (1.49)	.54 (.25)	-.15 (.10)
15. Japan	.62 (.15)		1.88 (.38)	.22 (.22)	2.08 (.35)	.78 (.25)	1.35 (.30)	1.15 (.32)		1 49 (.29)	-.37 (.10)
16. U.K.	.33 (.15)	1.03 (.17)	1.20 (.26)	.35 (.12)	2.14 (.22)	.61 (.59)	1.66 (.17)	1.34 (.25)	1.01 (.47)	1.17 (.15)	-.40 (.08)
17. Spain	.85 (.20)	.91 (.65)	1.29 (.34)	.19 (.30)	1.46 (.34)	.95 (.51)	2.37 (.35)	1.36 (.53)	.40 (.54)	.62 (.33)	-.29 (.08)
18. Italy	.86 (.10)	.70 (.26)	1.81 (.20)	.49 (.16)	1.53 (.23)	1.03 (.31)	1.42 (.18)	.67 (.25)	.62 (1.05)	.95 (.18)	- 18 (.07)
Mean	.55	.83	1.47	.28	1.72	.65	1.99	1.26	.67	1.00	-.45

for food in Canada and Switzerland seem to be on the high side. In all countries except Canada clothing is a luxury. Housing is a necessity and durables a luxury in all countries. In almost all countries, medical care is a necessity and transport and recreation are luxuries.

Column 12 gives the estimate of income flexibility ϕ. As can be seen, all ϕ-estimates are negative, as they should be, and the average is -.45. This value is in broad agreement with previous studies (Theil, 1980; Theil and Brooks, 1970/71).

Table 4.8 presents the own-price elasticities. With only a few exceptions, these elasticities are less than 1 in absolute value. Five of the elasticities are positive. It should be noted that these correspond to the five negative income elasticities.

4.11 More on the Elasticities

We noted previously that five of the income elasticities in Table 4.7 are negative. Taken literally, these goods are inferior. However, none of these negative elasticities is significant, which is fortunate as the assumption of preference independence rules out inferior goods (see Sections 1.5 and 1.13 for details). We shall now re-estimate the model for the relevant countries with the constraint that all income elasticities are positive. To do this, we specify the coefficient β_i of good i with negative income elasticity to be $\beta_i = -\min_t \overline{w}_{it}$, so that the income elasticity $\eta_{it} = 1 + \beta_i/\overline{w}_{it}$ is now constrained to be positive.

The countries involved are Denmark (for education), Iceland (housing and education) and Austria (medical care and education). It is to be noted that education is a troublemaker for all three countries. This suggests that either there may be some problems with the data for education or that the model is not satisfactory for this good. For the three countries we specify the β_i's for the relevant commodities. All other parameters are estimated in the same way as before by ML using model (8.3) with covariance

Table 4.8 Slutsky Own-Price Elasticities of 10 Commodities for 18 Countries

(Root-mean-square-errors are in parentheses)

Country	Food	Beverages	Clothing	Housing	Durables	Medical care	Transport	Recreation	Education	Miscellaneous
(1)	(2)	(3)	(4)	(5)	(6)	(7)	(8)	(9)	(10)	(11)
1. U.S.	-.22	-.11	-.46	-.14	-.58	-.14	-.56	-.43	-.31	-.24
	(.05)	(.12)	(.12)	(.05)	(11)	(.10)	(.09)	(.12)	(.18)	(.07)
2. Canada	-.45	-.32	-.42	-.02	-.75	-1.23	-.66	-.92	-.57	-.45
	(11)	(.17)	(.21)	(.12)	(.24)	(.35)	(.14)	(.27)	(.35)	(.16)
3. Sweden	-.28	-.58	-.74	-.09	-.93	-.03	-.84	-.79	-.33	-.55
	(.07)	(.12)	(.18)	(.08)	(.16)	(.13)	(.13)	(.14)	(.41)	(.16)
4. Switzerland	-.42	-.65	-.88	-.08	-.97	-.16	-.72	-.50		-.32
	(.06)	(.11)	(.17)	(.06)	(.16)	(.13)	(.12)	(.14)		(.14)
5. Denmark	-.16	-.30	-.67	-.16	-.63	-.22	-.69	-.52	.06	-.40
	(.07)	(.09)	(.14)	(.06)	(.11)	(.21)	(.11)	(.13)	(.29)	(.11)
6. Australia	-.11	-.35	-.53	-.26	-.84	-.31	-.53	-.91	-1.28	-.23
	(.09)	(.12)	(.13)	(.08)	(18)	(.18)	(.11)	(.19)	(.75)	(.12)
7. France	-.22	-.25	-.61	-.22	-.70	-.28	-.86	-.50	-.41	-.58
	(.09)	(.15)	(.14)	(.09)	(.14)	(.16)	(.14)	(.16)	(.64)	(.11)
8. Germany	-.31		-.76	-.09	- 72	-.49	-.97	-.56		-.40
	(.07)		(.15)	(.08)	(.14)	(.22)	(.15)	(.15)		(.11)
9. Belgium	-.06	-.12	-.13	-.07	-.15	-.07	-.10	-.11	-.01	-.22
	(.04)	(.09)	(.10)	(.04)	(.10)	(.07)	(07)	(.10)	(.30)	(.11)
10. Norway	-.11	-.50	-.51	-.00	-.55	-.37	-.89	-.46	-.25	-.37
	(.06)	(.10)	(.13)	(.08)	(.14)	(.17)	(.17)	(.17)	(.53)	(.11)
11. Netherlands	-.36	-.50	-1.21	-.46	-.98	-.49	-1.32	-.78	-.66	-.59
	(.12)	(.15)	(.16)	(.12)	(.18)	(.15)	(.17)	(.42)	(.32)	(.22)
12. Iceland	-.28	-.49	-.80	.03	-1.07	-.50	-1.21	-.92	.01	-1.09
	(.07)	(.15)	(.12)	(.08)	(16)	(.20)	(.16)	(.23)	(.91)	(.23)
13. Finland	-.18	-.43	-.54	-.06	-.52	-.24	-.51	-.64	-.43	-.25
	(.06)	(.14)	(.16)	(.09)	(.14)	(.25)	(.11)	(.18)	(.29)	(.13)
14. Austria	-.03	-.07	-.22	-.03	-.25	.12	-.28	-.12	.06	-.08
	(.04)	(.06)	(.15)	(.05)	(17)	(.12)	(.17)	(.11)	(24)	(.07)
15. Japan	-.19		-.59	-.08	-.66	-.27	-.44	-.38		-.43
	(.06)		(.21)	(.08)	(.16)	(.09)	(.13)	(.13)		(.14)
16. U.K.	-.12	-.38	-.43	-.13	-.71	-.24	-.51	-.47	-.39	-.37
	(.06)	(.07)	(.13)	(.05)	(16)	(.22)	(.10)	(.12)	(.19)	(.08)
17. Spain	-.18	-.26	-.32	-.05	- 37	-.27	-.53	-.37	-.12	-.17
	(.06)	(.19)	(.12)	(.09)	(12)	(.16)	(.13)	(.14)	(.17)	(.10)
18 Italy	-.12	-.12	-.28	-.09	- 25	-.18	-.22	-.12	-.11	-.15
	(.05)	(.08)	(.12)	(.04)	(.09)	(.09)	(.09)	(.06)	(.21)	(.07)
Mean	- 21	-.34	-.56	-.11	- 65	- 30	-.66	-.53	-.32	- 38

matrix Σ^*. Table 4.9 presents the elasticities and the income flexibility with and without the restrictions. Comparing the two rows for each country, we see that the restrictions result in only minor changes for Denmark and Austria, while for Iceland the changes are somewhat larger.

To test the validity of the restrictions, we use the likelihood ratio statistic $-2 \log \lambda = -2[\log L_r - \log L_u]$, where L_r and L_u represent the log-likelihood values for the restricted and unrestricted models, respectively. This test statistic has an asymptotic χ^2 distribution with degrees of freedom equal to the number of restrictions. Table 4.10 presents for each country the log-likelihood values; the observed value of the test statistic; and the critical value at the 5 percent level. As can be seen, we are unable to reject the restrictions for all three countries. The conclusion is that the income elasticities jointly are not significantly negative. This agrees with the individual insignificance of the negative elasticities.

4.12 Conclusion

It is well documented in the demand analysis literature that the rejection of the demand theory hypotheses homogeneity, symmetry and preference independence are at least in part due to the failure of the asymptotic theory. In this chapter, we discussed the recent developments in testing demand theory hypotheses using the distribution-free Monte Carlo procedure which do not require any asymptotic theory. We illustrated their applications using data from 18 OECD countries. In contrast to most previous studies, we found evidence in support of the three hypotheses. Finally, the implications of the estimates were explored by tabulating and analysing the implied demand elasticities.

Table 4.9 Unrestricted and Restricted Demand Elasticities for 10 Commodities in 3 Countries

(Root-mean-square-errors are in parentheses)

Country	Food	Beverages	Clothing	Housing	Durables	Medical care	Transport	Recreation	Education	Miscellaneous	ϕ Income flexibility
(1)	(2)	(3)	(4)	(5)	(6)	(7)	(8)	(9)	(10)	(11)	(12)
Income elasticities and income flexibility											
1. Denmark											
Unrestricted	.36	.69	1.63	.38	1.59	.49	2.25	1.24	-.14	.95	- 46
	(.16)	(.19)	(.23)	(.12)	(.16)	(.46)	(.14)	(.23)	(.61)	(.20)	(.08)
Restricted	.35	.69	1.63	.37	1.59	.48	2.24	1.24	.46	.95	-.47
	(.16)	(.19)	(.23)	(.12)	(.16)	(.46)	(.14)	(.23)	(-)	(.20)	(.08)
2. Iceland											
Unrestricted	.45	.74	1.34	-.04	1.89	.76	2.49	1.44	-.01	1.72	-.69
	(.11)	(.21)	(.16)	(.11)	(.19)	(.28)	(.18)	(.35)	(1.30)	(.30)	(.09)
Restricted	.40	.69	1.27	.23	1.82	.71	2.40	1.39	.11	1.65	-.72
	(.11)	(.22)	(.15)	(-)	(.19)	(.28)	(18)	(.35)	(-)	(.30)	(.09)
3. Austria											
Unrestricted	.21	.50	1.79	.18	1.95	-.73	3.11	.80	-.40	.54	-.15
	(.21)	(.32)	(.25)	(.24)	(.34)	(.53)	(.29)	(.41)	(1.49)	(.25)	(.10)
Restricted	.18	.43	1.77	.16	1.92	.27	3.03	.75	.31	.50	-.18
	(.21)	(.32)	(.25)	(.24)	(.35)	(-)	(.29)	(.42)	(-)	(.25)	(.10)
Slutsky own-price elasticities											
4. Denmark											
Unrestricted	-.16	-.30	-.67	-.16	-.63	-.22	-.69	-.52	.06	-.40	
	(.07)	(.09)	(.14)	(.06)	(.11)	(.21)	(.11)	(.13)	(.29)	(.11)	
Restricted	-.15	-.30	-.68	-.16	-.64	-.22	-.70	-.52	-.21	-.40	
	(.08)	(.09)	(.14)	(.05)	(.11)	(.18)	(.11)	(.12)	(-)	(.11)	
5. Iceland											
Unrestricted	-.28	-.49	-.80	.03	-1.07	-.50	-1.21	-.92	.01	-1.09	
	(.07)	(.15)	(.12)	(.08)	(.16)	(.20)	(.16)	(.23)	(.91)	(.23)	
Restricted	-.18	-.39	-.75	-.16	-1.10	-.56	-1.23	-.99	-.08	-1.14	
	(.08)	(.16)	(.12)	(-)	(.16)	(.20)	(.16)	(.26)	(-)	(.24)	
6. Austria											
Unrestricted	-.03	-.07	-.22	-.03	.25	.12	-.28	-.12	.06	-.08	
	(.04)	(.06)	(.15)	(.05)	(.17)	(.12)	(.17)	(.11)	(.24)	(.07)	
Restricted	-.03	-.08	-.25	-.02	-.28	-.05	-.32	-.13	-.06	-.08	
	(.04)	(.07)	(.15)	(.06)	(.17)	(-)	(.17)	(11)	(-)	(.07)	

For the restricted estimates, the income elasticities are constrained to be positive. The restrictions take the form $\beta_i = -\min_t \bar{w}_{it}$ for i = education in Denmark; housing and education in Iceland; and medical care and education in Austria. The unrestricted estimates are from Tables 4.7 and 4.8 .

Table 4.10 Tests of Restrictions of the Income Elasticities for 3 Countries

Country	Log-likelihood values		Likelihood ratio test statistic	Critical value at 5% level
	Unrestricted	Restricted		
(1)	(2)	(3)	(4)	(5)
1. Denmark	184.32	183.88	.89	3.84
2. Iceland	74.08	71.34	5.48	5.99
3. Austria	199.05	197.14	3.82	5.99

Appendices to Chapter 4

A4.1 Estimation Under Preference Independence with the Usual Covariance Matrix

For convenience, we reproduce model (8.3),

$$y_{it} = \beta_i DQ_t + \phi z_{it} + \varepsilon_{it}, \qquad \text{(A1.1)}$$

where $y_{it} = \bar{w}_{it}(Dq_{it} - DQ_t)$,

$$z_{it} = (\bar{w}_{it} + \beta_i)\left[Dp^*_{it} - \sum_{j=1}^{n-1} (\bar{w}_{jt} + \beta_j)Dp^*_{jt}\right]$$

and $Dp^*_{it} = Dp_{it} - Dp_{nt}$.

For reasons described in Section 4.2, we confine ourselves to (A1.1) for i=1,...,n-1. In vector form (A1.1) can be written as

$$\mathbf{y}_t = \mathbf{X}_t\boldsymbol{\theta} + \boldsymbol{\varepsilon}_t, \qquad \text{(A1.2)}$$

where $\mathbf{y}_t = [y_{it}]$; $\mathbf{X}_t = [DQ_t I \;\; z_t]$, I being the identity matrix of order n-1; $\mathbf{z}_t = [z_{it}]$; $\theta = [\boldsymbol{\beta}' \; \phi]' = [\beta_1 \ldots \beta_{n-1} \; \phi]'$; and $\varepsilon_t = [\varepsilon_{it}]$.

Assuming that the ε_t's are independent normal vectors with zero mean and non-singular covariance matrix $\boldsymbol{\Sigma}$, the log-likelihood function of the $\mathbf{y}_t$'s is given by

$$L(\boldsymbol{\theta},\Sigma;\mathbf{y}) = C + \frac{T}{2}\log\left|\Sigma^{-1}\right| - \frac{1}{2}\sum_{t=1}^{T}(\mathbf{y}_t - \mathbf{X}_t\boldsymbol{\theta})'\Sigma^{-1}(\mathbf{y}_t - \mathbf{X}_t\boldsymbol{\theta}), \tag{A1.3}$$

where C is a constant; and T is the sample size. The first-order conditions for a maximum of (A1.3) are

$$\frac{\partial L}{\partial \boldsymbol{\Sigma}^{-1}} = \frac{T}{2}\boldsymbol{\Sigma} - \frac{1}{2}\sum_{t=1}^{T}(\mathbf{y}_t - \mathbf{X}_t\boldsymbol{\theta})(\mathbf{y}_t - \mathbf{X}_t\boldsymbol{\theta})' = 0 \tag{A1.4}$$

and

$$\frac{\partial L}{\partial \boldsymbol{\theta}'} = \sum_{t=1}^{T}(\mathbf{y}_t - \mathbf{X}_t\boldsymbol{\theta})'\Sigma^{-1}\frac{\partial \mathbf{X}_t\boldsymbol{\theta}}{\partial \boldsymbol{\theta}'} = 0, \tag{A1.5}$$

where

$$\frac{\partial \mathbf{X}_t\boldsymbol{\theta}}{\partial \boldsymbol{\theta}'} = \left[DQ_t I + \phi\frac{\partial z_t}{\partial \boldsymbol{\beta}'} \quad z_t\right]; \tag{A1.6}$$

$$\frac{\partial z_t}{\partial \boldsymbol{\beta}'} = \left[\frac{\partial z_{it}}{\partial \beta_j}\right];$$

and

$$\frac{\partial z_{it}}{\partial \beta_j} = -(\bar{w}_{it} + \beta_i)Dp^*_{jt} + \delta_{ij}\left[Dp^*_{it} - \sum_{k=1}^{n-1}(\bar{w}_{kt} + \beta_k)Dp^*_{kt}\right].$$

From the first-order condition (A1.4), we have

$$\hat{\Sigma} = \frac{1}{T}\sum_{t=1}^{T} (y_t - X_t\hat{\theta})(y_t - X_t\hat{\theta})'.$$

This is the usual ML estimator of Σ. In Section 4.8 we denote this estimator by S_P.

It follows from (A1.5) that

$$\frac{\partial^2 L}{\partial \Sigma^{-1} \partial \theta'} = \sum_{t=1}^{T} (y_t - X_t\theta)\left[\frac{\partial X_t\theta}{\partial \theta'}\right]'. \qquad \text{(A1.7)}$$

Since $E[(y_t - X_t\theta)] = E[\varepsilon_t] = 0$, the expected value of the right-hand side of (A1.7) vanishes, so that the information matrix of the ML procedure is block-diagonal with respect to θ and Σ^{-1}. From (A1.5) we also have

$$\frac{\partial^2 L}{\partial\theta\partial\theta'} = -\sum_{t=1}^{T} \frac{\partial (X_t\theta)'}{\partial\theta} \Sigma^{-1} \frac{\partial (X_t\theta)}{\partial\theta'} + \sum_{t=1}^{T} (y_t - X_t\theta)' \, \Sigma^{-1} \frac{\partial^2 (X_t\theta)}{\partial\theta\partial\theta'}.$$

The second term on the right-hand side has zero expectation. Therefore, the asymptotic covariance matrix of the ML estimator of θ is

$$V = -\left[E\left[\frac{\partial^2 L}{\partial\theta\partial\theta'}\right]\right]^{-1} = \left[\sum_{t=1}^{T} \frac{\partial (X_t\theta)'}{\partial\theta} \Sigma^{-1} \frac{\partial (X_t\theta)}{\partial\theta'}\right]^{-1}.$$

The ML estimator of θ is obtained by means of Newton's iterative scheme based on successive estimates of V and Σ. The asymptotic standard errors are the square roots of the diagonal elements of V with ML-estimates substituted for the unknown parameters in V.

When constant terms (α_i) are included in the model, (A1.1) becomes

$$y_{it} = \alpha_i + \beta_i DQ_t + \phi z_{it} + \varepsilon_{it}.$$

This can be written in vector form as equation (A1.2) provided we redefine the parameter vector $\boldsymbol{\theta}$ as $[\boldsymbol{\beta}' \ \ \phi \ \ \boldsymbol{\alpha}']'$, with $\boldsymbol{\alpha}' = [\alpha_1 \ldots \alpha_{n-1}]$; $\mathbf{X}_t$ as $[DQ_tI \ \ z_t \ \ I]$; and all other notation remains the same. The only modification is that equation (A1.6) becomes

$$\frac{\partial \mathbf{X}_t \boldsymbol{\theta}}{\partial \boldsymbol{\theta}'} = \left[DQ_tI + \phi \frac{\partial \mathbf{z}_t}{\partial \boldsymbol{\beta}'} \quad z_t \quad \mathbf{I} \right].$$

The rest of the procedure is as before.

A4.2 Estimation Under Preference Independence with the Alternative Covariance Matrix

When the covariance matrix is specified as $\Sigma^* = \lambda^2 \Omega$, the log-likelihood function (A1.3) becomes

$$L(\boldsymbol{\theta},\lambda^2;\mathbf{y}) = C + \frac{T}{2} \log \lambda^{-2(n-1)} - \frac{1}{2\lambda^2} \sum_{t=1}^{T} (\mathbf{y}_t - \mathbf{X}_t\boldsymbol{\theta})'\boldsymbol{\Omega}^{-1}(\mathbf{y}_t - \mathbf{X}_t\boldsymbol{\theta}). \qquad \text{(A2.1)}$$

The first-order conditions for a maximum of (A2.1) are

$$\frac{\partial L}{\partial \lambda^2} = -\frac{T(n-1)}{2\lambda^2} + \frac{1}{2\lambda^4} \sum_{t=1}^{T} (\mathbf{y}_t - \mathbf{X}_t\boldsymbol{\theta})'\boldsymbol{\Omega}^{-1}(\mathbf{y}_t - \mathbf{X}_t\boldsymbol{\theta}) = 0 \qquad \text{(A2.2)}$$

and

$$\frac{\partial L}{\partial \boldsymbol{\theta}'} = \frac{1}{\lambda^2} \sum_{t=1}^{T} (\mathbf{y}_t - \mathbf{X}_t\boldsymbol{\theta})'\boldsymbol{\Omega}^{-1} \frac{\partial \mathbf{X}_t\boldsymbol{\theta}}{\partial \boldsymbol{\theta}'} = 0, \qquad \text{(A2.3)}$$

where $\partial(\mathbf{X}_t\boldsymbol{\theta})/\partial\boldsymbol{\theta}'$ is given by (A1.6).

The first-order condition (A2.2) implies

$$\hat{\lambda}^2 = \frac{1}{T(n-1)} \sum_{t=1}^{T} (\mathbf{y}_t - \mathbf{X}_t\hat{\boldsymbol{\theta}})'\boldsymbol{\Omega}^{-1}(\mathbf{y}_t - \mathbf{X}_t\hat{\boldsymbol{\theta}}).$$

This is the ML estimator of λ^2. Note that the estimator of λ^2 presented in (9.2) is the LS version.

From (A2.3),

$$\frac{\partial^2 L}{\partial\lambda^2 \partial\boldsymbol{\theta}'} = -\frac{1}{\lambda^4} \sum_{t=1}^{T} (\mathbf{y}_t - \mathbf{X}_t\boldsymbol{\theta})'\boldsymbol{\Omega}^{-1} \frac{\partial \mathbf{X}_t\boldsymbol{\theta}}{\partial\boldsymbol{\theta}'},$$

which has zero expectation. Thus the information matrix is block-diagonal with respect to $\boldsymbol{\theta}$ and λ^2. From (A2.3) we also have

$$\frac{\partial^2 L}{\partial\boldsymbol{\theta}\partial\boldsymbol{\theta}'} = -\frac{1}{\lambda^2} \sum_{t=1}^{T} \frac{\partial(\mathbf{X}_t\boldsymbol{\theta})'}{\partial\boldsymbol{\theta}} \boldsymbol{\Omega}^{-1} \frac{\partial(\mathbf{X}_t\boldsymbol{\theta})}{\partial\boldsymbol{\theta}'} + \frac{1}{\lambda^2} \sum_{t=1}^{T} (\mathbf{y}_t - \mathbf{X}_t\boldsymbol{\theta})' \boldsymbol{\Omega}^{-1} \frac{\partial^2(\mathbf{X}_t\boldsymbol{\theta})}{\partial\boldsymbol{\theta}\partial\boldsymbol{\theta}'}.$$

The second term on the right-hand side has zero expectation. Therefore, the asymptotic covariance matrix of the ML estimator of $\boldsymbol{\theta}$ is

$$\mathbf{V}^* = -\left[E\left[\frac{\partial^2 L}{\partial\boldsymbol{\theta}\partial\boldsymbol{\theta}'}\right]\right]^{-1} = \left[\frac{1}{\lambda^2} \sum_{t=1}^{T} \frac{\partial(\mathbf{X}_t\boldsymbol{\theta})'}{\partial\boldsymbol{\theta}} \boldsymbol{\Omega}^{-1} \frac{\partial(\mathbf{X}_t\boldsymbol{\theta})}{\partial\boldsymbol{\theta}'}\right]^{-1}.$$

The ML estimator of $\boldsymbol{\theta}$ is obtained by means of Newton's scheme based on successive estimates of $\mathbf{V}^*$ and λ^2. The asymptotic standard errors are the square roots of the diagonal elements of $\mathbf{V}^*$ with ML-estimates substituted for the unknown parameters in $\mathbf{V}^*$.

When constants are included, the adjustments are exactly the same as those presented at the end of Appendix A4.1.

References

Barnard, G.A. (1963). 'In discussion,' *Journal of the Royal Statistical Society*, Series B, 25: 294.

Barten, A.P. (1969). 'Maximum Likelihood Estimation of a Complete System of Demand Equations,' *European Economic Review* 1: 7-73.

Barten, A.P. (1977). 'The Systems of Consumer Demand Functions Approach: A Review,' *Econometrica* 45: 23-51.

Barten, A.P. and H. Theil (1964). 'Simultaneous Estimation of a Complete System of Demand Equations,' unpublished manuscript, Econometric Institute Report 6405, Netherlands School of Economics.

Bera, A.K., R.P. Byron and C.M. Jarque (1981). 'Further Evidence on Asymptotic Tests for Homogeneity and Symmetry in Large Demand Systems,' *Economics Letters* 8: 101-105.

Besag, J. and P.J. Diggle (1977). 'Simple Monte Carlo Tests for Spatial Patterns,' *Applied Statistics* 26: 327-333.

Bewley, R.A. (1983). 'Tests of Restrictions in Large Demand System,' *European Economic Review* 20: 257-269.

Deaton A. (1975). *Models and Projections of Demand in Post-War Britain*, Chapman and Hall, London.

Laitinen, K. (1978). 'Why is Demand Homogeneity So Often Rejected?' *Economics Letters* 1: 187-191.

Marriot, F.H.C. (1979). 'Barnard's Monte Carlo Tests: How Many Simulations?' *Applied Statistics* 28: 75-77.

Meisner, J.F. (1979). 'The Sad Fate of the Asymptotic Slutsky Symmetry Test for Large Systems,' *Economics Letters* 2: 231-233.

Selvanathan, E.A. (1985). 'An Even Simpler Differential Demand System,' *Economics Letters* 19: 343-347.

Selvanathan, E.A. (1987). *Explorations in Consumer Demand*, Ph.D. Thesis, Murdoch University, Western Australia.

Selvanathan, S. (1987). 'A Monte Carlo Test of Preference Independence,' *Economics Letters* 25: 259-261.

Selvanathan, S. (1988). *A System-Wide Analysis of International and Interregional Consumption Patterns*, Ph.D. Thesis, The University of Western Australia.

Selvanathan, S. (1991). 'The Reliability of ML Estimators of Systems of Demand Equations: Evidence from 18 Countries,' *Review of Economics and Statistics*, LXXIII: 338-346.

Selvanathan, S. (1993). *A System-Wide Analysis of International Consumption Patterns*, Kluwer Academic Publishers, Boston.

Theil, H. (1967). *Economics and Information Theory*, North-Holland Publishing Company, Amsterdam.

Theil, H. (1971). *Principles of Econometrics*, John Wiley and Sons, New York.

Theil, H. (1980). *The System-Wide Approach to Microeconomics*. University of Chicago Press, Chicago.

Theil, H. (1987). 'The Economics of Demand Systems,' Chapter 3 in H. Theil, H. and K.W. Clements (eds.), *Applied Demand Analysis: Results from System-wide Approaches*, Ballinger Publishing Company, Cambridge, MA.

Theil, H. and R.B. Brooks (1970/71). 'How Does the Marginal Utility of Income Change When Real Income Changes?' *European Economic Review* 2: 218-240.

Working, H. (1943). 'Statistical Laws of Family Expenditure,' *Journal of the American Statistical Association* 38: 43-56.

5 Undersized Samples and Demand Analysis

C. Dongling
Economic Research Centre, The University of Western Australia.

5.1 Introduction

To estimate the model $y_t = \Sigma_{i=1}^{k} \beta_i x_{ti} + \varepsilon_t$ (t = 1,...T observations) by least squares, the $T \times k$ matrix of independent variables $[x_{ti}]$ must be of full column rank. This requires that the number of observations T exceeds k, the number of independent variables. If this condition is not satisfied, the sample is said to be *undersized.*

Consider a system of demand equations of the form $q_{it} = \alpha_i + \beta_i Q_t + \Sigma_{j=1}^{n} \gamma_{ij} p_{jt} + \varepsilon_{it}$ (i = 1,...,n goods; t = 1,...,T years). Here there are $n \times T$ data points and $n(2 + n)$ unknown parameters. Thus it would seem that for the sample not be undersized we need $nT > n(2 + n)$ or $T > 2 + n$, which is equivalent to the single–equation case above with $k = 2 + n$. In a demand system, however, there are two additional complications: (i) There are cross–equation restrictions on the parameters; and (ii) the disturbance terms ε_{it} are correlated across equations due to the budget constraint. These complications mean that the n equations of the system have to be estimated simultaneously using the information contained in the $n \times n$ disturbance covariance matrix, to be denoted by Σ. The joint estimation of Σ together with the parameters of the system has more stringent data requirements. Accordingly, the problem of undersized samples is of practical importance in demand analysis. For example, Deaton (1975) applied the linear expenditure system with n = 37 goods; as there were only T = 17 years of data, to estimate he had to (loosely speaking) fix the covariance matrix in advance.

As Theil (1987) points out, until recently the area of estimation and testing in demand systems was thought to be well understood. In the linear case, it belonged to the domain of seemingly unrelated regressions or, if there were nonlinearities, maximum likelihood. However, a series of highly influential simulation studies by Theil and his associates (Fiebig and Theil, 1983; Laitinen, 1978; Meisner, 1979; and Theil, 1987) showed that these standard methods perform very poorly when the size of the system (n) is large relative to the number of observations. These studies revealed that (i) the conventional tests of homogeneity and symmetry are seriously biased against the null; and (ii) the standard errors of the estimators grossly understate the true sampling variability. The source of the problem is the estimation of the n^2 elements of the disturbance covariance matrix Σ. Basically, the problem is one of attempting to estimate too much with too little data, or, in other words, an undersized (or near undersized) sample.

As a demand system has the same structure as a reduced form, undersized samples in demand analysis is closely related to the question of sample size requirements for the simultaneous equation model. Key references in this area include Brown (1981), Klein (1971), Maddala (1981), Sargan (1975), Swamy and Holmes (1971) and Theil and Laitinen (1980).

In this chapter, we estimate a demand system for the world as a whole by using the Lluch, Powell and Williams (1977, hereafter LPW) cross–country data. As the number of goods is large relative to the number of countries, the sample is undersized and the usual GLS estimators are undefined. Various specifications of the disturbance covariance matrix are investigated as solutions to the problem. The structure of the chapter is as follows. In Section 5.2 we introduce the demand model, the database and the initial estimates. Details of the estimation procedures and alternative covariance matrices are given in the next two sections. The latter parts of the chapter contain extensive simulation results which evaluate the performance of the various covariance matrices.

5.2 Working's Model

For good i, the Working's (1943) model takes the form [see equation (2.1) of Chapter 4]

$$y_{it} = \beta_i DQ_t + \sum_{j=1}^{n} \pi_{ij} Dp_{jt} + \varepsilon_{it}, \tag{2.1}$$

where $y_{it} = \bar{w}_{it}(Dq_{it} - DQ_t)$; β_i is the income coefficient of i; π_{ij} is the (i,j)-*th* Slutsky coefficient; and ε_{ij} is a zero–mean disturbance.

As each equation of (2.1) has the same explanatory variables, it can be estimated by single–equation least square (LS). We apply it to the cross–coutry data of LPW for 8 commodity groups and 13 countries. This involves using the within–country mean for each variable and reinterpreting t as a country subscript; thus, n=8 and T=13. See Chapter 2 for details of the LPW data. The first part of Table 5.1 gives the estimates. As can be seen, only few of the coefficients are significant which is not surprising with 13 observations.

We now impose the homogeneity restriction $\Sigma_{j=1}^{n}\pi_{ij} = 0$, i=1,...,n. Equation (2.1) then becomes

$$y_{it} = \beta_i DQ_t + \sum_{j=1}^{n-1} \pi_{ij}(Dp_{jt} - Dp_{nt}) + \varepsilon_{it}, \tag{2.2}$$

which can also be estimated by LS. The second part of Table 5.1 contains the results. There is now some improvement in the precision of the estimates.

Next, we impose Slutsky symmetry $\pi_{ij} = \pi_{ji}$, i,j=1,...,n. As this is a cross–equation restriction, single–equation LS is no longer applicable. We use a systems GLS procedure which involves the inverse of the unknown covariance matrix of disturbances. Due to the undersized sample, the usual GLS estimator of this matrix is singular and thus can not be used. The GLS estimator uses residuals from the homogeneity–constrained model; instead, we use residuals from the preference independence version of the demand model; see the next section for details. The third part of Table 5.1 contains the symmetry–constrained estimates. There is a further improvement in the estimates, but still one diagonal Slutsky coefficient has wrong sign.

Finally, we impose preference independence. The Slutsky coefficients then take the form

$$\pi_{ij} = \phi(\beta_i + \bar{w}_{it})(\delta_{ij} - \beta_j - \bar{w}_{jt}), \tag{2.3}$$

where ϕ is the income flexibility; and δ_{ij} is the Kronecker delta, see equation (8.1) of Chapter 4. Let $DP'_t = \Sigma_{i=1}^n(\beta_i + \bar{w}_{it})Dp_{it}$ be the Frisch price index. Substituting (2.3) into (2.1) then yields the demand equation for good i under preference independence:

$$y_{it} = \beta_i DQ_t + \phi(\beta_i + \bar{w}_{it})(Dp_{it} - DP'_t) + \varepsilon_{it}. \tag{2.4}$$

The model becomes nonlinear in the parameters ϕ, $\beta_1,\ldots,\beta_n$ and we use an ML estimation procedure described in the next section. This yields $\hat{\phi} = -.240$ with asymptotic standard error .057. The estimates of β_i are given in the fourth part of column 2 of Table 5.1; the Slutsky coefficients given in this part of the table are computed from the estimates of ϕ and the β_i according to equation (2.3) with the budget shares $\bar{w}_{it}$ replaced with their means over the 13 countries, $\bar{w}_i$. The imposition of preference independence substantially reduces the standard errors, especially for the Slutsky coefficients.

Table 5.1 Estimates of Demand Equations for 8 Commodities (Standard errors are in parentheses)

Commodity	Income coefficient	Slutsky coefficients							
	β_i	π_{i1}	π_{i2}	π_{i3}	π_{i4}	π_{i5}	π_{i6}	π_{i7}	π_{i8}
(1)	(2)	(3)	(4)	(5)	(6)	(7)	(8)	(9)	(10)
				Unrestricted					
Food	-9.68	.21	18.02	9.61	-7.65	-8.50	-6.49	-7.91	1.35
	(6.11)	(12.65)	(10.18)	(7.00)	(9.60)	(6.60)	(11.00)	(12.74)	(10.43)
Clothing	4.70	-1.60	-8.09	-5.62	7.49	2.74	4.82	-2.57	1.20
	(1.65)	(3.42)	(2.75)	(1.89)	(2.59)	(1.78)	(2.97)	(3.44)	(2.82)
Housing	1.34	-4.02	1.19	.52	3.32	2.18	-3.22	-2.03	.79
	(3.42)	(7.07)	(5.69)	(3.91)	(5.36)	(3.69)	(6.15)	(7.12)	(5.83)
Durables	-.31	4.60	-3.02	-.71	-4.77	-1.02	5.70	.31	.31
	(1.90)	(3.93)	(3.16)	(2.18)	(2.98)	(2.05)	(3.42)	(3.96)	(3.24)
Personal care	-.69	3.51	3.31	3.46	-2.59	-1.88	-5.99	-2.00	3.00
	(.99)	(2.04)	(1.64)	(1.13)	(1.55)	(1.06)	(1.77)	(2.05)	(1.68)
Transport	2.18	-.69	-5.29	-.73	.56	1.36	.38	10.81	-3.77
	(3.27)	(6.76)	(5.44)	(3.74)	(5.13)	(3.53)	(5.88)	(6.81)	(5.58)
Recreation	1.93	.36	-2.96	-5.29	1.40	2.69	6.95	-1.91	-1.26
	(1.61)	(3.32)	(2.67)	(1.84)	(2.52)	(1.73)	(2.89)	(3.35)	(2.74)
Other services	.54	-2.51	-3.04	-1.24	2.14	2.44	-2.17	5.27	-1.46
	(1.60)	(3.31)	(2.66)	(1.83)	(2.51)	(1.73)	(2.88)	(3.33)	(2.73)
				Homogeneity imposed					
Food	-11.19	3.37	17.68	10.61	-8.59	-9.38	-5.66	-8.15	.10
	(4.45)	(9.17)	(9.26)	(6.00)	(8.51)	(5.71)	(9.87)	(11.62)	(9.12)
Clothing	2.89	2.16	-8.49	-4.43	6.37	1.71	5.81	-2.86	-.28
	(1.59)	(3.27)	(3.31)	(2.14)	(3.04)	(2.04)	(3.52)	(4.15)	(3.25)
Housing	-.06	-1.10	.88	1.45	2.46	1.37	-2.45	-2.25	-.36
	(2.57)	(5.30)	(5.36)	(3.47)	(4.92)	(3.30)	(5.71)	(6.72)	(5.27)
Durables	1.23	1.38	-2.69	-1.73	-3.82	-.13	4.85	.55	1.58
	(1.63)	(3.36)	(3.40)	(2.20)	(3.12)	(2.09)	(3.62)	(4.26)	(3.34)
Personal care	.22	1.61	3.51	2.86	-2.02	-1.35	-6.49	-1.86	3.75
	(.88)	(1.82)	(1.84)	(1.19)	(1.69)	(1.14)	(1.96)	(2.31)	(1.81)
Transport	5.07	-6.71	-4.66	-2.63	2.34	3.02	-1.21	11.26	-1.40
	(2.88)	(5.95)	(6.01)	(3.89)	(5.53)	(3.70)	(6.41)	(7.54)	(5.91)
Recreation	1.90	.41	-2.97	-5.27	1.38	2.68	6.97	-1.91	-1.28
	(1.14)	(2.36)	(2.38)	(1.54)	(2.19)	(1.47)	(2.54)	(2.99)	(2.35)
Other services	-.09	-1.19	-3.18	-.82	1.74	2.07	-1.82	5.17	-1.98
	(1.20)	(2.47)	(2.50)	(1.62)	(2.30)	(1.54)	(2.66)	(3.14)	(2.46)

All the entries are to be divided by 100.

(continued)

Table 5.1 (Cont.)

Commodity	Income coefficient	Slutsky coefficients							
	β_i	r_{i1}	r_{i2}	r_{i3}	r_{i4}	r_{i5}	r_{i6}	r_{i7}	r_{i8}
(1)	(2)	(3)	(4)	(5)	(6)	(7)	(8)	(9)	(10)
				Symmetry imposed					
Food	-11.89	-6.88	4.72	2.96	.80	-.44	-3.52	2.13	.22
	(2.35)	(6.30)	(3.08)	(2.55)	(2.34)	(1.84)	(3.69)	(2.90)	(1.97)
Clothing	.54		-6.48	-1.80	1.09	1.73	2.93	-.45	-1.74
	(1.43)		(3.51)	(1.87)	(2.10)	(1.83)	(2.88)	(2.31)	(1.56)
Housing	-1.90			1.26	-.14	.77	.25	-3.15	-.15
	(1.16)			(1.95)	(1.46)	(1.13)	(2.31)	(1.58)	(1.13)
Durables	2.40				-3.65	-.78	1.77	-.89	1.80
	(1.17)				(2.23)	(1.22)	(2.08)	(1.80)	(1.29)
Personal care	.73					-1.62	-1.98	1.12	1.20
	(.93)					(1.35)	(1.68)	(1.39)	(.98)
Transport	8.07						-2.44	4.06	-1.07
	(1.63)						(4.14)	(2.34)	(1.71)
Recreation	1.40							-3.52	.69
	(1.26)							(2.72)	(1.61)
Other services	.65								-.95
	(1.15)								(1.84)
				Preference independence imposed					
Food	-12.67	-4.97	.80	1.01	.63	.41	1.14	.64	.35
	(1.89)	(1.36)	(.22)	(.26)	(.18)	(.14)	(.38)	(.21)	(.12)
Clothing	1.20		-2.42	.39	.24	.16	.44	.25	.14
	(.81)		(.57)	(.10)	(.05)	(.04)	(.10)	(.06)	(.03)
Housing	-1.40			-2.94	.31	.20	.56	.31	.17
	(.81)			(.72)	(.07)	(.06)	(.15)	(.08)	(.05)
Durables	3.07				-1.95	.12	.35	.19	.11
	(.54)				(.44)	(.03)	(.06)	(.04)	(.02)
Personal care	.91					-1.31	.23	.13	.07
	(.54)					(.35)	(.05)	(.03)	(.02)
Transport	6.03						-3.25	.35	.19
	(1.12)						(.84)	(.07)	(.04)
Recreation	2.34							-1.97	.11
	(.70)							(.50)	(.03)
Other Services	.51								-1.12
	(.56)								(.30)
Income flexibility ϕ	-23.96								
	(5.69)								

All the entries are to be divided by 100. The standard errors in the last part of the table (preference independence imposed) are asymptotic.

5.3 Estimation Procedures

As (2.1) for i=1,...,n is an allocation model, one equation can be deleted. We delete the n-*th* equation. Let $y_i = [y_{it}]$ be a T–vector, $\mathbf{Y} = [y_1, ..., y_{n-1}]$, $\mathbf{DQ} = [DQ_t]$, $\mathbf{Dp}_i = [Dp_{it}]$, $\mathbf{X} = [\mathbf{DQ}, \mathbf{Dp}_1, ..., \mathbf{Dp}_n]$, $\gamma_i = [\beta_i, \pi_{i1}, ..., \pi_{in}]'$, $\mathbf{G} = [\gamma_1, ..., \gamma_{n-1}]$, $\varepsilon_i = [\varepsilon_{it}]$ and $\mathbf{E} = [\varepsilon_1, ..., \varepsilon_{n-1}]$. We can then write (2.1) for i=1,...,n-1 and t=1,...,T as $\mathbf{Y} = \mathbf{XG} + \mathbf{E}$ or

$$y = (\mathbf{I} \otimes \mathbf{X})\gamma + \varepsilon, \tag{3.1}$$

where $y = \text{vec}\, \mathbf{Y}$, $\gamma = \text{vec}\, \mathbf{G}$ and $\varepsilon = \text{vec}\, \mathbf{E}$.

When homogeneity is imposed on (2.1) we obtain (2.2). This can be written in the same form as (3.1):

$$y = (\mathbf{I} \otimes \mathbf{X}^*)\gamma^* + \varepsilon^*, \tag{3.2}$$

where y is as before; $\mathbf{X}^*$ is a $T \times n$ matrix whose t-*th* row equals (DQ_t, $Dp_{1t} - Dp_{nt}, ..., Dp_{n-1,t} - Dp_{nt}$); and γ^* is an n(n-1)–vector consisting of n-1 subvectors $\gamma_i^* = [\beta_i, \pi_{i1}, ..., \pi_{i,n-1}]'$. We assume that the disturbances ε^* are normally distributed with $E(\varepsilon^*) = 0$ and var $\varepsilon^* = \Sigma \otimes \mathbf{I}_T$.

The symmetry restriction takes the form

$$\mathbf{R}\gamma^* = 0, \tag{3.3}$$

where $\mathbf{R}$ is a $q \times n(n-1)$ matrix with $q = (n-1)(n-2)/2$; each row of $\mathbf{R}$ consists of zeros except a 1 and a -1 corresponding to π_{ij} and π_{ji} for some $i \neq j$ (the non–zero elements of $\mathbf{R}$ take the form $r_{ij} = 1$, $r_{ik} = -1$, where $j = (\ell-1)n+m+1$ and $k = (m-1)n+\ell+1$ for $i = 1,...,(n-1)(n-2)/2$, $\ell = 1,...,n-1$ and $m = \ell+1,...,n-1$). If Σ is known, the symmetry–constrained ML estimator of γ^* in (3.2) is equivalent to the GLS estimator:

$$\hat{\gamma}^* = \mathbf{d} - \mathrm{C}(\Sigma)\mathbf{R}'[\mathbf{R}\mathrm{C}(\Sigma)\mathbf{R}']^{-1}\mathbf{R}\mathbf{d}, \tag{3.4}$$

where $\mathbf{d} = \mathrm{vec}[(\mathbf{X}^{*\prime}\mathbf{X}^*)^{-1}\mathbf{X}^{*\prime}\mathbf{Y}]$ and $\mathrm{C}(\Sigma) = \Sigma \otimes (\mathbf{X}^{*\prime}\mathbf{X}^*)^{-1}$.

The covariance matrix of $\hat{\gamma}^*$ is

$$\mathrm{var}\,\hat{\gamma}^* = \mathrm{C}(\Sigma) - \mathrm{C}(\Sigma)\mathbf{R}'[\mathbf{R}\mathrm{C}(\Sigma)\mathbf{R}']^{-1}\mathbf{R}\mathrm{C}(\Sigma). \tag{3.5}$$

If Σ is unknown it is usually replaced in (3.4) and (3.5) with its GLS estimator:

$$\hat{\Sigma} = \frac{1}{T-n}\hat{\mathbf{E}}'\hat{\mathbf{E}}, \tag{3.6}$$

where $\hat{\mathbf{E}}$ is the $T \times (n-1)$ matrix of homogeneity–constrained LS residuals. ML obtains by replacing (T-n) with T in (3.6) and then iterating between that equation and (3.4).

Both GLS and ML require that $\mathbf{A} = \mathbf{R}\mathrm{C}(\hat{\Sigma})\mathbf{R}'$ be nonsingular. In the context of the unrestricted model (2.1) for i=1,...,n-1, Laitinen (1978) shows that the condition for the GLS estimator of the disturbance covariance matrix to be nonsingular is $T \geq 2n$. For the homogeneity–constrained model, this becomes $T \geq 2n - 1$. This is a sufficient, not necessary, condition for $|\mathbf{A}| \neq 0$. A necessary, but not sufficient, condition for $|\mathbf{A}| \neq 0$ is when $T \geq 3(n-1)/2 + 1/n$; see Appendix A5.1 for details. Our case, $T = 13$ and $n = 8$, falls in between the sufficient and necessary conditions. With our data the rank of $\mathbf{A}$ is equal to 20, less than its order of 21; hence $|\mathbf{A}| = 0$. One way of dealing with the undersized sample is to estimate the covariance matrix by using the residuals from the preference–independence version of the model, $\tilde{\mathbf{E}}$, rather than their homogeneity–constrained counterparts $\hat{\mathbf{E}}$. This yields

$$\hat{\Sigma}_1 = \frac{1}{T}\tilde{\mathbf{E}}'\tilde{\mathbf{E}}. \tag{3.7}$$

The results given in the third part of Table 5.1 are obtained by using $\hat{\Sigma}_1$ to replace Σ in equations (3.4) and (3.5). There are n unconstrained parameters in equation (2.4) for i=1,...,n-1, viz. $\beta_1,\ldots,\beta_{n-1}$ and ϕ. Consequently, there are n/(n-1) parameters per equation; and the degrees of freedom for the sum of squared residuals of each equation is approximately equal to T - n/(n-1). In (3.7) we approximate this by T as $n/(n-1) \approx 1$ for n=8.

The demand model under preference independence is (2.4). Using $\Sigma_{j=1}^{n}(\beta_j + \bar{w}_{jt}) = 1$, this can be written as

$$y_{it} = \beta_i DQ_t + \phi(\beta_i + \bar{w}_{it})\left[Dp^*_{it} - \sum_{j=1}^{n-1}(\beta_j + \bar{w}_{jt})Dp^*_{jt}\right] + \varepsilon_{it}, \tag{3.8}$$

where $Dp^*_{it} = Dp_{it} - Dp_{nt}$. Let

$$a_{it} = (\beta_i + \bar{w}_{it})\left[Dp^*_{it} - \sum_{j=1}^{n-1}(\beta_j + \bar{w}_{jt})Dp^*_{jt}\right],$$

so that (3.8) becomes $y_{it} = \beta_i DQ_t + \phi a_{it} + \varepsilon_{it}$. We write (3.8) for t=1,...T, in vector form as

$$\mathbf{y}_i = \mathbf{Z}_i \boldsymbol{\theta}_i + \boldsymbol{\varepsilon}_i, \tag{3.9}$$

where $\mathbf{y}_i = [y_{it}]$ is a T–vector; $\mathbf{Z}_i = [\mathbf{DQ}, \mathbf{a}_i]$ is a $T \times 2$ matrix with $\mathbf{DQ} = [DQ_t]$ and $\mathbf{a}_i = [a_{it}]$ being T–vectors; $\boldsymbol{\theta}_i = [\beta_i \ \phi]'$ is a vector of two parameters; and $\boldsymbol{\varepsilon}_i = [\varepsilon_{it}]$ is a T–vector. If we sum both sides of equation (3.8) over i=1,...,n, we get $\Sigma_{i=1}^{n}\varepsilon_{it} = 0$ for t=1,...,T, where we have used $\Sigma_{i=1}^{n}\beta_i = \Sigma_{i=1}^{n}a_{it} = 0$. Therefore the ε_{it}'s are linearly dependent and we need only consider equations (3.8) and (3.9) for i=1,...,n-1. We write (3.9) for i=1,...,n-1 as

$$\mathbf{y} = \mathbf{Z}\boldsymbol{\theta} + \boldsymbol{\varepsilon}, \tag{3.10}$$

where $\mathbf{y} = [\mathbf{y}_1',...,\mathbf{y}_{n-1}']'$; $\mathbf{Z} = \text{diag}[\mathbf{Z}_1,...,\mathbf{Z}_{n-1}]$; $\boldsymbol{\theta} = [\boldsymbol{\theta}_1',...,\boldsymbol{\theta}_{n-1}']'$ and $\boldsymbol{\varepsilon} = [\boldsymbol{\varepsilon}_1',...,\boldsymbol{\varepsilon}_{n-1}']'$.

Let $\boldsymbol{\varepsilon}_t = [\varepsilon_{1t},...,\varepsilon_{n-1,t}]'$ be a vector of the n-1 error terms at time t. If $\boldsymbol{\varepsilon}_1,...,\boldsymbol{\varepsilon}_T$ are independent normal vectors with zero mean and nonsingular covariance matrix $\boldsymbol{\Sigma}$, the log–likelihood function is then

$$\ell(\boldsymbol{\theta},\boldsymbol{\Sigma};\mathbf{y}) = \text{constant} - \frac{T}{2}\log|\boldsymbol{\Sigma}| - \frac{1}{2}(\mathbf{y} - \mathbf{Z}\boldsymbol{\theta})'(\boldsymbol{\Sigma}^{-1} \otimes \mathbf{I})(\mathbf{y} - \mathbf{Z}\boldsymbol{\theta}), \tag{3.11}$$

with

$$\frac{\partial \ell}{\partial \boldsymbol{\theta}'} = (\mathbf{y} - \mathbf{Z}\boldsymbol{\theta})'(\boldsymbol{\Sigma}^{-1} \otimes \mathbf{I})\frac{\partial(\mathbf{Z}\boldsymbol{\theta})}{\partial \boldsymbol{\theta}'}. \tag{3.12}$$

The (i,j)-*th* block of the matrix $\partial(\mathbf{Z}\boldsymbol{\theta})/\partial\boldsymbol{\theta}'$ is

$$\frac{\partial(\mathbf{Z}_i\boldsymbol{\theta}_i)}{\partial\boldsymbol{\theta}_j'} = \left[\delta_{ij}\mathbf{DQ} + \phi\frac{\partial \mathbf{a}_i}{\partial \beta_j}, \mathbf{a}_i\right],$$

with $\partial \mathbf{a}_i/\partial\beta_j = [\partial a_{it}/\partial\beta_j]$; and $\partial a_{it}/\partial\beta_j = -(\bar{w}_{it} + \beta_i)Dp_{jt}^* + \delta_{ij}\left[Dp_{it}^* - \sum_{k=1}^{n-1}(\bar{w}_{kt} + \beta_k)Dp_{kt}^*\right]$, where δ_{ij} is the Kronecker delta.

Since $E(\mathbf{y} - \mathbf{Z}\boldsymbol{\theta}) = E(\boldsymbol{\varepsilon}) = \mathbf{0}$, equation (3.12) implies that the matrix $\partial^2\ell/\partial\boldsymbol{\theta}\partial\boldsymbol{\Sigma}^{-1}$ has zero expectation. Consequently, the information matrix of the maximum likelihood (ML) procedure is block–diagonal with respect to $\boldsymbol{\theta}$ and $\boldsymbol{\Sigma}^{-1}$ and the asymptotic covariance matrix of the ML estimate of $\boldsymbol{\theta}$ is

$$\mathbf{V} = \left[-E\left[\frac{\partial^2 \ell}{\partial\boldsymbol{\theta}\partial\boldsymbol{\theta}'}\right]\right]^{-1} = \left[\frac{\partial(\mathbf{Z}\boldsymbol{\theta})'}{\partial\boldsymbol{\theta}}(\boldsymbol{\Sigma}^{-1} \otimes \mathbf{I})\frac{\partial(\mathbf{Z}\boldsymbol{\theta})}{\partial\boldsymbol{\theta}'}\right]^{-1}. \tag{3.13}$$

Setting $\partial\ell/\partial\boldsymbol{\Sigma}^{-1} = \mathbf{0}$ yields (3.7). The ML estimates are obtained by setting (3.12) to zero and successively estimating $\boldsymbol{\Sigma}$ and $\mathbf{V}$ using Newton's method.

The estimates of β_i and ϕ given in the fourth part of Table 5.1 are the ML estimates under preference independence; the standard errors are the square roots of the diagonal elements of **V**, defined in (3.13), with ML–estimates substituted for unknown parameters. The corresponding Slutsky coefficients are computed according to equation (2.3) with budget shares replaced with their cross–country means; see Appendix 5.2 for details of the asymptotic standard errors of these coefficients.

5.4 Alternative Covariance Matrices

In addition to covariance matrix Σ_1, we also use

$$\Sigma_2 = \sigma_2^2(\mathbf{I} - n^{-1}\boldsymbol{\iota}\boldsymbol{\iota}'), \tag{4.1}$$

$$\Sigma_3 = \sigma_3^2(\bar{\mathbf{W}} - \bar{\mathbf{w}}\,\bar{\mathbf{w}}'), \tag{4.2}$$

$$\Sigma_4 = \mathbf{D} - k^{-1}\mathbf{d}\mathbf{d}', \tag{4.3}$$

where σ_2^2 and σ_3^2 are unknown parameters; **I** is the $n \times n$ identity matrix; $\boldsymbol{\iota}$ is an n–vector of unit elements; $\bar{\mathbf{W}} = \text{diag}[\,\bar{\mathbf{w}}\,]$, with $\bar{\mathbf{w}} = [\,\bar{w}_i\,]$ an n–vector of mean budget shares; $\mathbf{D} = \text{diag}[\mathbf{d}]$, $k = \boldsymbol{\iota}'\mathbf{d}$ and $\mathbf{d} = [d_i]$ is an n–vector of parameters.

Equation (4.1) is an augmented identity matrix and has been used by Deaton (1975) and Theil (1987). In equation (4.2) the variances and covariances are allowed to vary with the relative sizes of the commodity groups, as measured by the budget shares (Barten and Theil, 1964; Deaton, 1975; S. Selvanathan, 1988; and Theil, 1987). Specification (4.3) was introduced by de Boer and Harkema (1986a, 1986b, 1990) and is obviously a generalization of Σ_2 and Σ_3. These covariance matrices Σ_i (i=2,...,4) are all $n \times n$ and the last row and column is to be deleted when they replace Σ in (3.4) and (3.5).

To apply Σ_i defined in (4.1)–(4.3), we need estimates of the additional unknown parameters. Let α_2 be $(\mathbf{I} - n^{-1}\iota\iota')$ with the last row and column deleted; and α_3 be $(\bar{\mathbf{W}} - \bar{\mathbf{w}}\,\bar{\mathbf{w}}')$ also with the last row and column deleted. Then the GLS estimator of σ_i^2 in (4.1) and (4.2) is

$$\hat{\sigma}_i^2 = \frac{1}{(T-n-1)(n-1)}\,\hat{\varepsilon}'(\alpha_i^{-1} \otimes I)\hat{\varepsilon}, \qquad i=2,3, \tag{4.4}$$

where $\hat{\varepsilon}$ is the T(n-1)–vector of homogeneity–constrained LS residuals and I is the identity matrix of order T. The estimator of k and the d_i in (4.3) is obtained from (de Boer and Harkema, 1986b)

$$\hat{d}_i - \frac{1}{\hat{k}}\hat{d}_i^2 = \frac{1}{T}\hat{\varepsilon}_i'\hat{\varepsilon}_i, \qquad i=1,\ldots,n, \tag{4.5}$$

where $\hat{\varepsilon}_i$ is the i-*th* sub–vector of $\hat{\varepsilon}$.

We use (4.4) and (4.5) in (4.1)–(4.3) to yield three additional estimators of the covariance matrix $\hat{\Sigma}_i$. These then replace Σ in (3.4) and (3.5) to yield three additional sets of symmetry–constrained estimates and covariance matrices for the cross–country data. Table 5.2 presents the results. For convenience, the upper part of this table reproduces the estimates from the third part of Table 5.1 which use $\hat{\Sigma}_1$, the preference independence covariance matrix.

5.5 A Simulation Experiment

In this section we conduct a Monte Carlo simulation experiment to analyse the quality of the estimates.

This and the subsequent two sections deal exclusively with symmetry–constrained estimation. Thus, in order to simplify the notation, we write $\hat{\gamma}$ for the symmetry–constrained estimator, defined by

Table 5.2 Four Sets of Symmetry Constrained Estimates of Demand Equations for 8 Commodities (Standard errors are in parentheses)

Commodity	Income coefficient	Slutsky coefficients							
	β_i	τ_{i1}	τ_{i2}	τ_{i3}	τ_{i4}	τ_{i5}	τ_{i6}	τ_{i7}	τ_{i8}
(1)	(2)	(3)	(4)	(5)	(6)	(7)	(8)	(9)	(10)
				$\hat{\Sigma}_1$ (Preference Independence)					
Food	-11.89	-6.88	4.72	2.96	.80	-.44	-3.52	2.13	.22
	(2.35)	(6.30)	(3.08)	(2.55)	(2.34)	(1.84)	(3.69)	(2.90)	(1.97)
Clothing	.54		-6.48	-1.80	1.09	1.73	2.93	-.45	-1.74
	(1.43)		(3.51)	(1.87)	(2.10)	(1.83)	(2.88)	(2.31)	(1.56)
Housing	1.90			1.26	-.14	.77	.25	-3.15	-.15
	(1.16)			(1.95)	(1.46)	(1.13)	(2.31)	(1.58)	(1.13)
Durables	2.40				-3.65	-.78	1.77	-.89	1.80
	(1.17)				(2.23)	(1.22)	(2.08)	(1.80)	(1.29)
Personal care	.73					-1.62	-1.98	1.12	1.20
	(.93)					(1.35)	(1.68)	(1.39)	(.98)
Transport	8.07						-2.44	4.06	-1.08
	(1.63)						(4.14)	(2.34)	(1.71)
Recreation	1.40							-3.52	.69
	(1.26)							(2.72)	(1.61)
Other services	.65								-.95
	(1.15)								(1.84)
				$\hat{\Sigma}_2$ (Augmented Identity)					
Food	-10.48	-1.76	8.72	6.40	-.99	-5.18	-3.87	-2.80	-.52
	(1.93)	(4.13)	(3.05)	(2.22)	(3.07)	(2.27)	(3.21)	(3.62)	(2.97)
Clothing	1.24		-5.30	-.06	1.41	1.40	-.27	-4.54	-1.37
	(1.94)		(4.41)	(2.25)	(3.19)	(2.49)	(3.39)	(3.43)	(3.03)
Housing	-1.34			2.52	-.54	.16	-1.58	-6.82	-.09
	(1.58)			(2.35)	(2.15)	(1.77)	(2.59)	(2.40)	(2.17)
Durables	2.24				-3.77	-.66	.88	2.94	.73
	(2.19)				(3.97)	(2.26)	(3.14)	(3.23)	(2.88)
Personal care	.34					-.44	.11	2.97	1.64
	(1.71)					(2.67)	(2.40)	(2.47)	(2.28)
Transport	6.03						-3.22	9.25	-1.30
	(1.96)						(4.87)	(3.63)	(3.21)
Recreation	2.02							-2.01	1.00
	(1.99)							(5.42)	(3.79)
Other services	-.05								-.09
	(2.27)								(4.49)

All the entries are to be divided by 100.

(*continued*)

Table 5.2 (Cont.)

Commodity	Income coefficient	Slutsky coefficients							
	β_i	π_{i1}	π_{i2}	π_{i3}	π_{i4}	π_{i5}	π_{i6}	π_{i7}	π_{i8}
(1)	(2)	(3)	(4)	(5)	(6)	(7)	(8)	(9)	(10)
				$\hat{\Sigma}_3$ (Budget Shares)					
Food	-10.67	-5.48	6.24	5.05	1.37	-2.20	-4.49	-.29	-.21
	(2.11)	(5.07)	(3.02)	(2.53)	(2.65)	(2.03)	(3.13)	(3.00)	(2.26)
Clothing	1.51		-4.23	-.28	1.30	1.44	1.00	-3.17	-2.28
	(1.59)		(3.61)	(1.96)	(2.40)	(1.86)	(2.86)	(2.56)	(2.06)
Housing	-1.13			2.56	.00	.37	-1.07	-6.19	-.45
	(1.43)			(2.27)	(1.66)	(1.32)	(2.33)	(1.85)	(1.48)
Durables	1.75				-5.00	-1.22	1.28	1.17	1.09
	(1.52)				(2.82)	(1.52)	(2.45)	(2.30)	(1.84)
Personal care	.20					-1.00	-.98	1.80	1.78
	(1.10)					(1.67)	(1.87)	(1.70)	(1.37)
Transport	6.78						-3.40	8.87	-1.20
	(1.62)						(4.23)	(2.78)	(2.25)
Recreation	1.68							-3.93	1.74
	(1.42)							(3.83)	(2.49)
Other services	-.12								-.46
	(1.36)								(2.65)
				$\hat{\Sigma}_4$ (De Boer and Harkema)					
Food	-11.45	-7.99	4.25	3.76	1.81	-.23	-3.00	.86	.54
	(1.54)	(3.71)	(1.59)	(1.79)	(1.70)	(.90)	(2.52)	(1.38)	(1.28)
Clothing	1.61		-6.30	-2.13	2.66	2.20	4.23	-2.48	-2.43
	(.80)		(1.75)	(1.06)	(1.32)	(.81)	(1.71)	(1.15)	(1.06)
Housing	-1.57			2.03	.58	1.58	-.02	-5.52	-.27
	(.92)			(1.50)	(1.07)	(.60)	(1.82)	(.87)	(.85)
Durables	1.68				-5.99	-1.58	.79	.84	.89
	(.98)				(1.77)	(.75)	(1.71)	(1.12)	(1.05)
Personal care	.18					-1.23	-4.01	1.37	1.91
	(.47)					(.64)	(.98)	(.71)	(.65)
Transport	8.04						-3.95	7.46	-1.50
	(1.23)						(3.41)	(1.39)	(1.38)
Recreation	1.80							-3.45	.93
	(.64)							(1.69)	(1.17)
Other services	-.29								-.08
	(.75)								(1.39)

All the entries are to be divided by 100.

equation (3.4), rather then $\hat{\gamma}^*$. This estimate depends on Σ, the disturbance covariance matrix, for which we have four estimators $\hat{\Sigma}_i$ (i=1,...,4). To indicate this dependence, we write $\hat{\gamma}_i$ and var $\hat{\gamma}_i$ when $\hat{\Sigma}_i$ is used in equations (3.4) and (3.5). There should be no confusion between $\hat{\gamma}_i$ here and γ_i of Section 5.3 which is the i-*th* sub–vector of γ.

The simulation proceeds as follows:

Step 1: Generate a pseudo–normal random error vector, $\tilde{\varepsilon}_i$, with zero mean and covariance matrix $\hat{\Sigma}_i \otimes \mathbf{I}_T$. This error vector has $(n-1) \times T$ elements.

Step 2: Use (i) the data–based estimates $\hat{\gamma}_i$; (ii) the observed values of the independent variables $\mathbf{X}$; and (iii) the error $\tilde{\varepsilon}_i$ to form the simulated value of the dependent variable vector as $\tilde{y}_i = (\mathbf{I} \otimes \mathbf{X})\hat{\gamma}_i + \tilde{\varepsilon}_i$ (we use a tilde (˜) to denote a simulated variable. Also, it is to be understood that $\mathbf{X}$ here is $\mathbf{X}^*$ of Section 5.3).

Step 3: Re–estimate Σ_i with $\tilde{y}_i$ and $\mathbf{X}$ by applying equation (3.7) or the procedures of Section 5.4 (as the case may be). Denote the estimate by $\hat{\Sigma}_i^*$, (we use an asterisk (*) to denote an estimate obtained with simulated data).

Step 4: Re–estimate γ and var γ with the simulated data and $\hat{\Sigma}_i^*$ by applying equations (3.4) and (3.5). Denote these estimates by $\hat{\gamma}_i^*$ and var $\hat{\gamma}_i^*$.

Step 5: Repeat Steps 1–4 N times to obtain $\hat{\gamma}_i^{*(j)}$ and var $\hat{\gamma}_i^{*(j)}$, j=1,...,N.

We start with $\hat{\Sigma}_1$, the covariance matrix based on preference independence, and perform 500 trials. Table 5.3 summarizes the results. As can be seen, the estimated bias (the mean of the 500 estimates minus

Table 5.3 Monte Carlo Simulation Results with the Preference Independence Version of the Covariance Matrix

Commodity subscripts i (1)	j (2)	True value (3)	Bias (4)	RMSE (5)	RMSSE (6)
		Income coefficients β_i			
1	-	-11.89	-.23	2.21	2.27
2	-	.54	.07	1.47	1.44
3	-	-1.90	.18	1.15	1.21
4	-	2.40	.12	1.09	1.05
5	-	.73	.14	.92	.91
6	-	8.07	-.38	1.63	1.58
7	-	1.40	.14	1.22	1.28
Average			.18	1.38	1.39
		Diagonal Slutsky coefficients π_{ii}			
1	1	-6.87	.18	5.93	6.14
2	2	-6.48	.72	3.43	3.45
3	3	1.26	-.54	1.92	2.01
4	4	-3.64	.53	2.11	1.90
5	5	-1.62	.03	1.33	1.31
6	6	-2.44	-.20	3.88	4.01
7	7	-3.51	.39	2.53	2.71
Average			.37	3.02	3.08
		Off-diagonal Slutsky coefficients π_{ij}			
1	2	4.72	-.21	2.85	3.09
1	3	2.96	-.57	2.45	2.53
1	4	.80	-.31	2.20	2.15
1	5	-.44	.06	1.74	1.80
1	6	-3.52	.81	3.45	3.50
1	7	2.12	-.19	2.83	2.98
2	3	-1.80	.42	1.92	1.83
2	4	1.08	-.34	1.98	1.85
2	5	1.73	-.31	1.78	1.77
2	6	2.93	-.62	2.80	2.80
2	7	-.44	-.05	2.21	2.29
3	4	-.14	.11	1.41	1.32
3	5	.77	-.27	1.14	1.09
3	6	.25	.23	2.12	2.23
3	7	-3.15	.57	1.61	1.63
4	5	-.78	.36	1.14	1.07
4	6	1.77	-.19	1.90	1.85
4	7	-.89	.30	1.66	1.64
5	6	-1.98	.53	1.74	1.62
5	7	1.12	-.16	1.31	1.36
6	7	4.06	-.87	2.27	2.29
Average			.36	2.02	2.03

All entries are to be divided by 100.
The average biases ignore the signs.

the true value) is very small, as it should be. The root–mean–squared errors (RMSEs) are close to the root–mean–squared standard errors (RMSSEs), thus indicating that the standard errors are on average of the correct size. The RMSSEs are obtained by summing over the 500 trials each diagonal element of the covariance matrix var $\hat{\gamma}_i^{*(j)}$ with i=1, dividing the sum by 500, and then taking the square root.

Next, we re–do the simulation with the covariance matrix $\hat{\Sigma}_1$ replaced everywhere with $\hat{\Sigma}_2$, the augmented identity matrix. This yields another set of results analogous to Table 5.3. The average biases, RMSEs and RMSSEs from this simulation are given in rows 2, 7 and 12 of Table 5.4. For convenience, rows 1, 6 and 11 of this table reproduce the averages from Table 5.3. The results for $\hat{\Sigma}_3$ and $\hat{\Sigma}_4$ are given in rows 3, 4, 8, 9, 13 and 14 of Table 5.4. The covariance matrix $\hat{\Sigma}_5$ of rows 5, 10 and 15 of the table is new; it is equal to $[T/(T\text{-}n)]\hat{\Sigma}_4$, where T is the sample size and n is the number of commodities. This $\hat{\Sigma}_5$ is a bias–adjusted version of $\hat{\Sigma}_4$.

Looking at rows 1 to 5 of Table 5.4, all the biases are, on average, very small, although those from $\hat{\Sigma}_1$ are relatively larger. Rows 6 to 10, for the RMSEs, indicate that the estimates derived from $\hat{\Sigma}_4$ are the most efficient; then follows the estimates derived from $\hat{\Sigma}_1$. A comparison of rows 6–10 with 11–15 shows that the RMSEs and RMSSEs are all very close, which indicates that the standard errors are on average of the correct size. The only exception is $\hat{\Sigma}_4$ where the RMSEs are substantially above the corresponding RMSSEs.

5.6 More Simulations

Underlying the simulations of the previous section is the true covariance matrix $\hat{\Sigma}_i$ which generates the errors $\tilde{\varepsilon}_i$. There is also the covariance

Table 5.4 Monte Carlo Simulation Results with Different Covariance Matrices

True and estimated covariance matrix (1)	Income coefficients β_i (2)	Slutsky coefficients Diagonal π_{ii} (3)	Slutsky coefficients Off-diagonal π_{ij} (4)
		Average absoluted bias	
1. $\hat{\Sigma}_1$ Preference Independence	.18	.37	.36
2. $\hat{\Sigma}_2$ Augmented Identity	.08	.09	.11
3. $\hat{\Sigma}_3$ Budget Shares	.06	.08	.09
4. $\hat{\Sigma}_4$ de Boer and Harkema	.03	.05	.05
5. $\hat{\Sigma}_5$ Bias Adjusted $\hat{\Sigma}_4$	.05	.08	.08
		Average root-mean sqared error	
6. $\hat{\Sigma}_1$ Preference Independence	1.38	3.02	2.02
7. $\hat{\Sigma}_2$ Augmented Identity	1.91	3.96	2.76
8. $\hat{\Sigma}_3$ Budget Shares	1.54	3.34	2.27
9. $\hat{\Sigma}_4$ de Boer and Harkema	.97	2.11	1.40
10. $\hat{\Sigma}_5$ Bias Adjusted $\hat{\Sigma}_4$	1.56	3.41	2.25
		Average root-mean squared standard error	
11. $\hat{\Sigma}_1$ Preference Independence	1.39	3.08	2.03
12. $\hat{\Sigma}_2$ Augmented Identity	1.88	3.94	2.75
13. $\hat{\Sigma}_3$ Budget Shares	1.53	3.33	2.26
14. $\hat{\Sigma}_4$ de Boer and Harkema	.56	1.23	.72
15. $\hat{\Sigma}_5$ Bias Adjusted $\hat{\Sigma}_4$	1.45	3.19	1.88

All entries are to be divided by 100.

estimated with the simulated data $\hat{\Sigma}_i^*$. It is to be noted that the *form* of these two matrices is the same by assumption. In most applications, however, the truth is unknown and the hope is that the form of the estimated covariance matrix at least approximates the true matrix. In this section we persue this idea by analysing the quality of the estimates when the true and estimated covariance matrices differ; consequently, in a certain sense, we make a specification error. One of our objectives is to analyse the robustness of the estimated covariance matrices with respect to the underlying true matrix.

We use a simulation procedure which is similar to that of the previous section. It involves the following steps:

Step 1: Generate a pseudo–normal random error vector, $\tilde{\varepsilon}_i$, with zero mean and covariance matrix $\hat{\Sigma}_i \otimes I_T$.

Step 2: Use (i) the data–based estimates $\hat{\gamma}_i$; (ii) the observed values of the independent variables $\mathbf{X}$; and (iii) the error $\tilde{\varepsilon}_i$ to form the simulated value of the dependent variable vector as $\tilde{y}_i = (\mathbf{I} \otimes \mathbf{X})\hat{\gamma}_i + \tilde{\varepsilon}_i$.

Step 3: Estimate Σ_j with $\tilde{y}_i$ and $\mathbf{X}$ by applying equation (3.7) or the procedures of Section 5.4. In general, Σ_j has a form different to $\hat{\Sigma}_i$, the matrix which generated $\tilde{\varepsilon}_i$. Denote the estimate of Σ_j by $\hat{\Sigma}_{ij}^*$ (i = true and j = estimated covariance matrix).

Step 4: Re–estimate γ and var γ with the simulated data and $\hat{\Sigma}_{ij}^*$ by applying equations (3.4) and (3.5). Denote these estimates by $\hat{\gamma}_{ij}^*$ and var $\hat{\gamma}_{ij}^*$.

Step 5: Repeat Steps 1–4 N times to obtain $\hat{\gamma}_{ij}^{*(k)}$ and var $\hat{\gamma}_{ij}^{*(k)}$, k=1,...,N.

Step 3 above is different to the procedure of Section 5.5. The covariance matrix $\hat{\Sigma}^*_{ij}$ from this step for i = j coincides with $\hat{\Sigma}^*_i$ of Section 5.5. Similarly, $\hat{\gamma}^*_{ii}$ is $\hat{\gamma}^*_i$ of Section 5.5.

Table 5.5 contains the results for 500 trials. This table has nine blocks. Consider the top left–hand block. The main diagonal of the 5×5 matrix in this block gives the average biases of the β_i when the five estimated and true covariance matrices coincide. These five diagonal elements are the same as the first five entries in column 2 of Table 5.4. The off–diagonal elements are the biases when the true and estimated covariances differ.

In practice we usually do not know the form of the true covariance matrix. Suppose that any of the five true covariance matrices are equally likely to occur. Continuing to concentrate on the top left–hand block of Table 5.5, the averages in column 7 then tell us which estimated covariance performs best with respect to the biases of the β_i. As can be seen, $\hat{\Sigma}_4$ and $\hat{\Sigma}_5$ are the best. This is also true for the biases of the coefficients π_{ii} and π_{ij}, but it needs to be remembered that all the biases are small.

Regarding the RMSEs, the central three blocks of Table 5.5 indicate that on average $\hat{\Sigma}_1$ produces the most efficient estimates of β_i, π_{ii} and π_{ij}. Note the tendency for the diagonal element to be the smallest in each relevant column of these blocks. This indicates that the estimates tend to be more efficient when the estimated covariance matrix is the same as the true, as expected. The bottom three blocks of the table confirm that the standard errors are, on average, of the correct size, except when $\hat{\Sigma}_4$ is used. Whenever this is the estimated covariance matrix, the standard errors substantially understate the true sampling variability of the estimates.

Our conclusions for this section are as follows: (i) The estimates based on the five covariance matrices are all approximately unbiased; (ii) on the basis of efficiency and robustness, we prefer the preference independence covariance matrix; and (iii) the de Boer and Harkema covariance matrix performs very well when it is bias corrected, but the associated standard errors are too small.

Table 5.5 Monte Carlo Simulation Results with Various Combinations of the Estimated and True Covariance Matrices

Estimated covariance matrix	Income coefficients β_i						Diagonal Slutsky coefficients π_{ii}						Off-diagonal Slutsky coefficients π_{ij}					
	True covariance matrix					Average	True covariance matrix					Average	True covariance matrix					Average
	$\hat{\Sigma}_1$	$\hat{\Sigma}_2$	$\hat{\Sigma}_3$	$\hat{\Sigma}_4$	$\hat{\Sigma}_5$		$\hat{\Sigma}_1$	$\hat{\Sigma}_2$	$\hat{\Sigma}_3$	$\hat{\Sigma}_4$	$\hat{\Sigma}_5$		$\hat{\Sigma}_1$	$\hat{\Sigma}_2$	$\hat{\Sigma}_3$	$\hat{\Sigma}_4$	$\hat{\Sigma}_5$	
(1)	(2)	(3)	(4)	(5)	(6)	(7)	(8)	(9)	(10)	(11)	(12)	(13)	(14)	(15)	(16)	(17)	(18)	(19)
							Average absolute bias											
1. $\hat{\Sigma}_1$ Preference Independence	.18	.18	.19	.20	.23	.20	.37	.54	.46	.39	.51	.45	.36	.80	.59	.42	.55	.54
2. $\hat{\Sigma}_2$ Augment Identity	.06	.08	.07	.05	.07	.07	.09	.09	.08	.05	.07	.07	.08	.11	.09	.06	.10	.09
3. $\hat{\Sigma}_3$ Budget Shares	.05	.08	.06	.04	.06	.06	.10	.09	.08	.05	.09	.08	.07	.11	.09	.05	.09	.08
4. $\hat{\Sigma}_4$ De Boer and Harkema	.06	.07	.06	.03	.05	.05	.09	.08	.07	.05	.08	.07	.09	.10	.08	.05	.08	.08
5. $\hat{\Sigma}_5$ Bias adjusted $\hat{\Sigma}_4$	.06	.07	.06	.03	.05	.05	.09	.08	.07	.05	.08	.07	.09	.10	.08	.05	.08	.08
6. Average						.09						.15						.17
							Average root-mean squared error											
7. $\hat{\Sigma}_1$ Preference Independence	1.38	1.86	1.51	1.01	1.52	1.46	3.02	3.92	3.29	2.28	3.36	3.17	2.02	2.82	2.29	1.51	2.18	2.17
8. $\hat{\Sigma}_2$ Augment Identity	1.75	1.91	1.65	1.11	1.79	1.64	3.87	3.96	3.47	2.32	3.73	3.47	2.82	2.76	2.46	1.70	2.74	2.50
9. $\hat{\Sigma}_3$ Budget Shares	1.59	2.00	1.54	.97	1.56	1.53	3.58	4.10	3.34	2.10	3.38	3.30	2.42	2.94	2.27	1.39	2.25	2.25
10. $\hat{\Sigma}_4$ De Boer and Harkema	1.61	1.99	1.60	.97	1.56	1.55	3.60	4.12	3.47	2.11	3.41	3.34	2.48	3.05	2.49	1.40	2.25	2.33
11. $\hat{\Sigma}_5$ Bias adjusted $\hat{\Sigma}_4$	1.61	1.99	1.60	.97	1.56	1.55	3.60	4.12	3.47	2.11	3.41	3.34	2.48	3.05	2.49	1.40	2.25	2.33
12. Average						1.55						3.32						2.32
							Average root-mean squared standard error											
13. $\hat{\Sigma}_1$ Preference Independence	1.39	1.93	1.58	1.16	1.59	1.53	3.08	4.08	3.48	2.67	3.52	3.37	2.03	2.82	2.33	1.78	2.27	2.25
14. $\hat{\Sigma}_2$ Augment Identity	1.80	1.88	1.67	1.18	1.90	1.69	3.76	3.94	3.50	2.46	3.96	3.52	2.62	2.75	2.44	1 72	2.77	2.46
15. $\hat{\Sigma}_3$ Budget Shares	1.48	2.05	1.53	.95	1.53	1.51	3.23	4.48	3.33	2.07	3.33	3.29	2.19	3.04	2.26	1.40	2.26	2.23
16. $\hat{\Sigma}_4$ De Boer and Harkema	.85	1.11	.90	.56	.90	.86	1.98	2.34	1.98	1.23	1.98	1.90	1.21	1.53	1.26	.72	1.17	1.18
17. $\hat{\Sigma}_5$ Bias adjusted $\hat{\Sigma}_4$	1.37	1.79	1.46	.90	1.45	1.39	3.19	3.77	3.20	1.98	3.19	3.06	1.95	2.46	2.04	1.17	1.88	1.90
18. Average						1.40						3.03						2.00

5.7 Hypothesis Testing

The log likelihood function for model (3.2) is ℓ = constant - $(T/2)\log|\Sigma| - (1/2)\varepsilon'(\Sigma^{-1} \otimes I)\varepsilon$. Substituting $\hat{\varepsilon}_i$ and $\hat{\Sigma}_i$ (i = 1,...,5) we obtain five likelihood values, which are shown in column 2 of Table 5.6. As can be seen, $\hat{\Sigma}_1$ and $\hat{\Sigma}_4$ yield the highest values. In general, however, the covariance matrices are non–nested. For instance, we cannot obtain Σ_2 by imposing restrictions on Σ_1 and vice versa. On the other hand, Σ_2 and Σ_3 are special cases of Σ_4 and Σ_5. Thus, we can test H_0: $\Sigma_i = \Sigma_j$ (i = 4,5, j = 2,3) against H_1: $\Sigma_i \neq \Sigma_j$. As can be seen from columns 3–6 of the table, we reject all the null hypotheses at the 5 percent level except in one case when we apply Italianer's (1985) correction factor to adjust for the small–sample bias of the likelihood ratio test statistic.

Next, as the likelihood ratio test is asymptotic and our sample small, we use a Monte Carlo procedure to evaluate the performance of the test under the null that the true covariance matrix is $\hat{\Sigma}_j$. The simulation procedure is same as Steps 1–4 of Section 5.6 except that now (i) we only use i = 4,5 and j = 2,3; and (ii) we have the additional steps:

<u>Step 5</u>: Form the simulated log likelihood value

$$\tilde{\ell}_{ji} = \text{constant} - \frac{T}{2}\log|\hat{\Sigma}^*_{ji}| - \frac{1}{2}\tilde{\varepsilon}_{ji}'(\hat{\Sigma}^{*-1}_{ji} \otimes I)\tilde{\varepsilon}_{ji},$$

where $\tilde{\varepsilon}_{ji} = \tilde{y}_j - (I \otimes X)\hat{\gamma}^*_{ji}$. This $\tilde{\ell}_{ji}$ is the likelihood value when $\hat{\Sigma}_j$ and $\hat{\Sigma}^*_{ji}$ are the true and estimated covariances, respectively.

<u>Step 6</u>: Compute the simulated test statistic $\tilde{\chi}^2_{ji} = -2(\tilde{\ell}_{jj} - \tilde{\ell}_{ji})$, where $\tilde{\ell}_{jj}$ is the likelihood value when $\hat{\Sigma}_j$ is simultaneously the true and estimated covariance. As the hypotheses all involve (n-1) = 7 independent restrictions, compare $\tilde{\chi}^2_{ji}$ with the critical value of the chi–square distribution with 7 degrees of

Table 5.6 Likelihood Values and Likelihood Ratio Test Statistics for Different Covariance Matrices

Covariance matrix	Log likelihood value	Likelihood ratio test statistics with the unrestricted covariance matrix specified as			
		$\hat{\Sigma}_4$		$\hat{\Sigma}_5$	
		Uncorrected	Corrected	Uncorrected	Corrected
(1)	(2)	(3)	(4)	(5)	(6)
1. $\hat{\Sigma}_1$	553.34				
2. $\hat{\Sigma}_2$	510.01	87.68*	49.62*	56.72*	32.10*
3. $\hat{\Sigma}_3$	530.16	47.37*	26.81*	16.42*	9.29
4. $\hat{\Sigma}_4$	553.85				
5. $\hat{\Sigma}_5$	538.37				

The likelihood ratio test statistic is defined as $\chi^2 = -2(\ell_r - \ell_u) \sim \chi^2(q)$, where ℓ_r and ℓ_u are the log likelihood values under null (given by the row) and the alternative (given by the column), respectively; and q is number of restrictions. The corrected likelihood ratio statistic is the uncorrected counterpart multiplied by Italianer's (1985) factor $\kappa = (df_0+df_1)/[2\times T(n-1)]$, where df_0 and df_1 are the degrees of freedom under the null and alternative hypotheses, respectively. In our case, $df_0 = T(n-1)-(n-1)-(n-1)n/2-n = 48$ and $df_1 = df_0+n-1 = 55$, so that $\kappa = (48+55)/(2\times 13\times 7) = .5659$. A * indicates significant at the 5 percent level.

freedom at the 5 percent level. Record a rejection if $\tilde{\chi}^2_{ji}$ exceeds the critical value.

Step 7: Repeat Steps 1–6 N times.

The upper parts of columns 2 and 3 of Table 5.7 present the simulation results with N = 1000 trials. The rejection rates are far above the nominal significance level of 5 percent indicating that the test is seriously biased against the null.

Next, we re–do the above simulation by multiplying the simulated test statistic $\tilde{\chi}^2_{ji}$ by Italianer's correction factor, $\kappa = .5659$ (see the notes to Table 5.6). As can be seen from the lower parts of columns 2 and 3 of Table 5.7, this has no effect when $\hat{\Sigma}_4$ is the unrestricted covariance, but reduces substantially the rejection rates when $\hat{\Sigma}_5$ is used in place of $\hat{\Sigma}_4$. But still the rejection rates are well above the nominal significance level.

Finally, we apply Barnard's (1963) Monte Carlo test procedure to the 1000 simulated chi–square values (see Section 4.5). In general, this procedure can be explained as follows. Let T_1 be the data–based value of a test statistic. We then simulate data sets under null hypothesis N-1 times, yielding N-1 additional test statistics $T_2,...,T_N$. The null is then rejected at the 5 percent significance level if T_1 is among the N' largest values of the T_i's such that $N'/N = .05$. The hypothesis to be tested is H_0: $\Sigma_4 = \Sigma_2$. Using the likelihood ratio test statistic, $T_1 = 87.68$ (see the first entry in column 3 of Table 5.6). As this T_1 is the second largest of the 1001, we reject the null. Columns 4 and 5 of Table 5.7 contain the rankings of the other three likelihood ratios. As the data–based likelihood ratio for $\hat{\Sigma}_3$ is ranked 457, we are unable to reject this covariance matrix on the basis of the Monte Carlo test. Note that as $\hat{\Sigma}_4$ and $\hat{\Sigma}_5$ differ only by a constant, the rankings in columns 4 and 5 coincide. It is also to be noted that application of Italianer's correction factor will not change the rankings.

We conclude this section with a summary of the findings: (i) The simulation results indicate that the asymptotic likelihood ratio test over–rejects the null hypothesis; (ii) Italianer's correction factor reduces the problem but the rejection rate is still too high; and (iii) Barnard's Monte Carlo test reveals that Σ_4 and Σ_3 are statistically equivalent.

Table 5.7 Simulation Results for Likelihood Ratio Tests

Null hypothesis	Percentage rejections with unrestricted covariance matrix specified as		Rank of the data-based test statistic with unrestricted covariance matrix specified as	
	$\hat{\Sigma}_4$	$\hat{\Sigma}_5$	$\hat{\Sigma}_4$	$\hat{\Sigma}_5$
(1)	(2)	(3)	(4)	(5)
		Uncorrected		
1. $\hat{\Sigma}_2$	100	66.3	1000	1000
2. $\hat{\Sigma}_3$	100	64.9	457	457
		Corrected		
3. $\hat{\Sigma}_2$	100	26.5	-	-
4. $\hat{\Sigma}_3$	100	26.8	-	-

For details of the correction to the likelihood ratio statistic, see the notes to Table 5.6.

5.8 Concluding Comments

A system of n demand equations has associated with it an $n \times n$ disturbance covariance matrix which is nondiagonal. The estimation of this matrix by the usual methods is problematic for anything but small systems (small n). Previous research has shown that this gives rise to fundamental difficulties for testing and estimation. The source of the problem is trying to estimate too much with too little data, i.e., one of undersized (or near undersized) samples.

This chapter has considered a demand system for the world as a whole. Data from 13 representative countries were used to estimate the model. As this sample is undersized, various specifications of the disturbance covariance matrix were investigated as solutions to the problem. On the basis of unbiasedness, efficiency and robustness, our preferred covariance matrix is that obtained from the preference independence version of the demand system. The results also reveal that the matrix suggested by de Boer and Harkema (1986a) performs creditably, especially when it is corrected for small–sample bias.

Appendices to Chapter 5

A5.1 When is the Sample Undersized?

Let **R** be the $q \times n(n-1)$ constraint matrix for symmetry defined in (3.3) of Section 5.3, where $q = (n-1)(n-2)/2$; $\hat{\mathbf{E}}$ be the $T \times (n-1)$ matrix of homogeneity–constrained LS residuals; and $\mathbf{S} = [1/(T-n)]\hat{\mathbf{E}}'\hat{\mathbf{E}}$ be the $(n-1) \times (n-1)$ matrix of mean squares and cross products. This **S** is the usual GLS estimator of Σ. Furthermore, let $\mathbf{A} = \mathbf{RC(S)R}'$ be a $q \times q$ matrix, where $C(\mathbf{S}) = \mathbf{S} \otimes (\mathbf{X}'\mathbf{X})^{-1}$ and **X** is the T×n matrix of explanatory variables (to simplify the notation, **X** here is $\mathbf{X}^*$ of Section 5.3). The inverse of **A** is used in equations (3.4) and (3.5); consequently, the sample is undersized when **A** is singular.

The matrix **S** is nonsingular when $T \geq 2n-1$ (see Section 5.3). In this case, **S** is positive definite, as is $\mathbf{X}'\mathbf{X}$. Consequently, there exists a nonsingular matrix **L** such that $\mathbf{LL}' = C(\mathbf{S})$ and **A** can then be written as $\mathbf{RLL}'\mathbf{R}'$, or $\mathbf{A} = \mathbf{BB}'$, where $\mathbf{B} = \mathbf{RL}$. As $r(\mathbf{B}) = q$, the rank of **A** is also q, the same as its order. Consequently, **A** is nonsingular. The requirement that $T \geq 2n-1$ is a sufficient condition for $|\mathbf{A}| \neq 0$. This, however, is not a necessary condition.

If **S** is singular, the rank of **A** is

$$r(\mathbf{A}) = r[\mathbf{R}C(\mathbf{S})\mathbf{R}'] \leq \min\left[r(\mathbf{R}), r[C(\mathbf{S})]\right]. \tag{A1.1}$$

The matrix **R** has rank q. The rank of C(**S**) is $r(S)r(\mathbf{X}'\mathbf{X}) = (T-n)n$. Equation (A1.1) thus becomes

$$r(\mathbf{A}) \leq \min[q, (T-n)n]. \tag{A1.2}$$

Since **A** is $q \times q$, a necessary condition for its nonsingularity is that $(T-n)n \geq q = (n-1)(n-2)/2$, or $T \geq 3(n-1)/2 + 1/n$. This is a necessary, not sufficient, condition for $|\mathbf{A}| \neq 0$.

The relationships between the sample size and the determinants of S and A are summarized in Table A5.1. When T falls in the ranges corresponding to either cases 1 or 3, the situation is unambiguous. That is, **A** is either singular or it is not. Case 2, however, defines an indeterminant range. Here the singularity of **A** has to be checked numerically.

A5.2 The Asymptotic Standard Errors of the Slutsky Coefficients Under Preference Independence

Equation (2.3) defines the (i,j)-*th* Slutsky coefficient under preference independence. We replace $\bar{w}_{it}$ in that equation with its cross–country average $\bar{w}_i$,

$$\pi_{ij} = \phi(\beta_i + \bar{w}_i)(\delta_{ij} - \beta_j - \bar{w}_j). \tag{A2.1}$$

Let $\hat{\theta} = (\hat{\beta}_1,...,\hat{\beta}_n, \hat{\phi})$ be the vector of ML estimates and s_i be an (n+1)–vector with all elements equal to zero except the i-*th*, which is unity. We replace the unknown parameters in equation (A2.1) with their

Table A5.1 The Sample Size and the Determinants of **S** and **A**

Case	Range of sample size, T	Determinant of	
		S	**A**
1.	$0 \leq T < \frac{3}{2}(n-1) + \frac{1}{n}$	0	0
2.	$\frac{3}{2}(n-1) + \frac{1}{n} \leq T < 2n - 1$	0	?
3.	$2n - 1 \leq T < \infty$	+	+

ML estimates and write it in the form

$$\hat{\pi}_{ij} = s'_{n+1}\hat{\boldsymbol{\theta}}\left[a_{ij} + (b_{ij}s'_i - \bar{w}_i s'_j)\hat{\boldsymbol{\theta}} + \hat{\boldsymbol{\theta}}' s_i s'_j \hat{\boldsymbol{\theta}}\right]. \tag{A2.2}$$

where $a_{ij} = \bar{w}_i b_{ij}$, $b_{ij} = \delta_{ij} - \bar{w}_j$ and δ_{ij} is Kronecker delta.

We write (A2.2) as $\hat{\pi}_{ij} = \pi_{ij}(\hat{\boldsymbol{\theta}})$ with

$$\frac{\partial \pi_{ij}}{\partial \hat{\boldsymbol{\theta}}} = s'_{n+1}\hat{\boldsymbol{\theta}}(s_i b_{ij} - s_j \bar{w}_i + s_i s'_j \hat{\boldsymbol{\theta}} + s_j s'_i \hat{\boldsymbol{\theta}})$$
$$+ s_{n+1}\left[a_{ij} + (b_{ij}s'_i - \bar{w}_i s'_j)\hat{\boldsymbol{\theta}} + \hat{\boldsymbol{\theta}}' s_i s'_j \hat{\boldsymbol{\theta}}\right].$$

Because $\hat{\pi}_{ij}$ is a totally differentiable nonlinear function of $\hat{\boldsymbol{\theta}}$, $\sqrt{T}\left[\pi_{ij}(\hat{\boldsymbol{\theta}}) - \pi_{ij}(\boldsymbol{\theta})\right]$ converges in distribution to a normal random variate with mean zero and asymptotic variance var $\hat{\pi}_{ij} = [\partial \pi_{ij}/\partial \hat{\boldsymbol{\theta}}']\hat{\Sigma}_{\boldsymbol{\theta}}[\partial \pi_{ij}/\partial \hat{\boldsymbol{\theta}}]$, where $\hat{\Sigma}_{\boldsymbol{\theta}} = \text{var}\ \hat{\boldsymbol{\theta}}$. The fourth part of Table 5.1 contains the estimates of the Slutsky coefficients under preference independence; the asymptotic standard errors are the square roots of var $\hat{\pi}_{ij}$.

References

Barnard, G.A. (1963). 'In discussion,' *Journal of the Royal Statistical Society*, Series B, 25: 294.

Barten, A.P. and H. Theil (1964). 'Simultaneous Estimation of a Complete System of Demand Equations,' Netherlands School of Economics, Econometric Institute, Report 6405.

Brown, B.W. (1981). 'Sample Size Requirements in Full Information Maximum likelihood Estimation,' *International Economic Review* 22: 443–459.

Deaton, A. (1975). *Models and Projections of Demand in Post–War Britain*. London: Chapman and Hall.

de Boer, P.M.C. and R. Harkema (1986a). 'Maximum Likelihood Estimation of Sum–Constrained Linear Models with Insufficient Observations,' *Economics Letters* 20: 325–329.

de Boer, P.M.C. and R. Harkema (1986b). 'An Algorithm for Maximum Likelihood Estimation of A New Covariance Matrix Specification for Sum–Constrained Models,' Report 8639, Econometric Institute, Erasmus University, Rotterdam.

de Boer, P.M.C. and R. Harkema (1990). 'Estimating the Consumption Block of the HERMES Models: An Application to the Netherlands,' *Applied Economics* 22: 1149–1165.

Fiebig, D.G. and H. Theil (1983). 'The Two Perils of Symmetry–Constrained Estimation of Demand Systems,' *Economics Letters* 13: 105–111.

Italianer, A. (1985). 'A Small–Sample Correction for the Likelihood Ratio Test,' *Economics Letters* 19: 315–317.

Klein, L.R. (1971). 'Forecasting and Policy Evaluation Using Large Scale Econometric Models: The State of the Art,' In M.D. Intriligator (ed), *Frontiers of Quantitative Economics*. Amsterdam: North Holland Publishing Company, 133–177.

Laitinen, K. (1978). 'Why Is Demand Homogeneity So Often Rejected?' *Economics Letters* 1: 187–191.

Lluch, C., A.A. Powell and R.A. Williams (1977). *Patterns in Household Demand and Saving.* Oxford: Oxford University Press.

Maddala, G.S. (1981). 'Statistical Inference in Relation to the Size of the Model,' In J. Kmenta and J.B. Ramsey (eds), *Large–Scale Macro–Econometric Models.* Amsterdam: North–Holland Publishing Company, 191–218.

Meisner, J.F. (1979). 'The Sad Fate of the Asymptotic Slutsky Symmetry Tests for Large Systems,' *Economics Letters* 2: 231–233.

Sargan, J.D. (1975). 'Asymptotic Theory and Large Models,' *International Economic Review* 16: 75–91.

Selvanathan, S. (1987). 'A Monte Carlo Test of Preference Independence,' *Economics Letters* 25: 259–261.

Selvanathan, S. (1991), The Reliability of ML Estimators of Systems of Demand Equations: Evidence from 18 Countries, *Review of Economics and Statistics*, LXXIII: 338-346.

Selvanathan, S. (1993), *A System-Wide Analysis of International Consumption Patterns*, Advanced Econometric Series, Boston: Kluwer Academic Publishers.

Swamy, P.A.V.B. and J. Holmes (1971). 'The Use of Undersized Samples in the Estimation of Simultaneous Equation Systems,' *Econometrica* 39: 455–459.

Theil, H. (1987). 'The Econometrics of Demand Systems,' Chapter 3 in H. Theil and K.W. Clements, *Applied Demand Analysis: Results from System–Wide Approaches.* Cambridge, Mass.: Ballinger Publishing Company, 101–162.

Theil, H. and K. Laitinen (1980). 'Singular Moments Matrices in Applied Econometrics,' In P.R. Krishnaiah (ed), *Multivariate Analysis–V.* Amsterdam: North–Holland Publishing Company, 629–649.

6 The Demand for Alcoholic Beverages

K.W. Clements[1] and S. Selvanathan[2]

[1] *Economic Research Centre, The University of Western Australia.*
[2] *Faculty of Commerce and Administration, Griffith University, Australia.*

6.1 Introduction

The consumption of alcoholic beverages is of interest to economists for at least three reasons. First, there is the basic challenge to analyse the extent to which alcohol consumption is amenable to economic analysis. Second, in many countries alcohol is heavily taxed. This raises interesting issues in public finance such as the welfare cost of these taxes, optimal taxation and externalities. Third, in many cases alcohol data are better than most as their basic source is the tax collection records.

The application of the system–wide approach to alcohol was initiated by Clements and Johnson (1983) who estimated demand equations for beer, wine and spirits. Other studies on this area include Adrian and Ferguson (1987), Clements and E.A. Selvanathan (1987), Duffy (1987), Fuss and Waverman (1987), Heien and Pompelli (1989), Holm (1989), Johnson et al. (1990), Jones (1989), Pearce (1986), Penm (1988), Quek (1988), E.A. Selvanathan (1988) and Wong (1988). This chapter extends previous research on alcohol in a number of directions. These extensions include the use of new distribution–free procedures discussed in Chapter 4 (which do not require any asymptotic theory) to test the validity of the hypotheses of demand homogeneity and Slutsky symmetry; the identification of an intriguing structure of preferences whereby wine consumption seems to be in a category by itself, one which is independent of beer and spirits; and an international comparison of alcohol consumption patterns which reveals fascinating similarities and differences across countries.

This chapter draws on Clements and S. Selvanathan (1991). For a more extensive version of this chapter, see Clements and S. Selvanathan (1989).

6.2 The Data

The data we use are for Australia (1955/56 – 1985/86) and come mainly from the Australian Bureau of Statistics; full details are given in Clements and S. Selvanathan (1989).

Let p_{it} and q_{it} be the price and per capita quantity consumed of good i (i=1,...,n) in year t; $M_t = \Sigma_{i=1}^{n} p_{it}q_{it}$ be total expenditure ("income" for short); $w_{it} = p_{it}q_{it}/M_t$ be the budget share of i; and $\bar{w}_{it} = \frac{1}{2}(w_{it} + w_{i,t-1})$ be the arithmetic average of the budget share over the years t-1 and t. If the three alcoholic beverages (beer, wine and spirits) are the first three goods, then $\bar{W}_{gt} = \Sigma_{i=1}^{3} \bar{w}_{it}$ is the (arithmetic average of the) budget share for total alcohol and $\bar{w}'_{it} = \bar{w}_{it}/\bar{W}_{gt}$ is the share of beverage i in total expenditure on alcohol; this $\bar{w}'_{it}$ is known as the (arithmetic average of the) conditional budget share of i.

Rows 1 and 2 of Table 6.1 give the sample means of $\bar{w}'_{it}$ and $\bar{W}_{gt}$. As can be seen, on average beer absorbs almost 70 percent of the drinker's budget and the remaining 30 percent is about evenly split between wine and spirits. Alcohol as a whole accounts for almost 6 percent of income. The first three entries in row 3 of the table contain the means of the log-changes in the prices, defined as $Dp_{it} = \log p_{it} - \log p_{i,t-1}$; when multiplied by 100 these are approximately equal to annual percentage changes. The fourth entry in row 3 is the mean of the Divisia price index of alcohol, $DP_{gt} = \Sigma_{i=1}^{3} \bar{w}'_{it}Dp_{it}$. The last row of the table contains the (means of the) quantity log-changes, $Dq_{it} = \log q_{it} - \log q_{i,t-1}$, and the

Table 6.1 Australian Alcohol Data: Means, 1955/56 - 1985/86

Variable	Beer	Wine	Spirits	Total alcohol
1. Conditional budget share ($\bar{w}'_{it}$)	68.56	15.40	16.04	
2. Budget share ($\bar{W}_{gt}$)				5.82
3. Log–change in price (Dp_{it}, DP_{gt})	6.68	6.30	6.17	6.43
4. Log–change in quantity (Dq_{it}, DQ_{gt})	.29	4.61	1.57	1.25

All entries are to be divided by 100.

Divisia volume index, $DQ_{gt} = \Sigma_{i=1}^{3} \bar{w}'_{it} Dq_{it}$. The rapid growth in wine consumption should be noted.

6.3 The Effects of Relative Prices and Income: A Preliminary Analysis

In this section we present some preliminary evidence about the price sensitivity of alcohol consumption. In later sections this evidence will be shown to be broadly consistent with more formal econometric results. This section is in the spirit of the data analysis presented in Chapter 3.

Figure 6.1 plots the relative growth in beer consumption, $(Dq_1 - DQ_g)$, against the growth in the relative price of that beverage, $(Dp_1 - DP_g)$. As can be seen, the points are scattered around a downward sloping least-squares (LS) regression line. Consequently, beer consumption grows less rapidly when its relative price rises. The slope of the regression line

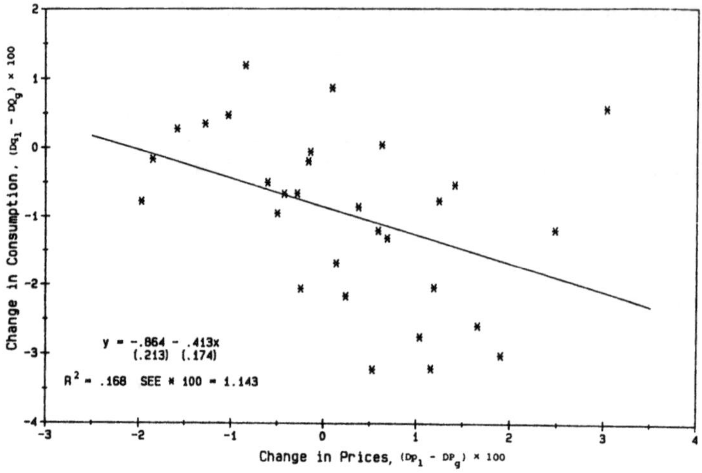

Fig. 6.1 Relative Consumption Against Relative Price of Beer, Australia, 1956/57-1985/86 (Annual log-changes ×100)

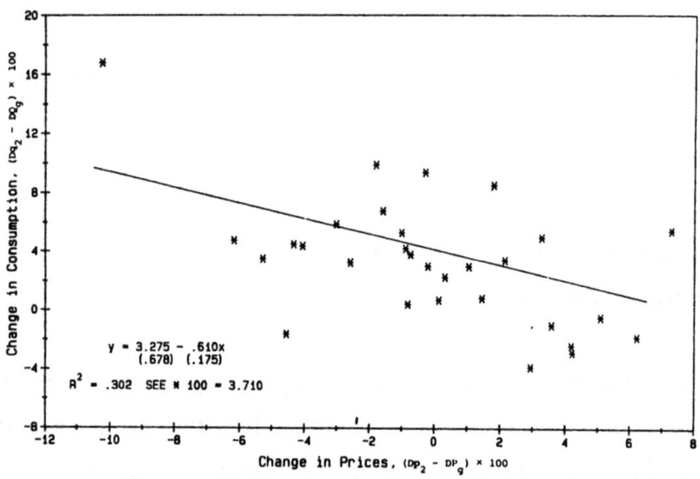

Fig. 6.2 Relative Consumption Against Relative Price of Wine, Australia, 1956/57-1985/86 (Annual log-changes ×100)

is -.41 with standard error .17, implying that the coefficient is significant. This slope can be interpreted as the conditional own-price elasticity of demand for beer under the assumption of a unitary conditional income elasticity. The intercept of the regression line is -.86 (s.e. = .21) which indicates that per capita beer consumption is falling autonomously at .9 percent p.a.

Figures 6.2-6.4 are similar scatterplots for the two other beverages and for total alcohol. In each case the slope of the regression line is negative and significant. The conclusion is that the law of demand holds even for alcohol. It is also to be noted that in each of the four cases, the own-price elasticity is of the order of $-\frac{1}{2}$.

In addition to relative prices, consumption also depends on income. Accordingly, we obtain some preliminary evidence about the income sensitivity of alcohol consumption. As before, this evidence will be shown to be consistent with econometric results presented in later sections.

To analyse the income responses we need to adjust observed consumption (Dq_i) for relative price changes ($Dp_i - DP_g$). Using an own-price elasticity of $-\frac{1}{2}$ (a value consistent with the above), the effect of prices on consumption is $-\frac{1}{2}(Dp_i - DP_g)$. Taking out this effect from observed consumption leaves

$$Dq_{it} + \tfrac{1}{2}(Dp_{it} - DP_{gt}). \tag{3.1}$$

Figure 6.5 plots (3.1) for i=1 (beer) and t = 1956/57,...,1985/86 against the growth in total alcohol consumption (DQ_{gt}). As can be seen, the observations are scattered around an upward sloping LS regression line. The slope can be interpreted as the conditional income elasticity of demand for beer. Its value is .85 (.07) which indicates that this beverage is a necessity.

Similar scatterplots for wine, spirits and total alcohol are given in Figures 6.6-6.8. These show that wine and total alcohol both have income elasticities close to unity, while the spirits elasticity is almost two. The

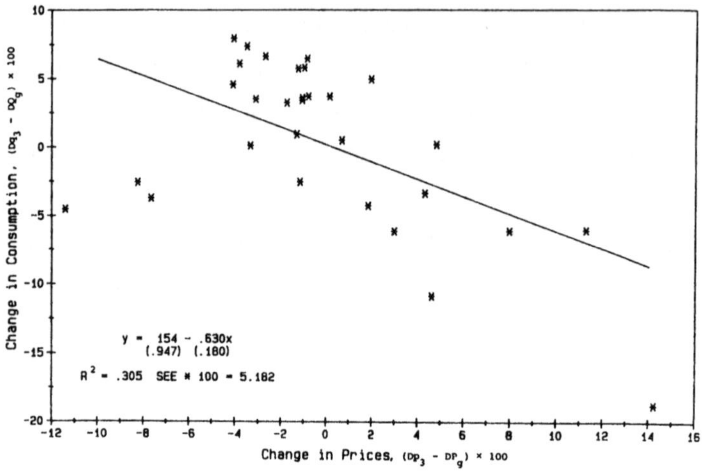

Fig. 6.3 Relative Consumption Against Relative Price of Spirits, Australia, 1956/57-1985/86 (Annual log-changes ×100)

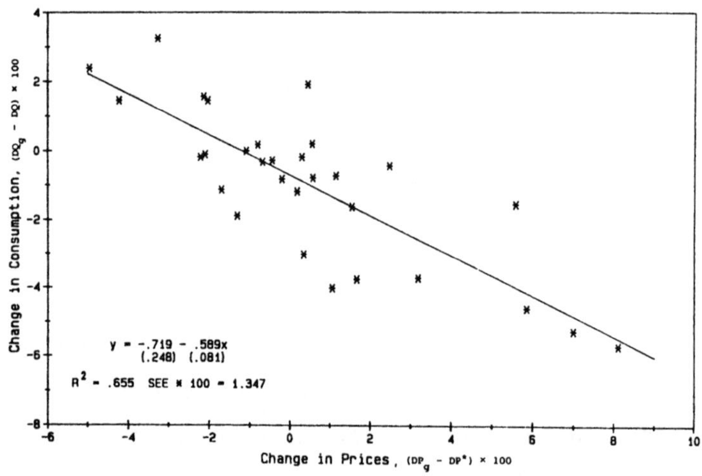

Fig. 6.4 Relative Consumption Against Relative Price of Alcohol, Australia, 1956/57-1985/86 (Annual log-changes ×100)

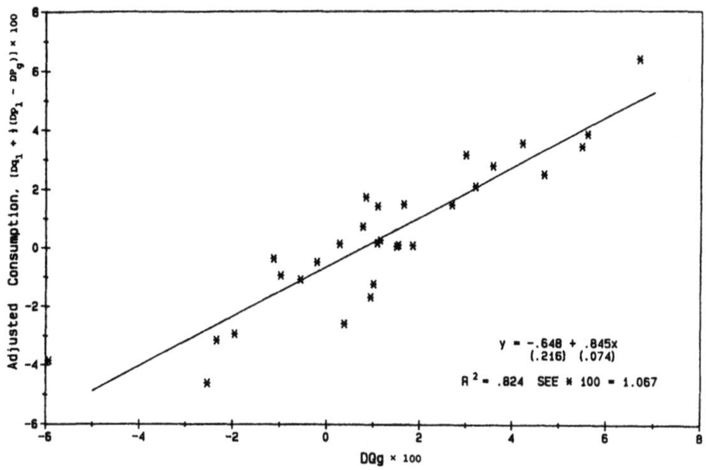

Fig. 6.5 Consumption of Beer Adjusted for Price Changes Against Total Alcohol Consumption: Australia, 1956/57-1985/86 (Annual log-changes ×100)

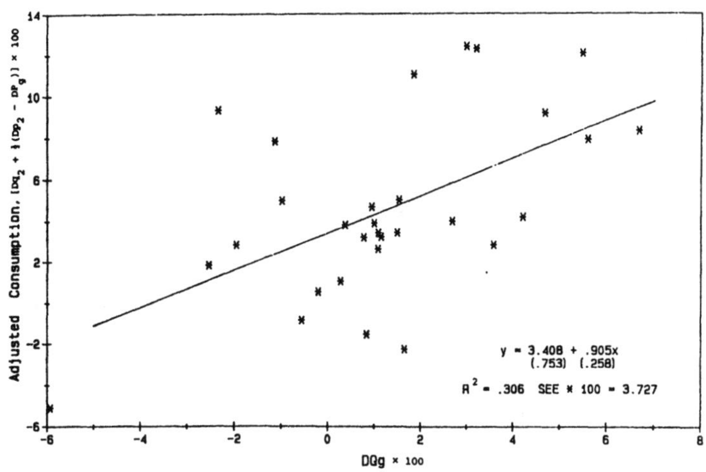

Fig. 6.6 Consumption of Wine Adjusted for Price Changes Against Total Alcohol Consumption: Australia, 1956/57-1985/86 (Annual log-changes ×100)

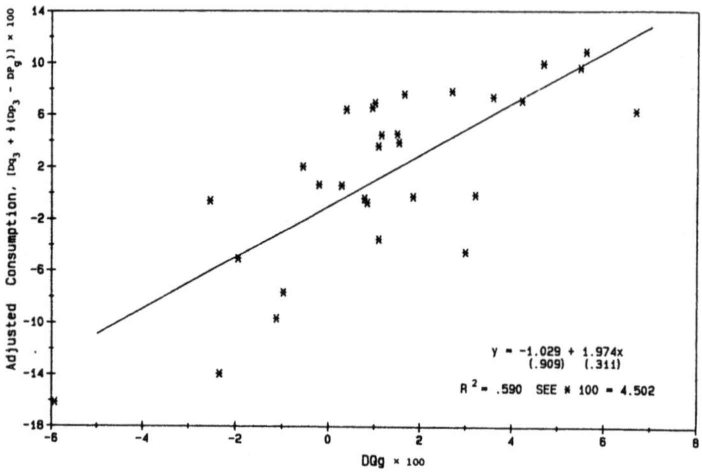

Fig. 6.7 Consumption of Spirits Adjusted for Price Changes Against Total Alcohol Consumption: Australia, 1956/57-1985/86 (Annual log-changes ×100)

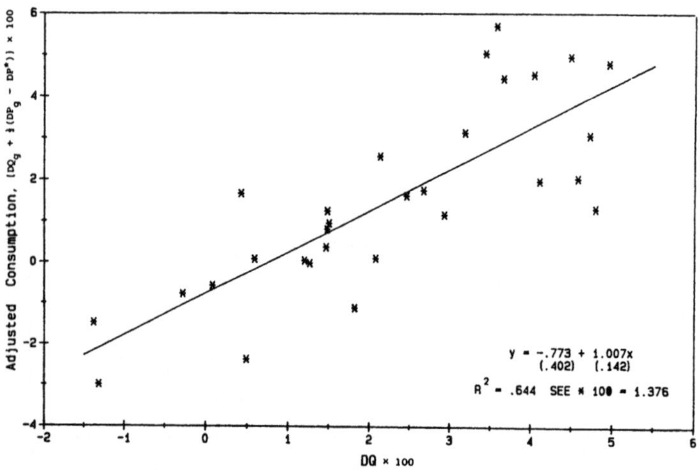

Fig. 6.8 Consumption of Alcohol Adjusted for Price Changes Against Real Income: Australia, 1956/57-1985/86 (Annual log-changes ×100)

result that spirits is a strong luxury seems to agree with the observation that, on the whole, it is the high-income earners in Australia who are spirits drinkers.

6.4 Testing Homogeneity and Symmetry

Consider the following conditional demand equation for beverage i

$$\bar{w}'_{it}(Dq_{it} - DQ_{gt}) = \alpha'_i + \beta'_i DQ_{gt} + \sum_{j=1}^{3} \pi'_{ij} Dp_{jt} + \varepsilon_{it}. \tag{4.1}$$

Here α'_i is a constant term satisfying $\Sigma_{i=1}^{3}\alpha'_i = 0$; β'_i is the conditional income coefficient of i with $\Sigma_{i=1}^{3}\beta'_i=0$; π'_{ij} is the (i,j)-*th* conditional Slutsky coefficient; and ε_{it} is a zero-mean error term. The income term of (4.1) uses Working's model with β'_i being 100 times the change in w'_i resulting from a one-percent increase in total alcohol expenditure; and the coefficient π'_{ij} measures the substitution effect of a change in the price of beverage j on the consumption of i. The π'_{ij}'s satisfy demand homogeneity,

$$\sum_{j=1}^{3} \pi'_{ij} = 0, \qquad i=1,2,3, \tag{4.2}$$

and Slutsky symmetry,

$$\pi'_{ij} = \pi'_{ji}, \qquad i,j=1,2,3. \tag{4.3}$$

Model (4.1) and the constraints are attractive in their simplicity: everything is linear in the parameters.

The variables on the right-hand side of equation (4.1), DQ_{gt} and Dp_{jt} (j=1,2,3), refer to the alcoholic beverages only; consumption of other goods and other prices play no role. Consequently, (4.1) for i=1,2,3 refers to the allocation of the alcohol budget to the three beverages and is known as a system of conditional (i.e., within alcohol) demand equations. These demand equations hold under the conditions of block independence with the alcoholic beverages comprising one block and all other goods another. Under block independence, the marginal utility of any member of the alcoholic beverages group is unaffected by the consumption of other goods (see Chapter 1 for details). For evidence in favour of block independence of alcohol, see Clements and E.A. Selvanathan (1988). Constraint (4.2) means that an equiproportional increase in the prices of the three beverages has no effect on the consumption of i, total alcohol consumption remaining unchanged. Constraint (4.3) implies that the substitution effects are symmetric in i and j. Dividing both sides of (4.1) by $\bar{w}'_{it}$ and rearranging, we obtain $1 + \beta'_i/\bar{w}'_{it}$ as the i-*th* conditional income elasticity and $\pi'_{ij}/\bar{w}'_{it}$ as the (i,j)-*th* conditional Slutsky price elasticity.

To test (4.2) and (4.3) we use distribution-free procedure introduced in Chapter 4. Briefly, this procedure involves drawing error terms to simulate a large number of values of the test statistic under the null hypothesis to construct its empirical distribution. The observed value of the test statistic is then compared to this distribution, rather than its asymptotic counterpart as in the conventional approach.

Let $\hat{\pi}'_{ij}$ be the least–squares (LS) estimate of π'_{ij} in (4.1). Then the test statistic for the homogeneity of the i-*th* equation is

$$\hat{\tau}_i = \sum_{j=1}^{3} \hat{\pi}'_{ij} \tag{4.4}$$

and the test statistic for the homogeneity of all three equations jointly is

$$\hat{\tau}^h = \sum_{i=1}^{3} |\hat{\tau}_i|. \tag{4.5}$$

Table 6.2 Monte Carlo Tests of Homogeneity (Standard errors in parentheses)

Beverage	Data-based value of the test statistic $\hat{\tau}_i, \hat{\tau}^h \times 10$	Rank of the data-based test statistic	
		Normal errors	Bootstrap errors
(1)	(2)	(3)	(4)
Beer	-.374 (.434)	22	11
Wine	.505 (.371)	91	97
Spirits	-.131 (.429)	35	33
All	1.009 (–)	59	78

Column 2 of Table 6.2 presents the data–based values of the test–statistics. To assess the significance of these values the Monte Carlo simulation procedure with quasi–normal error terms is used. Column 3 of the table presents the rank of the data-based value among the 99 simulated values. As can be seen from the last entry of this column, the rank of the test statistic for the homogeneity of the system as a whole is 59. As this value lies outside the right–hand tail of the empirical distribution which contains 5 percent of the drawings, homogeneity may not be rejected at the 5 percent level. Similarly, a two-tailed test for the homogeneity of the individual equations shows that this hypothesis is also acceptable at the 5 percent level for each of the three beverages. Reinforcing this finding is the insignificance of the values of the three $\hat{\tau}_i$'s (see column 2).

Let $\hat{\pi}_{ij}^{\prime h}$ be the homogeneity–constrained LS estimate of $\pi_{ij}^{\prime}$ (see Section 4.4 for details). The test statistic for symmetry given homogeneity is

$$\hat{\tau}^s = \sum_{i=1}^{3} \sum_{j=1}^{3} |\hat{\pi}_{ij}^{\prime h} - \hat{\pi}_{ji}^{\prime h}|. \tag{4.6}$$

The data–based value of $\hat{\tau}^s(\times 10) = .679$. To assess the significance of this value we proceed as before and compute the simulated value of the test statistic (4.6). The rank of the data-based $\hat{\tau}^s$ among the 99 simulated values is 23. Thus symmetry may not be rejected at the 5 percent level.

The above results are based on quasi–normal errors. In order to avoid the normality assumption entirely, Efron's (1979) bootstrap procedure is now used. This involves using bootstrap realizations of the residuals of the demand equations under the null hypothesis. To ensure that these disturbances have the same variances as in the previous simulations, we multiply each realization by $\sqrt{T/(T-K)}$, where T is the sample size and K is the number of independent variables in each demand equation. Proceeding as before, the simulated values of the test–statistics (4.4), (4.5) and (4.6) for 99 simulations are then obtained. For homogeneity, the ranks of the data–based test statistics are presented in column 4 of Table 6.2. As can be seen, homogeneity still may not be rejected at the 5 percent level for the three individual beverages as well as for alcohol as a whole; the rank for wine is on the high side, but still not significant (the 5 percent level critical values for a two-tail tests are 3 and 97). For symmetry, the rank is 23 (as before). Hence symmetry is also still acceptable at the 5 percent level.

6.5 The Utility Interactions Among Beverages

In this section the structure of preferences within the alcoholic beverages group is analysed.

The presentation begins with the homogeneity– and symmetry–constrained estimates of demand equation (4.1) for i = 1,2,3. The maximum likelihood (ML) estimates under the assumption that the errors are independent, multivariate normal with a constant covariance matrix are given in Table 6.3. Based on a preliminary analysis of the data, constant terms were added to the equations to take account of autonomous trends. As can be seen, all the constant terms are significant. It is to be noted that there are three sub–periods for the constants. The data are not incompatible with the restriction that the second constant in the wine equation is equal to the third constant for that beverage. This restriction is imposed in Table 6.3. As the estimates of β_i' for beer and wine are significantly negative, these two beverages are conditional necessities. Spirits is a conditional luxury as the estimate of β_3' is significantly positive. Regarding the estimated Slutsky coefficients, the three diagonal elements of the matrix $[\pi_{ij}']$ are significantly negative, as they should be.

The Slutsky coefficient π_{ij}' refers to the total substitution effect of a price change. This total effect comprises a specific and general substitution effect; the former, which holds the marginal utility of income constant, is related to the interactions in the utility function among the beverages. We now derive estimates of the specific substitution effects by decomposing the Slutsky coefficients. Let λ be the marginal utility of income; $M_g = \Sigma_{i=1}^{3} p_i q_i$ be total alcohol expenditure; u^{ij} be the (i,j)-*th* element of the inverse of the Hessian matrix of the utility function pertaining to alcohol; and $\nu_{ij}' = (\lambda / M_g) p_i p_j u^{ij}$. The coefficient ν_{ij}' represents the specific substitution effect and is related to π_{ij}' by [see equation (25.5) of Chapter 1]

$$\pi_{ij}' = \nu_{ij}' - \eta_{gg} \theta_i' \theta_j', \tag{5.1}$$

where $\eta_{gg} = \phi\theta_g / \bar{W}_g$ is the own–price elasticity of demand for alcohol as a group; ϕ is the income flexibility; θ_g is the marginal share for alcohol as a whole; $\bar{W}_g$ is the corresponding budget share; and $\theta_i' = \partial(p_i q_i) / \partial M_g$ is the conditional marginal share of beverage i. The coefficients ν_{ij}' are

Table 6.3 First Set of Estimates of Conditional Demand Equations for Alcoholic Beverages

$$\bar{w}'_{it}(Dq_{it} - DQ_{gt}) = \alpha'_i + \beta'_i DQ_{gt} + \sum_{j=1}^{3} \pi'_{ij} Dp_{jt}$$

(Asymptotic standard errors in parentheses)

Beverage	Constant $\alpha'_i \times 100$			Conditional income coefficient β'_i	Conditional Slutsky coefficients		
					$\pi'_{i1} \times 10$	$\pi'_{i2} \times 10$	$\pi'_{i3} \times 10$
	1956/57–1964/65	1965/66–1976/77	1977/78–1985/86				
Beer	0	0	-1.093(.194)	-.163(.038)	-.620(.293)	-.014(.225)	635(165)
Wine	0	.881(.122)	.881(.122)	-.073(.037)		-.453(214)	.467(131)
Spirits	0	-.881(.122)	.212(.183)	.236(.039)			-1 102(165)

symmetric in i and j and satisfy [see, equation (25.2) of Chapter 1]

$$\sum_{j=1}^{3} \nu'_{ij} = \eta_{gg}\theta'_i, \qquad i=1,2,3. \tag{5.2}$$

Let $DP'_{gt} = \Sigma_{i=1}^{3}\theta'_i Dp_{it}$ be the Frisch price index. Then, using (5.1) and (5.2), the substitution term of demand equation (4.1) becomes

$$\sum_{j=1}^{3} \pi'_{ij} Dp_{jt} = \sum_{j=1}^{3} \nu'_{ij}(Dp_{jt} - DP'_{gt}). \tag{5.3}$$

Accordingly, ν'_{ij} is the coefficient attached to the j-*th* relative price in the i-*th* demand equation, or the (i,j)-*th* price coefficient for short.

Consider the marginal utility of beverage i, $\partial u/\partial q_i$. Additional consumption of another beverage j causes this marginal utility to change by $\partial^2 u/\partial q_i \partial q_j$. All such changes are given by the 3×3 Hessian matrix of the utility function pertaining to alcohol, $\mathbf{U} = [\partial^2 u/\partial q_i \partial q_j]$. Suppose, for example, that the marginal utility of wine is independent of the consumption of beer and spirits. As Hessians are symmetric, in this case

$$\mathbf{U} = \begin{array}{c} \\ \text{beer} \\ \text{wine} \\ \text{spirits} \end{array} \begin{array}{c} \begin{array}{ccc} \text{beer} & \text{wine} & \text{spirits} \end{array} \\ \begin{bmatrix} \partial^2 u/\partial q_1^2 & 0 & \partial^2 u/\partial q_1 \partial q_3 \\ 0 & \partial^2 u/\partial q_2^2 & 0 \\ \partial^2 u/\partial q_3 \partial q_1 & 0 & \partial^2 u/\partial q_3^2 \end{bmatrix} \end{array} .$$

Here the beverages can be reordered so that $\mathbf{U}$ and $\mathbf{U}^{-1}$ are both block diagonal with beer and spirits in one block and wine in another. This can be described as block independence within alcohol or, more simply, wine independence. In this case, all the off-diagonal ν'_{ij}'s involving wine vanish and, according to (5.3), the relative price of wine has no effect on the consumption of the other two beverages.

Equation (5.1) is used in the form $\nu'_{ij} = \pi'_{ij} + \eta_{gg}\theta'_i\theta'_j$ to obtain estimates of the price coefficients from the Slutsky coefficients given in Table 6.3. The price elasticity of alcohol η_{gg} is set equal to -.6, a value obtained in Clements and S. Selvanathan (1989). Regarding the marginal shares θ'_i, these take the form $\beta'_i + \bar{w}'_{it}$ under model (4.1). Column 2 of Table 6.4 contains the estimates of the θ'_i's, obtained using the income coefficients of Table 6.3 and means of the $\bar{w}'_{it}$'s. These indicate that an additional \$1 of spending on alcohol results in beer expenditure increasing by 52 cents, wine by 8 cents and spirits by 40 cents. Columns 3–5 of the table contain the upper triangle of the $[\nu'_{ij}]$ matrix.

The two off-diagonal price coefficients involving wine (ν'_{12} and ν'_{23}) are both insignificant, which points in the direction that the marginal utility of this beverage is independent of the other two. Wine by itself satisfies a basic want of the consumer. Note also that the estimate of ν'_{13} (beer/spirits) is significantly negative; a rise in the relative price of

Table 6.4 Conditional Marginal Shares and Price Coefficients (Asymptotic standard errors in parentheses)

Beverage	Conditional marginal share θ_i'	Price coefficients × 10		
		ν_{i1}'	ν_{i2}'	ν_{i3}'
(1)	(2)	(3)	(4)	(5)
Beer	.523(.038)	-2.260(.317)	-.268(.213)	-.609(.191)
Wine	.081(.037)		-.492(.229)	.275(.159)
Spirits	.396(.039)			-2.045(.260)

spirits *decreases* beer consumption, indicating complementarity. There are good reasons to expect complementarity, however. At a formal dinner it is not unusual for beer to be consumed beforehand, to have wine during dinner and for spirits to be served afterwards. Additional consumption of one beverage consequently reinforces the pleasure of drinking the other two, provided consumption remains within the usual tolerance levels. In this sense the beverages are complements, rather than being competitive or substitutes. Even if some do not drink all three beverages sequentially, another line of argument establishes the presumption of complementarity. The utility at the margin of, say, a beer drinker may well be enhanced by additional consumption by spirits drinkers (and vice versa) due to the increased social interaction facilitated by the larger intake of alcohol as a whole. The finding that wine is an independent beverage suggests that wine consumers tend not to mix their drinks or they talk to themselves only at social occasions.

6.6 The Second Version of the Demand Model

In the previous section it was concluded that the data are not inconsistent with the proposition that the marginal utility of wine is independent of the consumption of the other two beverages. In this section this restriction is imposed and formally tested.

Equation (4.1) is a demand equation in absolute prices. Substituting (5.3) in (4.1) yields the following demand equation for i in terms of relative prices,

$$\bar{w}'_{it}(Dq_{it} - DQ_{gt}) = \beta'_i DQ_{gt} + \sum_{j=1}^{3} \nu'_{ij}(Dp_{jt} - DP'_{gt}) + \varepsilon_{it}. \tag{6.1}$$

This is the second version of the demand model, while (4.1) is the first. When wine is preference independent, the 3×3 symmetric matrix $[\nu'_{ij}]$ takes the form

$$\begin{matrix} \text{beer} \\ \text{wine} \\ \text{spirits} \end{matrix} \quad \begin{bmatrix} \nu'_{11} & 0 & \nu'_{13} \\ & \nu'_{22} & 0 \\ & & \nu'_{33} \end{bmatrix}. \tag{6.2}$$

As $\theta'_i = \beta'_i + \bar{w}'_{it}$, constraint (5.2) becomes

$$\sum_{j=1}^{3} \nu'_{ij} = \eta_{gg}(\beta'_i + \bar{w}'_{it}), \qquad i=1,2,3. \tag{6.3}$$

Constraint (6.3) means that the price coefficients cannot be constants; following Clements and E.A. Selvanathan (1987), ν'_{13} in (6.2) is specified to take the form

$$\nu'_{13} = \kappa\sqrt{\bar{w}'_{1t}\bar{w}'_{3t}}, \tag{6.4}$$

where κ is a constant. As $\nu'_{13} < 0$ in Table 6.4, κ is expected to be negative. It follows from (6.2)–(6.4) that

$$\left\{\begin{aligned} \nu'_{11} &= \eta_{gg}(\beta'_1 + \bar{w}'_{1t}) - \kappa\sqrt{\bar{w}'_{1t}\bar{w}'_{3t}} \\ \nu'_{22} &= \eta_{gg}(\beta'_2 + \bar{w}'_{2t}) \\ \nu'_{33} &= \eta_{gg}(\beta'_3 + \bar{w}'_{3t}) - \kappa\sqrt{\bar{w}'_{1t}\bar{w}'_{3t}}. \end{aligned}\right. \tag{6.5}$$

To derive the estimating equations, (6.2), (6.3) and (6.5) are substituted for ν'_{ij} in (6.1). After rearrangements, this yields the following conditional demand equation for beverage i:

$$\bar{w}'_{it}(Dq_{it} - DQ_{gt}) = \beta'_i DQ_{gt} + \eta_{gg} z_{it} + \kappa_i c_t + \varepsilon_{it}, \tag{6.6}$$

where

$$z_{it} = (\beta'_i + \bar{w}'_{it})\left[(Dp_{it} - Dp_{3t}) - \sum_{j=1}^{2} (\beta'_j + \bar{w}'_{jt})(Dp_{jt} - Dp_{3t})\right];$$

$$c_t = -\sqrt{\bar{w}'_{1t}\bar{w}'_{3t}}\,(Dp_{1t} - Dp_{3t});$$

and $\kappa_2 = 0$, $\kappa_1 = -\kappa_3 = \kappa$. To estimate (6.6) for i=1,2,3 constant terms are added, as before, and ML applied. The results are contained in Table 6.5. As can be seen, the estimates of the constants and income coefficients are quite similar to those in Table 6.3. The estimate of κ is negative, as expected, and significant. The value of η_{gg}, the own–price elasticity for alcohol, is fixed in the table as initial results indicated that it was not possible to obtain a precise estimate of this parameter. This

Table 6.5 Second Set of Estimates of Conditional Demand Equations

$$\bar{w}'_{it}(Dq_{it} - DQ_{gt}) = \alpha'_i + \beta'_i DQ_{gt} + \eta_{gg} z_{it} + \kappa_i c_t + \varepsilon_{it}$$

(Asymptotic standard errors are in parentheses)

Beverage	Constant $\alpha'_i \times 100$			Conditional income coefficient β'_i
	1956/57-1964/65	1965/66-1976/77	1977/78-1985/86	
Beer	0	0	-.963(.189)	-.187(.035)
Wine	0	.801(.117)	.801(.117)	-.054(.030)
Spirits	0	-.801(.117)	.162(.183)	.241(.039)
	κ = -.142(.048)		η_{gg} = -.6 (specified)	

Table 6.6 Means of Conditional Income and Price Elasticities

Beverage	Conditional income elasticity η'_i	Conditional price elasticities		
		η'_{i1}	η'_{i2}	η'_{i3}
Beer	.73	-.15	.04	.11
Wine	.61	.18	-.32	.15
Spirits	2.51	.46	.15	-.61

elasticity is set at -.6, as before. An analysis of the residuals indicates that autocorrelation is not a problem.

To test the hypothesis that wine is a preference independent beverage, the unrestricted model (4.1) is used for i=1,2 (one equation of the three is redundant) with restricted constant terms and homogeneity and symmetry imposed. The restricted model is (6.6) for i=1,2 with restricted constant terms. Let L_u and L_r be the log–likelihood values of the unrestricted and restricted models, respectively. The test statistic chosen was $-2(L_r - L_u)$ which has a data–based value of 6.59. To assess the significance of this value, the Monte Carlo procedure of Section 6.4 is used. A data set is simulated with quasi–normal error terms under the null hypothesis, the restricted and unrestricted models estimated and the simulated value of the test statistic computed. This procedure is repeated 999 times and the data–based value of the test statistic ranked among the 999 simulated values. The null is rejected at the 5 percent level if the rank of the data–based test statistic is greater than 950. As this rank is 620, the hypothesis that wine is preference independent is not rejected. This result is also confirmed by bootstrap simulations.

The means of the elasticities implied by the estimates in Table 6.5 are given in Table 6.6. Beer and wine are conditional necessities, while spirits is a strong luxury. The own–price Slutsky elasticities are -.2, -.3 and -.6 for beer, wine and spirits, respectively; most of the cross elasticities are small.

6.7 How Reliable are the ML Estimators?

In this section we use simulation experiments to assess the reliability of the maximum likelihood (ML) estimators of model (6.6). This material follows Clements and E.A. Selvanathan (1987, Section 5.15) and Theil (1987, Section 3.11).

Equation (6.6) for i=1,2,3 is an allocation model so that one equation is redundant. Consequently, we need only consider (6.6) for i=1,2. We generate T=30 (the sample size) quasi-normal error vectors with mean zero and covariance matrix **S**, the data-based ML estimate of the error covariance matrix **Σ**. We use these disturbances together with the observed values of the independent variables and the data-based ML estimates of the parameters given in Table 6.5 to obtain new values of the dependent variables of equation (6.6) for i=1,2. These values and the observed values of the independent variables are then used to re-estimate the model by ML. This procedure is repeated 1000 times.

The upper half of Table 6.7 summarizes the results. Column 2 gives the true values of the parameters, the estimates from Table 6.5. In column 3 we present the means over the 1000 trials. These estimates are quite close to the corresponding true values of column 2. Thus we conclude that the ML estimators are unbiased. Column 4 presents the root-mean-squared errors (RMSEs) computed around the true values, while column 5 gives the root-mean-squared asymptotic standard errors (RMSASEs). The RMSASEs are obtained by summing each diagonal element of the asymptotic covariance matrix over the 1000 trials, dividing by 1000 and then taking the square root. These RMSASEs are always below the corresponding RMSEs indicating that the asymptotic standard errors tend to overstate the precision of the point estimates. However, the differences are not too large. Thus we conclude that our asymptotic standard errors provide a fairly realistic picture of the sampling variability of the estimators.

In the above experiment the data-based ML estimate of **Σ**, **S**, is used to generate the disturbance terms. A new estimate of **Σ** is then obtained in each trial. In general, this estimate does not coincide with **S**, the covariance matrix which actually generated the disturbances. To analyse the effects of this, we redo the experiment by fixing this matrix at **S** in the ML procedure. In other words, we now treat **Σ** as being known. Columns 6-8 of Table 6.7 summarize these results. A comparison of columns 4 and 7 reveals that the RMSEs are only slightly larger when **Σ** is estimated. Thus there is not much of an efficiency loss as a result of estimating Σ. Comparing columns 5 and 8 we see that the RMSASEs are slightly larger when Σ is known.

The above experiments use pseudo-normal error vectors. To allow for the possibility of non-normal errors, we use the bootstrap procedure which is distribution-free. This involves redoing the experiments using for the disturbances bootstrap realizations of the data-based ML residuals of equation (6.6) for i=1,2. We then use exactly the same procedure as before. The results are summarized in the lower half of Table 6.7.

Looking at columns 4 and 5 of Table 6.7, it can be seen that with bootstrap errors the RMSASEs are not always below the corresponding RMSEs. This is in contrast to the previous results with normal errors. However, the RMSASEs still increase when Σ is known (compare columns 5 and 8). As before, the estimators are unbiased. An element-by-element comparison of the upper and lower halfs of columns 4 and 7 reveals that the RMSEs under normality tend to be higher than in the bootstrap case.

6.8 The Goodness of Fit of the Model

We use the estimates of equation (6.6) for i=1,2,3 to compute the predicted conditional budget shares as the actual shares minus the residuals.

The quality of these predictions can be analysed with the Strobel (1982) information inaccuracies (I_{it}) and their total (I_t),

$$I_{it} = \hat{w}'_{it} - w'_{it} + w'_{it} \log \frac{w'_{it}}{\hat{w}'_{it}}, \qquad i=1,2,3,$$

$$I_t = \sum_{i=1}^{3} I_{it},$$

Table 6.7 Simulation Results for 1000 Trials

Parameter (1)	True value (2)	Σ unknown Mean (3)	RMSE (4)	RMSASE (5)	Σ known Mean (6)	RMSE (7)	RMSASE (8)
		Normal errors					
β_i' Beer	-.187	-.188	.036	.033	-.188	.035	.035
Wine	-.054	-.054	.031	.029	-.054	.031	.030
Spirits	.241	.242	.041	.036	.242	.041	.039
κ (Beer/spirits)	-.142	-.138	.047	.045	-.138	.045	.049
α_i' Beer, 1977/78 1985/86	-.963	-.979	.202	.177	-.978	.197	.189
Wine, 1965/66-1985/86	.801	.802	.122	.112	.802	.120	.117
		Bootstrap errors					
β_i' Beer	-.187	-.190	.031	.032	-.190	.031	.035
Wine	-.054	-.053	.024	.023	-.053	.023	.030
Spirits	.241	.243	.036	.035	.243	.036	.039
κ (Beer/spirits)	-.142	-.141	.049	.045	-.141	.048	.048
α_i' Beer, 1977/78-1985/86	-.963	-.954	.161	.173	-.955	.161	.189
Wine, 1965/66-1985/86	.801	.801	.066	.090	.800	.069	.117

All entries for the constants are to be divided by 100.

where $\hat{w}_{it}'$ and w_{it}' are the predicted and actual conditional budget shares of beverage i in year t. Both I_{it} and I_t are non-negative and increase as the predictions deteriorate. In row 1 of Table 6.8 we present the means of these inaccuracies and in row 2 the means of the relative measures I_{it}/I_t. The general picture which emerges is that, on average, the spirits equation contributes more than 50 percent to the lack of fit of the model.

Consider the entropy of the relative Strobel measures, I_{1t}/I_t, I_{2t}/I_t, I_{3t}/I_t,

$$H_t = - \sum_{i=1}^{3} \frac{I_{it}}{I_t} \log \frac{I_{it}}{I_t}.$$

Table 6.8 Information Inaccuracies and Relative Strobel Measures: Means, 1956/57 - 1985/86

Variable	Beer	Wine	Spirits	Total alcohol
1. Information inaccuracy (I_{it}, I_t)	27.28	65.84	102.96	196.08
2. Strobel measure (I_{it}/I_t)	16.04	29.65	54.32	-

All entries in row 1 are to be divided by 10^6. All entries in row 2 are to be divided by 100.

This entropy varies between 0 and log 3 $\simeq$ 1.1 and takes smaller values when the proportions I_{it}/I_t are more unequal, i.e. when the total I_t is dominated by one or two equations. The mean of H_t is .69, which is a bit on the low side due to the dis-proportionality involving spirits.

6.9 The Demand for Alcohol as a Whole

The conditional demand equations relate to the allocation of total expenditure on alcohol to the three beverages; total alcohol consumption is held constant in these equations. In this section the analysis is extended by presenting estimates of the demand equation for alcohol as a whole, which shall be referred to as the composite demand equation. (See Section 1.22 for the relevant theory.)

The Divisia volume index for alcohol is a budget-share weighted mean of the three quantity log-changes, $DQ_{gt} = \Sigma_{i=1}^{3} \bar{w}_{it}' Dq_{it}$. For simplicity, DQ_g is expressed as a linear function of the log-change in per capita real income DQ and the relative price of alcohol $DP_g - DP^*$, where DP_g is the Divisia price index of alcohol and DP^* is the log–change in the price index of all goods,

$$DQ_{gt} = \eta_g DQ_t + \eta_{gg}(DP_{gt} - DP_t^*) + \mu_t, \tag{9.1}$$

with η_g the income elasticity for alcohol; η_{gg} the own–price elasticity; and μ_t an error term. The LS estimates of (9.1) are presented in Table 6.9. As before, constant terms have been added to take account of residuals trends. The income elasticity for alcohol as a whole is 1.0, while the price elasticity is -.6. Note that these elasticities are estimated precisely and that the estimate of η_{gg} is consistent with the value used previously.

Suppose the price of beverage i increases when real income and all other prices remain unchanged. This has two effects on the consumption of i. The first is a reallocation of a *given* total expenditure on alcohol. The increase in the relative price of i causes consumption of i to fall. This direct effect is given by the conditional demand equation for i. In addition, the price increase causes alcohol as a whole to become relatively more expensive. Total alcohol consumption thus falls. This reduction in real total expenditure then causes consumption of i to change, which is an indirect effect given by a combination of the composite and conditional demand equations. In what follow the direct and indirect effects are combined to obtain estimates of the total impact of all income and price changes.

The i-*th* conditional demand equation is given by (6.6). To simplify matters, we use a double–log approximation to this equation and omit the error term,

$$Dq_{it} = \eta_i' DQ_{gt} + \sum_{j=1}^{3} \eta_{ij}' Dp_{jt}, \tag{9.2}$$

where η_i' is the conditional income elasticity of demand for i; and η_{ij}' is the (i,j)-*th* conditional Slutsky price elasticity. The relative price of alcohol, $(DP_g - DP^*)$, in the composite demand equation (9.1) is the

Table 6.9 Estimates of Composite Demand Equation for Alcohol

$$DQ_{gt} = \alpha + \eta_g DQ_t + \eta_{gg}(DP_{gt} - DP_t^*)$$

(Standard errors are in parentheses)

Constant $\alpha \times 100$ 1956/57-1964/65	Constant $\alpha \times 100$ 1965/66-1976/77	Constant $\alpha \times 100$ 1977/78-1985/86	Income elasticity η_g	Price elasticity η_{gg}	R^2	SEE × 100	DW
-1.101 (.416)	-	-1.573 (.406)	1.004 (.087)	-.592 (.069)	.84	1.13	1.84

difference between the Divisia price index for alcohol and the log–change in the price index of all goods (including alcohol). The former index is defined as

$$DP_{gt} = \sum_{i=1}^{3} \bar{w}'_{it} Dp_{it}, \tag{9.3}$$

with $\bar{w}'_{it}$ the arithmetic average of the conditional budget share of i. The latter price index is expressed as a budget–share weighted average of the changes in the prices of all n goods,

$$DP_t^* = \sum_{i=1}^{n} \bar{w}_{it} Dp_{it}, \tag{9.4}$$

where $\bar{w}_{it}$ is the arithmetic average of the (unconditional) budget share of good i.

Recalling that the n goods are ordered such that the alcoholic beverages are the first three, $DP_{ot} = \Sigma_{i=4}^{n} \bar{w}'_{it} Dp_{it}$ is defined as an index of the prices of all other (i.e., nonalcoholic) goods. As the conditional budget share of beverage i is defined as $\bar{w}'_{it} = \bar{w}_{it}/\bar{W}_{gt}$, it follows from equations (9.3) and (9.4) that DP^*_t can be expressed as a weighted average of DP_{gt} and DP_{ot}, $DP^*_t = \bar{W}_{gt}DP_{gt} + (1 - \bar{W}_{gt})DP_{ot}$, so that

$$DP_{gt} - DP^*_t = (1 - \bar{W}_{gt})(DP_{gt} - DP_{ot}). \tag{9.5}$$

The time-dependent budget shares $(\bar{W}_{gt}, \bar{w}'_{it})$ are approximated with their sample means $(\bar{\bar{W}}_g, \bar{\bar{w}}'_i)$, so that (9.5) becomes

$$DP_{gt} - DP^*_t = (1 - \bar{\bar{W}}_g)\left[\sum_{i=1}^{3} \bar{\bar{w}}'_i Dp_{it} - DP_{ot}\right]. \tag{9.6}$$

We substitute the right-hand side of (9.6) for the relative price in the composite demand equation (9.1) and omit the error term to give

$$DQ_{gt} = \eta_g DQ_t + \sum_{j=1}^{3} \eta_{gj} Dp_{jt} + \eta_{go} DP_{ot}, \tag{9.7}$$

where

$$\eta_{gj} = \eta_{gg}(1 - \bar{\bar{W}}_g)\bar{\bar{w}}'_j, \qquad \eta_{go} = -\eta_{gg}(1 - \bar{\bar{W}}_g) \tag{9.8}$$

are price elasticities of demand for total alcohol. Using the values of $\bar{\bar{W}}_g$ and $\bar{\bar{w}}'_i$ given in Table 6.1, together with $\eta_{gg} = -.592$ (from Table 6.9) in equation (9.8) for j=1,2,3, the following results are obtained

Good j	Elasticity of demand for total alcohol with respect to price of good j η_{gj}
beer	-.382
wine	-.086
spirits	-.089
all other goods	.558.

(9.9)

Finally, we use equation (9.7) to substitute for DQ_{gt} in (9.2) to give

$$Dq_{it} = \eta_i DQ_t + \sum_{j=1}^{3} \eta_{ij} Dp_{jt} + \eta_{io} DP_{ot},$$

where

$$\eta_i = \eta_i' \eta_g, \quad \eta_{ij} = \eta_{ij}' + \eta_i' \eta_{gj} \quad \text{and} \quad \eta_{io} = \eta_i' \eta_{go} \tag{9.10}$$

are the total (or unconditional) income and price elasticities. The values of these elasticities are contained in Table 6.10 and are computed using in equation (9.10) for i,j=1,2,3, η_g=1.004 (from Table 6.9) and the elasticity values given in (9.9) and Table 6.6. A comparison of Tables 6.6 and 6.10 reveals that the unconditional income elasticities are almost exactly equal to their conditional counterparts (as $\eta_g \approx 1$). Also, the own–price elasticities in Table 6.10 are all larger (in absolute value) than those in Table 6.6 because of the indirect effects of the price changes. The negative cross–price elasticities in Table 6.10 indicate complementarity.

Table 6.10 Unconditional Income and Slutsky Price Elasticities

Beverage	Unconditional income elasticity η_i	Unconditional price elasticities			
		η_{i1}	η_{i2}	η_{i3}	η_{io}
Beer	.73	-.43	-.02	.05	.41
Wine	.61	-.05	-.37	.10	.34
Spirits	2.52	-.50	-.07	-.83	1.40

6.10 On Substitutes and Complements

In Section 6.5 it was shown that there is complementarity amongst the alcoholic beverages (see Table 6.4). However, all the cross-price elasticities in Table 6.6 are positive, indicating that the three beverages are pairwise substitutes. The occurrence of negative cross-price elasticities in Table 6.10 only serves to add to the apparent contradiction. In this section these findings are reconciled.

The explanation lies in different variables being held constant in the three tables. The measures based on the Hessian matrix of the utility function (Table 6.4) deal with only the specific part of the substitution effect and thus hold constant the marginal utility of income. By contrast, the conditional elasticities in Table 6.6 refer to both the specific and general components; as they are conditional, they hold constant total consumption of alcohol. Finally, the elasticities in Table 6.10 are unconditional and hold constant income rather than alcohol expenditure. Let $F_{ij} = \nu'_{ij}/w'_i$ be the elasticity of demand for beverage i with respect to the price of beverage j when the marginal utility of income is held constant (the F is for Frisch); here ν'_{ij} is the (i,j)-*th* price coefficient defined in Section 6.5 and w'_i is the conditional budget share of beverage i. The conditional Slutsky elasticity η'_{ij} is the same elasticity when real total expenditure on alcohol remains unchanged. It can then be shown that the relationship between η'_{ij} and F_{ij} is

$$\eta'_{ij} = F_{ij} - \eta_{gg} w'_i \eta'_i \eta'_j, \tag{10.1}$$

where η_{gg} is the own-price elasticity of demand for alcohol as a whole; and η'_i is the conditional income elasticity of demand for i. As $\eta_{gg} < 0$ and w'_i, η'_i, η'_j are all positive, equation (10.1) shows that the conditional Slutsky elasticity is algebraically larger than the corresponding Frisch elasticity. This explains why Table 6.6 reveals substitutability ($\eta'_{ij} > 0$ for $i \neq j$), whereas Table 6.4 indicates complementarity (ν'_{12}, $\nu'_{13} < 0$).

The relationship between the unconditional elasticity (η_{ij}) and its conditional counterpart is given in the middle part of equation (9.10), $\eta_{ij} = \eta'_{ij} + \eta'_i \eta_{gj}$, where η_{gj} is the elasticity of total alcohol with respect to the price of beverage j. As $\eta_{gj} < 0$, $j = 1,2,3$, this equation shows that $\eta_{ij} < \eta'_{ij}$, which explains the negative cross elasticities in Table 6.10. Take, for example, $i = 3$ (spirits) and $j = 1$ (beer). From Tables 6.6 and 6.10, $\eta'_{31} = .5$ (substitutes) and $\eta_{31} = -.5$ (complements). Here an increase in beer prices causes total alcohol to fall to such an extent that the indirect effect swamps the substitution effect, so that the total effect of the beer-price increase is for spirits' consumption to fall.

6.11 Comparison with Other Studies

Alcohol consumption patterns in several other countries have also been analysed recently at The University of Western Australia using a similar methodology to ours. These studies are summarised in Table 6.11. Note that beer is always a (conditional) necessity and, in every case except one, spirits a luxury. As can be seen, New Zealanders are the median drinkers. The last two rows of Table 6.11 reveals both similarities and

Table 6.11 Conditional Demand Elasticities for Alcohol from Recent Studies

Author	Country	Period	Income elasticities			Own-price Slutsky elasticities		
			Beer	Wine	Spirits	Beer	Wine	Spirits
Clements and E.A.Selvanathan (1987)	Australia	1956-1977	.73	.62	2.50	-.12	-.34	-.52
——— (1987)	U K.	1955-1975	.41	1.91	1.81	-.19	-.23	-.24
——— (1987)	U.S.	1949-1982	.75	.46	1.34	-.09	-.22	-.10
Pearce (1986)	New Zealand	1966-1982	.85	1.14	1.31	-.15	-.35	- 32
Quek (1988)	Canada	1953-1982	.77	1.12	1 20	-.28	- 58	-.30
E A.Selvanathan (1988)	U.K.	1955-1985	.55	1.23	1.82	-.13	- 37	-.32
Wong (1988)	U.K.	1920-1938	.94	1.62	.94	-.25	- 99	-.51
Median			.75	1.14	1.34	-.15	-.35	-.32
Current study	Australia	1956-1986	.73	.61	2.51	-.15	-.32	-.61

differences between the previous elasticities (as summarized by the medians) and those derived here. The major differences involve the income elasticities for wine and spirits and the price elasticity for spirits. The other three pairs of elasticities are quite similar. Note also it is reassuring that the old elasticities for Australia (given in the first row of the table) agree well with the new ones (last row).

Thus there are similarities and differences among the elasticities for different countries. To a certain extent, differences are to be expected for such finely-defined commodities as beer, wine and spirits. Presumably, if the three beverages were aggregated into total alcohol, there would be fewer differences. This matter is pursued by E.A. Selvanathan and Clements (1988) who analyse annual per capita alcohol data for Australia (1956–77), the UK (1955–75) and the US (1949–82). Figure 6.9 plots the change in alcohol consumption relative to income, $DQ_g - DQ$, against the change in the relative price, $DP_g - DP^*$. Both variables are multiplied by 100 in the figure so they are approximately percentage changes. The solid lines are the LS regression lines. As can be seen, there is a distinct negative relationship between consumption and the price

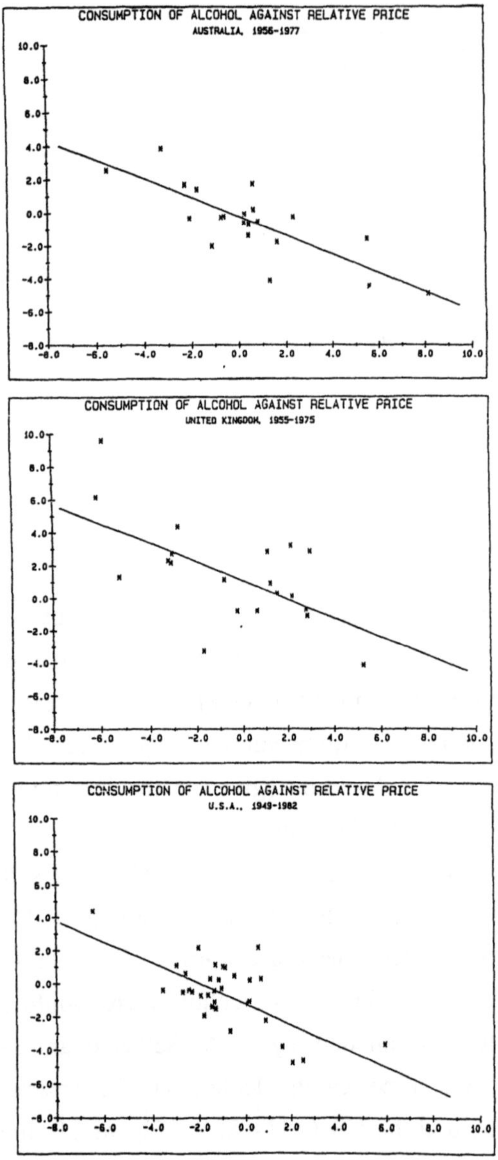

Fig. 6.9 Consumption of Alcohol Against Relative Price in 3 Countries

in each country. The slopes of the regression lines are (standard errors in parentheses) Australia -.56 (.10), UK -.61 (.17) and US -.63 (.12). The slopes, which are all highly significant, are interpreted as estimates of the own-price elasticity of demand for alcohol under the assumption of a unitary income elasticity. Note that these elasticities are very similar in the three countries. E.A. Selvanathan and Clements (1988), using formal methods, conclude that the elasticities are identical in the three countries. Their three-country pooled estimates are .81 (s.e. = .10) for the income elasticity and -.59 (.07) for the price elasticity. These values are not inconsistent with those given in Table 6.11.

This intriguing similarity of elasticities across countries points in the direction of tastes being identical. It could be argued this implies that tastes are a fundamental constant which transcend national boundaries. In other words, if differences in real incomes and relative prices are adjusted for, then consumption patterns are more or less the same internationally. Such an interpretation is appealing to economists like Stigler and Becker (1977) who emphasize the universal applicability of microeconomic theory and eschew the ad hocery of 'special case' explanations. On the other hand, it should be acknowledged that basic characteristics of Australians, the British and Americans are not too dissimilar, so that the finding of similar elasticities for alcohol should not come as such a great surprise.

6.12 Concluding Comments

This chapter has presented an extensive analysis of the consumption patterns of beer, wine and spirits. The hypotheses of demand homogeneity and Slutsky symmetry were tested. The results indicated that drinkers do not suffer from money illusion and are consistent in their choice of beverage, i.e., the substitution effects are symmetric. A feature of this hypothesis testing was the use of new Monte Carlo techniques which do not rely on the usual assumption of normality or asymptotic theory. Next, we showed that there was evidence of complementarity among the three beverages, contrary to popular belief. In particular, the results indicated that beer and spirits are specific complements in the sense that the marginal utility of beer increases with additional consumption of spirits. The marginal utility of wine, however, is independent of the consumption of the other two beverages, indicating that wine by itself satisfies a basic want of the consumer.

The conditional (i.e., within the alcoholic beverages group) income elasticities show that beer and wine are necessities, while spirits is a strong luxury. The conditional own-price Slutsky elasticities are -.2, -.3, and -.6 for beer, wine and spirits. The demand equation for alcohol as a whole reveals that the income and own-price elasticities are 1 and -.6, respectively. There are several other recent studies which apply a similar methodology to other countries. A systematic review of these highlights some intriguing similarities and differences in elasticities across countries. Beer is always a (conditional) necessity and, in every case except one, spirits a luxury. Also, the income and price elasticities for alcohol as a whole are not significantly different in Australia, the UK and the US, pointing in the direction of tastes being the same for the broader aggregates.

Based on the usual criteria of plausibility of the results, hypothesis testing and compatibility of the findings with previous studies, taken as a whole our approach of explaining alcohol demand in terms of the utility-maximizing theory of the consumer must be judged to be at least fairly successful. However, it should be acknowledged that there are still some important aspects of alcohol consumption patterns that remain unexplained in this work. In particular, constant terms are needed in all the demand equations to account for residual trends in consumption. These trends could reflect changing demographics, immigration, new packaging and so on. More research is required to explore systematically the role of these factors.

References

Adrian, M. and B.S. Ferguson (1987). 'Demand for Domestic and Imported Alcohol in Canada,' *Applied Economics* 19: 531–540.

Clements, K.W. and L.W. Johnson (1983). 'The Demand for Beer, Wine and Spirits: A System–Wide Analysis,' *Journal of Business* 56: 273–304. Reprinted in T.J. Coyne ed. 1985. *Reading in Managerial Economics*, 4th ed. Plano, Texas: Business Publications, Inc., pp.127–155.

Clements, K.W. and E.A. Selvanathan (1987). 'Alcohol Consumption,' Chapter 5 in H. Theil and K.W. Clements, *Applied Demand Analysis: Results from System–Wide Approaches*. Cambridge, Mass.: Ballinger Publishing Company, pp.185–264.

Clements, K.W. and E.A. Selvanathan (1988). 'The Rotterdam Demand Model and its Application in Marketing,' *Marketing Science* 7 (1988): 60-75.

Clements, K.W. and S. Selvanathan (1989). 'The Economic Determinants of Alcohol Consumption,' Discussion Paper 89.35, Department of Economics, The University of Western Australia, December 1989.

Clements, K.W. and S. Selvanathan (1991). 'The Economic Determinants of Alcohol Consumption,' *Australian Journal of Agricultural Economics* 35: 209-231.

Duffy, M.H. (1987). 'Advertising and the Inter–Product Distribution of Demand: A Rotterdam Model Approach,' *European Economic Review* 31: 1051–1070.

Efron, B. (1979). 'Bootstrap Methods: Another Look at the Jackknife,' *Annals of Statistics* 7: 1–26.

Fuss, M. and L. Waverman (1987). 'The Demand for Alcoholic Beverages in Canada: An Application of the Almost Ideal Demand System System,' Working Paper No. 8714, Department of Economics and Institute for Policy Analysis, University of Toronto.

Heien, D. and G. Pompelli (1989). 'The Demand for Alcoholic Beverages: Economic and Demographic Effects,' *Southern Economic Journal* 55: 759–770.

Holm, P. (1989). 'Advertising, Alcohol Content and Demand for Alcoholic Beverages: A System Approach,' Unpublished, Department of Economics, University of Helsinki.

Johnson, J.A., E.H. Oksanen, M.R. Veall and D. Fretz (1990). 'Alternative Approaches to the Measurement of Consumption and Price of Alcoholic Beverages, Canada, 1957–1983' *Journal of Studies on Alcohol* 51: 82–85.

Jones, A.M. (1989). 'A Systems Approach to the Demand for Alcohol and Tobacco,' *Bulletin of Economic Research* 41: 82–101.

Pearce, D. (1986). 'The Demand for Alcohol in New Zealand,' Discussion Paper No.86.02, Department of Economics, The University of Western Australia.

Penm, J.H. (1988). 'An Econometric Study of the Demand for Bottled, Canned and Bulk Beer,' *Economic Record* 64: 268–74.

Quek, K.E. (1988). 'The Demand for Alcohol in Canada: An Econometric Study,' Discussion Paper No.88.08, Department of Economics, The University of Western Australia.

Selvanathan, E.A. (1988). 'Alcohol Consumption in the UK, 1955–85: A System-Wide Analysis,' *Applied Economics* 20: 1071–86.

Selvanathan, E.A. and K.W. Clements (1988). 'Is the Elasticity of Demand for Alcohol an International Constant?' Economic Research Centre, Department of Economics, The University of Western Australia, unpublished paper.

Stigler, G.J. and G.S. Becker (1977). 'De Gustibus Non Est Disputandum,' *American Economic Review* 67: 76–90.

Strobel, D. (1982). 'Determining Outliers in Multivariate Surveys by Decomposition of a Measure of Information,' *Business and Economic Statistics Section, Proceedings of the American Statistical Association*, pp.31-35.

Theil, H. (1987). 'The Econometrics of Demand Systems,' Chapter 3 in H. Theil and K.W. Clements, *Applied Demand Analysis: Results from System-Wide Approaches*. Cambridge, Mass: Ballinger Publishing Company, pp. 101–62.

Wong, A.Y-T. (1988). 'The Demand for Alcohol in the UK 1920–1938: An Econometric Study,' Discussion Paper No. 88.13, Department of Economics, The University of Western Australia.

7 Advertising and Consumption: A Theoretical Analysis

E.A. Selvanathan
School of International Business Relations, Griffith University, Australia.

7.1 Introduction

In Chapters 1 to 6 we followed the traditional approach to consumption theory to analyse the demand for a commodity in terms of the consumer's income and prices. This chapter extends the differential approach to consumption theory (see Section 1.10) to analyse the effects of advertising. We give a comparative statics analysis of advertising and results on separability of the consumer's utility function in the presence of advertising. This chapter is exclusively theoretical. In Chapter 8 we apply this theoretical framework to U.K. alcohol data.

We commence this chapter by extending the usual consumer demand problem to deal with advertising. We then develop a differential demand system with advertising variables. Under block independence, we obtain demand equations for groups of goods in which income, prices and advertising of the group play a role. Block independence also leads to demand equations for goods within each group. We show that under certain assumptions, the within group (or conditional) demand equations contain only total consumption of the group, prices and advertising of goods within the group.

7.2 Advertising and Consumption

In this section initially we review the traditional consumer maximization problem and the solution to Barten's (1964) fundamental matrix equation discussed in Section 1.10. Then we extend the analysis for advertising.

A Brief Review of Previous Results

The consumer's utility function is

$$u = u(\mathbf{q}), \tag{2.1}$$

where $\mathbf{q} = [q_1 \dots q_n]'$ is the quantity vector. To maximize $u(\mathbf{q})$ subject to the budget constraint, $\mathbf{p}'\mathbf{q} = M$, we form the Lagrangian function $u^*(\mathbf{q},\lambda) = u(\mathbf{q}) - \lambda(\mathbf{p}'\mathbf{q} - M)$, where λ is the Lagrangian multiplier; $\mathbf{p} = [p_1 \dots p_n]'$ is the price vector; and M is income. The first-order conditions are

$$\frac{\partial u}{\partial \mathbf{q}} = \lambda \mathbf{p} \tag{2.2}$$

and

$$\mathbf{p}'\mathbf{q} = M. \tag{2.3}$$

The solution to the first-order conditions results in a system of demand equations of the form

$$\mathbf{q} = \mathbf{q}(M,\mathbf{p}) \qquad \text{or} \qquad q_i = q_i(M,p_1,\dots,p_n), \qquad i=1,\dots,n. \tag{2.4}$$

By differentiating the first-order conditions (2.2) and (2.3) with respect to $\mathbf{p}$ and M we obtain

$$U\frac{\partial \mathbf{q}}{\partial \mathbf{p}'} = \lambda I + \mathbf{p}\frac{\partial \lambda}{\partial \mathbf{p}'}, \qquad \mathbf{p}'\frac{\partial \mathbf{q}}{\partial \mathbf{p}'} = -\mathbf{q}', \tag{2.5}$$

$$U\frac{\partial \mathbf{q}}{\partial M} = \frac{\partial \lambda}{\partial M}\mathbf{p}, \qquad \mathbf{p}'\frac{\partial \mathbf{q}}{\partial M} = 1, \tag{2.6}$$

where $U = [\partial^2 u/\partial q_i \partial q_j]$ is the Hessian matrix of the utility function, which is symmetric negative definite. Combining equations (2.5) and (2.6) yields Barten's (1964) fundamental matrix equation, equation (10.3) of Chapter 1. The solution for the compensated-price derivatives of the demand equations is

$$\frac{\partial q^*}{\partial p'} = \lambda U^{-1} - \frac{\lambda}{\partial\lambda/\partial M}\frac{\partial q}{\partial M}\frac{\partial q'}{\partial M}, \tag{2.7}$$

where $\partial q^*/\partial p' = \partial q/\partial p' + (\partial q/\partial M)q'$. It is obvious from equation (2.7) and the symmetry of U^{-1} that the compensated-cross-price slopes are symmetric,

$$\frac{\partial q^*}{\partial p'} = \frac{\partial q^*}{\partial p}. \tag{2.8}$$

Premultiplying both sides of the first equation of (2.6) by U^{-1} and taking the transpose we get

$$\frac{\partial q'}{\partial M} = \frac{\partial\lambda}{\partial M}p'U^{-1},$$

where we have used the symmetry of U^{-1}. Premultiplying both sides of (2.7) by p' and using the above result we obtain

$$p'\frac{\partial q^*}{\partial p'} = \lambda p'U^{-1} - \frac{\lambda}{\partial\lambda/\partial M}p'\frac{\partial q}{\partial M}\frac{\partial q'}{\partial M} = 0, \tag{2.9}$$

where we have also used the second equation in (2.6).

Extension for Advertising

Let a_i be the advertising of good i (i=1,...,n) and $\mathbf{a} = [a_i]$ be the corresponding vector. We assume that a_i is outside the control of the consumer, like p_i and M. Following Barten (1977), we now postulate that the consumer's preferences can be described by means of a utility function of the form

$$u = u(\mathbf{q},\mathbf{a}). \tag{2.10}$$

We write the Hessian matrix of the utility function as

$$\frac{\partial^2 u}{\partial\boldsymbol{\zeta}\partial\boldsymbol{\zeta}'} = \begin{bmatrix} \mathbf{U} & \mathbf{V} \\ \mathbf{V}' & \mathbf{F} \end{bmatrix}, \tag{2.11}$$

where $\boldsymbol{\zeta} = [\mathbf{q}' \ \mathbf{a}']'$; $\mathbf{U} = \partial^2 u/\partial\mathbf{q}\partial\mathbf{q}'$; $\mathbf{V} = \partial^2 u/\partial\mathbf{q}\partial\mathbf{a}'$; and $\mathbf{F} = \partial^2 u/\partial\mathbf{a}\partial\mathbf{a}'$. As before, we assume that this Hessian is symmetric negative definite, which is needed for a budget-constrained utility maximum.

The Lagrangian for the maximization problem is now $u^*(\mathbf{q},\lambda) = u(\mathbf{q},\mathbf{a}) - \lambda(\mathbf{p}'\mathbf{q} - M)$. The first-order conditions are equations (2.2) and (2.3) with u given by (2.10). This maximization problem will result in a system of demand equations of the form

$$\mathbf{q} = \mathbf{q}(M,\mathbf{p},\mathbf{a}) \qquad \text{or} \qquad q_i = q_i(M,p_1,\ldots,p_n,a_1,\ldots,a_n), \quad i=1,\ldots,n. \tag{2.12}$$

This is an extended version of the demand system (2.4).

7.3 The Comparative Statics of Advertising

In this section we shall analyse the effects of advertising on consumption by deriving the partial derivative matrix $\partial\mathbf{q}/\partial\mathbf{a}' = [\partial q_i/\partial a_j]$ and some related measures.

Differentiating (2.2) and (2.3) with respect to **a** we obtain

$$\mathbf{U}\frac{\partial\mathbf{q}}{\partial\mathbf{a}'} + \mathbf{V} = \mathbf{p}\frac{\partial\lambda}{\partial\mathbf{a}'}, \qquad \mathbf{p}'\frac{\partial\mathbf{q}}{\partial\mathbf{a}'} = \mathbf{0}, \tag{3.1}$$

where **V** is a component of the Hessian matrix of the utility function defined in (2.11); and $\partial\lambda/\partial \mathbf{a} = [\partial\lambda/\partial a_i]$. In scalar form the second equation in (3.1) is $\Sigma_{i=1}^{n} p_i(\partial q_i/\partial a_j) = 0$ for j=1,...,n. This means that a change in the demand for one good due to advertising has to be compensated by a change in the demand for all other goods so that total expenditure remains constant. This property is analogous to (2.9).

Premultiplying both sides of (2.7) by **U** and using the first equation of (2.6) we obtain

$$\mathbf{U}\frac{\partial \mathbf{q}^*}{\partial \mathbf{p}'} = \lambda \mathbf{I} - \frac{\lambda}{\partial\lambda/\partial M}\mathbf{U}\frac{\partial \mathbf{q}}{\partial M}\frac{\partial \mathbf{q}'}{\partial M} = \lambda \mathbf{I} - \lambda \mathbf{p}\frac{\partial \mathbf{q}'}{\partial M}.$$

Taking the transpose of the above equation and post multiplying both sides by $\partial\mathbf{q}/\partial\mathbf{a}'$ gives

$$\frac{\partial \mathbf{q}^*}{\partial \mathbf{p}'}\mathbf{U}\frac{\partial \mathbf{q}}{\partial \mathbf{a}'} = \lambda\left[\mathbf{I} - \frac{\partial \mathbf{q}}{\partial M}\mathbf{p}'\right]\frac{\partial \mathbf{q}}{\partial \mathbf{a}'} = \lambda\frac{\partial \mathbf{q}}{\partial \mathbf{a}'}, \tag{3.2}$$

where we have used equation (2.8), the symmetry of **U** and the second equation in (3.1). Premultiplying both sides of the first equation in (3.1) by $\partial \mathbf{q}^*/\partial \mathbf{p}'$ we obtain

$$\frac{\partial \mathbf{q}^*}{\partial \mathbf{p}'}\mathbf{U}\frac{\partial \mathbf{q}}{\partial \mathbf{a}'} = -\frac{\partial \mathbf{q}^*}{\partial \mathbf{p}'}\mathbf{V} + \frac{\partial \mathbf{q}^*}{\partial \mathbf{p}'}\mathbf{p}\frac{\partial \lambda}{\partial \mathbf{a}'}$$

$$= -\frac{\partial \mathbf{q}^*}{\partial \mathbf{p}'}\mathbf{V},$$

where the second step is based on (2.8) and (2.9). Combining this with equation (3.2) gives

$$\frac{\partial \mathbf{q}}{\partial \mathbf{a}'} = -\frac{1}{\lambda}\frac{\partial \mathbf{q}^*}{\partial \mathbf{p}'}\mathbf{V}. \tag{3.3}$$

In scalar form, using equation (2.2) and the definition of **V**, equation (3.3) can be written as

$$\frac{\partial q_i}{\partial a_k} = -\sum_{j=1}^{n} \frac{\partial q_i^*}{\partial p_j} \frac{p_j}{a_k} \frac{\partial\left[\log \frac{\partial u}{\partial q_j}\right]}{\partial(\log a_k)},$$

which is the well-known 'Tintner-Basmann' equation (see Basmann, 1956). This equation shows that the effects of advertising on consumption are related to the substitution effects of price changes.

We define μ_{ij} as the elasticity of the marginal utility of good i with respect to advertising of good j,

$$\frac{\partial\left[\log \frac{\partial u}{\partial q_i}\right]}{\partial(\log a_j)} = \mu_{ij}. \tag{3.4}$$

We can rewrite (3.4) as

$$\frac{\partial\left[\frac{\partial u}{\partial q_i}\right]}{\partial a_j} = \frac{\mu_{ij}\left[\frac{\partial u}{\partial q_i}\right]}{a_j} = \lambda \frac{p_i \mu_{ij}}{a_j},$$

where for the second step we have used (2.2) in its scalar form. Noting that the left-hand side of the above equation is $\partial^2 u/\partial q_i \partial a_j$, it can be written for i,j=1,...,n as

$$\mathbf{V} = \lambda \mathbf{P} \boldsymbol{\mu} \mathbf{A}^{-1}, \tag{3.5}$$

where $\mathbf{V} = \partial^2 u/\partial \mathbf{q} \partial \mathbf{a}'$; $\mathbf{P} = \text{diag}[p_1 \dots p_n]$; $\boldsymbol{\mu} = [\mu_{ij}]$; and $\mathbf{A} = \text{diag}[a_1 \dots a_n]$. Premultiplying both sides of (3.5) by $\partial \mathbf{q}^*/\partial \mathbf{p}'$ gives

$$\frac{\partial \mathbf{q}^*}{\partial \mathbf{p}'} \mathbf{V} = \lambda \frac{\partial \mathbf{q}^*}{\partial \mathbf{p}'} \mathbf{P} \boldsymbol{\mu} \mathbf{A}^{-1},$$

which when combined with (3.3) yields

$$\frac{\partial \mathbf{q}}{\partial \mathbf{a}'} = -\frac{\partial \mathbf{q}^*}{\partial \mathbf{p}'} \mathbf{P}\boldsymbol{\mu}\mathbf{A}^{-1}. \tag{3.6}$$

Equation (3.6) can be expressed in elasticity form as

$$\boldsymbol{\tau} = \frac{\partial(\log \mathbf{q})}{\partial(\log \mathbf{a}')} = -\boldsymbol{\eta}^* \boldsymbol{\mu} \quad \text{or} \quad \tau_{ij} = \frac{\partial(\log q_i)}{\partial(\log a_j)} = -\sum_{k=1}^{n} \eta^*_{ik}\mu_{kj}, \tag{3.7}$$

where $\boldsymbol{\tau} = [\tau_{ij}] = [\partial(\log q_i)/\partial(\log a_j)]$ is the matrix of advertising elasticities; and $\boldsymbol{\eta}^* = [\eta^*_{ij}]$ is the matrix of compensated price elasticities. Equation (3.7) is a simple result showing again the link between the effects of advertising and the substitution effects.

7.4 Two Special Cases

In this section we analyse the implications of two special cases of the matrix $[\mu_{ij}]$.

The First Special Case

Consider the special case when the elasticity of the marginal utility of each good with respect to its own advertising is unity and when all the corresponding cross elasticities are zero. That is,

$$\mu_{ij} = \begin{cases} 1 & \text{if } i=j \\ 0 & \text{otherwise,} \end{cases} \tag{4.1}$$

so that $\boldsymbol{\mu} = \mathbf{I}$, the $n \times n$ identity matrix. In this situation (3.7) implies

$$\tau_{ij} = -\eta^*_{ij}, \qquad i,j=1,\dots,n.$$

In words, the elasticity of consumption of i with respect to advertising of j is the negative of the corresponding (compensated) price elasticity. This means that $\tau_{ii} > 0$ for i=1,...,n; $\tau_{ij} < 0$ if i and j are net substitutes; and $\tau_{ij} > 0$ if i and j are net complements. These results make sense since it is reasonable to expect that advertising will depress the sales of products which are substitutes for the good in question ($\eta^*_{ij} > 0$); and vice versa for complements.

The Second Special Case

Next, consider the slightly more general case

$$\mu_{ij} = \begin{cases} \mu & \text{if } i=j \\ 0 & \text{otherwise,} \end{cases} \tag{4.2}$$

where μ is a scalar, so that $\boldsymbol{\mu} = \mu \mathbf{I}$. This kind of restriction has been considered by Theil (1980). Here again all cross-advertising elasticities of the marginal utilities are zero, but now the own elasticities are non-unity. In this situation, the advertising elasticities of consumption are a constant multiple $-\mu$ of the corresponding price elasticities.

7.5 Indexes of Advertising

Consider the change in the marginal utility of j resulting from changes in the advertising of the n goods. In logarithmic form this is

$$d\left[\log \frac{\partial u}{\partial q_j}\right] = \sum_{k=1}^{n} \frac{\partial\left[\log \frac{\partial u}{\partial q_j}\right]}{\partial(\log a_k)} d(\log a_k)$$

$$= \sum_{k=1}^{n} \mu_{jk} d(\log a_k),$$

where the second step follows from definition (3.4). The right-hand side of the above equation can be considered as an index of advertising, where the "weights" are the elasticities μ_{jk}. We shall write $d(\log \tilde{a}_j)$ for this index,

$$d(\log \tilde{a}_j) = \sum_{k=1}^{n} \mu_{jk} d(\log a_k). \tag{5.1}$$

We define a marginal-share-weighted average of $d(\log \tilde{a}_1),\ldots,d(\log \tilde{a}_n)$ as

$$d(\log \tilde{A}') = \sum_{j=1}^{n} \theta_j d(\log \tilde{a}_j), \tag{5.2}$$

where $\theta_j = \partial(p_j q_j)/\partial M$ is the marginal share of commodity j. This can be considered as an index of $d(\log \tilde{a}_1),\ldots,d(\log \tilde{a}_n)$. Substituting for $d(\log \tilde{a}_j)$ from (5.1) in (5.2) we can also express this index in terms of the n original advertising variables, $d(\log a_1),\ldots,d(\log a_n)$,

$$d(\log \tilde{A}') = \sum_{j=1}^{n} \theta_j \sum_{k=1}^{n} \mu_{jk} d(\log a_k)$$

$$= \sum_{k=1}^{n} h_k d(\log a_k), \tag{5.3}$$

where

$$h_k = \sum_{j=1}^{n} \theta_j \mu_{jk}.$$

Consider the situation when there is an equiproportionate change in advertising on each good, $d(\log a_i) = d(\log a)$ for i=1,...,n. In this situation equation (5.1) becomes

$$d(\log \tilde{a}_j) = \mu_j d(\log a), \tag{5.4}$$

where $\mu_j = \Sigma_{k=1}^{n} \mu_{jk}$. This μ_j is interpreted as the percentage increase in the marginal utility of j resulting from a one percent increase in the advertising of each of the n goods. Using (5.4), (5.2) becomes

$$d(\log \tilde{A}') = d(\log a) \sum_{j=1}^{n} \theta_j \mu_j. \tag{5.5}$$

Let μ_j be the same for all j and equal to a constant μ_o, i.e.,

$$\mu_j = \mu_o, \qquad j=1,...,n. \tag{5.6}$$

Then (5.4) and (5.5) imply that $d(\log \tilde{a}_j) = \mu_o d(\log a)$ and $d(\log \tilde{A}') = \mu_o d(\log a)$, respectively, where we have used $\Sigma_{j=1}^{n} \theta_j = 1$. With restriction (5.6), an equiproportionate change in advertising of each good causes the relative advertising index, $d(\log \tilde{a}_j/\tilde{A}')$, to vanish:

$$d\left[\log \frac{\tilde{a}_j}{\tilde{A}'}\right] = d(\log \tilde{a}_j) - d(\log \tilde{A}') = 0.$$

In what follows, to ensure that the relative advertising index vanishes for an equiproportionate change in advertising of all n goods, we shall impose constraint (5.6).

We return to the special case (4.1) whereby $\mu_{jk} = \delta_{jk}$, δ_{jk} being the Kronecker delta. Here $d(\log \tilde{a}_j)$ becomes $d(\log a_j)$ and consequently $d(\log \tilde{A}')$ becomes a marginal-share-weighted average of $d(\log a_1),...,d(\log a_n)$, which we write as

$$d(\log A') = \sum_{j=1}^{n} \theta_j d(\log a_j). \tag{5.7}$$

This can be described as a Frisch index. In the second special case (4.2), $\mu_{jk} = \mu\delta_{jk}$, $d(\log \tilde{a}_j) = \mu d(\log a_j)$ and the advertising index $d(\log \tilde{A}')$ is a multiple μ of the Frisch index. It is to be noted that these two special cases satisfy constraint (5.6), so that $d(\log \tilde{a}_j/\tilde{A}')$ vanishes for an equiproportionate change in advertising on all n goods.

7.6 A Differential Demand System with Advertising

In this section we shall briefly review the differential demand system associated with (2.4) previously discussed in Section 1.12. We then derive a differential demand system with advertising.

Previous Results

The total differential of (2.4) is

$$dq_i = \frac{\partial q_i}{\partial M} dM + \sum_{j=1}^{n} \frac{\partial q_i}{\partial p_j} dp_j, \qquad i=1,\dots,n.$$

Transforming the above equation to logarithmic differential form by multiplying both sides by p_i/M and using $w_i = p_i q_i/M$, we obtain

$$w_i d(\log q_i) = \frac{\partial (p_i q_i)}{\partial M} d(\log M) + \sum_{j=1}^{n} \frac{p_i p_j}{M} \frac{\partial q_i}{\partial p_j} d(\log p_j)$$

$$= \theta_i d(\log Q) + \sum_{j=1}^{n} \nu_{ij} d\left[\log \frac{p_j}{P'}\right], \tag{6.1}$$

where $d(\log Q) = \Sigma_{i=1}^{n} w_i d(\log q_i)$ is the Divisia volume index; ν_{ij} is the (i,j)-*th* price coefficient; and $d(\log P') = \Sigma_{j=1}^{n} \theta_j d(\log p_j)$ is the Frisch price index. The price coefficients are symmetric in i and j and satisfy

$$\sum_{j=1}^{n} \nu_{ij} = \phi\theta_i, \qquad i=1,\ldots,n, \tag{6.2}$$

where ϕ is the income flexibility. Equation (6.1) is the i-*th* differential demand equation in terms of relative prices.

To formulate demand equations in terms of the absolute prices we use the Slutsky coefficients defined as

$$\pi_{ij} = \nu_{ij} - \phi\theta_i\theta_j, \qquad i,j=1,\ldots,n. \tag{6.3}$$

The Slutsky coefficients are obviously also symmetric and, in view of (6.2), satisfy

$$\sum_{j=1}^{n} \pi_{ij} = 0, \qquad i=1,\ldots,n, \tag{6.4}$$

which is the homogeneity constraint. If we substitute for ν_{ij} from (6.3), the price term of (6.1) becomes

$$\sum_{j=1}^{n} \nu_{ij} d\left[\log \frac{p_j}{P'}\right] = \sum_{j=1}^{n} \pi_{ij} d(\log p_j), \tag{6.5}$$

so that (6.1) takes the form

$$w_i d(\log q_i) = \theta_i d(\log Q) + \sum_{j=1}^{n} \pi_{ij} d(\log p_j). \tag{6.6}$$

This is the differential demand equation for good i in terms of absolute prices.

An Extension

The total differential of (2.12) is

$$dq_i = \frac{\partial q_i}{\partial M} dM + \sum_{j=1}^{n} \frac{\partial q_i}{\partial p_j} dp_j + \sum_{j=1}^{n} \frac{\partial q_i}{\partial a_j} da_j, \qquad i=1,\dots,n.$$

As before, we transform the above equation to logarithmic differential form by multiplying both sides by p_i/M and using $w_i = p_i q_i/M$ to give

$$w_i d(\log q_i) = \frac{\partial (p_i q_i)}{\partial M} d(\log M) + \sum_{j=1}^{n} \frac{p_i p_j}{M} \frac{\partial q_i}{\partial p_j} d(\log p_j)$$
$$+ \sum_{j=1}^{n} \frac{p_i a_j}{M} \frac{\partial q_i}{\partial a_j} d(\log a_j). \tag{6.7}$$

From equation (6.1) we have that the first two right-hand side terms of (6.7) equal $\theta_i d(\log Q) + \Sigma_{j=1}^{n} \nu_{ij} d[\log (p_j/P')]$, where $d(\log Q)$ and $d(\log P')$ are as before.

In Section 7.7 we show that the advertising term in (6.7) can be simplified to

$$\sum_{j=1}^{n} \frac{p_i a_j}{M} \frac{\partial q_i}{\partial a_j} d(\log a_j) = - \sum_{j=1}^{n} \nu_{ij} d\left[\log \frac{\tilde{a}_j}{\tilde{A}'}\right], \tag{6.8}$$

where $d[\log \tilde{a}_j/\tilde{A}'] = d(\log \tilde{a}_j) - d(\log \tilde{A}')$ with $d(\log \tilde{a}_j)$ and $d(\log \tilde{A}')$ as defined in (5.1) and (5.2), respectively. In view of (6.8) equation (6.7) becomes

$$w_i d(\log q_i) = \theta_i d(\log Q) + \sum_{j=1}^{n} \nu_{ij} \left[d\left[\log \frac{p_j}{P'}\right] - d\left[\log \frac{\tilde{a}_j}{\tilde{A}'}\right]\right]. \tag{6.9}$$

This is the *relative price version of the extended differential demand equation* for commodity i. Equation (6.9) shows that the demand for good i depends on total consumption, the relative price and relative advertising of each good. Under restriction (5.6), when there is an equiproportionate change in the advertising of all goods the relative advertising term in (6.9) vanishes.

Below equation (5.6) we pointed out that when $\mu = I$, $d(\log \tilde{a}_j) = d(\log a_j)$ and $d(\log \tilde{A}') = d(\log A')$. Consequently, in this case the j-*th* relative advertising term in equation (6.9) simplifies to $d(\log a_j/A')$, so that the last term in that equation becomes

$$\sum_{j=1}^{n} \nu_{ij}\left[d\left[\log \frac{p_j}{P'}\right] - d\left[\log \frac{a_j}{A'}\right]\right].$$

The j-*th* term in this sum involves only the relative price and advertising of good j. This is not true in equation (6.9) as in general $d(\log \tilde{a}_j)$ involves the advertising of all goods; see equation (5.1).

Below equation (5.7) we showed that when $\mu = \mu I$, $d(\log \tilde{a}_j) = \mu d(\log a_j)$, and $d(\log \tilde{A}') = \mu d(\log A')$. Hence the relative advertising index $d(\log \tilde{a}_j/\tilde{A}')$ becomes a multiple μ of $d(\log a_j/A')$. Consequently, the last term in equation (6.9) simplifies to

$$\sum_{j=1}^{n} \nu_{ij}\left[d\left[\log \frac{p_j}{P'}\right] - \mu d\left[\log \frac{a_j}{A'}\right]\right].$$

Again the j-*th* term in this sum involves only the j-*th* relative price and advertising.

Equation (6.9) is formulated in terms of relative (or deflated) prices and advertising. To obtain the demand equation in absolute (or undeflated) terms we write (6.9) as

$$w_i d(\log q_i) = \theta_i d(\log Q) + \sum_{j=1}^{n} \nu_{ij} d\left[\log \frac{p_j}{P'}\right] - \sum_{j=1}^{n} \nu_{ij} d\left[\log \frac{\tilde{a}_j}{\tilde{A}'}\right]. \tag{6.10}$$

In Section 7.7 we show that

$$\sum_{j=1}^{n} \nu_{ij} d\left[\log \frac{\tilde{a}_j}{\tilde{A}'}\right] = - w_i \sum_{j=1}^{n} \tau_{ij} d(\log a_j), \tag{6.11}$$

where $w_i = p_i q_i/M$ is the *i-th* budget share; and τ_{ij} is the advertising elasticity defined in equation (3.7). Using (6.5) and (6.11), (6.10) becomes

$$w_i d(\log q_i) = \theta_i d(\log Q) + \sum_{j=1}^{n} \pi_{ij} d(\log p_j) + \sum_{j=1}^{n} \lambda_{ij} d(\log a_j), \tag{6.12}$$

where $\lambda_{ij} = w_i \tau_{ij}$ is the *(i,j)-th* advertising coefficient. The above equation is the *extended differential demand equation for commodity i in terms of undeflated variables.*

In Section 7.7 we show that under restriction (5.6) the advertising coefficients λ_{ij} satisfy

$$\sum_{j=1}^{n} \lambda_{ij} = 0, \qquad i=1,...,n. \tag{6.13}$$

Equation (6.13) implies that a proportionate change in all the advertising variables does not affect the demand for any good, income and prices remaining unchanged. The Slutsky coefficients π_{ij} continue to satisfy (6.4).

Below equation (4.1) we showed that $\mu_{ij} = \delta_{ij}$ implies that $\tau_{ij} = - \eta^*_{ij}$. Therefore, $\lambda_{ij} = - w_i \eta^*_{ij} = - \pi_{ij}$ in this case. In view of this result, the demand equation (6.12) becomes

$$w_i d(\log q_i) = \theta_i d(\log Q) + \sum_{j=1}^{n} \pi_{ij} [d(\log p_j) - d(\log a_j)]. \tag{6.14}$$

Here advertising acts as the deflator of each good's price change.

Below equation (4.2) we showed that when $\mu_{ij} = \mu\delta_{ij}$, $\tau_{ij} = -\mu\eta^*_{ij}$. This implies that $\lambda_{ij} = -\mu w_i \eta^*_{ij} = -\mu\pi_{ij}$, so that (6.12) becomes

$$w_i d(\log q_i) = \theta_i d(\log Q) + \sum_{j=1}^{n} \pi_{ij}[d(\log p_j) - \mu d(\log a_j)]. \qquad (6.15)$$

7.7 Derivations

We first derive result (6.8). The advertising term in (6.7) can be considered as the i-*th* element of the n × 1 vector

$$\left[\sum_{j=1}^{n} \frac{p_i a_j}{M} \frac{\partial q_i}{\partial a_j} d(\log a_j)\right].$$

This vector can be expressed as

$$\left[\sum_{j=1}^{n} \frac{p_i a_j}{M} \frac{\partial q_i}{\partial a_j} d(\log a_j)\right] = \frac{1}{M}\mathbf{P}\frac{\partial \mathbf{q}}{\partial \mathbf{a}'}\mathbf{A}d(\log \mathbf{a}), \qquad (7.1)$$

where $\mathbf{P} = \text{diag}[p_1 \dots p_n]$; $\partial\mathbf{q}/\partial\mathbf{a}' = [\partial q_i/\partial a_j]$; $\mathbf{A} = \text{diag}[a_1 \dots a_n]$; and $d(\log \mathbf{a}) = [d(\log a_i)]$.

Premultiplying both sides of (3.6) by (1/M)**P** and then post multiplying by **A**, we obtain

$$\frac{1}{M}\mathbf{P}\frac{\partial \mathbf{q}}{\partial \mathbf{a}'}\mathbf{A} = -\frac{1}{M}\mathbf{P}\frac{\partial \mathbf{q}^*}{\partial \mathbf{p}'}\mathbf{P}\mu\mathbf{A}^{-1}\mathbf{A} = -\frac{1}{M}\mathbf{P}\frac{\partial \mathbf{q}^*}{\partial \mathbf{p}'}\mathbf{P}\mu. \qquad (7.2)$$

Substituting for $\partial\mathbf{q}^*/\partial\mathbf{p}'$ from (2.7), the far right-hand side of the above equation becomes

$$-\frac{1}{M}\mathbf{P}\frac{\partial \mathbf{q}^*}{\partial \mathbf{p}'}\mathbf{P}\boldsymbol{\mu} = -\frac{1}{M}\mathbf{P}\left[\lambda \mathbf{U}^{-1} - \frac{\lambda}{\partial\lambda/\partial M}\frac{\partial \mathbf{q}}{\partial M}\frac{\partial \mathbf{q}'}{\partial M}\right]\mathbf{P}\boldsymbol{\mu}$$

$$= -\left[\frac{\lambda}{M}\mathbf{P}\mathbf{U}^{-1}\mathbf{P} - \frac{\lambda/M}{\partial\lambda/\partial M}\mathbf{P}\frac{\partial \mathbf{q}}{\partial M}\frac{\partial \mathbf{q}'}{\partial M}\mathbf{P}'\right]\boldsymbol{\mu}$$

$$= -[\boldsymbol{\nu} - \phi\boldsymbol{\theta}\boldsymbol{\theta}']\boldsymbol{\mu}$$

$$= -\boldsymbol{\nu}[\mathbf{I} - \boldsymbol{\iota}\boldsymbol{\theta}']\boldsymbol{\mu}, \tag{7.3}$$

where the second step uses $\mathbf{P} = \mathbf{P}'$; the third step uses the definitions $\boldsymbol{\nu} = (\lambda/M)\mathbf{P}\mathbf{U}^{-1}\mathbf{P}$, $\phi = \frac{\lambda/M}{\partial\lambda/\partial M}$ and $\boldsymbol{\theta} = [\theta_i] = \mathbf{P}(\partial\mathbf{q}/\partial M)$; and the last step uses constraint (6.2) in the form $\boldsymbol{\nu\iota} = \phi\boldsymbol{\theta}$, where $\boldsymbol{\iota} = [1 \ldots 1]'$. Combining equations (7.2) and (7.3) yields

$$\frac{1}{M}\mathbf{P}\frac{\partial \mathbf{q}}{\partial \mathbf{a}'}\mathbf{A} = -\boldsymbol{\nu}[\mathbf{I} - \boldsymbol{\iota}\boldsymbol{\theta}']\boldsymbol{\mu}. \tag{7.4}$$

We write (5.1) for j=1,...,n as

$$d(\log \tilde{\mathbf{a}}) = \boldsymbol{\mu} d(\log \mathbf{a}), \tag{7.5}$$

where $d(\log \tilde{\mathbf{a}}) = [d(\log \tilde{a}_j)]$; $\boldsymbol{\mu} = [\mu_{jk}]$; and $d(\log \mathbf{a}) = [d(\log a_k)]$. We also write (5.2) in the form

$$d(\log \tilde{A}') = \boldsymbol{\theta}' d(\log \tilde{\mathbf{a}}). \tag{7.6}$$

Post multiplying both sides of (7.4) by d(log **a**) gives

$$\frac{1}{M}\mathbf{P}\frac{\partial \mathbf{q}}{\partial \mathbf{a}'}\mathbf{A}d(\log \mathbf{a}) = -\boldsymbol{\nu}[\mathbf{I} - \boldsymbol{\iota}\boldsymbol{\theta}']\boldsymbol{\mu} d(\log \mathbf{a})$$

$$= -[\boldsymbol{\nu}\, d(\log \tilde{\mathbf{a}}) - \boldsymbol{\nu\iota}\, d(\log \tilde{A}')]$$

$$= \left[- \sum_{j=1}^{n} \nu_{ij} d\left[\log \frac{\tilde{a}_j}{\tilde{A}'}\right]\right], \tag{7.7}$$

where the second step uses (7.5) and (7.6); and the last member of (7.7) represents an $n \times 1$ vector.

Combining equations (7.1) and (7.7) gives

$$\sum_{j=1}^{n} \frac{p_i a_j}{M} \frac{\partial q_i}{\partial a_j} d(\log a_j) = - \sum_{j=1}^{n} \nu_{ij} d\left[\log \frac{\tilde{a}_j}{\tilde{A}'}\right], \tag{7.8}$$

which is the result given in equation (6.8).

To derive (6.11) consider the negative of the right-hand side of equation (7.8)

$$\sum_{j=1}^{n} \nu_{ij} d\left[\log \frac{\tilde{a}_j}{\tilde{A}'}\right] = \sum_{j=1}^{n} \nu_{ij} d(\log \tilde{a}_j) - \sum_{j=1}^{n} \nu_{ij} d(\log \tilde{A}')$$

$$= \sum_{j=1}^{n} \nu_{ij} d(\log \tilde{a}_j) - \phi\theta_i d(\log \tilde{A}'), \tag{7.9}$$

where the second step is based on (6.2). Using (6.3) to substitute $\pi_{ij} + \phi\theta_i\theta_j$ for ν_{ij} in the above equation, we obtain

$$\sum_{j=1}^{n} \nu_{ij} d(\log \tilde{a}_j) - \phi\theta_i d(\log \tilde{A}')$$

$$= \sum_{j=1}^{n} (\pi_{ij} + \phi\theta_i\theta_j) d(\log \tilde{a}_j) - \phi\theta_i d(\log \tilde{A}')$$

$$= \sum_{j=1}^{n} \pi_{ij} d(\log \tilde{a}_j) + \phi\theta_i \sum_{j=1}^{n} \theta_j d(\log \tilde{a}_j) - \phi\theta_i d(\log \tilde{A}')$$

$$= \sum_{j=1}^{n} \pi_{ij} d(\log \tilde{a}_j), \tag{7.10}$$

where the last step uses (5.2). Combining (7.9) and (7.10) gives

$$\sum_{j=1}^{n} \nu_{ij} d\left[\log \frac{\tilde{a}_j}{\tilde{A}'}\right] = \sum_{j=1}^{n} \pi_{ij} d(\log \tilde{a}_j). \tag{7.11}$$

Using (5.1) we write (7.11) as

$$\begin{aligned}\sum_{j=1}^{n} \nu_{ij} d\left[\log \frac{\tilde{a}_j}{\tilde{A}'}\right] &= \sum_{j=1}^{n} \pi_{ij}\left[\sum_{k=1}^{n} \mu_{jk} d(\log a_k)\right] \\ &= w_i \sum_{k=1}^{n}\left[\sum_{j=1}^{n} \eta^*_{ij}\mu_{jk}\right] d(\log a_k) \\ &= - w_i \sum_{k=1}^{n} \tau_{ik} d(\log a_k),\end{aligned} \tag{7.12}$$

where the second step uses $\pi_{ij} = w_i\eta^*_{ij}$ and the last step uses (3.7). Equation (7.12) is equivalent to (6.11).

Finally, we derive equation (6.13). Multiplying both sides of the scalar form of equation (3.7) by w_i and substituting $\lambda_{ij} = w_i\tau_{ij}$ and $\pi_{ij} = w_i\eta^*_{ij}$, we obtain

$$\lambda_{ij} = - \sum_{k=1}^{n} \pi_{ik}\mu_{kj}. \tag{7.13}$$

If we sum both sides of the above equation over j=1,...,n we obtain

$$\sum_{j=1}^{n} \lambda_{ij} = - \sum_{j=1}^{n}\left[\sum_{k=1}^{n} \pi_{ik}\mu_{kj}\right] = - \sum_{k=1}^{n}\left[\sum_{j=1}^{n} \mu_{kj}\right]\pi_{ik} = - \mu_o \sum_{k=1}^{n} \pi_{ik} = 0,$$

where the third step uses (5.6) and the last step uses (6.4). This is equation (6.13).

7.8 Block Independence

In this section initially we review the material on block independence discussed in Sections 1.21-1.23. We then discuss extensions for advertising.

Previous Results

We partition the n goods into G groups, $S_1,...,S_G$. The *g-th* group consists of n_g goods so that $\Sigma_{g=1}^{G} n_g = n$. Under block independence the consumer's utility function (2.1) becomes

$$u(\mathbf{q}) = \sum_{g=1}^{G} u_g(\mathbf{q}_g), \tag{8.1}$$

where $\mathbf{q}_g$ is the vector of q_i's that fall under S_g. Specification (8.1) implies that price coefficient matrix is block diagonal,

$$\boldsymbol{\nu} = \text{diag}[\boldsymbol{\nu}_1 \; ... \; \boldsymbol{\nu}_G]. \tag{8.2}$$

In other words, $\nu_{ij} = 0$ for $i \in S_g$ and $j \notin S_g$.

In view of (8.2), under block independence the demand equation (6.1) for $i \in S_g$ becomes

$$w_i d(\log q_i) = \theta_i d(\log Q) + \sum_{j \in S_g} \nu_{ij} d\left[\log \frac{p_j}{P'}\right]. \tag{8.3}$$

An Extension

Under block independence the consumer's utility function (2.10) becomes

$$u(\mathbf{q},\mathbf{a}) = \sum_{g=1}^{G} u_g(\mathbf{q}_g,\mathbf{a}_g), \tag{8.4}$$

where a_g is the sub-vector of **a** containing the goods that fall under S_g. This formulation of the utility function is the natural extension of (8.1). As before with specification (8.1), (8.4) implies that the price coefficient matrix is block diagonal as indicated by (8.2).

Under (8.4) we have

$$\frac{\partial^2 u}{\partial q_i \partial a_j} = 0, \qquad \text{for every } i \in S_g,\ j \in S_h,\ g \neq h. \tag{8.5}$$

In words, (8.5) states that the marginal utility of a good which belongs to group S_g does not depend on the advertising of a good belonging to some other group. From (8.5) it is clear that the Hessian of the utility function (8.4) is block diagonal. Using equation (3.4), equation (8.5) implies

$$\mu_{ij} = 0, \qquad i \in S_g,\ j \in S_h,\ g \neq h. \tag{8.6}$$

We return to restriction (5.6) and write it in the form

$$\sum_{j=1}^{n} \mu_{ij} = \mu_o, \qquad i=1,\ldots,n.$$

In view of (8.6), for $i \in S_g$ this becomes

$$\sum_{j \in S_g} \mu_{ij} = \mu_o. \tag{8.7}$$

Equation (8.7) says that for any given $i \in S_g$, the sum of the advertising elasticities over $j \in S_g$ is a constant μ_o. This constant is interpreted as the percentage increase in the marginal utility of i resulting from a one percent increase in advertising of each of the goods belonging to the same group as i.

Under block independence the demand equation (6.9) for $i \in S_g$ becomes

$$w_i d(\log q_i) = \theta_i d(\log Q) + \sum_{j \in S_g} \nu_{ij} \left[d\left[\log \frac{p_j}{P'}\right] - d\left[\log \frac{\tilde{a}_j}{\tilde{A}'}\right]\right]. \tag{8.8}$$

Under restrictions (8.6) and (8.7), an equiproportionate change in all advertising variables in S_g implies that $d(\log \tilde{a}_j) = \mu_o d(\log a)$; this follows from (5.1). Equation (5.3) implies that $d(\log \tilde{A}') = \mu_o d(\log a)$. Hence the relative advertising term in (8.8), $d(\log \tilde{a}_j/\tilde{A}')$, will be zero.

Below equation (5.6) we pointed out that $d(\log \tilde{a}_j) = d(\log a_j)$ and $d(\log \tilde{A}') = d(\log A')$ when $\mu_{ij} = \delta_{ij}$. In this case the last term of equation (8.8) becomes

$$\sum_{j \in S_g} \nu_{ij} \left[d\left[\log \frac{p_j}{P'}\right] - d\left[\log \frac{a_j}{A'}\right]\right]. \tag{8.9}$$

Below equation (5.7) we showed that $\mu_{ij} = \mu\delta_{ij}$ implies $d(\log \tilde{a}_i) = \mu d(\log a_i)$ and $d(\log \tilde{A}') = \mu d(\log A')$. Thus the last term of equation (8.8) simplifies to

$$\sum_{j \in S_g} \nu_{ij} \left[d\left[\log \frac{p_j}{P'}\right] - \mu d\left[\log \frac{a_j}{A'}\right]\right]. \tag{8.10}$$

As can be seen from equations (8.9) and (8.10), under these two special cases, the demand equation for good $i \in S_g$, equation (8.8), contains only the advertising of goods which belong to the same group as does i.

7.9 A Groupwise Index of Advertising

In Section 7.5 we introduced indexes of advertising of all n goods. In this section we develop an index of advertising for a group of commodities.

This group index will be used in the composite and conditional demand equations which are derived in subsequent sections.

Consider a conditional-marginal-share-weighted average of $\{d(\log \tilde{a}_k), k \in S_g\}$,

$$d(\log \tilde{A}'_g) \doteq \sum_{k \in S_g} \theta'_k d(\log \tilde{a}_k), \tag{9.1}$$

where $\theta'_k = \theta_k/\Theta_g$ is the conditional marginal share of i; and Θ_g is the group marginal share. The above advertising index aggregates consistently since a group-marginal-share-weighted average of $d(\log \tilde{A}'_1),...,d(\log \tilde{A}'_G)$ equals the overall advertising index $d(\log \tilde{A}')$ defined by (5.2):

$$\sum_{g=1}^{G} \Theta_g d(\log \tilde{A}'_g) = \sum_{g=1}^{G} \Theta_g \sum_{k \in S_g} \theta'_k d(\log \tilde{a}_k) = \sum_{k=1}^{n} \theta_k d(\log \tilde{a}_k) = d(\log \tilde{A}').$$

Substituting for $d(\log \tilde{a}_k)$ from (5.1) in (9.1) and using (8.6) we can express the group advertising index in terms of $\{d(\log a_j), j \in S_g\}$:

$$\begin{aligned} d(\log \tilde{A}'_g) &= \sum_{j \in S_g} \theta'_j d(\log \tilde{a}_j) \\ &= \sum_{j \in S_g} \theta'_j \sum_{k=1}^{n} \mu_{jk} d(\log a_k) \\ &= \sum_{j \in S_g} \theta'_j \sum_{k \in S_g} \mu_{jk} d(\log a_k) \\ &= \sum_{k \in S_g} h'_k d(\log a_k), \end{aligned} \tag{9.2}$$

where

$$h'_k = \sum_{j \in S_g} \theta'_j \mu_{jk}. \tag{9.3}$$

Under constraint (8.6) the weights used in equation (5.3), h_k for $k \in S_g$, become

$$h_k = \sum_{j \in S_g} \theta_j \mu_{jk} = \Theta_g h'_k,$$

where we have used (9.3) and $\theta_j = \Theta_g \theta'_j$. Equation (9.2) shows that the weighted average given by (9.1) can be considered as an index of the advertising of the goods in S_g only. If we sum both sides of (9.3) over $k \in S_g$ we get

$$\sum_{k \in S_g} h'_k = \sum_{k \in S_g} \sum_{j \in S_g} \theta'_j \mu_{jk} = \sum_{j \in S_g} \theta'_j \left[\sum_{k \in S_g} \mu_{jk} \right] = \mu_o, \tag{9.4}$$

where the last step uses $\Sigma_{j \in S_g} \theta'_j = 1$ and equation (8.7). Furthermore, this result implies that

$$\sum_{k \in S_g} h_k = \Theta_g \sum_{k \in S_g} h'_k = \Theta_g \mu_o.$$

When $\mu_{jk} = \delta_{jk}$, $d(\log \tilde{A}'_g)$ becomes a conditional marginal-share-weighted average of $\{d(\log a_i), i \in S_g\}$ which we write as

$$d(\log A'_g) = \sum_{i \in S_g} \theta'_i d(\log a_i). \tag{9.5}$$

This is a Frisch index of advertising for the group S_g. If $\mu_{jk} = \mu\delta_{jk}$, then the advertising index $d(\log \tilde{A}'_g)$ is a multiple of μ of the Frisch index for the group.

Consider

$$d\left[\log \frac{\tilde{A}'_g}{\tilde{A}'}\right] = d(\log \tilde{A}'_g) - d(\log \tilde{A}'). \tag{9.6}$$

Equation (9.2) shows that the index $d(\log \tilde{A}'_g)$ can be expressed as a weighted sum of the advertising of goods that belong to S_g. Therefore the index $d(\log \tilde{A}'_g/\tilde{A}')$ can be considered as a relative advertising index for the group S_g. This index is analogous to the index of the relative price of S_g, $d(\log P'_g/P')$.

Consider the situation when there is an equiproportionate change in the advertising of each good, so that $d(\log a_i) = d(\log a)$ for all i. Then from (5.1) we have $d(\log \tilde{a}_j) = \Sigma_{k=1}^{n} \mu_{jk} d(\log a_k) = \mu_o d(\log a)$. Substituting this result in (5.2) and (9.1) we get $d(\log \tilde{A}') = \mu_o d(\log a)$ and $d(\log \tilde{A}'_g) = \mu_o d(\log a)$. Hence the advertising index defined in (9.6) becomes $d(\log \tilde{A}'_g/\tilde{A}') = d(\log \tilde{A}'_g) - d(\log \tilde{A}') = 0$. Consequently, the relative advertising index of S_g vanishes when there is an equiproportionate change in the advertising of all members of S_g.

7.10 The Composite Demand Equation

In this section initially we give a brief summary of the results on composite demand equation for the group S_g from Section 1.22 and then extend the composite demand equation to deal with advertising.

Previous Results

Summation of both sides of equation (8.3) over $i \in S_g$ yields the composite demand equation for S_g,

$$W_g d(\log Q_g) = \Theta_g d(\log Q) + \phi\Theta_g d\left[\log \frac{P'_g}{P'}\right], \tag{10.1}$$

where $W_g = \Sigma_{i \in S_g} w_i$ is the group budget share; $d(\log Q_g)$ is the Divisia volume index of S_g; $\Theta_g = \Sigma_{i \in S_g} \theta_i$ is the marginal share of S_g; $d(\log Q)$ is the change in real income; ϕ is the income flexibility; $d(\log P'_g) = \Sigma_{i \in S_g} \theta'_i d(\log p_i)$ is the Frisch price index of S_g; and $d(\log P')$ is the overall Frisch price index.

An Extension

If we add (8.8) over $i \in S_g$ we get $W_g d(\log Q_g)$ on the left and $\Theta_g d(\log Q)$ as the first term on the right. The term dealing with price substitution and advertising is

$$\sum_{i \in S_g} \sum_{j \in S_g} \nu_{ij} \left[d\left[\log \frac{p_j}{P'}\right] - d\left[\log \frac{\tilde{a}_j}{\tilde{A}'}\right] \right]. \tag{10.2}$$

The double summation of the price term can be expressed as

$$\sum_{i \in S_g} \sum_{j \in S_g} \nu_{ij} d\left[\log \frac{p_j}{P'}\right] = \phi\Theta_g d\left[\log \frac{P'_g}{P'}\right]. \tag{10.3}$$

In Section 7.14 we show that

$$\sum_{i \in S_g} \sum_{j \in S_g} \nu_{ij} d\left[\log \frac{\tilde{a}_j}{\tilde{A}'}\right] = \phi\Theta_g d\left[\log \frac{\tilde{A}'_g}{\tilde{A}'}\right], \tag{10.4}$$

which is analogous to (10.3).

Using (10.3) and (10.4), the composite demand equation for S_g is thus

$$W_g d(\log Q_g) = \Theta_g d(\log Q) + \phi\Theta_g \left[d\left[\log \frac{P'_g}{P'}\right] - d\left[\log \frac{\tilde{A}'_g}{\tilde{A}'}\right] \right]. \tag{10.5}$$

Equation (10.5) is the *extended composite demand equation for* S_g as a group. This equation shows that under block independence, the demand for a group as a whole depends on real income, the relative price of the group, $d(\log P_g'/P')$, and the relative advertising of the group, $d(\log \tilde{A}_g'/\tilde{A}')$. From the discussion given below equation (9.6) it is clear that the relative advertising index of the group $d(\log \tilde{A}_g'/\tilde{A}')$ depends only on those goods that belong to S_g. Thus the relative prices and relative advertising of goods outside the group do not play any role in the extended composite demand equation. As stated below equation (9.6), an equiproportionate change in the advertising of all goods means that the relative advertising term becomes zero. Dividing both sides of equation (10.5) by W_g we find that the elasticity of the demand for S_g as a whole with respect to its relative advertising is $-\phi\Theta_g/W_g$, which is the same in absolute value as the elasticity with respect to the relative price. This result implies that under block independence, groups of goods which are more price sensitive (i.e., those which have more substitutes) are more responsive to advertising.

Under the special case (4.1), $d(\log \tilde{a}_j) = d(\log a_j)$, $d(\log \tilde{A}') = d(\log A')$ and $d(\log \tilde{A}_g') = d(\log A_g')$. Hence the last term of the composite demand equation (10.5) becomes

$$\phi\Theta_g\left[d\left[\log \frac{P_g'}{P'}\right] - d\left[\log \frac{A_g'}{A'}\right]\right]. \tag{10.6}$$

For the other special case, $\mu = \mu I$, $d(\log \tilde{a}_j) = \mu d(\log a_j)$, $d(\log \tilde{A}') = \mu d(\log A')$ and $d(\log \tilde{A}_g') = \mu d(\log A_g')$. Therefore the last term of (10.5) simplifies to

$$\phi\Theta_g\left[d\left[\log \frac{P_g'}{P'}\right] - \mu d\left[\log \frac{A_g'}{A'}\right]\right]. \tag{10.7}$$

7.11 Conditional Demand Equations

In this section we first give a brief review of the results on conditional demand equations from Section 1.23. We then analyse the extension for advertising.

Previous Results

By combining equations (8.3) and (10.1) to eliminate d(log Q) and d(log P′) we obtain the conditional demand equations for $i \in S_g$,

$$w_i d(\log q_i) = \theta_i' W_g d(\log Q_g) + \sum_{j \in S_g} \nu_{ij} d\left[\log \frac{p_j}{P_g'}\right]. \tag{11.1}$$

This shows that only variables pertaining to the group S_g to which i belongs affect the demand for that good.

An Extension

To obtain the advertising extension of (11.1), we combine equations (8.8) and (10.5) to give

$$w_i d(\log q_i) = \theta_i' W_g d(\log Q_g) + \sum_{j \in S_g} \nu_{ij} \left[d\left[\log \frac{p_j}{P_g'}\right] - d\left[\log \frac{\tilde{a}_j}{\tilde{A}_g'}\right]\right]. \tag{11.2}$$

This is the *extended version of the conditional demand equation for i in terms of relative prices and advertising.*

When $\mu_{ij} = \delta_{ij}$, we have $d(\log \tilde{a}_j) = d(\log a_j)$ and $d(\log \tilde{A}_g') = d(\log A_g')$. Consequently the last term of the above equation becomes

$$\sum_{j \in S_g} \nu_{ij} \left[d\left[\log \frac{p_j}{P_g'}\right] - d\left[\log \frac{a_j}{A_g'}\right]\right].$$

For the case $\mu_{ij} = \mu\delta_{ij}$, this last term simplifies to

$$\sum_{j\in S_g} \nu_{ij}\left[d\left[\log \frac{p_j}{P'_g}\right] - \mu d\left[\log \frac{a_j}{A'_g}\right]\right].$$

7.12 Conditional Demand Equations in Absolute Prices

In the last section we derived the extended version of the conditional demand equations in relative prices and advertising. In this section we formulate these demand equations in terms of absolute prices and advertising. As before, we commence with a brief restatement of the previous results from Section 1.25.

Previous Results

We define the conditional Slutsky coefficients as

$$\pi^g_{ij} = \nu_{ij} - \phi\Theta_g\theta'_i\theta'_j, \qquad i,j\in S_g. \tag{12.1}$$

These Slutsky coefficients satisfy symmetry

$$\pi^g_{ij} = \pi^g_{ji}, \qquad i,j\in S_g,$$

and homogeneity

$$\sum_{j\in S_g} \pi^g_{ij} = 0, \qquad i\in S_g. \tag{12.2}$$

Equations (12.1) and (12.2) are the conditional versions of equations (6.3) and (6.4).

Substituting for ν_{ij} from (12.1) we can write the price substitution term in (11.1) as

$$\sum_{j \in S_g} \nu_{ij} d\left[\log \frac{p_j}{P'_g}\right] = \sum_{j \in S_g} \pi^g_{ij} d(\log p_j). \tag{12.3}$$

This is the conditional version of (6.5). In view of (12.3), the conditional demand equation (11.1) can be written as

$$w_i d(\log q_i) = \theta'_i W_g d(\log Q_g) + \sum_{j \in S_g} \pi^g_{ij} d(\log p_j). \tag{12.4}$$

This is the conditional demand equation for $i \in S_g$ in terms of absolute prices.

An Extension

We define

$$\lambda^g_{ij} = - \sum_{k \in S_g} \pi^g_{ik} \mu_{kj}, \qquad i,j \in S_g. \tag{12.5}$$

In Section 7.14 we show that the negative of the advertising term of equation (11.2) is

$$\sum_{j \in S_g} \nu_{ij} d\left[\log \frac{\tilde{a}_j}{\tilde{A}'_g}\right] = - \sum_{j \in S_g} \lambda^g_{ij} d(\log a_j). \tag{12.6}$$

Using the above result and (12.3) we can write equation (11.2) as

$$w_i d(\log q_i) = \theta'_i W_g d(\log Q_g) + \sum_{j \in S_g} \pi^g_{ij} d(\log p_j) + \sum_{j \in S_g} \lambda^g_{ij} d(\log a_j). \tag{12.7}$$

This is the *extended version of the conditional demand equation for commodity i in terms of absolute prices and advertising*. The coefficient

λ^g_{ij} measures the effect of a change in the advertising of good j on the consumption of good i (i,j $\in S_g$) under the conditions that prices, the advertising of goods other than j and total consumption of the group remain constant.

Obviously, in general, $\lambda^g_{ij} \neq \lambda^g_{ji}$. Summing both sides of (12.5) over $j \in S_g$ and using (8.7) and (12.2) we obtain, for $i \in S_g$,

$$\sum_{j\in S_g} \lambda^g_{ij} = - \sum_{k\in S_g} \left[\sum_{j\in S_g} \mu_{kj}\right] \pi^g_{ik} = - \mu_o \sum_{k\in S_g} \pi^g_{ik} = 0. \tag{12.8}$$

Using (12.7) we can interpret (12.8) as stating that an equiproportionate change in all the advertising variables a_j, $j \in S_g$, has no effect on consumption of good $i \in S_g$ under the condition that total consumption of the group and prices of all goods belonging to S_g remain constant.

When $\mu_{ij} = \delta_{ij}$, equation (12.5) implies that

$$\lambda^g_{ij} = - \pi^g_{ij}.$$

Consequently, the last two terms of (12.7) become

$$\sum_{j\in S_g} \pi^g_{ij}[d(\log p_j) - d(\log a_j)].$$

It also follows from (12.5) that when $\mu_{ij} = \mu\delta_{ij}$, $\lambda^g_{ij} = - \mu\pi^g_{ij}$. In this case the last two terms of (12.7) simplify to

$$\sum_{j\in S_g} \pi^g_{ij}[d(\log p_j) - \mu d(\log a_j)]. \tag{12.9}$$

It should also be noted that both special cases imply that $\lambda^g_{ij} = \lambda^g_{ji}$ for $i, j \in S_g$.

7.13 The Unconditional Demand Equations

In Section 7.6 we derived the unconditional demand equations. In Sections 7.10-7.12 we derived the composite and conditional demand equations under block independence. In this section we develop the relationship between the conditional price and advertising coefficients, on the one hand, and their unconditional counterparts, on the other.

We re-write the relative price and advertising terms of the composite demand equation (10.5) in the form

$$d\left[\log \frac{P'_g}{P'}\right] = \sum_{j \in S_g} \theta'_j d(\log p_j) - d(\log P') \tag{13.1}$$

and

$$d\left[\log \frac{\tilde{A}'_g}{\tilde{A}'}\right] = \sum_{j \in S_g} h'_j d(\log a_j) - d(\log \tilde{A}'), \tag{13.2}$$

where we have used equation (9.2). Thus equation (10.5) can be expressed as

$$W_g d(\log Q_g) = \Theta_g d(\log Q) + \phi\Theta_g \left[\sum_{j \in S_g} \theta'_j d(\log p_j) - d(\log P')\right]$$
$$- \phi\Theta_g \left[\sum_{j \in S_g} h'_j d(\log a_j) - d(\log \tilde{A}')\right]. \tag{13.3}$$

According to the conditional demand equation (12.7), consumption of good i depends on the total consumption of the group and the prices and advertising of the goods in the group. Equation (13.3) shows the dependence of total consumption of the group on the price of good j and its advertising. Thus a change in p_j or a_j has a direct effect on i, via the conditional demand equation, and an indirect effect via the composite demand equation. These two effects can be combined to give the total effect by substituting the right-hand side of (13.3) for $W_g d(\log Q_g)$ in the conditional demand equation (12.7).

In Section 7.14 we show that the above substitution yields

$$w_i d(\log q_i) = \theta_i d(\log Q) + \sum_{j\in S_g} \pi_{ij} d(\log p_j) + \pi_{io} d(\log P_o) + \sum_{j\in S_g} \lambda_{ij} d(\log a_j) + \lambda_{io} d(\log A_o), \tag{13.4}$$

where $\theta_i = \Theta_g \theta_i'$ is the unconditional marginal share of i;

$$\pi_{ij} = \pi_{ij}^g + \phi\Theta_g(1 - \Theta_g)\theta_i'\theta_j' \quad \text{and} \quad \pi_{io} = -\phi\Theta_g(1 - \Theta_g)\theta_i' \tag{13.5}$$

are the unconditional Slutsky coefficients;

$$\lambda_{ij} = \lambda_{ij}^g - \phi\Theta_g(1 - \Theta_g)\theta_i' h_j' \quad \text{and} \quad \lambda_{io} = \mu_o \phi\Theta_g(1 - \Theta_g)\theta_i' \tag{13.6}$$

are the unconditional advertising coefficients;

$$d(\log P_o) = \sum_{i\notin S_g} \frac{\theta_i}{1-\Theta_g} d(\log p_i)$$

is the Frisch price index of goods outside of S_g; and

$$d(\log A_o) = \sum_{j\notin S_g} \frac{h_j}{\mu_o(1-\Theta_g)} d(\log a_j)$$

is an analogous index of advertising.

The unconditional Slutsky coefficients given by (13.5) satisfy symmetry and homogeneity,

$$\pi_{ij} = \pi_{ji}, \qquad i,j \in S_g, \tag{13.7}$$

$$\sum_{j \in S_g} \pi_{ij} + \pi_{io} = 0, \qquad i \in S_g. \tag{13.8}$$

On the other hand, the advertising coefficients given by (13.6) are asymmetric. However, in the special cases when $\mu_{kj} = \mu\delta_{kj}$ and $\mu_{kj} = \delta_{kj}$, $\lambda^g_{ij} = \lambda^g_{ji}$, $\theta'_i h'_j = \theta'_j h'_i$ and hence $\lambda_{ij} = \lambda_{ji}$. The advertising coefficients always satisfy

$$\sum_{j \in S_g} \lambda_{ij} + \lambda_{io} = 0, \qquad i \in S_g. \tag{13.9}$$

In deriving (13.9) we have used (12.8) and (9.4).

7.14 More Derivations

We first derive result (10.4). The negative of the advertising term in equation (10.2) is

$$\sum_{i \in S_g} \sum_{j \in S_g} \nu_{ij} d\left[\log \frac{\tilde{a}_j}{\tilde{A}'}\right] = \sum_{j \in S_g} \left[\sum_{i \in S_g} \nu_{ij}\right] d(\log \tilde{a}_j) - \sum_{j \in S_g} \left[\sum_{i \in S_g} \nu_{ij}\right] d(\log \tilde{A}')$$

$$= \phi\Theta_g \sum_{j \in S_g} \theta'_j d(\log \tilde{a}_j) - \phi\Theta_g d(\log \tilde{A}')$$

$$= \phi\Theta_g d(\log \tilde{A}'_g) - \phi\Theta_g d(\log \tilde{A}')$$

$$= \phi\Theta_g d\left[\log \frac{\tilde{A}'_g}{\tilde{A}'}\right], \tag{14.1}$$

where the second step uses (6.2) and (8.2); and the third step uses (9.1). Equation (14.1) is equivalent to (10.4).

To derive (12.6) we substitute for π^g_{ij} from (12.1) in (12.5) to give

$$\lambda^g_{ij} = -\sum_{k \in S_g} (\nu_{ik} - \phi\Theta_g \theta'_i \theta'_k)\mu_{kj}$$

$$= -\sum_{k \in S_g} \nu_{ik}\mu_{kj} + \phi\Theta_g \theta'_i h'_j,$$

where we have used (9.3). Multiplying both sides of the above equation by $-d(\log a_j)$ and summing over $j \in S_g$ we obtain

$$-\sum_{j \in S_g} \lambda^g_{ij} d(\log a_j) = \sum_{k \in S_g} \nu_{ik}\left[\sum_{j=1}^{n} \mu_{kj}\, d(\log a_j)\right] - \phi\Theta_g \theta'_i \sum_{j \in S_g} h'_j d(\log a_j)$$

$$= \sum_{k \in S_g} \nu_{ik} d(\log \tilde{a}_k) - \sum_{k \in S_g} \nu_{ik} d(\log \tilde{A}'_g)$$

$$= \sum_{j \in S_g} \nu_{ij} d\left[\log \frac{\tilde{a}_j}{\tilde{A}'_g}\right],$$

where the first step uses (8.6); and the second step uses (5.1), (9.2) and $\Sigma_{j \in S_g} \nu_{ij} = \phi\Theta_g \theta'_i$. This is equation (12.6).

Finally, we derive (13.4). Substituting the right-hand side of (13.3) for $W_g d(\log Q_g)$ in equation (12.7) we obtain

$$w_i d(\log q_i) = \theta'_i \left[\Theta_g d(\log Q) + \phi\Theta_g \left[\sum_{j \in S_g} \theta'_j d(\log p_j) - d(\log P')\right]\right.$$

$$\left. - \phi\Theta_g \left[\sum_{j \in S_g} h'_j d(\log a_j) - d(\log \tilde{A}')\right]\right] + \sum_{j \in S_g} \pi^g_{ij} d(\log p_j) + \sum_{j \in S_g} \lambda^g_{ij} d(\log a_j). \quad (14.2)$$

We write the overall Frisch price index d(log P′) as

$$d(\log P') = \sum_{j=1}^{n} \theta_j d(\log p_j)$$

$$= \Theta_g \sum_{j \in S_g} \theta'_j d(\log p_j) + (1 - \Theta_g) \sum_{j \notin S_g} \frac{\theta_j}{1 - \Theta_g} d(\log p_j)$$

$$= \Theta_g \sum_{j \in S_g} \theta'_j d(\log p_j) + (1 - \Theta_g) d(\log P_0), \qquad (14.3)$$

where $d(\log P_0) = \Sigma_{j \notin S_g} [\theta_j/(1-\Theta_g)] d(\log p_j)$ is the Frisch price index of the goods not in S_g.

Similarly, we write the overall advertising index $d(\log \tilde{A}')$ as

$$d(\log \tilde{A}') = \sum_{j=1}^{n} h_j d(\log a_j)$$

$$= \Theta_g \sum_{j \in S_g} h'_j d(\log a_j) + \mu_0 (1 - \Theta_g) \sum_{j \notin S_g} \frac{h_j}{\mu_0 (1 - \Theta_g)} d(\log a_j)$$

$$= \Theta_g \sum_{j \in S_g} h'_j d(\log a_j) + \mu_0 (1 - \Theta_g) d(\log A_0), \qquad (14.4)$$

where $d(\log A_0) = \Sigma_{j \notin S_g} [h_j/\mu_0(1-\Theta_g)] d(\log a_j)$ and $h_k = \Theta_g h'_k$.

Substituting the right-hand sides of equations (14.3) and (14.4) for $d(\log P')$ and $d(\log \tilde{A}')$ in (14.2) and rearrangement of that equation gives

$$w_i d(\log q_i) = \theta_i d(\log Q) + \sum_{j \in S_g} \pi_{ij} d(\log p_j) + \pi_{io} d(\log P_o)$$

$$+ \sum_{j \in S_g} \lambda_{ij} d(\log a_j) + \lambda_{io} d(\log A_o), \tag{14.5}$$

where $\theta_i = \Theta_g \theta_i'$;

$$\pi_{ij} = \pi_{ij}^g + \phi\Theta_g(1 - \Theta_g)\theta_i'\theta_j';$$

$$\pi_{io} = -\phi\Theta_g(1 - \Theta_g)\theta_i';$$

$$\lambda_{ij} = \lambda_{ij}^g - \phi\Theta_g(1 - \Theta_g)\theta_i' h_j';$$

and

$$\lambda_{io} = \phi\Theta_g(1 - \Theta_g)\mu_o\theta_i'.$$

This is equation (13.4).

References

Barten, A.P. (1964). 'Consumer Demand Functions Under Conditions of Almost Additive Preferences,' *Econometrica* 32 : 1-38.

Barten, A.P. (1977). 'The Systems of Consumer Demand Functions Approach: A Review,' *Econometrica* 45: 23-51.

Basmann, R.L. (1956). 'A Theory of Demand with Variables Consumer Preferences,' *Econometrica* 24: 47-58

Theil, H. (1980). *System-Wide Explorations in International Economics, Input-Output Analysis, and Marketing Research.* Amsterdam: North-Holland Publishing Company.

8 The Effects of Advertising on Alcohol Consumption: An Empirical Analysis

E.A. Selvanathan
School of International Business Relations, Griffith University, Australia.

8.1 Introduction

In Chapter 7 we used the differential approach to derive demand equations to deal with advertising. The main aim of this chapter is to demonstrate the applications of those demand equations by obtaining estimates of advertising elasticities for alcoholic beverages. We use the UK alcohol consumption data used in Chapter 3 and the advertising data from McGuinness (1980, App. 2). As advertising data are available to us only for the years 1955-1975, we restrict the analysis in this chapter to that period.

The chapter proceeds by firstly presenting the UK alcohol advertising data. We then extend the Divisia moments methodology presented in Chapters 1, 2 and 3 to analyse the effects of advertising on consumption. This methodology is applied to the UK data in Sections 8.3 - 8.7. These results can be viewed as simple summary measures of the data and as an informal way of obtaining parameter estimates.

We present estimates of income, price and advertising elasticities in Sections 8.8 - 8.9 and, in Section 8.10, carry out causality tests of advertising and consumption. Section 8.11 summarizes the results by presenting the unconditional demand elasticities. These elasticities are then compared (in Section 8.12) with previous studies.

8.2 The UK Alcohol Advertising Data

In this section we give the UK advertising data for alcohol. McGuinness (1980, App.2) gives real advertising expenditure for beer, wine, spirits and cider. He gives wine and cider advertising separately; we add these and denote the total 'wine' advertising as the consumption of wine and cider are available only in combined form. The advertising variables are measured by McGuinness in per adult terms. As in Chapter 3, we convert the data from per adult to per capita and columns 2-5 of Table 8.1 contain these data. We plot these data in Figure 8.1.

Columns 6-8 of Table 8.1 give the log-changes in advertising. As can be seen, on average per capita advertising increased by about 7.2, 6.2 and 3.9 percent per annum for beer, wine and spirits, respectively. Figure 8.2 plots the log-changes in advertising.

8.3 Divisia Indexes of Alcohol Advertising

In this section we use the methodology of Divisia moments to deal with advertising. We then apply these extensions to the UK data.

Let a_{1t}, a_{2t} and a_{3t} be the advertising of beer, wine and spirits in year t, and Da_{1t}, Da_{2t} and Da_{3t} be the corresponding log-changes. We define the *Divisia volume index of advertising* of alcohol as

$$DA_{gt} = \sum_{i=1}^{3} \overline{w}'_{it} Da_{it}, \tag{3.1}$$

where $\overline{w}'_{it} = \overline{w}_{it}/\overline{W}_{gt}$ is the conditional budget share of i; $\overline{w}_{it} = \frac{1}{2}(w_{it} + w_{i,t-1})$; and $\overline{W}_{gt} = \Sigma_{i=1}^{3} \overline{w}_{it}$. This is a weighted first-order moment of Da_1, Da_2 and Da_3 which measures the change in the advertising of alcohol as a whole. The corresponding second-order

Table 8.1 Advertising of Beer, Wine and Spirits: United Kingdom, 1955-1975

	Advertising a_{it}				Log-changes in Advertising Da_{it}		
Year (1)	Beer (2)	Wine (3)	Spirits (4)	Total (5)	Beer (6)	Wine (7)	Spirits (8)
1955	4.014	3.416	3.161	10.591			
1956	4.937	4.561	3.288	12.786	20.710	28.895	3.956
1957	5.710	5.325	3.452	14.487	14.542	15.490	4.858
1958	6.230	6.668	3.983	16.881	8.710	22.502	14.312
1959	6.338	6.969	4.654	17.961	1.730	4.408	15.568
1960	7.674	8.335	5.488	21.497	19.128	17.904	16.474
1961	9.319	9.227	5.958	24.504	19.421	10.160	8.214
1962	8.734	8.812	6.602	24.149	-6.483	-4.594	10.275
1963	8.761	9.134	6.904	24.799	.304	3.584	4.465
1964	8.762	9.104	7.626	25.492	.016	-.335	9.946
1965	8.576	8.807	7.470	24.852	-2.150	-3.313	-2.069
1966	8.109	8.251	6.857	23.217	-5.603	-6.519	-8.559
1967	8.797	8.768	6.175	23.739	8.145	6.074	-10.476
1968	9.168	10.263	6.031	25.462	4.135	15.744	-2.359
1969	10.630	10.210	6.050	26.891	14.796	-.512	.323
1970	13.915	10.104	5.844	29.862	26.929	-1.051	-3.477
1971	15.231	10.262	6.101	31.594	9.035	1.558	4.305
1972	15.346	10.773	6.303	32.421	.750	4.855	3.258
1973	15.417	10.959	8.198	34.574	.462	1.717	26.285
1974	16.338	12.488	8.318	37.145	5.807	13.057	1.463
1975	16.909	11.698	6.900	35.506	3.430	-6.533	-18.701
Mean	9.948	8.768	5.970	24.686	7.191	6.155	3.903

The advertising expenditures given in columns 2-5 are in 1970 pence per capita. Entries in columns 6-8 are to be divided by 100.

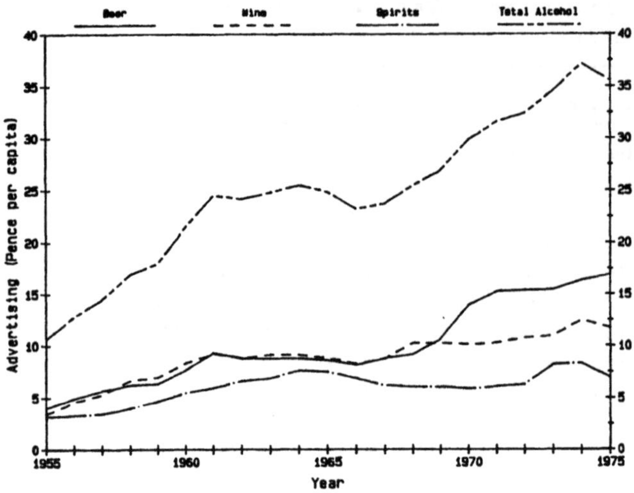

Fig. 8.1 Alcohol Advertising: United Kingdom, 1955-1975

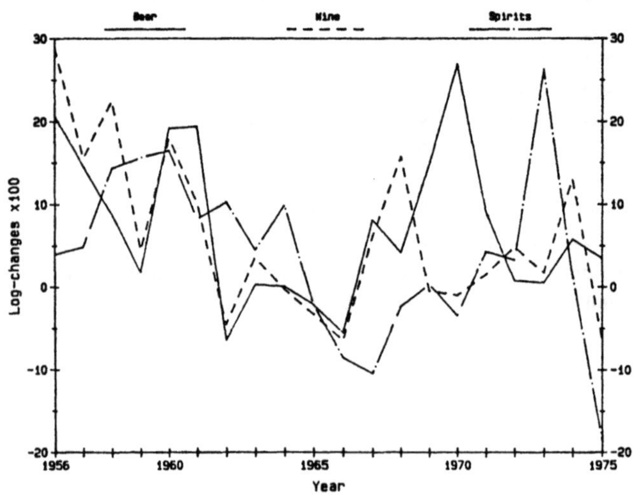

Fig. 8.2 Log-changes in Alcohol Advertising: United Kingdom, 1955-1975

moment is the *Divisia advertising variance*,

$$\alpha_{gt} = \sum_{i=1}^{3} \overline{w}'_{it}(Da_{it} - DA_{gt})^2. \tag{3.2}$$

This measures the extent to which advertising on the three beverages changes disproportionately. We use the UK data to evaluate these two measures and the results are presented in columns 2 and 3 of Table 8.2. On average, the per capita advertising of alcohol increases by about 6.1 percent per annum. Looking at column 3 we see that in some years there is a great deal of variation in advertising among the three beverages.

We define the *Divisia quantity-advertising covariance* as

$$B_{gt} = \sum_{i=1}^{3} \overline{w}'_{it}(Dq_{it} - DQ_{gt})(Da_{it} - DA_{gt}), \tag{3.3}$$

where $DQ_{gt} = \Sigma_{i=1}^{3} \overline{w}'_{it} Dq_{it}$ is the Divisia volume index of alcohol and $Dq_{it} = \log q_{it} - \log q_{i,t-1}$. This measures the joint movement of alcohol consumption and advertising. Thus, B_{gt} is positive when, on average, those beverages with above-average growth rates experience greater than average advertising, and vice versa. We also define the corresponding *Divisia correlation coefficient* as

$$V_{gt} = \frac{B_{gt}}{\sqrt{K_{gt}\alpha_{gt}}}, \tag{3.4}$$

where $K_{gt} = \Sigma_{i=1}^{3} \overline{w}'_{it}(Dq_{it} - DQ_{gt})^2$ is the Divisia quantity variance. Column 4 of Table 8.2 gives the values of V_{gt}. As can be seen, there is a great deal of variation in this coefficient and it has an average .2. In 13 out of the 20 cases V_{gt} is positive.

Table 8.2 Divisia Moments of Alcohol Advertising and Related Measures: United Kingdom, 1955-1975

Year	Volume Index	Volume Variance	Divisia Correlation Coefficient: Quantity-Advertising, Uncorrected	Quantity-Advertising, Corrected, First Set	Quantity-Advertising, Corrected, Second Set	Price-Advertising	Estimates of Advertising Elasticity of Marginal Utility: First Set	Second Set
	DA_g ×100	α_g ×10000	V_g	V'_g	V'_g	R_g	μ	μ
(1)	(2)	(3)	(4)	(5)	(6)	(7)	(8)	(9)
1956	17.12	67.94	-.70	-.92	-1.00	-.22	-.31	-.61
1957	12.07	18.84	.09	.76	.26	.88	.37	.11
1958	11.64	19.60	.93	.76	.83	-.72	.56	2.17
1959	5.88	36.96	.70	.84	.92	.93	.74	.28
1960	18.22	1.39	-.37	-.79	.62	-.59	-2.62	1.27
1961	14.99	27.96	-.38	-.98	.83	-.84	-.34	.45
1962	- 1.20	57.47	.07	-.39	.86	-.28	-.13	.09
1963	1.92	3.77	.91	.32	.73	-.42	1.35	1.61
1964	2.86	20.62	.21	.33	-.97	.68	.29	-.57
1965	- 2.28	.17	.19	.30	.09	.98	3.98	.97
1966	- 6.55	1.65	-.06	-.06	-.31	.03	-.09	-.53
1967	2.74	66.65	.31	.61	.62	.54	.25	.37
1968	4.06	31.38	.59	.42	.57	-.78	.38	1.67
1969	8.61	53.21	.98	.89	.99	-.04	.83	.90
1970	14.85	211.35	-.73	-.42	.13	1.00	-.13	.07
1971	6.68	8.66	-.86	-.64	.15	.94	-1.07	.39
1972	2.06	2.61	.95	.97	.95	-.90	3.30	.66
1973	7.92	131.77	.71	.73	.68	-.18	.78	.12
1974	5.85	14.97	-.48	.61	-.68	.79	.29	-2.65
1975	- 4.65	91.98	.85	.78	.61	-.89	.48	.35
Mean	6.14	43.45	.20	.21	.34	.05	.45	.36

The year 1956, for example, refers to the transition from 1955 to 1956.

We define the *Divisia price-advertising covariance* and the corresponding *Divisia price-advertising correlation* as

$$C_{gt} = \sum_{i=1}^{3} \overline{w}'_{it}(Dp_{it} - DP_{gt})(Da_{it} - DA_{gt}) \tag{3.5}$$

and

$$R_{gt} = \frac{C_{gt}}{\sqrt{\Pi_{gt}\alpha_{gt}}}, \tag{3.6}$$

where $DP_{gt} = \Sigma_{i=1}^{3} \overline{w}'_{it} Dp_{it}$ is the Divisia price index of alcohol; $Dp_{it} = \log p_{it} - \log p_{i,t-1}$; and $\Pi_{gt} = \Sigma_{i=1}^{3} \overline{w}'_{it}(Dp_{it} - DP_{gt})^2$ is the Divisia price variance. This R_{gt} measures the extent to which those beverages that are intensively advertised have above-average price increases. Column 7 of Table 8.2 gives R_{gt}. The value of this correlation also fluctuates a great deal and has an average of .05. We shall discuss columns 5-6 and 8-9 of the table in Sections 8.6 and 8.7.

8.4 The Extended Generalized Rotterdam Model

In Section 7.12 we derived the extended conditional demand equations to deal with advertising. These equations were formulated in terms of infinitesimal changes. A finite-change version of equation (12.7) of Section 7.12 with $n_g = 3$ is

$$\overline{w}_{it}Dq_{it} = \theta'_i \overline{W}_{gt} DQ_{gt} + \sum_{j=1}^{3} \pi^g_{ij} Dp_{jt} + \sum_{j=1}^{3} \lambda^g_{ij} Da_{jt}, \tag{4.1}$$

where θ'_i is the i-*th* conditional marginal share; and π^g_{ij} and λ^g_{ij} are the (i,j)-*th* Slutsky and advertising coefficients.

If we treat the coefficients of (4.1) as constants, then that equation for i = 1,2,3 can be considered as an extended Rotterdam model. To allow more flexibility with the marginal shares, we now use Working's model (see Section 1.8) whereby these shares are variables. Under Working's model the conditional marginal shares take the form

$$\theta_i' = \beta_i' + \bar{w}_{it}', \qquad i=1,2,3, \tag{4.2}$$

where β_i' is a constant such that $\Sigma_{i=1}^{3} \beta_i' = 0$. Substituting this in (4.1) and dividing both sides by $\bar{W}_{gt}$, we obtain

$$\bar{w}_{it}'(Dq_{it} - DQ_{gt}) = \beta_i' DQ_{gt} + \sum_{j=1}^{3} \pi_{ij}' Dp_{jt} + \sum_{j=1}^{3} \lambda_{ij}' Da_{jt}, \tag{4.3}$$

where $\pi_{ij}' = \pi_{ij}^g/\bar{W}_{gt}$ and $\lambda_{ij}' = \lambda_{ij}^g/\bar{W}_{gt}$. From equations (12.2) and (12.8) of Section 7.12 we have $\Sigma_{j=1}^{3} \pi_{ij}^g = 0$, $\Sigma_{j=1}^{3} \lambda_{ij}^g = 0$, i=1,2,3; and $\pi_{ij}^g = \pi_{ji}^g$, i,j=1,2,3. Dividing both sides of these equations by $\bar{W}_{gt}$ it follows that the price and advertising coefficients in (4.3) satisfy

$$\sum_{j=1}^{3} \pi_{ij}' = 0, \qquad \sum_{j=1}^{3} \lambda_{ij}' = 0, \qquad i=1,2,3, \tag{4.4}$$

and

$$\pi_{ij}' = \pi_{ji}', \qquad i,j=1,2,3. \tag{4.5}$$

8.5 The Corrected Quantity-Advertising Indexes

The quantity-advertising covariance (3.3) relates the *total* change in consumption of the three beverages to advertising. As consumption changes on account of changes in income, prices and advertising, included in this covariance are the effects of income and price changes, as well as any effects of advertising. In other words, the covariance could be positive for reasons other than advertising. For example, if the advertising of conditional luxuries grows more rapidly than that of necessities, then income growth will cause (3.3) to be positive even if advertising has no independent effect on consumption. In this section we correct the covariance (3.3) and the associated correlation (3.4) by removing the effects of income and relative prices.

The Covariance

Using $\Sigma_{j=1}^{3} \lambda'_{ij} = 0$, equation (4.3) can be written as

$$\bar{w}'_{it}(Dq_{it} - DQ_{gt}) = \beta'_i DQ_{gt} + \sum_{j=1}^{3} \pi'_{ij} Dp_{jt} + \sum_{j=1}^{3} \lambda'_{ij}(Da_{jt} - DA_{gt}). \tag{5.1}$$

Rearrangement of the above equation yields

$$\bar{w}'_{it}\left[Dq_{it} - DQ_{gt} - \frac{\beta'_i}{\bar{w}'_{it}} DQ_{gt} - \sum_{j=1}^{3} \frac{\pi'_{ij}}{\bar{w}'_{it}} Dp_{jt}\right] = \sum_{j=1}^{3} \lambda'_{ij}(Da_{jt} - DA_{gt}). \tag{5.2}$$

We define the log-change in the consumption of i after allowing for the effects of income and prices as

$$Dq^*_{it} = Dq_{it} - DQ_{gt} - \frac{\beta'_i}{\bar{w}'_{it}} DQ_{gt} - \sum_{j=1}^{3} \frac{\pi'_{ij}}{\bar{w}'_{it}} Dp_{jt}. \tag{5.3}$$

For short, we shall refer to Dq^*_{it} as the corrected quantity change of i. Using $\Sigma_{i=1}^{3} \bar{w}'_{it} = 1$, $\Sigma_{i=1}^{3} \beta'_i = 0$ and $\Sigma_{i=1}^{3} \pi'_{ij} = 0$, it can be shown that the Divisia mean of the corrected quantity changes is zero,

$$\sum_{i=1}^{3} \bar{w}'_{it} Dq^*_{it} = 0. \tag{5.4}$$

Multiplying both sides of equation (5.2) by $(Da_{it} - DA_{gt})$, summing over i = 1,2,3 and then using (5.3) we obtain

$$\sum_{i=1}^{3} \bar{w}'_{it} Dq^*_{it}(Da_{it} - DA_{gt}) = \sum_{i=1}^{3} \sum_{j=1}^{3} (Da_{it} - DA_{gt})\lambda'_{ij}(Da_{jt} - DA_{gt}) \tag{5.5}$$

$$= B'_{gt} \text{ (say).}$$

In view of (5.4), the left-hand side of (5.5) is the Divisia covariance between the corrected quantity changes and advertising. Consequently, we shall call B'_{gt} the *corrected quantity-advertising covariance.*

The Correlation

The weighted second-order moment about zero of Dq^*_{1t}, Dq^*_{2t}, Dq^*_{3t} is interpreted as a weighted variance as the weighted mean is zero [see equation (5.4)]. Thus the *corrected quantity variance* corresponding to B'_{gt} is

$$K'_{gt} = \sum_{i=1}^{3} \bar{w}'_{it}\left[Dq^*_{it}\right]^2. \tag{5.6}$$

Consequently, the *corrected quantity-advertising correlation* is

$$V'_{gt} = \frac{B'_{gt}}{\sqrt{K'_{gt}\alpha_{gt}}}. \tag{5.7}$$

This is the corrected version of (3.4).

Special Cases

In Section 7.3 we introduced the coefficient μ_{ij}, the elasticity of the marginal utility of good i with respect to advertising of j. From equation (12.5) of Chapter 7, we also have the relationship $\lambda^g_{ij} = -\Sigma_{k=1}^{3} \pi^g_{ik}\mu_{kj}$, so that the advertising coefficients λ'_{ij} in demand equation (5.1) are related to the μ_{ij}'s and the π'_{ij}'s. Dividing both sides of the above result by $\bar{W}_{gt}$, this relationship can be expressed as

$$\lambda'_{ij} = - \sum_{k=1}^{3} \pi'_{ik}\mu_{kj}. \tag{5.8}$$

In Section 7.4 we considered the special case when $\mu_{ij} = \mu\delta_{ij}$, where δ_{ij} is the Kronecker delta and μ is a constant. In this case, equation (5.8) implies that $\lambda'_{ij} = - \mu\pi'_{ij}$. Defining $x_{it} = (Da_{it} - DA'_{gt})$, from equation (5.5) we can write the covariance B'_{gt} as a quadratic form,

$$B'_{gt} = - \mu\mathbf{x}'_t\boldsymbol{\pi}'\mathbf{x}_t, \tag{5.9}$$

where $\mathbf{x}_t = [x_{it}]$ and $\boldsymbol{\pi}' = [\pi'_{ij}]$. As $\boldsymbol{\pi}'$ is negative semidefinite, $\mathbf{x}'_t\boldsymbol{\pi}'\mathbf{x}_t \leq 0$. Therefore, B'_{gt} and μ have the same sign.

In Section 7.4 we also considered the special case, $\mu_{ij} = \delta_{ij}$. Equation (5.8) then implies that $\lambda'_{ij} = - \pi'_{ij}$. In this case (5.9) becomes $B'_{gt} = - \mathbf{x}'_t\boldsymbol{\pi}'\mathbf{x}_t$, which is always non-negative as $\boldsymbol{\pi}'$ is negative semidefinite.

8.6 Estimates of the Corrected Quantity-Advertising Correlation

The corrected quantity-advertising covariance and the corrected quantity variance depend on the unknown parameters β'_i and π'_{ij}. To evaluate these measures we have to either eliminate these unknown parameters or use some estimates. In this section we shall employ both ways to obtain numerical values of V'_{gt}.

The First Set of Estimates

We commence by eliminating the unknown parameters by assuming (i) preference independence and (ii) unitary conditional income elasticities. Preference independence means that the (i,j)-*th* conditional Slutsky coefficient takes the form

$$\pi^g_{ij} = \phi\Theta_g\theta'_i(\delta_{ij} - \theta'_j), \tag{6.1}$$

where ϕ is the income flexibility; Θ_g is the group marginal share; θ'_i is the conditional marginal share of i; and δ_{ij} is the Kronecker delta. The assumption of unitary income elasticities implies that

$$\theta'_i = \bar{w}'_{it}, \qquad \beta'_i = 0, \qquad \Theta_g = \bar{W}_{gt}. \tag{6.2}$$

Consequently, when we divide (6.1) by $\bar{W}_{gt}$ we obtain

$$\pi'_{ij} = \phi\bar{w}'_{it}(\delta_{ij} - \bar{w}'_{jt}), \tag{6.3}$$

where $\pi'_{ij} = \pi^g_{ij}/\bar{W}_{gt}$.

Using (6.2) and (6.3), the corrected quantity change of i defined by equation (5.3) becomes

$$Dq^*_{it} = Dq_{it} - DQ_{gt} - \phi\sum_{j=1}^{3}(\delta_{ij} - \bar{w}'_{jt})Dp_{jt}$$

$$= (Dq_{it} - DQ_{gt}) - \phi(Dp_{it} - DP_{gt}),$$

where $DP_{gt} = \Sigma_{i=1}^{3}\ \bar{w}'_{it}Dp_{it}$. The corrected quantity-advertising covariance (5.5) then becomes

$$B'_{gt} = B_{gt} - \phi C_{gt}, \tag{6.4}$$

where we have used (3.3) and (3.5). Thus the corrected quantity-advertising covariance is the difference between the uncorrected version and ϕ times the Divisia price-advertising covariance. As $\phi < 0$ we can write $B'_{gt} - B_{gt} = |\phi| C_{gt}$. Therefore $B'_{gt} > B_{gt}$ when the relative prices of those beverages with high advertising intensities increase. This is simply because these increases in relative prices cause consumption of these beverages to grow less rapidly; and this slower growth is included in the uncorrected covariance B_{gt}.

Under (6.2) and (6.3) the corrected quantity variance (5.6) becomes

$$K'_{gt} = \sum_{i=1}^{3} \bar{w}'_{it}[(Dq_{it} - DQ_{gt}) - \phi(Dp_{it} - DP_{gt})]^2$$

$$= K_{gt} + \phi^2 \Pi_{gt} - 2\phi\Gamma_{gt}, \tag{6.5}$$

where K_{gt} and Π_{gt} are the Divisia quantity and price variances; and Γ_{gt} is the Divisia price-quantity covariance. We use (6.4) and (6.5) with $\phi = -.7$ to evaluate (5.7). [In this chapter we use the ϕ-value of -.7 which is the average of the estimates of this parameter presented in Selvanathan (1987b, Table A5.6), where the same data set for the years 1955-1975 is used.] Column 5 of Table 8.2 gives the corrected quantity-advertising correlation. As before, in 13 out of 20 cases the correlation is positive and its average value is .21, which is close to the average of V_g given in column 4 of the same table. One reason why the means of V'_g and V_g are approximately equal is that the mean of the price-advertising covariance C_g is about zero; see equation (6.4). However, a comparison of the individual entries in column 4 with those in column 5 shows that in some years the difference between V_g and V'_g is very large; and in some cases they even have the opposite sign.

The Second Set of Estimates

We now abandon the assumption of preference independence and unitary income elasticities and evaluate V'_{gt} by using estimates of the unknown parameters. Here we employ Working's model in absolute prices. We use the estimates of this model given in Table 8.3 below. These estimates are used in equations (5.3), (5.5), (5.6) and (5.7) to obtain V'_{gt} and the results are presented in column 6 of Table 8.2. As can be seen, in 16 out of 20 cases the correlation is positive with an average of .34, which is larger than before.

8.7 Estimates of the Elasticity of Marginal Utility

We return to the special case when $\mu_{ij} = \mu\delta_{ij}$. In this section we obtain informal estimates of the parameter μ, the elasticity of the marginal utility of consumption of i with respect to the advertising of i. This parameter takes the same value for all i in this special case. As before, we proceed in two ways. First, we assume preference independence and unitary income elasticities. Second, we use estimates of β'_i and π'_{ij}.

We write equation (5.9) in the form

$$\mu = \frac{-B'_{gt}}{x'_t\pi' x_t}. \tag{7.1}$$

Using this equation we can obtain an estimate of μ for each period t. We use the assumptions of preference independence and unitary income elasticities by employing (6.3) and $\phi = -.7$ to evaluate $x'_t\pi' x_t$. To evaluate B'_{gt}, we use (3.3), (3.5) and (6.4) with $\phi = -.7$. We then obtain numerical values for μ from (7.1) and column 8 of Table 8.2 presents the results. The average value of μ over the twenty-year period is .45. This means that, under the stated assumptions, the advertising elasticity of the marginal utility of each beverage is .45.

Table 8.3 Estimates of Conditional Demand Equations for Alcoholic Beverages: United Kingdom, 1955-1975

$$\overline{w}'_{it}(Dq_{it} - DQ_{gt}) = \alpha'_i + \beta'_i DQ_{gt} + \sum_{j=1}^{3} \pi'_{ij} Dp_{jt}$$

(Asymptotic standard errors are in parentheses)

Beverage	Constant	Conditional Income Coefficient	Conditional Slutsky Coefficients		
	$\alpha'_i \times 100$	β'_i	$\pi'_{i1} \times 10$	$\pi'_{i2} \times 10$	$\pi'_{i3} \times 10$
(1)	(2)	(3)	(4)	(5)	(6)
Beer	.537 (.204)	-.347 (.046)	-1.207 (.590)	.269 (.324)	.938 (.408)
Wine*	-	.126 (.025)		-.169 (.261)	-.100 (.216)
Spirits	-.537 (.204)	.222 (.040)			-.838 (.357)

Log-likelihood value = 22.15

* Initial estimation results suggest that the constant term for the wine equation is insignificant. Consequently, we estimated that equation without a constant term.

Next, we use the approach of the second subsection of the previous section to compute μ by using the estimates of β'_i and π'_{ij} presented in Table 8.3. We use these values to evaluate Dq^*_{it} from (5.3), B'_{gt} from (5.5), $x'_t\pi'x_t$ and then μ from (7.1). Column 9 of Table 8.2 presents the results. The mean of μ is .36 which is not too different from the .45 value obtained before.

8.8 Estimates of the Conditional Demand Equations

In this section we initially estimate the conditional demand equations of the form (4.3) without advertising variables. We then estimate (4.3) with the UK data.

Results without Advertising

The estimation results of the conditional demand equations without advertising variables,

$$\bar{w}'_{it}(Dq_{it} - DQ_{gt}) = \beta'_i DQ_{gt} + \sum_{j=1}^{3} \pi'_{ij} Dp_{jt}, \tag{8.1}$$

are presented in Table 8.3. We take the total consumption of alcohol and prices to be predetermined and use Wymer's (1977) program RESIMUL for estimation.

Results with Advertising

We now estimate the extended conditional demand equations (4.3) with the UK data. As before, we take the total consumption of alcohol, the prices and the advertising variables to be predetermined and use Wymer's (1977) program RESIMUL for estimation. Table 8.4 contains the ML estimates constrained by (4.4) and (4.5). As before, we have added constant terms to the beer and spirits equations.

As can be seen, the constant terms and the conditional income coefficients are highly significant, as before. The Slutsky coefficients π'_{11}, π'_{13} and π'_{33} are also highly significant. The coefficients λ'_{11} and λ'_{22} are significantly positive indicating that the advertising of beer and wine increases the consumption of these beverages. On the other hand, λ'_{33} is negative but is insignificant. The advertising coefficients for beer/wine and wine/beer are significantly negative indicating that the advertising of wine decreases the beer consumption and vise versa. The advertising of

Table 8.4 Estimates of Extended Conditional Demand Equations for Alcoholic Beverages: United Kingdom, 1955-1975

$$\bar{w}'_{it}(Dq_{it} - DQ_{gt}) = \alpha'_i + \beta'_i DQ_{gt} + \sum_{j=1}^{3} \pi'_{ij} Dp_{jt} + \sum_{i=1}^{3} \lambda'_{ij} Da_{jt}$$

(Asymptotic standard errors are in parentheses)

Beverage	Constant	Conditional Income Coefficient	Conditional Slutsky Coefficients		
	$\alpha'_i \times 100$	β'_i	$\pi'_{i1} \times 10$	$\pi'_{i2} \times 10$	$\pi'_{i3} \times 10$
(1)	(2)	(3)	(4)	(5)	(6)
Beer	.508 (.191)	-.348 (.039)	-1.410 (.420)	.381 (.232)	1.029 (.317)
Wine	-	.127 (.020)		-.222 (.198)	-.159 (.186)
Spirits	-.508 (.191)	.221 (.040)			-.870 (.324)

	Conditional Advertising Coefficients		
	$\lambda'_{i1} \times 10$	$\lambda'_{i2} \times 10$	$\lambda'_{i3} \times 10$
	(7)	(8)	(9)
Beer	.593 (.139)	-.561 (.166)	-.032 (.122)
Wine	-.348 (.101)	.299 (.120)	.049 (.082)
Spirits	-.246 (.146)	.262 (.174)	-.017 (.128)

Log-likelihood value = 30.02

spirits has no significant effect on the consumption of the other two beverages. A comparison of Table 8.3 with Table 8.4 shows that the differences are minor except that the standard errors are lower in Table 8.4.

The log-likelihood values given in Tables 8.3 and 8.4 can be used to test the null hypothesis that all the advertising coefficients are zero. Under the null hypothesis, the test statistic $-2(L_r - L_u)$ has an asymptotic $\chi^2(4)$ distribution, where $L_r = 22.15$ is the log-likelihood value under the null hypothesis; and $L_u = 30.02$ is the log-likelihood under the alternative. The value of the test statistic is thus -2(22.15-30.02) = 15.74. As this value is very much higher than the critical value of $\chi^2_{.05}(4) = 9.49$, we reject the null hypothesis.

We now re-estimate model (4.3) under the restriction that $\mu_{ij} = \mu\delta_{ij}$ for i,j=1,2,3. This is one of the special cases considered previously. The ML estimates are presented in Table 8.5. The estimates for the conditional income coefficients are more or less the same as those in Table 8.4. Only major changes relative to Table 8.4 involve π'_{13} and π'_{33}. The estimate of μ is .52 and significant. This value indicates that when advertising of a beverage is increased by ten percent the marginal utility of that beverage increases by 5.2 percent, all other variables remaining unchanged. Note that this estimate of μ is not significantly different from unity which corresponds to the other special case discussed before. It is also to be noted that the μ-value of .52 is quite close to the informal estimate of .45 which was discussed below equation (7.1).

The log-likelihood values associated with Tables 8.4 and 8.5 can be used to test the null hypothesis that $\mu_{ij} = \mu\delta_{ij}$ for i,j=1,2,3. Under the null hypothesis, the test statistic $-2(L_r - L_u)$ has an asymptotic $\chi^2(3)$ distribution, where $L_r = 26.29$ is the log- likelihood value under the null hypothesis; and $L_u = 30.02$ is the log-likelihood under the alternative. Therefore the value of the test statistic is -2(26.29-30.02) = 7.46. As this is less than the critical value of $\chi^2_{.05}(3) = 7.81$, we have no evidence to reject the null hypothesis.

The log-likelihood values presented in Tables 8.3 and 8.5 can also be used to test the null hypothesis that $\mu = 0$. The value of the test statistic is -2(22.15 - 26.29) = 8.28, which is far above the critical value of $\chi^2_{.05}(1) = 3.84$. Hence we reject the null hypothesis.

Table 8.5 Estimates of Extended Conditional Demand Equations for Alcoholic Beverages with Scalar μ: United Kingdom, 1955-1975

$$\bar{w}'_{it}(Dq_{it} - DQ_{gt}) = \alpha'_i + \beta'_i DQ_{gt} + \sum_{j=1}^{3} \pi'_{ij}(Dp_{jt} - \mu Da_{jt})$$

(Asymptotic standard errors are in parentheses)

Beverage	Constant	Conditional Income Coefficient	Conditional Slutsky Coefficients		
	$\alpha'_i \times 100$	β'_i	$\pi'_{i1} \times 10$	$\pi'_{i2} \times 10$	$\pi'_{i3} \times 10$
(1)	(2)	(3)	(4)	(5)	(6)
Beer	.325 (.210)	-.321 (.043)	-1.009 (.445)	.554 (.238)	.455 (.275)
Wine	-	.121 (.021)		-.381 (.179)	-.173 (.154)
Spirits	-.325 (.210)	.200 (.044)			-.283 (.241)
Log-likelihood = 26.29		Advertising elasticity of marginal utility of consumption		μ = .522 (.245)	

Table 8.6 explores the implications of the estimates presented in Table 8.5 by presenting the conditional income, price and advertising elasticities. Dividing both sides of (4.3) by $\bar{w}'_{it}$, we obtain the income elasticity $\eta'_{it} = 1 + \beta'_i/\bar{w}'_{it}$, the price elasticity $\eta'_{ijt} = \pi'_{ij}/\bar{w}'_{it}$ and the advertising elasticity $\tau'_{ijt} = \lambda'_{ij}/\bar{w}'_{it}$. We evaluate these elasticities at sample means. Column 2 gives the income elasticities, while columns 3-5 give the price elasticities. The income elasticities are .5, 1.9 and 1.7 for beer, wine and spirits, respectively. These estimates indicate that within alcohol, beer is a necessity whereas wine and spirits are luxuries. The own-price elasticities are -.2, -.3 and -.1 (in the same order).

Columns 6-8 of Table 8.6 present the advertising elasticities. As can be seen from the first row, the own-advertising elasticity of beer is .09. This indicates that a ten percent increase in the advertising of beer raises

Table 8.6 Conditional Income, Price and Advertising Elasticities for Alcoholic Beverages: United Kingdom, 1955-1975

Beverage	Income	Price			Advertising		
	η'_i	η'_{i1}	η'_{i2}	η'_{i3}	τ'_{i1}	τ'_{i2}	τ'_{i3}
(1)	(2)	(3)	(4)	(5)	(6)	(7)	(8)
Beer	.45	-.17	.09	.08	.09	-.05	-.04
Wine	1.90	.41	-.28	-.13	-.22	.15	.07
Spirits	1.72	.16	-.06	-.10	-.09	.03	.05

beer sales by .9 percent (all other variables held constant). The elasticity of beer consumption with respect to advertising of wine is -.05, which implies that a ten percent rise in wine advertising depresses beer sales by .5 percent, so that beer and wine are competitive, as expected. The other advertising elasticities are interpreted in the same way. It is to be noted that the row sums of the advertising elasticities are zero. This means that an equiproportional increase in the advertising of all beverages has a canceling effect; this follows directly from the second equation in constraint (4.4).

8.9 Advertising in Stock Form

In this section we investigate the possibility that the effects of advertising last more than one year. We do this by considering a *stock* of advertising which depreciates in the consumer's mind with the passage of time. The annual *flow* of advertising plays the role of investment which serves to increases the stock. This approach is to be contrasted with the previous treatment whereby it was only the current flow of advertising which played any role. Indeed, this previous treatment is a special case of the stock approach in the sense that when the annual depreciation rate is 100 percent, the stock coincides with the flow.

The conclusion of this section is that with the UK data we are unable to reject the hypothesis that the depreciation rate is in fact 100 percent. Consequently, the preferred estimates are still those given in Table 8.5 which treated advertising as a flow.

We denote by $\log s_{it}$ the logarithm of the stock of advertising of beverage i, i=1,2,3, in year t. This stock is equal to what it was last year ($\log s_{i,t-1}$) minus a depreciation component ($\lambda \log s_{i,t-1}$, $0 \leq \lambda \leq 1$) plus this year's advertising ($\log a_{it}$),

$$\begin{aligned} \log s_{it} &= \log s_{i,t-1} - \lambda \log s_{i,t-1} + \log a_{it} \\ &= (1 - \lambda) \log s_{i,t-1} + \log a_{it}. \end{aligned} \tag{9.1}$$

In finite-change form we have

$$Ds_{it} = (1 - \lambda) Ds_{i,t-1} + Da_{it}. \tag{9.2}$$

Assuming $Ds_{i0} = 0$ for i=1,2,3, we evaluate Ds_{it} by specifying the value of λ. Tables A8.1-A8.3 of the appendix to this chapter contain Ds_{it} for i=1,2,3 for various values of λ.

We now reinterpret Da_{jt} in (4.3) as Ds_{jt} and re-estimate that model for various values of the depreciation rate. As before, we impose the constraint $\mu_{ij} = \mu \delta_{ij}$ for i,j=1,2,3. The results are presented in Table 8.7.

For $\lambda = 1$, equation (9.2) implies that $Ds_{it} = Da_{it}$. Therefore, the estimates corresponding to 100 percent depreciation presented in Table 8.7 are exactly the same as those of Table 8.5. The estimates of the income coefficients are more or less the same for all values of λ. Even though some price coefficients and their standard errors change with λ, the associated t-values remain more or less constant. The estimate of μ decreases with decreasing values of λ; however, μ is significant at all depreciation rates. Looking at the log-likelihood values we see that the

Table 8.7 Estimates of Extended Conditional Demand Equations for Alcoholic Beverages, with Advertising in Stock Form: United Kingdom, 1955-1975

$$\bar{w}'_{it}(Dq_{it} - DQ_{gt}) = \alpha'_i + \beta'_i DQ_{gt} + \sum_{j=1}^{3} \pi'_{ij}(Dp_{jt} - \mu Ds_{jt})$$

(Asymptotic standard errors are in parentheses)

Beverage	Constant	Conditional Income Coefficient	Conditional Slutsky Coefficients		
	$\alpha'_i \times 100$	β'_i	$\pi'_{i1} \times 10$	$\pi'_{i2} \times 10$	$\pi'_{i3} \times 10$
(1)	(2)	(3)	(4)	(5)	(6)
Depreciation rate = 100 percent per annum					
Beer	.325 (.210)	-.321 (.043)	-1.009 (.445)	.554 (.238)	.455 (.275)
Wine	-	.121 (.021)		-.381 (.179)	-.173 (.154)
Spirits	-.325 (.210)	.200 (.044)			-.283 (.241)
Log-likelihood = 26.29					μ = .522 (.245)
Depreciation rate = 75 percent per annum					
Beer	.377 (.205)	-.322 (.043)	-1.450 (.509)	.665 (.269)	.785 (.342)
Wine	-	.120 (.022)		-.421 (.212)	-.244 (.184)
Spirits	-.377 (.205)	.202 (.042)			-.541 (.304)
Log-likelihood = 25.03					μ = .292 (.121)
Depreciation rate = 50 percent per annum					
Beer	.437 (.203)	-.336 (.043)	-1.647 (.564)	.675 (.306)	.972 (.378)
Wine	-	.123 (.023)		-.396 (.238)	-.279 (.202)
Spirits	-.437 (.203)	.214 (.041)			-.693 (.330)
Log-likelihood = 23.88					μ = .186 (.083)
Depreciation rate = 25 percent per annum					
Beer	.485 (.204)	-.360 (.044)	-1.755 (.600)	.691 (.321)	1.064 (.402)
Wine	-	.129 (.023)		-.380 (.240)	-.311 (.211)
Spirits	-.485 (.204)	.232 (.041)			-.753 (.348)
Log-likelihood = 23.48					μ = .138 (.062)

Table 8.7 (Continued next page)

Table 8.7 (Cont.)

Beverage	Conditional Constant Coefficient	Income	Conditional Slutsky Coefficients		
	$\alpha'_i \times 100$	β'_i	$\pi'_{i1} \times 10$	$\pi'_{i2} \times 10$	$\pi'_{i3} \times 10$
(1)	(2)	(3)	(4)	(5)	(6)
		Depreciation rate = 10 percent per annum			
Beer	.497 (.208)	-.378 (.046)	-1.794 (.599)	.705 (.310)	1.089 (.411)
Wine	-	.133 (.023)		-.377 (.225)	-.328 (.212)
Spirits	-.497 (.208)	.245 (.042)			-.760 (.362)
Log-likelihood = 23.66					μ = .125 (.052)
		Depreciation rate = 5 percent per annum			
Beer	.494 (.212)	-.382 (.046)	-1.787 (.595)	.691 (.305)	1.096 (.413)
Wine	-	.134 (.023)		-.364 (.219)	-.328 (.213)
Spirits	-.494 (.212)	.248 (.043)			-.769 (.368)
Log-likelihood = 23.72					μ = .119 (.050)

maximum of 26.29 is achieved for $\lambda = 1$. Thus we can interpret this as the ML estimate of λ. This result implies that the advertising stock depreciates fully in one year.

8.10 Is Advertising Predetermined?

When we estimated the extended demand equations we treated the advertising variables as predetermined. In this section we give some statistical evidence to support this assumption using Granger (1969) causality tests.

Consider the following simple causal model:

$$Da_{it} = c_i + \sum_{k=1}^{n} \gamma_{ik} Da_{i,t-k} + \sum_{r=1}^{m} \delta_{ir} Dq_{i,t-r} + v_{it}, \quad i=1,2,3, \tag{10.1}$$

where c_i, γ_{ik} and δ_{ir} are all constants; and v_{it} is a stochastic disturbance. If advertising is determined by factors other than consumption, then given its own history, the history of consumption should not help explain it. Thus, a test of the null hypothesis that $\delta_{i1} = \ldots = \delta_{im} = 0$ for i=1,2,3 is a test of the hypothesis that consumption does not cause advertising.

We set the lag lengths at m=n=3 and estimate (10.1) with the UK data by LS. For each beverage we test the null hypothesis $\delta_{i1} = \delta_{i2} = \delta_{i3} = 0$ by employing the usual F-test. Table 8.8 reports the results. Column 2 gives the observed F-values; column 3 gives the corresponding critical values; and column 4 presents the Box-Pierce (1970) Q-statistic which tests for autocorrelation of the residuals. As can be seen, the result is that consumption does not cause advertising for any beverage. The Q-statistic show that the residuals are serially uncorrelated and thus the inferences based on the F-tests are valid.

8.11 The Unconditional Elasticities

In this section we use the results of Section 7.13 and the estimates presented in Table 8.5 to obtain values of the unconditional income, price and advertising elasticities.

From Section 7.13 we have that the extended unconditional demand equation for i is

$$w_i d(\log q_i) = \theta_i d(\log Q) + \sum_{j=1}^{3} \pi_{ij} d(\log p_j) + \pi_{io} d(\log P_o)$$

$$+ \sum_{j=1}^{3} \lambda_{ij} d(\log a_j) + \lambda_{io} d(\log A_o). \tag{11.1}$$

Table 8.8 Results of Granger Causality Tests

$$Da_{it} = c_i + \sum_{k=1}^{3} \gamma_{ik} Da_{i,t-k} + \sum_{r=1}^{3} \delta_{ir} Dq_{i,t-r} + v_{it}$$

Beverage (1)	F-value for $\delta_{i1}=\delta_{i2}=\delta_{i3}=0$ (2)	Critical F-value at 5% (3)	Box-Pierce Q-statistic (4)	Critical χ^2 at 5% (1%) (5)
Beer	1.13	3.71	4.75	7.82 (11.34)
Wine	3.41	3.71	9.87	7.82 (11.34)
Spirits	1.44	3.71	4.65	7.82 (11.34)

In this equation,

$$\theta_i = \Theta_g \theta_i' \tag{11.2}$$

is the unconditional marginal share of i;

$$\pi_{ij} = \pi_{ij}^g + \phi\Theta_g(1-\Theta_g)\theta_i'\theta_j', \qquad \pi_{io} = -\phi\Theta_g(1-\Theta_g)\theta_i' \tag{11.3}$$

are the unconditional Slutsky coefficients; and

$$\lambda_{ij} = \lambda_{ij}^g - \phi\Theta_g(1-\Theta_g)\theta_i' h_j', \qquad \lambda_{io} = \mu_o\phi\Theta_g(1-\Theta_g)\theta_i' \tag{11.4}$$

are the unconditional advertising coefficients. These coefficients satisfy $\Sigma_{i=1}^3 \theta_i = \Theta_g$, $\pi_{ij} = \pi_{ji}$, $\Sigma_{j=1}^3 \pi_{ij} + \pi_{io} = 0$ and $\Sigma_{j=1}^3 \lambda_{ij} + \lambda_{io} = 0$. The variables $d(\log P_0)$ and $d(\log A_0)$ are, respectively, the change in the price and advertising of all other goods.

In Section 8.8 we found that the data are not incompatible with the special case $\mu_{ij} = \mu\delta_{ij}$. Accordingly, this restriction will be employed in what follows. As $h'_j = \Sigma_{k=1}^{3} \theta'_k \mu_{kj}$ and $\mu_o = \Sigma_{j=1}^{3} \mu_{ij}$, under this special case we have $h'_j = \mu\theta'_j$ and $\mu_o = \mu$. Substituting these results in (11.4) we obtain

$$\lambda_{ij} = \lambda^g_{ij} - \mu\phi\Theta_g(1-\Theta_g)\theta'_i\theta'_j, \qquad \lambda_{io} = \mu\phi\Theta_g(1-\Theta_g)\theta'_i. \tag{11.5}$$

Dividing both sides of (11.1) by w_i we obtain the i-*th* unconditional income elasticity

$$\eta_i = \frac{\theta_i}{w_i}. \tag{11.6}$$

Similarly, the unconditional price elasticities are

$$\eta^*_{ij} = \frac{\pi_{ij}}{w_i}, \qquad \eta^*_{io} = \frac{\pi_{io}}{w_i}; \tag{11.7}$$

and the unconditional advertising elasticities are

$$\tau_{ij} = \frac{\lambda_{ij}}{w_i}, \qquad \tau_{io} = \frac{\lambda_{io}}{w_i}. \tag{11.8}$$

Substituting for θ_i from (11.2) in (11.6) and then dividing and multiplying the right-hand side by W_g we obtain

$$\eta_i = \eta'_i\eta_g, \tag{11.9}$$

where $\eta'_i = \theta'_i/w'_i$ and $\eta_g = \Theta_g/W_g$ are the conditional and group income elasticities.

Substituting for π_{ij} and π_{io} from (11.3) in (11.7) we obtain

$$\eta^*_{ij} = \frac{\pi^g_{ij}}{w_i} + \phi\Theta_g(1-\Theta_g)\frac{\theta'_i}{w_i}\theta'_j, \qquad \eta^*_{io} = -\phi\Theta_g(1-\Theta_g)\frac{\theta'_i}{w_i},$$

$$= \frac{\pi'_{ij}}{w'_i} + \phi\frac{\Theta_g}{W_g}(1-\Theta_g)\frac{\theta'_i}{w'_i}\theta'_j, \qquad = -\phi\frac{\Theta_g}{W_g}(1-\Theta_g)\frac{\theta'_i}{w'_i},$$

$$= \eta'_{ij} + \eta_{gg}(1-\Theta_g)\eta'_i\theta'_j, \qquad = -\eta_{gg}(1-\Theta_g)\eta'_i, \tag{11.10}$$

where $\eta'_{ij} = \pi'_{ij}/w'_i$ is the (i,j)-*th* conditional price elasticity with $\pi'_{ij} = \pi^g_{ij}/W_g$; and $\eta_{gg} = \phi\Theta_g/W_g$ is the own-price elasticity for the group.

Substituting for λ_{ij} and λ_{io} from (11.5) in (11.8) we obtain

$$\tau_{ij} = \frac{\lambda^g_{ij}}{w_i} - \mu\phi\Theta_g(1-\Theta_g)\frac{\theta'_i}{w_i}\theta'_j, \qquad \tau_{io} = \mu\phi\Theta_g(1-\Theta_g)\frac{\theta'_i}{w_i},$$

$$= \frac{\lambda'_{ij}}{w'_i} - \mu\phi\frac{\Theta_g}{W_g}(1-\Theta_g)\frac{\theta'_i}{w'_i}\theta'_j, \qquad = \mu\phi\frac{\Theta_g}{W_g}(1-\Theta_g)\frac{\theta'_i}{w'_i},$$

$$= \tau'_{ij} + \tau_{gg}(1-\Theta_g)\eta'_i\theta'_j, \qquad = -\tau_{gg}(1-\Theta_g)\eta'_i, \tag{11.11}$$

where $\tau'_{ij} = \lambda'_{ij}/w'_i$ is the (i,j)-*th* conditional advertising elasticity; $\lambda'_{ij} = \lambda^g_{ij}/W_g$; and $\tau_{gg} = -\mu\phi\Theta_g/W_g$ is the elasticity of demand for the group with respect to advertising [see equation (A8.5) of the appendix to this chapter].

We evaluate the unconditional elasticities at sample means. To implement these elasticities we set $\theta'_i = \beta'_i$ + mean of $\overline{w}'_{it}$ and $\Theta_g = B_g$ + mean of W_{gt}. We use the estimates of β'_i from Table 8.5 and for B_g the average value of the estimates of that parameter presented in Selvanathan (1987, Table A5.3), $B_g = .005$. For the conditional elasticities we use the values presented in Table 8.6 (which are at means and are based on the Table 8.5 estimates) and for the group elasticities we use the averages of the estimates presented in Table A8.7. These elasticity values are $\eta_g = 1.1$, $\eta_{gg} = -.6$ and $\tau_{gg} = .03$. Table 8.9 presents the resulting unconditional elasticities.

As can be seen, the unconditional income elasticity for beer is .5, for wine 2.0 and for spirits 1.8. These estimates indicate that beer is a necessity and that wine and spirits are luxuries. The own-price elasticities are -.2, -.6 and -.6. The elasticity of wine with respect to the price of spirits is -.6, indicating that wine and spirits are complements. The own-advertising elasticities are .1, .2 and .1. These unconditional advertising elasticities are close to the conditional ones presented in Table 8.6 as $\tau_{gg} \approx 0$; see equation (11.11).

8.12 Previous Studies

Several papers have recently appeared in the literature which examine, among other things, the effect of advertising on the consumption of alcoholic beverages. In this section we survey eleven such studies, most of which are summarized in Table 8.10. Six use UK data and the others use US and Canadian data. Below we discuss each in turn. We also compare these studies with our results presented in Table 8.9.

The UK

Duffy (1982) uses quarterly data for the period 1963-1978 for alcoholic beverages as a whole to estimate a log-linear demand equation. The demand equation expresses consumption of alcohol as a function of real income, the relative price of alcohol and the relative advertising of alcohol. His results provide no evidence of a link between total consumption and advertising. In the same study Duffy also estimates log-linear demand equations for each beverage with quarterly data for the

Table 8.9 Unconditional Income, Price and Advertising Elasticities for Alcoholic Beverages: United Kingdom, 1955-1975

Beverage	Income	Price				Advertising			
	η_i	η^*_{i1}	η^*_{i2}	η^*_{i3}	η^*_{io}	τ_{i1}	τ_{i2}	τ_{i3}	τ_{io}
(1)	(2)	(3)	(4)	(5)	(6)	(7)	(8)	(9)	(10)
Beer	.48	-.24	.03	-.04	.25	.09	-.05	-.04	-.01
Wine	2.02	.13	-.55	-.63	1.06	-.20	.16	.09	-.05
Spirits	1.83	-.09	-.31	-.56	.96	-.07	.04	.07	-.04

period 1971-1978 and finds that all the advertising elasticities are insignificant.

In a subsequent paper, Duffy (1983) uses quarterly data for the period 1963-1978. He estimates demand equations in log-linear form which express the consumption of each beverage as a function of real income, the own relative price and the own advertising deflated by the advertising of all other goods. He finds that beer and spirits advertising have significant effects on consumption, while the wine advertising does not.

Hagman and Waterson (1983) use quarterly data for the period 1962-1980 and estimate a double-log demand equation which expresses real expenditure on alcohol as a function of real income, the real price of alcohol, the stock of advertising of alcohol and a lagged dependent variable. The advertising stock variable is the accumulated flow of advertising, with an assumed depreciation rate of 70 percent per quarter. These authors also estimate disaggregated demand equations. They find that none of the advertising elasticities (at both the aggregate and disaggregate levels) is significant.

McGuinness (1980) uses annual data for the period 1956-1975 to estimate a linear demand equation with total alcohol consumption as the dependent variable. The real price of alcohol, real income, real advertising of beer, wine and spirits (individually) and the number of licensed

Table 8.10 Effects of Income, Prices and Advertising on Consumption of Beer, Wine and Spirits

Beverage	Income Elasticity	Price Elasticities				Advertising Elasticities			
		Beer	Wine	Spirits	All	Beer	Wine	Spirits	All
United Kingdom									
Duffy (1982): 1963(1)-1978(4)									
All	1.41*				-.64*				.09
Duffy (1982): 1971(1)-1978(4)									
Beer	.46*	-.01				.18			
Wine	1.03*		-1.40*				.23		
Spirits	1.52*			-.91*				.08	
Duffy (1983): 1963(1)-1978(4)									
Beer	.85*	.20				.17*			
Wine	2.22*		-1.00*				.18		
Spirits	1.67*			-.77*				.12*	
Hagman and Waterson (1983): 1962(2)-1980(4)									
All	.59*				-.79*				-.03
Beer	.04	-.34*				-.02			
Wine	1.25*		-.40				-.17		
Spirits	1.56*			-.95*				.07	
McGuinness (1980): 1956-1975									
All	.18				-.26*				.19*
McGuinness (1983): 1956-1979									
Beer	.13	-.30*	.03	.12*		.16*	-.03	-.01	
Wine	1.11*	-.18	-.17	-.30		-.05	.01	.16	
Spirits	1.54*	-.15	-.15	-.38		.09	-.15	.13	

Table 8.10 (Continued next page)

Table 8.10 (Cont.)

Beverage	Income Elasticity	Price Elasticities				Advertising Elasticities			
		Beer	Wine	Spirits	All	Beer	Wine	Spirits	All
United Kingdom *(Cont.)*									
Walsh (1982): 1956-1975									
Beer	.13	-.13	-.03	.06		.10	.03	.03	
Wine	.51	-.12	-.28*	-.36*		-.21	.17	.31*	
Spirits	1.20	.17	-.27*	-.47*		-.05	.12	.21*	
United States of America									
Comanor and Wilson (1974): 1947-1964									
Beer	-.18	-.56*				.01			
Wine	.41		-.68*				.97*		
Spirits	.18			-.25				.64*	
Grabowski (1976): 1956-1972									
All									-.01
Norman (1975): 1953-1970									
Beer						.06*			

* Significant at 5 percent level; a blank indicates not applicable.

premises are the explanatory variables. The initial estimates of the coefficients of advertising of beer and wine are insignificant; McGuinness re-estimates with these two advertising variables omitted, so that only the advertising of spirits is included. His results indicate that spirits advertising has a significant effect on the total consumption of alcohol.

In a subsequent study McGuinness (1983) uses annual data from 1956 to 1979. He estimates separate linear demand equations for beer, wine and spirits with the volume of consumption of each beverage as the dependent variable. In each equation the explanatory variables are a time trend, the real prices of three beverages, real income, the number of licensed premises and real advertising of the three beverages as well as that of cider. The main difference between this study and the previous one is that total alcohol consumption is now disaggregated into beer, wine and spirits. The results of this study indicate that beer advertising has a significant effect on beer consumption; however, none of the other (individual) advertising elasticities is significant.

Walsh (1982) commented on McGuinness (1980) regarding the regression of aggregate consumption on disaggregated advertising and the aggregated real price of alcohol. He then estimates demand equations for beer, wine and spirits individually (like McGuinness, 1983). He finds that spirits advertising has a significant effect on the consumption of wine and spirits.

The US and Canada

Comanor and Wilson (1974), who use annual US data from 1947 to 1964, find significant and positive advertising elasticities for wine and spirits. Grabowski (1976), using US data for the period 1956-1972, finds an insignificant relationship between total alcoholic beverages sales and advertising. Norman (1975) analyses US beer consumption for the period 1953-1970. His results indicate that advertising has some effect on its own demand.

Two other studies, one by Ogbourne and Smart (1980) for the US and Canada and the other by Smart and Cutler (1976) for the Canadian provinces of British Columbia and Ontario, report that there is no significant effect of alcohol advertising on consumption.

A Comparison

We now compare our elasticity estimates presented in Table 8.9 with the estimates from the UK studies presented in Table 8.10. These estimates are comparable in the sense that they are all unconditional. It is to be noted that in most of the previous studies income and prices play a significant role in determining the demand for alcohol.

In most of the UK alcohol studies presented in Table 8.10 beer is a necessity, while wine and spirits are luxuries. This is true in our study too. Regarding the price elasticities, we found that all own-price elasticities are less than unity; this is also the case in most of the studies summarized in Table 8.10. McGuinness (1983) and Walsh (1982) find that wine and spirits are pair wise complements in the UK, which is consistent with our findings. Our own-advertising elasticities for beer and wine are reasonably close to the ones presented by Walsh (1982). On the other hand, however, the advertising elasticity of spirits presented in that study is three times larger than ours. Among the cross-advertising elasticities, our estimates for wine/beer and spirits/beer are very close to the ones obtained by Walsh (1982); and our estimate for beer/wine is reasonably close to the estimate given in McGuinness (1983).

All in all, we conclude that most of our elasticity estimates are reasonably consistent with the previous findings.

Appendix to Chapter 8

In this appendix initially we give the advertising data in stock form. Then we present a summary of the estimation results for the composite demand equation obtained in Selvanathan (1987, Chapter 5). Next, we derive the estimating form of the extended composite demand equation and present Frisch advertising indexes. Finally, we give the estimation results for the extended composite demand equation.

Advertising Data in Stock Form

We present in Tables A8.1-A8.3 the values of Ds_{it} for i = beer, wine and spirits corresponding to various depreciation rates. These values are calculated according to equation (9.2) with $Ds_{io} = 0$.

Table A8.1 Per Capita Stock of Beer Advertising in Log-change Form: United Kingdom, 1955-1975

	Annual Percentage Depreciation Rate					
Year	100	75	50	25	10	5
1956	20.71	20.71	20.71	20.71	20.71	20.71
1957	14.54	19.72	24.90	30.07	33.18	34.22
1958	8.71	13.64	21.16	31.27	38.57	41.22
1959	1.73	5.14	12.31	25.18	36.45	40.89
1960	19.13	20.41	25.28	38.01	51.93	57.97
1961	19.42	24.53	32.06	47.93	66.16	74.49
1962	-6.48	-.35	9.55	29.47	53.06	64.29
1963	.30	.22	5.08	22.40	48.06	61.37
1964	.02	.07	2.56	16.82	43.27	58.32
1965	-2.15	-2.13	-.87	10.46	36.79	53.26
1966	-5.60	-6.14	-6.04	2.24	27.51	44.99
1967	8.15	6.61	5.13	9.83	32.90	50.89
1968	4.14	5.79	6.70	11.51	33.75	52.48
1969	14.80	16.24	18.14	23.43	45.17	64.65
1970	26.93	30.99	36.00	44.50	67.58	88.34
1971	9.04	16.78	27.04	42.41	69.86	92.96
1972	.75	4.95	14.27	32.56	63.62	89.06
1973	.46	1.70	7.60	24.88	57.72	85.07
1974	5.81	6.23	9.60	24.47	57.76	86.63
1975	3.43	4.99	8.23	21.78	55.41	85.72
Mean	7.19	9.50	13.97	25.50	46.97	62.38

The year 1956, for example, refers to the transition from 1955 to 1956. All entries are to be divided by 100.

We define the *Divisia volume index of the stock of advertising* for alcohol as

$$DS_{gt} = \sum_{i=1}^{3} \bar{w}'_{it} Ds_{it}.$$

The values of DS_{gt} are presented in Table A8.4.

Table A8.2 Per Capita Stock of Wine Advertising in Log-Change Form: United Kingdom, 1955-1975

	Annual Percentage Depreciation Rate					
Year	100	75	50	25	10	5
1956	28.90	28.90	28.90	28.90	28.90	28.90
1957	15.49	22.71	29.94	37.16	41.50	42.94
1958	22.50	28.18	37.47	50.37	59.85	63.30
1959	4.41	11.45	23.14	42.19	58.27	64.54
1960	17.90	20.77	29.48	49.54	70.35	79.22
1961	10.16	15.35	24.90	47.32	73.47	85.42
1962	-4.59	-.76	7.86	30.90	61.53	76.55
1963	3.58	3.40	7.51	26.76	58.96	76.31
1964	-.34	.51	3.42	19.73	52.73	72.16
1965	-3.31	-3.19	-1.60	11.49	44.15	65.24
1966	-6.52	-7.32	-7.32	2.10	33.21	55.46
1967	6.07	4.25	2.41	7.65	35.97	58.76
1968	15.74	16.81	16.95	21.48	48.11	71.56
1969	-.51	3.69	7.96	15.60	42.79	67.47
1970	-1.05	-.13	2.93	10.65	37.46	63.05
1971	1.56	1.53	3.02	9.54	35.27	61.45
1972	4.86	5.24	6.37	12.01	36.60	63.24
1973	1.72	3.03	4.90	10.73	34.66	61.79
1974	13.06	13.81	15.51	21.10	44.25	71.76
1975	-6.53	-3.08	1.22	9.29	33.29	61.64
Mean	6.15	8.26	12.25	23.22	46.57	64.54

See notes to Table A8.1.

Previous Estimates of the Composite Demand Equation

Selvanathan (1987, Chapter 5) estimated the composite demand equation with three different parameterizations, namely, Rotterdam, Working's and the constant elasticity model. The latter model takes the form

$$DQ_{gt} = \eta_g DQ_t + \eta_{gg}(DP'_{gt} - DP'_t), \tag{A8.1}$$

where $DQ_{gt} = \Sigma_{i=1}^{3} \overline{w}'_{it} Dq_{it}$; $DQ_t = \Sigma_{i=1}^{n} \overline{w}_{it} Dq_{it}$, n being the total

Table A8.3 Per Capita Stock of Spirits Advertising in Log-Change Form: United Kingdom, 1955-1975

	Annual Percentage Depreciation Rate					
Year	100	75	50	25	10	5
1956	3.96	3.96	3.96	3.96	3.96	3.96
1957	4.86	5.85	6.84	7.83	8.42	8.62
1958	14.31	15.77	17.73	20.18	21.89	22.50
1959	15.57	19.51	24.43	30.70	35.27	36.94
1960	16.47	21.35	28.69	39.50	48.21	51.57
1961	8.21	13.55	22.56	37.84	51.61	57.20
1962	10.28	13.66	21.56	38.66	56.72	64.62
1963	4.47	7.88	15.24	33.46	55.52	65.85
1964	9.95	11.92	17.57	35.04	59.91	72.51
1965	-2.07	.91	6.71	24.21	51.85	66.81
1966	-8.56	-8.33	-5.20	9.60	38.11	54.91
1967	-10.48	-12.56	-13.08	-3.28	23.82	41.69
1968	-2.36	-5.50	-8.90	-4.82	19.08	37.25
1969	.32	-1.05	-4.13	-3.29	17.49	35.71
1970	-3.48	-3.74	-5.54	-5.94	12.27	30.45
1971	4.31	3.37	1.54	-.15	15.35	33.23
1972	3.26	4.10	4.03	3.14	17.07	34.83
1973	26.29	27.31	28.30	28.64	41.65	59.37
1974	1.46	8.29	15.61	22.95	38.95	57.86
1975	-18.70	-16.63	-10.90	-1.49	16.35	36.27
Mean	3.90	5.48	8.35	15.84	31.67	43.61

See notes to Table A8.1.

number of goods; $DP'_{gt} = \Sigma_{i=1}^{3} \theta'_i Dp_{it}$; $DP'_t = \Sigma_{i=1}^{n} \theta_i Dp_{it}$; and η_g and η_{gg} are the income and price elasticities of the alcoholic beverages group.

Selvanathan (1987, Chapter 5) found that the estimates were robust with respect to the three parameterizations. Consequently, we shall concentrate exclusively on model (A8.1). In Table A8.5 we present the estimation results for (A8.1). These results, which are from Selvanathan (1987, Table A5.4), were obtained under the simplification of replacing the Frisch price index, DP', with the CPI log-change, DP^*. Here there are three specifications of the conditional marginal shares, θ'_i. These shares are contained in the variable DP'_{gt}.

Table A8.4 Per Capita Stock of Alcohol Advertising in Log-change Form: United Kingdom, 1955-1975

	Annual Percentage Depreciation Rate					
Year	100	75	50	25	10	5
1956	17.12	17.12	17.12	17.12	17.12	17.12
1957	12.07	16.35	20.63	24.91	27.48	28.34
1958	11.64	15.73	21.95	30.32	36.37	38.56
1959	5.88	9.81	16.85	28.62	38.61	42.51
1960	18.22	20.67	26.64	39.68	52.96	58.60
1961	14.99	20.15	28.31	44.75	62.65	70.65
1962	-1.20	3.83	12.95	32.35	55.18	65.92
1963	1.92	2.88	8.39	26.18	51.58	64.54
1964	2.86	3.58	7.05	22.49	49.28	64.17
1965	-2.28	-1.39	1.24	14.59	42.07	58.68
1966	-6.55	-6.90	-5.93	4.39	31.31	49.19
1967	2.74	1.02	-.22	6.03	30.92	49.47
1968	4.06	4.32	3.95	8.59	31.89	51.06
1969	8.61	9.69	10.58	15.05	37.31	57.12
1970	14.85	17.27	20.14	26.14	48.43	69.11
1971	6.68	10.99	16.75	26.28	50.26	72.33
1972	2.06	4.81	10.43	21.77	47.30	70.77
1973	7.92	9.13	13.14	24.25	50.49	75.16
1974	5.85	8.13	12.42	24.03	51.29	77.25
1975	-4.65	-2.62	1.56	13.38	41.51	68.74
Mean	6.14	8.23	12.20	22.55	42.70	57.46

See notes to Table A8.1.

The Extended Composite Demand Equation

The extended composite demand equation is given by equation (10.5) of Section 7.10. In finite-change form this becomes

$$\overline{W}_{gt} DQ_{gt} = \Theta_g DQ_t + \gamma(DP'_{gt} - DP'_t) - \gamma(D\tilde{A}'_{gt} - D\tilde{A}'_t), \qquad \text{(A8.2)}$$

where DQ_{gt}, DQ_t, DP'_{gt} and DP'_t are as before; $D\tilde{A}'_{gt} = \Sigma_{i=1}^{3} h'_i Da_{it}$; $D\tilde{A}'_t = \Sigma_{i=1}^{n} h_i Da_{it}$; $h'_i = \Sigma_{j=1}^{3} \theta'_j \mu_{ji}$; $h_i = \Sigma_{j=1}^{n} \theta_j \mu_{ji}$; Θ_g is the marginal share of the group; $\gamma = \phi\Theta_g$; and ϕ is the income flexibility.

Table A8.5 Estimates of the Composite Demand Equation: United Kingdom, 1955-1975

$$DQ_{gt} = \alpha + \eta_g DQ_t + \eta_{gg}(DP'_{gt} - DP^*_t)$$

(Standard errors are in parentheses)

Specification of Conditional Marginal Share θ'_i (1)	Constant $\alpha \times 100$ (2)	Income Elasticity η_g (3)	Price Elasticity η_{gg} (4)
$\overline{w}'_{it}$	1.380 (.900)	.877 (.382)	-.624 (.182)
	-	1.328 (.252)	-.601 (.188)
$\beta'_i + \bar{w}'_i$	.930 (.910)	.968 (.381)	-.578 (.174)
	-	1.262 (.251)	-.590 (.173)
$\beta'_i + \overline{w}'_{it}$	.965 (.907)	.954 (.381)	-.579 (.173)
	-	1.260 (.251)	-.589 (.173)
Mean		1.108	-.594

β'_i = conditional income coefficient in Working's model; $\bar{w}'_i$ = mean of $\overline{w}'_{it}$.

As we do not have any information on the advertising of all goods, $D\tilde{A}'_t$, we absorb this into a constant term c_0. Furthermore, to simplify the estimation procedure we consider the special case when $\mu_{ij} = \mu\delta_{ij}$. Under this special case we have $D\tilde{A}'_{gt} = \mu DA'_{gt}$, where

$$DA'_{gt} = \sum_{j=1}^{3} \theta'_j Da_{jt} \qquad \text{(A8.3)}$$

is the finite-change form of the Frisch-advertising index for the group. Consequently, we can write (A8.2) as

$$\bar{W}_{gt}DQ_{gt} = c_o + \Theta_g DQ_t + \gamma(DP'_{gt} - DP'_t) + \delta DA'_{gt}, \tag{A8.4}$$

where $\delta = -\gamma\mu$. By dividing both sides of (A8.4) by $\bar{W}_{gt}$ we obtain

$$DQ_{gt} = c + \eta_g DQ_t + \eta_{gg}(DP'_{gt} - DP'_t) + \tau_{gg} DA'_{gt}, \tag{A8.5}$$

where $c = c_o/\bar{W}_{gt}$; η_g and η_{gg} are the income and price elasticities; and $\tau_{gg} = \delta/\bar{W}_{gt}$ is the advertising elasticity.

The Frisch Indexes

As before, we evaluate the Frisch indexes in (A8.5), DP'_{gt} and DA'_{gt}, by using three specifications of the conditional marginal shares, θ'_i: (i) The corresponding arithmetic averages of the conditional budget shares, $\bar{w}'_{it}$, so that Frisch indexes become Divisia. (ii) The variable conditional marginal shares implied by the estimates of Working's model given in Selvanathan (1987, Table 5.2), evaluated at sample means. These are defined as β'_i + mean of $\bar{w}'_{it}$. (iii) The same as (ii) except that the mean of $\bar{w}'_{it}$ is replaced with $\bar{w}'_{it}$, so that the conditional marginal shares are now truly variable. Table A8.6 presents the three versions of DA'_{gt} defined by (A8.3). As can be seen, the columns 3 and 4 indexes are on average a little below the column 2 index.

Estimates of the Extended Composite Demand Equation

Now we use the UK alcohol data to estimate equation (A8.5). For DQ_{gt} and DQ_t we use the values presented in Tables 3.7 and 3.10. We approximate the overall Frisch-price index DP'_t with the CPI log-change DP^*_t and use the values presented in columns 3-5 of Selvanathan (1987, Table A5.1) for $(DP'_{gt} - DP^*_t)$. For DA'_{gt} we use the values presented in columns 2-4 of Table A8.6.

Table A8.6 Three Versions of the Frisch-Advertising Index of Alcohol: United Kingdom, 1955-1975

Year	Specification of the Conditional Marginal Share θ'_i		
	$\bar{w}'_{it}$	β'_i + mean of $\bar{w}'_{it}$	$\beta'_i + \bar{w}'_{it}$
(1)	(2)	(3)	(4)
1956	17.118	14.455	14.266
1957	12.074	9.941	9.978
1958	11.638	15.108	14.549
1959	5.877	9.356	9.350
1960	18.215	17.480	17.465
1961	14.985	11.398	11.333
1962	-1.204	2.399	2.842
1963	1.919	3.242	3.256
1964	2.856	4.896	5.079
1965	-2.283	-2.412	-2.402
1966	-6.551	-7.322	-7.334
1967	2.742	-1.717	-1.751
1968	4.063	3.908	3.957
1969	8.609	3.562	3.495
1970	14.848	4.417	4.599
1971	6.677	4.719	4.713
1972	2.059	3.075	3.117
1973	7.924	13.717	13.962
1974	5.847	5.521	5.715
1975	-4.649	-10.245	-10.876
Mean	6.138	5.275	5.266

The year 1956, for example, refers to the transition from 1955 to 1956. All entries are to be divided by 100.

The LS estimates of (A8.5) are presented in Table A8.7. As can be seen, the income and price elasticities are always highly significant. The income and price elasticity estimates are fairly robust with respect to the specification of the conditional marginal shares. A comparison of Table A8.5 with Table A8.7 shows that the income and price elasticities are approximately equal in both tables. It is to be noted that the advertising elasticity is always low and insignificant.

Table A8.7 Estimates of the Extended Composite Demand Equation: United Kingdom, 1955-1975

$$DQ_{gt} = c + \eta_g DQ_t + \eta_{gg}(DP'_{gt} - DP^*_t) + \tau_{gg} DA'_{gt}$$

(Standard errors are in parentheses)

Specification of Conditional Marginal Share θ'_i (1)	Constant $c \times 100$ (2)	Income Elasticity η_g (3)	Price Elasticity η_{gg} (4)	Advertising Elasticity τ_{gg} (5)
$\bar{w}'_{it}$	1.258 (1.037)	.869 (.394)	-.607 (.199)	.023 (.090)
	-	1.182 (.302)	-.554 (.197)	.073 (.082)
$\beta'_i + \bar{w}'_i$	.928 (.953)	.966 (.418)	-.577 (.202)	.001 (.101)
	-	1.225 (.322)	-.571 (.202)	.019 (.099)
$\beta'_i + \bar{w}'_{it}$	.946 (.949)	.938 (.418)	-.569 (.200)	.011 (.100)
	-	1.203 (.323)	-.562 (.200)	.029 (.099)
Mean		1.064	-.573	.026

We now estimate the composite demand equation (A8.5) with the specification $\theta'_i = \bar{w}'_{it}$ and the advertising variable DA'_{gt} replaced with the stock DS_{gt}. With these replacements, equation (A8.5) becomes

$$DQ_{gt} = c + \eta_g DQ_t + \eta_{gg}(DP_{gt} - DP^*_t) + \tau_{gg} DS_{gt}. \tag{A8.6}$$

We estimate (A8.6) by LS for various values of λ, the depreciation rate. The values of DS_{gt} are given in Table A8.4. Table A8.8 presents the estimation results.

As can be seen, the constant term is significant only at the implausibly low depreciation rates. As before, the income elasticity is highly

Table A8.8 Estimates of the Extended Composite Demand Equation with Advertising in Stock Form: United Kingdom, 1955-1975

$$DQ_{gt} = c + \eta_g DQ_t + \eta_{gg}(DP_{gt} - DP_t^*) + \tau_{gg} DS_{gt}$$

(Standard errors are in parentheses)

Annual Percentage Depreciation Rate $\lambda \times 100$ (1)	Constant $c \times 100$ (2)	Income Elasticity η_g (3)	Price Elasticity η_{gg} (4)	Advertising Elasticity τ_{gg} (5)
100	1.258 (1.037)	.869 (.394)	-.607 (.199)	.023 (.090)
	-	1.182 (.302)	-.554 (.197)	.073 (.082)
75	1.316 (1.093)	.873 (.395)	-.617 (.199)	.009 (.081)
	-	1.163 (.317)	-.560 (.196)	.061 (.070)
50	1.353 (1.176)	.875 (.398)	-.622 (.198)	.003 (.070)
	-	1.111 (.344)	-.564 (.193)	.052 (.056)
25	.875 (1.481)	.834 (.404)	-.612 (.189)	.026 (.060)
	-	.899 (.381)	-.592 (.183)	.054 (.037)
10	-2.995 (2.054)	.715 (.348)	-.652 (.163)	.109 (.047)
	-	.659 (.357)	-.644 (.168)	.046 (.019)
5	-3.834 (1.829)	.860 (.311)	-.637 (.148)	.091 (.029)
	-	.669 (.326)	-.639 (.162)	.035 (.013)

significant and not too far from unity. The price elasticity is also highly significant, in the order of -.6. All the estimates of the advertising elasticity are extremely low and most are not significantly different from zero; they only become significant at implausibly low depreciation rates (10 and 5 percent per annum). These results indicate that there is not much to be gained by using the stock of advertising approach for the composite demand equation. This was also the conclusion for the conditional demand equations (see Section 8.9). Accordingly, our preferred estimates of the composite demand equations are those presented in Table A8.7.

References

Box, G.E.P. and D.A. Pierce (1970). 'Distribution of Residual Autocorrelations in Autoregressive-Integrated Moving Average Models,' *Journal of the American Statistical Association* 65: 1509-26.

Comanor, W.S. and A.T. Wilson (1974). *Advertising and Market Power*. Cambridge : Harvard University Press, 1974.

Duffy, M. (1982). 'The Effect of Advertising on the Total Consumption of Alcoholic Drinks in the United Kingdom: Some Econometric Estimates,' *Journal of Advertising* 1: 105-117.

Duffy, M. (1983). 'The Demand for Alcoholic Drink in the United Kingdom: 1963-78,' *Applied Economics* 15: 125-140.

Grabowski, H.G. (1976). 'The Effects of Advertising on the Inter-industry Distribution of Demand,' *Explorations in Economic Research* 3: 21-75.

Granger, C.W.J. (1969). 'Investigating Causal Relations by Econometric Models and Cross-Spectral Methods,' *Econometrica* 37: 425-438.

Hagman, L.W. and M.J. Waterson (1983). *The Impact of Advertising on the United Kingdom Alcohol Drink Market.* Published by the Advertising Association: London.

McGuinness, T. (1980). 'An Econometric Analysis of Total Demand for Alcoholic Beverages in the U.K., 1956-75,' *Journal of Industrial Economics* 29: 85-109. Published with data listing as *Scottish Health Education Unit Report*, 1979.

McGuinness, T. (1983). 'The Demand for Beer, Spirits and Wine in the U.K., 1956-1979,' in M. Grant , M. Plant and A. Williams (eds.), *Economics and Alcohol: Consumption and Controls.* London, New York: Croom Helm and Gardner Press, Inc.

Norman, D. (1975). 'Structural Change and Performance in the Brewing Industry,' Unpublished dissertation, University of California, Los Angeles.

Ogborne, A.C. and R.G. Smart (1980). 'Will Restrictions on Alcohol Advertising Reduce Alcohol Consumption?' *The British Journal of Addiction* 75: 293-6.

Selvanathan, E.A. (1987). *Explorations in Consumer Demand.* Ph.D. thesis, Department of Economics, Murdoch University.

Smart, R.G. and R.E. Cutler (1976). 'The Alcohol Advertising Ban in British Columbia: Problems and Effects on Beverage Consumption,' *The British Journal of Addiction* 7: 13-21.

Theil, H. (1967). *Economics and Information Theory.* New York: American Elsevier Publishing Company, and Amsterdam: North-Holland Publishing Company.

Walsh, B.M. (1982). 'The Demand for Alcohol in the U.K.: A Comment,' *Journal of Industrial Economics* 30: 439-46.

Wymer, C.R. (1977) 'Computer Programs: RESIMUL Manual,' Mimeographed. Washington, D.C. International Monetary Fund.

9 Rotterdam Model in Forecasting: An Application to the Alcohol Market

E.A. Selvanathan
School of International Business Relations, Griffith University, Australia.

9.1 Introduction

In Chapters 7 and 8 we showed how the differential demand equations can be used to analyse the effects of advertising on consumption. In this chapter we demonstrate the use of the differential demand system in forecasting the market shares and consumption of goods. The forecasting approach discussed in this chapter, in general, will be useful to researchers working in public and private enterprises in developing policies and marketing strategies. The applications are illustrated with UK data. For related research, see Clements and Selvanathan (1988), Finke et al. (1984) and Lee (1988).

The chapter is structured as follows. In Section 9.2 we present the Rotterdam model and in Section 9.3 we use that model to identify the UK alcohol market structure. Section 9.4 describes the forecasting procedure and Section 9.5 illustrates its application with the UK consumption data. In Section 9.6 we apply Efron's (1979) distribution-free bootstrap technique to evaluate the standard errors of the forecasts. Section 9.7 analyses the quality of the forecasts. Finally, in Section 9.8 we give our concluding comments.

9.2 The Rotterdam Demand Model

In this section we briefly review the Rotterdam demand system introduced in Chapter 1. In the following section we use this system to model the UK alcohol market.

The relative price version of the Rotterdam demand equation for good i under Working's (1943) specification of the marginal shares can be expressed as [see equation (15.1) of Chapter 1]

$$\bar{w}_{it}(Dq_{it} - DQ_t) = \alpha_i + \beta_i DQ_t + \sum_{j=1}^{n} \nu_{ij}(Dp_{jt} - DP'_t) + \varepsilon_{it}, \qquad (2.1)$$

where α_i is a constant term that captures any systematic trend and satisfies $\sum_{i=1}^{n} \alpha_i = 0$; β_i is a constant satisfying $\sum_{i=1}^{n} \beta_i = 0$; ε_{it} is the usual error term; and

$$\nu_{ij} = \frac{\lambda}{M} p_i u^{ij} p_j \qquad (2.2)$$

is the (i,j)-*th* price coefficient with λ (> 0) the marginal utility of income and u^{ij} the (i,j)-*th* element of the inverse of the Hessian matrix of the utility function $[\partial^2 u/\partial q_i \partial q_j]^{-1}$. The price coefficients are symmetric and satisfy

$$\sum_{j=1}^{n} \nu_{ij} = \phi\, \theta_i, \qquad i=1,\ldots,n, \qquad (2.3)$$

where ϕ is income flexibility.

We assume that the errors ε_{it}'s are serially uncorrelated and normally distributed with zero mean and a constant contemporaneous covariance matrix. As $\sum_{i=1}^{n} \varepsilon_{it} = 0$, the errors are linearly independent. This means that one of the equations is redundant and can be deleted. Barten (1969) shows that it does not matter which equation is deleted. So we delete the n-*th* equation from the system (2.1) for estimation.

9.3 Block Structure of Alcohol Market

As in Section 6.5, we analyse the block structure among the n goods by asking, how does the marginal utility of one good change with increased consumption of the others? The most convenient way to do this is via the ν_{ij}'s defined in equation (2.2). If the marginal utility of good i is independent of the consumption of all other goods then $\partial^2 u/\partial q_i \partial q_j = 0$, $i \neq j=1,...,n$. From equation (2.2) we can easily see that the above condition is equivalent to $\nu_{ij} = 0$, for $i \neq j=1,...,n$. Then we can block the n goods into two groups: (i) good i and (ii) all other goods (j=1,2, ...,i-1,i+1, ...,n).

Now we apply this approach to model the UK consumer goods market. We consider four goods; namely, beer (i=1), wine (i=2), spirits (i=3) and all other goods (i=4) and identify the block structure of these 4 goods for the UK consumers. We use the UK consumption data over a 31-year period from 1955 to 1985. (The same data were used in Chapter 3.) As the ν_{ij}'s are not identified without additional constraints (see Theil 1975, p.55), initially we specify the value of ϕ and obtain estimates for the ν_{ij}'s. Using these estimates we identify the block structure of $[\nu_{ij}]$. We then test the resulting block structure without specifying ϕ using a likelihood ratio test.

Following Sections 2.8 and 3.4, we specify $\phi = -.5$ and estimate (2.1) by maximum likelihood. Table 9.1 presents the estimates obtained for the price coefficients. As can be seen, none of the point estimates ν_{ij}, $i \neq j=1,2,3,4$ are significantly different from zero. This means that we can block the 4 goods into 4 blocks, with each block comprising one good. Such a block structure is known as preference independence (see Sections 1.5 and 1.13, for details). We now impose the restriction that $\nu_{ij} = 0$, $i \neq j=1,2,3,4$, and re-estimate the model.

Under preference independence, equation (2.3) becomes

$$\nu_{ii} = \phi\theta_i = \phi(\bar{w}_{it} + \beta_i) \tag{3.1}$$

Table 9.1 Estimates of the Price Coefficients
(Asymptotic standard errors are in parentheses)

Commodity i	Beer ν_{i1}	Wine ν_{i2}	Spirits ν_{i3}	All other ν_{i4}
Beer	-.828 (.461)	.115 (.191)	-.248 (.201)	.278 (.729)
Wine		-.542 (.158)	-.160 (.113)	-.323 (.343)
Spirits			-1.555 (.196)	.048 (.524)
All other				-46.496 (1.691)

and equation (2.1) reduces to

$$y_{it} = \alpha_i + \beta_i DQ_t + \phi a_{it} + \varepsilon_{it}, \qquad i=1,2,3,4, \tag{3.2}$$

where $y_{it} = \bar{w}_{it}(Dq_{it} - DQ_t)$; and

$$a_{it} = \theta_{it}(Dp_{it} - DP'_t) = (\bar{w}_{it} + \beta_i)[Z_{i4t} - \sum_{k=1}^{3}(\bar{w}_{kt} + \beta_k)Z_{k4t}] \tag{3.3}$$

with $Z_{ijt} = Dp_{it} - Dp_{jt}$. Equation (3.2) is identical to equation (8.3) of Chapter 4, except that a constant term is included in (3.2). For estimation, we write equation (3.2) for i=1,2,3 in vector form as

$$\mathbf{Y}_t = \mathbf{X}_t\boldsymbol{\theta} + \boldsymbol{\varepsilon}_t, \tag{3.4}$$

where $\mathbf{Y}_t = [y_{1t}\ y_{2t}\ y_{3t}]'$; $\mathbf{X}_t\boldsymbol{\theta} = [\mathrm{I}_3\ \mathrm{I}_3 DQ_t\ \mathbf{a}_t]$; I_3 is the 3×3 identity matrix; $\mathbf{a}_t = [a_{1t}\ a_{2t}\ a_{3t}]'$; $\boldsymbol{\theta} = [\alpha_1\ \alpha_2\ \alpha_3\ \beta_1\ \beta_2\ \beta_3\ \phi]'$ and $\boldsymbol{\varepsilon}_t = [\varepsilon_{1t}\ \varepsilon_{2t}\ \varepsilon_{3t}]'$.

Now we estimate (3.4) with the UK data for the period 1955-1985 and the resulting estimates are:

$$\hat{\beta}_1 = -.0203 \quad \hat{\beta}_2 = .0065 \quad \hat{\beta}_3 = .0202 \quad \hat{\beta}_4 = -.0065 \quad \hat{\phi} = -.3689$$
$$(.0061) \qquad (.0038) \qquad (.0068) \qquad (.0127) \qquad (.0787)$$

$$\hat{\alpha}_1 = .1084 \quad \hat{\alpha}_2 = .2568 \quad \hat{\alpha}_3 = -.2268 \quad \hat{\alpha}_4 = -.1384\,, \tag{3.5}$$
$$(.1780) \qquad (.1057) \qquad (.1843) \qquad (.3384)$$

where the asymptotic standard errors are in parentheses and the estimates $\hat{\alpha}$'s are to be divided by 1000. The signs of the β estimates indicate that beer and all other goods are necessities ($\hat{\beta}_1$, $\hat{\beta}_4 < 0$) and wine and spirits are luxuries ($\hat{\beta}_2$, $\hat{\beta}_3 > 0$) in the UK. The estimate of ϕ is consistent with previous econometric findings. All the constant terms are not significantly different from zero except the one for wine.

Under the null hypothesis of preference independence, the test statistic $-2(L_r - L_u)$ has an asymptotic $\chi^2(5)$ distribution, where $L_r = 245.98$ is the log-likelihood value under the null and $L_u = 249.49$ is the likelihood value under the alternative. The value of the test statistic is thus $-2(245.98 - 249.49) = 7.02$. As this value is less than the critical value of $\chi^2_{.05}(5) = 11.07$, we are unable reject the null hypothesis. Thus the conclusion is that the marginal utility of each good is independent of consumption of any of the other 3 goods. That is, we can block the four goods into four independent groups: (i) beer, (ii) wine, (iii) spirits, and (iv) all other goods.

9.4 The Forecasting Procedure

In this section we set out the procedure to use the demand model to predict the market shares and consumption of beer, wine and spirits for an out-of-sample year.

We proceed in three steps. First, we forecast the exogenous variables income and prices by models external to our demand model. Second, we predict $y_{it} = \overline{w}_{it}(Dq_{it} - DQ_t)$ by using the estimates of our demand equations (3.2) given in equation (3.5) and replacing the ε_{it}'s by their expectation zero. Third we use an iterative procedure to obtain forecasts for the market share and consumption of each beverage.

To predict DQ_t (the log-change in per capita income) we found a constant mean model

$$DQ_t = \mu + u_t \tag{4.1}$$

to be adequate, where u_t is a zero-mean disturbance term. The estimate of μ can be obtained as the arithmetic average of DQ_t. Thus for the UK data, model (4.1) gives $\hat{\mu} = .0187$.

For the prediction of Dp_{it} we follow the approach of Clements and Izan (1987) and Selvanathan (1989). We write Dp_{it} as the sum of the common trend in all prices at time t (or the rate of inflation) λ_t, a commodity specific component γ_i and a zero-mean random component ξ_{it},

$$Dp_{it} = \lambda_t + \gamma_i + \xi_{it}, \qquad i=1,2,3,4. \tag{4.2}$$

For details of the estimation procedure of (4.2), see Clements and Izan (1987). The GLS estimates of the γ_i's and their standard errors (× 100) are

$$\underset{(.3510)}{\hat{\gamma}_1 = 1.1280} \quad \underset{(.6757)}{\hat{\gamma}_2 = -.6662} \quad \underset{(.5128)}{\hat{\gamma}_3 = -1.0651} \quad \underset{(.0191)}{\hat{\gamma}_4 = -.0181.} \tag{4.3}$$

To predict the DQ_t and the Z_{ijt}'s, we use (4.1) and (4.2) and set the u_t's and the ξ_{it}'s at their expected values of zero to yield

$$\hat{DQ}_t = \hat{\mu}; \qquad \hat{Z}_{ijt} = \hat{Dp}_{it} - \hat{Dp}_{jt} = \hat{\gamma}_i - \hat{\gamma}_j, \quad i \neq j=1,2,3,4. \tag{4.4}$$

By taking the differential of $w_i = p_i q_i / M$, we obtain

$$dw_i = w_i d(\log p_i) + w_i d(\log q_i) - w_i d(\log M).$$

A finite-change version of the above equation is

$$w_{it} - w_{i,t-1} = \bar{w}_{it} Dp_{it} + \bar{w}_{it} Dq_{it} - \bar{w}_{it} DM_t, \quad i=1,2,3,4, \tag{4.5}$$

where $\bar{w}_{it} = (w_{it} + w_{i,t-1})/2$, as before, and $DM_t = \ln M_t - \ln M_{t-1}$. If we sum both sides of (4.5) over i=1,2,3,4, we obtain

$$DM_t = DP_t + DQ_t, \tag{4.6}$$

where $DP_t = \Sigma_{i=1}^4 \bar{w}_{it} Dp_{it}$ is the overall Divisia price index and $DQ_t = \Sigma_{i=1}^4 \bar{w}_{it} Dq_{it}$. Substituting for DM_t from (4.6) in (4.5), we get

$$w_{it} - w_{i,t-1} = y_{it} + \bar{w}_{it} b_{it}, \qquad i=1,2,3,4, \tag{4.7}$$

where $y_{it} = \bar{w}_{it}(Dq_{it} - DQ_t)$ and

$$b_{it} = \sum_{k=1}^{4} \bar{w}_{kt} Z_{ikt}. \tag{4.8}$$

In order to predict the values of w_{it} for i=1,2,3,4 in an out-of-sample period τ, we use an iterative procedure. The iterations are needed because of the presence of $\bar{w}_{it}$ on the right-hand side of (3.2) and (4.7). This $\bar{w}_{it}$ equals $\frac{1}{2}(w_{it} + w_{i,t-1})$, and w_{it} is unknown when t is an out-of-sample period. We replace in (3.2) and (4.7) the unknown parameters with estimates, disturbances with zeros and independent variables with their predictions. Then, for an out-of-sample period τ for the r-*th* iteration, these equations become

$$\hat{y}^r_{i\tau} = \hat{\alpha}_i + \hat{\beta}_i D\hat{Q}_\tau + \hat{\phi}\,\hat{a}^r_{i\tau} \tag{4.9}$$

and

$$\hat{w}^r_{i\tau} = w_{i,\tau-1} + \hat{y}^r_{i\tau} + \bar{w}^r_{i\tau}\hat{b}^r_{i\tau} \tag{4.10}$$

where

$$\hat{a}^r_{i\tau} = (\bar{w}^r_{i\tau} + \hat{\beta}_i)\left[\hat{Z}_{i4\tau} - \sum_{k=1}^{3}(\bar{w}^r_{k\tau} + \hat{\beta}_k)\hat{Z}_{k4\tau}\right] \tag{4.11}$$

and

$$\hat{b}^r_{i\tau} = \sum_{k=1}^{4} \bar{w}^r_{k\tau}\hat{Z}_{ik\tau}. \tag{4.12}$$

The terms $\hat{\alpha}_i$, $\hat{\beta}_i$ and $\hat{\phi}$ in (4.9) and (4.11) are the parameter estimates given in equation (3.5) and $D\hat{Q}_\tau$ and $\hat{Z}_{jk\tau}$ are the predicted values of the independent variables given by (4.4).

Let τ be the first out-of-sample year (τ=1986). We use the following iterative procedure:

<u>Step 0</u>: Initially for r=0 and we set for i=1,2,3,4,

$$\bar{w}^0_{i\tau} = w_{i,\tau-1}.$$

<u>Step 1</u>: Substituting for $\bar{w}^r_{i\tau}$, find $\hat{a}^r_{i\tau}$ from (4.11) and then obtain $\hat{y}^r_{i\tau}$ from (4.9).

Step 2: Obtain $\hat{b}^r_{i\tau}$ from (4.12). Substitute $\hat{y}^r_{i\tau}$, $\bar{w}^r_{i\tau}$ and $\hat{b}^r_{i\tau}$ in (4.10) and obtain $\hat{w}^r_{i\tau}$. If r=0 go to Step 4; otherwise go to Step 3.

Step 3: If $\hat{w}^r_{i\tau} = \hat{w}^{r-1}_{i\tau}$ (a test of convergence) for i=1,2,3,4, set $w^*_{i\tau} = \hat{w}^r_{i\tau}$ and go to Step 5; otherwise go to Step 4.

Step 4: Take $\bar{w}^{r+1}_{i\tau} = \frac{1}{2}(\hat{w}^r_{i\tau} + w_{i,\tau-1})$ and set r=r+1. Go to Step 1.

Step 5: Stop and take $\hat{w}_{i\tau} = w^*_{i\tau}$ and $\hat{\bar{w}}_{i\tau} = \frac{1}{2}(\hat{w}_{i\tau} + w_{i,\tau-1})$.

For the second out-of-sample period τ=1987 in step 0 we set $\bar{w}^0_{i\tau} = \hat{w}_{i,\tau-1}$, which is the converged value of the first out-of-sample year 1986, and replace $w_{i,\tau-1}$ in equation (4.10) and Steps 4 and 5 with $\hat{w}_{i,\tau-1}$. We repeat this iterative procedure for each of the out-of-sample period.

To evaluate the prediction of the consumption of good i (in log-change form) we use equation (4.7) in the form

$$D\hat{q}_{i\tau} = D\hat{Q}_{\tau} - \hat{b}_{i\tau} + (\hat{w}_{i\tau} - \hat{w}_{i,\tau-1})/\hat{\bar{w}}_{i\tau}.$$

We then compute the consumption of i for the first out-of-sample year τ=1986 as $\hat{q}_{i\tau} = \hat{q}_{i,\tau-1}$ exp $(D\hat{q}_{i\tau})$ with $\hat{q}_{i,1985} = q_{i,1985}$. For the second out-of-sample year τ=1987, $\hat{q}_{i\tau} = \hat{q}_{i,\tau-1}$ exp $(D\hat{q}_{i\tau})$. We repeat this for each of the out-of-sample period.

9.5 The Forecasts

In this section we use the above forecasting procedure to predict the consumption and the market shares (within the alcohol market) of beer, wine and spirits in the UK for the out-of-sample years 1986-1993. We evaluate the market shares of beer, wine and spirits within the alcohol market as $w'_{it} = w_{it}/\Sigma_{i=1}^{3} w_{it}$, i=1,2,3. These market shares are the proportion of alcohol expenditure devoted to each beverage. Table 9.2 presents the results.

From columns 2-4 of the table we see that the market share of beer falls from 53.1 percent in 1986 to 51.7 in the year 1993. The wine share increases from 22.5 percent to 24.2 while spirits share falls from 24.5 to 24.1. The next three columns of the table give the predictions of the per capita volume of consumption of the three beverages. As can be seen, per capita consumption of beer increases from 109.7 per capita in 1986 to 117.2 litres in the year 1993; and wine and spirits consumption increases from 17.3 and 4.4 liters per capita in 1986 to 23.2 and 5.6 in the year 1993, respectively. We shall discuss columns 8-13 in the following section.

9.6 The Bootstrap Standard Errors of the Forecasts

In this section we apply the bootstrap simulation technique, a distribution-free statistical procedure developed by Efron (1979) to evaluate the standard errors of the forecasts. This technique was used in Chapter 5 and has been applied to econometric time series models by Freedman and Peters (1984a, 1984b), Finke et al. (1984), Rao and Selvanathan (1991), Selvanathan (1989), Theil (1987) and Theil et al. (1984). We describe below the application of the bootstrap technique to a system of equations to obtain pseudo values for the dependent variables and bootstrap estimates for the model parameters.

Consider a system of equations of the form $y_{it} = \Sigma_{j=1}^{m} \delta_{ij} x_{jt} + v_{it}$, i=1,...,n and t=1,...,T, where the δ_{ij}'s are the parameters to be estimated and v_{it} is a stochastic disturbance term. Let $\hat{\delta}_{ij}$ be the data-based estimate of δ_{ij}. We use the $\hat{\delta}_{ij}$'s together with the observed values of the dependent variables and independent variables to evaluate the residuals

Table 9.2 Predicted Alcohol Market Shares, Consumption and their Root-Mean-Square Forecast Errors: United Kingdom, 1986-1993

Year	Forecasts						Root-mean-square forecast errors					
	Market shares			Consumption			Market shares			Consumption		
	Beer	Wine	Spirits	Beer	Wine	Spirits	Beer	Wine	Spirits	Beer	Wine	Spirits
(1)	(2)	(3)	(4)	(5)	(6)	(7)	(8)	(9)	(10)	(11)	(12)	(13)
1986	.5310	.2246	.2445	109.63	17.26	4.44	.0130	.0082	.0095	2.66	.72	.37
1987	.5288	.2273	.2440	110.67	18.03	4.59	.0133	.0080	.0097	2.76	.77	.41
1988	.5266	.2299	.2435	111.72	18.82	4.75	.0139	.0089	.0100	2.69	.75	.42
1989	.5245	.2325	.2430	112.78	19.64	4.91	.0135	.0087	.0098	2.70	.75	.42
1990	.5224	.2350	.2425	113.86	20.49	5.08	.0136	.0092	.0096	2.90	.75	.45
1991	.5204	.2375	.2421	114.94	21.36	5.25	.0134	.0087	.0097	2.84	.81	.44
1992	.5185	.2399	.2416	116.04	22.27	5.42	.0133	.0091	.0095	3.13	.91	.53
1993	.5165	.2423	.2411	117.15	23.20	5.61	.0132	.0084	.0095	3.14	1.02	.63

$\hat{v}_{it} = y_{it} - \sum_{j=1}^{m} \hat{\delta}_{ij} x_{jt}$, for i=1,...,n and t=1,...,T. Let $\hat{v}_t = [\hat{v}_{1t} \ldots \hat{v}_{nt}]'$ be the residual vector for the year t. We have T such residual vectors. We generate a new set of pseudo dependent variables y^*_{it} for i=1,...,n and t=1,...,T in the following manner.

We assign mass 1/T to each residual vector $\hat{v}_t$, t=1,...,T. We draw T uniform random numbers with replacement in the range 1 to T and write v^*_t for the tth draw. We then generate pseudo dependent variables as $y^*_{it} = \sum_{j=1}^{m} \hat{\delta}_{ij} x_{jt} + v^*_{it}$, i=1,...,n and t=1,...,T. Using these y^*_{it}'s and the observed values of the x_{it}'s we re-estimate the model to obtain bootstrap estimates δ^*_{ij}'s for the δ_{ij}'s.

Now we describe the application of the bootstrap simulation technique to forecasting. The application of bootstrapping to forecasting involves four new concepts: (i) The simulated-actual values of the independent variables; (ii) the simulated-actual values of the dependent variable; (iii) the simulated-predictions of the independent variables; and (iv) the simulated-predictions of the dependent variables. We explain each of these concepts in turn.

We start by applying the bootstrap procedure to the exogenous variable DQ_t and Z_{ijt}. We obtain the residuals for DQ_t by substituting the estimate of μ in (4.1),

$$\hat{u}_t = DQ_t - \hat{\mu}, \qquad t=1,\ldots,30. \tag{6.1}$$

Using the estimates of λ_t (which are not reported in this chapter) and γ_i in (4.2) we obtain the residuals

$$\hat{\xi}_{it} = Dp_{it} - \hat{\lambda}_t - \hat{\gamma}_i, \qquad i=1,\ldots,4, \qquad t=1,\ldots,30, \tag{6.2}$$

and define the vector $\hat{\xi}_t = [\hat{\xi}_{1t}\ \hat{\xi}_{2t}\ \hat{\xi}_{3t}\ \hat{\xi}_{4t}]'$.

Next, we assign mass 1/30 to each $\hat{u}_t$ and draw a residual u^*_τ from the distribution $\{\hat{u}_t$: t=1,...,30} for the first out-of-sample year τ. Similarly, we assign mass 1/30 to each ξ_t and draw a residual vector ξ^*_τ from the distribution $\{\hat{\xi}_t$: t=1,...,30}. Then we compute

$$DQ^*_\tau = \hat{\mu} + u^*_\tau, \tag{6.3}$$

and

$$Z^*_{ij\tau} = Dp^*_{i\tau} - Dp^*_{j\tau} = \hat{\gamma}_i - \hat{\gamma}_j + \xi^*_{i\tau} - \xi^*_{j\tau}, \quad i,j=1,...,4, \tag{6.4}$$

where $\hat{\mu}$ and $\hat{\gamma}_i$ are the data based estimates presented below equation (4.1) and in equation (4.3). These are the *simulated-actual values of the independent variables.*

To apply the bootstrap procedure for the dependent variable, we use the data-based estimates of the parameters given in (3.5) together with the observed values of the dependent and independent variables to yield the residuals

$$\hat{\varepsilon}_{it} = y_{it} - \hat{\alpha}_i - \hat{\beta}_i DQ_t - \hat{\phi} a_{it}, \qquad i=1,2,3, \; t=1,...,30.$$

Let $\hat{\varepsilon}_t = [\hat{\varepsilon}_{1t}\ \hat{\varepsilon}_{2t}\ \hat{\varepsilon}_{3t}]'$ be the residual vector for the year t. We assign mass 1/30 to each residual vector $\hat{\varepsilon}_t$, t=1,...,30, and draw a residual vector ε^*_τ from this distribution for the out-of-sample period τ.

We replace DQ_t and Z_{ijt} in (3.2) with their 'starred' counterparts defined in (6.3) and (6.4). We also use in (3.2) the data-based parameter estimates and the bootstrap values of the disturbance term:

$$y^*_{i\tau} = \hat{\alpha}_i + \hat{\beta}_i DQ^*_\tau + \hat{\phi} a^*_{i\tau} + \varepsilon^*_{i\tau}, \tag{6.5}$$

where $a^*_{i\tau} = (\overline{w}_{i\tau} + \hat{\beta}_i)[Z^*_{i4\tau} - \Sigma^3_{k=1} (\overline{w}_{k\tau} + \hat{\beta}_k)Z^*_{k4\tau}]$ and $\overline{w}_{i\tau}$ is the arithmetic average of $w^*_{i\tau}$ and $w^*_{i,\tau-1}$ which are the converged values of the budget shares in the out-of-sample periods τ and τ-1. For τ=1986, we take $w^*_{i,\tau-1} = w_{i,\tau-1}$. We call $y^*_{i\tau}$ given by (6.5) the *simulated-actual values of the dependent variables.* This y^*_{it} involves three set of residuals, ε^*_τ, u^*_τ, ξ^*_τ, the data-based estimates (the 'hatted' values) and the simulated-actual values of the independent variables.

To obtain the simulated-predicted values of the independent variables, in (4.1) and (4.2) for the out-of-sample year τ we replace (i) the parameters with their bootstrap estimates and (ii) the disturbances with their expected values of zero:

$$D\hat{Q}^*_\tau = \mu^* \tag{6.6}$$

and

$$\hat{Z}^*_{ij\tau} = D\hat{p}^*_{i\tau} - D\hat{p}^*_{j\tau} = \gamma^*_i - \gamma^*_j, \quad i,j=1,\ldots,4. \tag{6.7}$$

These are the *simulated-predicted values of the independent variables.* The bootstrap estimates μ^* and γ^*_i were obtained for models (4.1) and (4.2) using the bootstrap simulation procedure described in paragraphs 2 and 3 of this section.

To obtain the *simulated-predicted values of the dependent variables* we generate y_{it} from (3.2) by (i) replacing the parameters with their bootstrap estimates and (ii) setting the error terms at their expected values of zero. We also use in (3.2) the simulated-predictions of the exogenous variables defined in (6.6) and (6.7). The simulated-predicted value of the i-*th* dependent variable is thus

$$\hat{y}^*_{i\tau} = \alpha^*_i + \beta^*_i D\hat{Q}^*_\tau + \phi^* \hat{a}^*_{i\tau} \tag{6.8}$$

where $\hat{a}^*_{i\tau} = (\overline{w}_{i\tau} + \beta^*_i)[\hat{Z}^*_{i4\tau} - \Sigma^3_{k=1} (\overline{w}_{k\tau} + \beta^*_k)\hat{Z}^*_{k4\tau}]$, with $\overline{w}_{i\tau}$ defined below (6.5). The bootstrap estimates α^*_i, β^*_i and ϕ^* of α_i, β_i and ϕ in model (3.2) are obtained using the simulation procedure described in paragraphs 2 and 3 of this section.

Comparing (6.5) and (6.8), we see that the difference between the simulated-actual and simulated-predicted values of y_{it} is threefold. First, (6.5) uses the data-based parameter estimates ($\hat{\alpha}_i$, $\hat{\beta}_i$ and $\hat{\phi}$), whereas (6.8) uses the bootstrap estimates (α^*_i, β^*_i and ϕ^*). Second, for the exogenous variables, (6.5) uses the simulated-actual values (DQ^*_τ and $a^*_{i\tau}$), which are obtained with the data-based estimates. By contrast, (6.8) uses the simulated-predictions ($\hat{DQ}^*_\tau$ and $\hat{a}^*_{i\tau}$) from the bootstrap estimates. Third, (6.5) has a disturbance ($\varepsilon^*_{i\tau}$), while (6.8) does not.

Finally, for both the simulated-actual and simulated-predicted values of the dependent variable, we apply the iterative procedure described in Section 9.4 to obtain the simulated-actual and simulated-predicted market shares and consumption of the three beverages. For each out-of-sample year τ, we carry out 1000 trials and obtain 1000 bootstrap forecast errors, defined as the difference between the simulated-actual and simulated-predicted values.

Columns 8-13 of Table 9.2 present the root-mean-square of these 1000 forecast errors for each of the out-of-sample period. These standard errors can be used to assess the quality of our forecasts and to construct confidence intervals for the forecasts.

9.7 Forecasts versus Observed

In this section we present a comparison of our out-of-sample predictions with the observed values.

The observed values for the market shares and consumption of beer, wine and spirits in the UK for the out-of-sample years 1986-1988 are now available. Therefore, we could use these values to assess our predictions. Table 9.3 presents the forecasts and observed values for these three out-of-sample years. It can be seen from the table that the observed values are quite close to our predictions for the three beverages and almost all are within one standard error of the forecasts. This indicates that our approach seems to work satisfactorily.

References

Barten, A.P. (1969). 'Maximum Likelihood Estimation of a Complete System of Demand Equations,' *European Economic Review* 1: 7-73.

Clements, K.W. and H.Y. Izan (1987). 'The Measurement of Inflation: A Stochastic Approach,' *Journal of Business and Economic Statistics* 5: 339-50.

Clements, K.W. and E.A. Selvanathan (1988). 'The Rotterdam Demand Model and Its Application in Marketing Research,' *Marketing Science* 7: 60-75.

Efron, B. (1979). 'Bootstrap Methods: Another Look at the Jacknife,' *Annals of Statistics* 7: 1-26.

Finke, R., L.R. Flood and H. Theil (1984). 'The Budget Share of Food in 1990: Bootstrapping for Distribution-Free Prediction Intervals,' McKethan-Matherly Discussion Paper MM2, September 1984, Graduate School of Business, University of Florida.

Finke, R., L.R. Flood and H. Theil (1984b). 'Bootstrapping an Econometric Model: Some Empirical Results,' *Journal of Business and Economic Statistics* 2: 150-158.

Freedman, D.A. and S.C. Peters (1984a). 'Bootstrapping a Regression Equation: Some Empirical Results,' *Journal of the American Statistical Association* 79: 97-106.

Table 9.3 Observed and Predicted Market Shares and Consumption of Beer, Wine and Spirits: United Kingdom, 1986-1988

	Market Shares						Consumption					
	Beer		Wine		Spirits		Beer		Wine		Spirits	
Year	F	O	F	O	F	O	F	O	F	O	F	O
1986	.5310	.5412	.2246	.2174	.2445	.2414	109.63	107.84	17.26	17.03	4.44	4.28
	(.0130)		(.0082)		(.0095)		(2.66)		(.72)		(.37)	
1987	.5288	.5319	.2273	.2254	.2440	.2428	110.67	108.86	18.03	17.64	4.59	4.32
	(.0133)		(.0080)		(.0097)		(2.76)		(.77)		(.41)	
1988	.5266	.5264	.2299	N/A	.2435	N/A	111.72	111.43	18.82	17.84	4.75	4.53
	(.0139)		(.0089)		(.0100)		(2.69)		(.75)		(.42)	

F = Forecast; O = Observed; and N/A = Not available. The forecast values and the root-mean-square errors of the forecast errors (in parentheses) are reproduced from Table 2. The observed values are from the Annual Abstract of Statistics, 1989 and Monthly Digest of Statistics, 1989.

Lee, J.C. (1988). 'Nested Rotterdam Model: Applications to Marketing Research with Special Reference to Telecommunications Demand,' *International Journal of Forecasting* 4: 193-206.

Rao, D.S.P. and E.A. Selvanathan (1991). 'Standard Errors for Geary-Khamis Parities and International Prices,' *Journal of Business and Economic Statistics*, forthcoming.

Selvanathan, E.A. (1988). 'Alcohol Consumption in the UK, 1955-1985: A System-Wide Analysis,' *Applied Economics* 20: 1071-1086.

Selvanathan, E.A. (1989). 'A Note on the Stochastic Approach to Index Numbers,' *Journal of Business and Economic Statistics* 7, 471-474.

Theil, H. (1975). *Theory and Measurement of Consumer Demand*, Vol.1, North-Holland.

Theil, H. (1987). 'The Econometrics of Demand Systems,' Chapter 3 in H.Theil and K.W. Clements, *Applied Demand Analysis: Results from System-wide Approaches*. Cambridge, Mass.: Ballinger Publishing Company, pp.101-162.

Theil, H., M.C. Rosalsky and R. Finke (1984). 'A Comparison of Normal and Discrete Bootstraps for Standard Errors in Equation Systems,' *Statistics and Probability Letters* 2: 175-180.

Working, H. (1943). 'Statistical Laws of Family Expenditure,' *Journal of the American Statistical Association* 38: 43-56.

10 Aggregation and Consumer Demand

E.A. Selvanathan
School of International Business Relations, Griffith University, Australia.

10.1 Introduction

The term *aggregation* has two meanings in consumer demand analysis. One refers to *aggregation over commodities* and the other is the *aggregation over consumers*. In this chapter we shall consider both types of aggregation.

We will first look at the aggregation over commodities. Consider the situation where a consumer derives utility from the purchase of n commodities. In this situation the utility maximization problem will result in n basic demand equations; one for each commodity. However, in practice, it may not be possible to analyse the demand for each good for reasons such as limitations on data availability, the difficulties in estimating a large demand system etc. To overcome this problem it is essential to group the n commodities into a smaller number of groups, such as food, clothing, housing etc. This is termed "aggregation over commodities". We will show in this chapter that the aggregate demand equation for a group reflects the basic properties of the individual demand equations.

Now consider aggregation over consumers. With the introduction of flexible functional forms such as translog and almost ideal demand systems (e.g. Deaton and Muellbauer, 1980; Christensen, Jorgenson and Lau, 1973; Diewert, 1974), the differential demand systems came under severe criticism. One of the criticisms is based on the aggregation of the systems over consumers. As the differential demand equations we used in the last nine chapters are derived from the utility-maximizing theory of a single consumer, they are micro in nature. Usually since data are obtainable in some aggregate form (e.g. per capita), we estimate the aggregate (or macro) form of the micro demand system. The critics argue that the theoretical properties of the micro system (such as demand homogeneity and Slutsky symmetry) will not carry over to the macro system. Sonnenschein (1973) concluded that with respect to market demand functions, there is only little left of demand theory beyond homogeneity. In a similar vein, Shafer and Sonnenschein (1982) consider the conditions under which a market demand function has the same characteristics as a demand function for an individual consumer. They conclude that the required conditions are strong. These conclusions are pessimistic indeed.

The first response to these criticisms was offered by Barnett (1979a, 1979b, 1981). More recently Selvanathan (1991) also provided additional response. These authors use a completely different approach to attack the problem, an approach which uses statistical tools of analysis (Theil, 1971). This yields much more encouraging results about the properties of market demand function.

Theil (1971) aggregates differential demand equations in relative prices under fairly strong assumptions about the macro parameters and variables. Barnett (1979a, 1979b) relaxes these assumptions but works with absolute (undeflated) prices. Selvanathan (1991) extended Theil's work under the weaker assumptions of Barnett and derived macro demand equations in relative prices. The results show that the properties of the macrocoefficients are analogous to those of the microcoefficients.

The organisation of this chapter is as follows. In Section 10.2 we discuss the aggregation of the demand equations over commodities. In the following section we introduce Theil's (1971, 1975/76) convergence approach to aggregation which forms the base for the forthcoming sections. In Sections 10.4-10.6 we look at the problems of aggregation of the demand equations over consumers in absolute prices and in the remainder of the chapter we consider the aggregation over consumers in relative prices.

10.2 Aggregation over Commodities

Let there be n=6 goods, bread (i=1), meat (i=2), vegetables (i=3), clothing (i=4), housing (i=5), and other (i=6). Assume that these goods are divided into G=2 groups, food (S_f) and non-food (S_{nf}), which are block independent in the consumer's utility function. If we further assume that the non-food items are preference independent then we can write the utility function as

$$u(q_1,\ldots,q_6) = u_f(q_1,q_2,q_3) + \sum_{i=4}^{6} u_i(q_i), \tag{2.1}$$

where u_f, u_4, u_5 and u_6 are the sub-utility functions of food, clothing, housing and all other goods, respectively. Then the demand equation for the food items are [see equation (12.9) of Chapter 1]

$$w_i d(\log q_i) = \theta_i d(\log Q) + \sum_{j=1}^{3} \nu_{ij} d\left[\log \frac{p_j}{P'}\right], \qquad i \in S_f. \tag{2.2}$$

The demand equation for the non-food items are [see equation (13.7) of Chapter 1]

$$w_i d(\log q_i) = \theta_i d(\log Q) + \phi\theta_i d\left[\log \frac{p_i}{P'}\right], \qquad i \in S_{nf}. \tag{2.3}$$

Suppose the analyst combines the 3 food items into one group called "food", so that n is now equal to 4. What is the relationship of (i) the food demand equation to (2.2) and (ii) the new demand equations for the non-food items to (2.3)? If we sum both sides of (2.2) over $i \in S_f$, we obtain the composite or group demand equation for food,

$$W_f d(\log q_f) = \Theta_f d(\log Q) + \phi\Theta_f d\left[\log \frac{P'_f}{P'}\right]. \tag{2.4}$$

Consequently, the smaller system of n=4 equations comprises (2.4) plus (2.3). As the structure of (2.4) is identical to that of (2.3), if we now reinterpret the notation appropriately, the whole system can be written as

$$w_i d(\log q_i) = \theta_i d(\log Q) + \phi\theta_i d\left[\log \frac{p_i}{P'}\right], \qquad i=1,\ldots,4.$$

The appealing result is that (i) the aggregate food demand equation reflects the properties of the demand equations for the individual food items; and (ii) the demand equations for the non-food items are unaffected by the aggregation of food. In this sense there is no aggregation bias. These results hold when preferences are of the form (2.1).

10.3 The Convergence Approach to Linear Aggregation

In this section we consider the convergence approach to aggregation. The material of this section is based on Theil (1971, 1975/76).

Consider the demand equation for good i and the c-*th* consumer:

$$q_{ic} = q_{ic}(M_c, \mathbf{p}), \qquad \begin{array}{l} i=1,\ldots,n, \\ c=1,\ldots,N, \end{array} \tag{3.1}$$

where M_c is the income of consumer c; and we make the assumption that each consumer faces the same price vector **p**; and where N is the total number of consumers. For commodity i, if we sum (3.1) over c=1,...,N and divide both sides by N, we obtain

$$\bar{q}_i = \frac{1}{N}\sum_{c=1}^{N} q_{ic}(M_c, \mathbf{p}) = f_i(M_1,\ldots,M_N, \mathbf{p}), \qquad i=1,\ldots,n, \tag{3.2}$$

for some functions f_i. In (3.2), $\bar{q}_i$ is the average consumption of commodity i per consumer, or per capita consumption of i for short. If exact aggregation is possible then for some functions g_i, i=1,...,n, we can write (3.2) in the form

$$\bar{q}_i = g_i(\bar{M},p), \qquad i=1,\ldots,n, \tag{3.3}$$

where $\bar{M}$ is the per capita income. Equation (3.3) is the per capita analogue, or the macro analogue, of the micro equation (3.1).

The problem is that the functions g_i do not, in general, exist. Let us consider (3.1) in linear form,

$$q_{ic} = \alpha_{ic} + \beta_{ic}M_c, \qquad i=1,\ldots,n, \quad c=1,\ldots,N, \tag{3.4}$$

where α_{ic} is a constant term and β_{ic} is the income parameter. For simplicity, prices have been omitted from (3.4). If we sum both sides of the micro relation (3.4) over c=1,...,N and divide both sides by N, we obtain the macro relation,

$$\bar{q}_i = \bar{\alpha}_i + \frac{1}{N}\sum_{c=1}^{N} \beta_{ic}M_c, \tag{3.5}$$

or equivalently,

$$\bar{q}_i = \bar{\alpha}_i + \frac{\sum_{c=1}^{N} \beta_{ic}M_c}{\sum_{c=1}^{N} M_c}\bar{M}, \tag{3.6}$$

where $\bar{\alpha}_i = (1/N)\sum_{c=1}^{N} \alpha_{ic}$ and we have assumed that $\sum_{c=1}^{N} M_c \neq 0$. Generally, equation (3.6) cannot be considered as a linear macro relation in $\bar{q}_i$ and $\bar{M}$. To consider (3.6) as an approximate linear macro relation, we apply the Theil's (1971,1975/76) *convergence approach to aggregation* in the following manner.

Let us assume that the N consumers are independent random elements of an infinite consumer population and that the coefficients $\beta_{i1},...,\beta_{iN}$ are identically independently distributed and come from a probability distribution having mean β_i and finite variance σ^2. We shall also initially assume that $M_1,...,M_N$ are nonstochastic. Then the coefficient of $\bar{M}$ in (3.6) is a random variable with expectation

$$E\left[\frac{\sum_{c=1}^{N} \beta_{ic} M_c}{\sum_{c=1}^{N} M_c}\right] = \beta_i \tag{3.7}$$

and has the following variance

$$E\left[\frac{\sum_{c=1}^{N} \beta_{ic} M_c}{\sum_{c=1}^{N} M_c} - \beta_i\right]^2 = E\left[\frac{\sum_{c=1}^{N} (\beta_{ic} - \beta_i) M_c}{\sum_{c=1}^{N} M_c}\right]^2$$

$$= \frac{\sum_{c=1}^{N} M_c^2 \, E[(\beta_{ic} - \beta_i)^2]}{\left[\sum_{c=1}^{N} M_c\right]^2}$$

$$= \sigma^2 \frac{\sum_{c=1}^{N} M_c^2}{\left[\sum_{c=1}^{N} M_c\right]^2},$$

where we have used the fact the β_{ic}'s are identically independently distributed. As $\bar{M} = (1/N) \Sigma_{c=1}^{N} M_c$ and $\Sigma_{c=1}^{N} (M_c - \bar{M})^2 = \Sigma_{c=1}^{N} M_c^2 - N\bar{M}^2$, the above variance can now be written as

$$E\left[\frac{\sum_{c=1}^{N} \beta_{ic} M_c}{\sum_{c=1}^{N} M_c} - \beta_i\right]^2 = \frac{\sigma^2}{N}\left[1 + \frac{\frac{1}{N}\sum_{c=1}^{N} (M_c - \bar{M})^2}{\bar{M}^2}\right]. \tag{3.8}$$

When $(1/N)\,\Sigma_{c=1}^{N} (M_c - \bar{M})^2 < \infty$, we have

$$\lim_{N\to\infty} E\left[\frac{\sum_{c=1}^{N} \beta_{ic} M_c}{\sum_{c=1}^{N} M_c} - \beta_i\right]^2 \to 0. \tag{3.9}$$

Using Chebyshev's inequality we can conclude that

$$\frac{\sum_{c=1}^{N} \beta_{ic} M_c}{\sum_{c=1}^{N} M_c} \text{ converges in probability to } \beta_i.$$

Therefore for sufficiently large N, we can write equation (3.6) as

$$\bar{q}_i \approx \bar{\alpha}_i + \beta_i \bar{M}, \tag{3.10}$$

which is a linear macro relation in per capita variables $\bar{q}_i$ and $\bar{M}$ with constant coefficients.

Now we shall consider the case when $M_1, \ldots, M_N$ are stochastic and redefine

$$\beta_i = \frac{E[\beta_{ic} M_c]}{E[M_c]}. \tag{3.11}$$

Let us assume that (i) M_c, c=1,...,N are identically independently distributed; (ii) $\beta_{ic}M_c$, c=1,...,N are also identically independently distributed at each point in time; and (iii) that $E[M_c]$ and $E[\beta_{ic}M_c]$ exist and are finite.

Applying Khinchine's theorem

$$\bar{M} = E[M_c] + o_p(1), \tag{3.12}$$

where $o_p(1)$ denotes a random variable that converges in probability to zero as N tends to infinity. Assuming that $E[M_c] > 0$, applying Slutsky's theorem, we get

$$\frac{1}{\bar{M}} = \frac{1}{E[M_c]} + o_p(1). \tag{3.13}$$

As $\beta_{ic}M_c$, c=1,...,N are identically independently distributed, using Khinchine's theorem, we get

$$\frac{1}{N}\sum_{c=1}^{N} \beta_{ic}M_c = E[\beta_{ic}M_c] + o_p(1). \tag{3.14}$$

Therefore from equations (3.11), (3.13) and (3.14) we have

$$\frac{\frac{1}{N}\sum_{c=1}^{N}\beta_{ic}M_c}{\frac{1}{N}\sum_{c=1}^{N}M_c} = \frac{E[\beta_{ic}M_c]}{E[M_c]} + o_p(1) = \beta_i + o_p(1).$$

Now taking the limit as N tends to infinity of both sides of the above equation we get

$$\lim_{N\to\infty} \frac{\frac{1}{N}\sum_{c=1}^{N}\beta_{ic}M_c}{\frac{1}{N}\sum_{c=1}^{N}M_c} = \beta_i, \tag{3.15}$$

where we have used $\text{plim}_{N\to\infty}\, o_p(1) = 0$. Thus for sufficiently large N, (3.6) becomes equivalent to (3.10) even when income is random.

10.4 Demand Equations in Absolute Prices

In this section, we shall apply the convergence approach to develop a macro differential demand system. This section deals with differential demand equations in absolute prices. The material of this section and Sections 10.5 and 10.6 are based on Barnett (1979a). The relative price version will be considered in Section 10.7.

The Micro Demand Equation

Consider the absolute price version of the differential demand equation for good i [see equation (13.11) of Chapter 1]. As that equation refers to an individual consumer we add a consumer subscript c and the *micro demand equation* can be written as,

$$w_{ic}\, d(\log q_{ic}) = \theta_{ic}\, d(\log Q_c) + \sum_{j=1}^{n} \pi_{ijc}\, d(\log p_j), \tag{4.1}$$

where $w_{ic} = p_i q_{ic}/M_c$ is the budget share of good i for consumer c (=1,...,N); q_{ic} is the quantity consumed of i by c; p_i is the price of i which is assumed to be the same for all consumers; M_c is the income of c; $\theta_{ic} = \partial(p_i q_{ic})/\partial M_c$ is the marginal share of i; $d(\log Q_c) = d(\log M_c) - \Sigma_{\ell=1}^{n} w_{\ell c}\, d(\log p_\ell)$ is the change in the real income of consumer c; and π_{ijc} is the (i,j)-*th* Slutsky coefficient. The *microcoefficients* θ_{ic} and π_{ijc} of the micro demand equation (4.1) are functions of income M_c and prices p_i's. Consequently, we can consider the microcoefficients of equation (4.1) as random coefficients. These microcoefficients satisfy

$$\sum_{i=1}^{n} \theta_{ic} = 1, \tag{4.2}$$

$$\sum_{j=1}^{n} \pi_{ijc} = 0 \qquad i=1,\dots,n, \quad c=1,\dots,N, \tag{4.3}$$

with $[\pi_{ijc}]$ an $n \times n$ symmetric negative semidefinite matrix of order n-1.

The Macro Demand Equation

Now let us define the per capita variables which we shall refer to as the *macrovariables*

$$\bar{q}_i = \frac{1}{N} \sum_{c=1}^{n} q_{ic}, \quad \bar{M} = \frac{1}{N} \sum_{c=1}^{n} M_c = \sum_{i=1}^{n} p_i \bar{q}_i, \quad \bar{w}_i = \frac{p_i \bar{q}_i}{\bar{M}}, \quad i=1,\dots,n. \tag{4.4}$$

Our objective is to develop a *macro demand equation* in terms of macro variables and macrocoefficients which is analogous to the micro demand equation (4.1). To obtain this, first let us multiply both sides of (4.1) by $M_c/N\bar{M}$ and take the summation over c=1,...,N,

$$\sum_{c=1}^{N} \frac{M_c}{N\bar{M}} w_{ic} d(\log q_{ic}) = \sum_{c=1}^{N} \frac{M_c}{N\bar{M}} \theta_{ic} \left[d(\log M_c) - \sum_{k=1}^{n} w_{kc} d(\log p_k) \right]$$

$$+ \sum_{c=1}^{N} \sum_{j=1}^{n} \frac{M_c}{N\bar{M}} \pi_{ijc} d(\log p_j). \tag{4.5}$$

The left-hand term of (4.5) is

$$\sum_{c=1}^{N} \frac{M_c}{N\bar{M}} w_{ic} d(\log q_{ic}) = \sum_{c=1}^{N} \frac{M_c}{N\bar{M}} \frac{p_i q_{ic}}{M_c} \frac{dq_{ic}}{q_{ic}}$$

$$= \frac{p_i}{N\bar{M}} \sum_{c=1}^{N} dq_{ic}$$

$$= \frac{p_i d\bar{q}_i}{\bar{M}}$$

$$= \bar{w}_i d(\log \bar{q}_i), \tag{4.6}$$

which is the macro analogue of the left-hand side variable of equation (4.1).

In the following section, we shall show that under certain plausible assumptions, we can aggregate the real-income and price terms of (4.5) such that the final form of the macro demand model becomes

$$\bar{w}_i d(\log \bar{q}_i) = \bar{\theta}_i d(\log \bar{Q}) + \sum_{j=1}^{n} \bar{\pi}_{ij} d(\log p_j), \tag{4.7}$$

where $\bar{\theta}_i$ and $\bar{\pi}_{ij}$ are the macrocoefficients analogous to the microcoefficients θ_{ic} and π_{ijc}. These macrocoefficients shall be defined in the next section. Equation (4.7) is a macro analogue of the micro relation (4.1).

10.5 Derivations

In this section, we make certain assumptions about the parameters and variables in order to derive the aggregate real income and price terms given on the right-hand side of the macro demand model (4.7).

Assumptions

Let $K_{ic} = M_c(\theta_{ic} - \bar{\theta}_i)$ and $V_c = d(\text{loq } Q_c) = d(\log M_c) - \sum_{j=1}^{n} w_{jc} d(\log p_j)$. We shall make the following assumptions about the parameters and variables in order to simplify the right-hand side of equation (4.5). We assume that M_c, c=1,...,N, are identically independently distributed and that the moments $E[M_c]$, $E[V_c]$, $E\theta_{\theta ic}]$,

$E[M_c\pi_{ijc}]$, $E[K_{ic}V_c]$ and $E[K_{ic}\pi_{ijc}]$ exist and are finite. We also assume that the *macrocoefficients* defined as

$$\bar{\theta}_i = \frac{E[M_c\theta_{ic}]}{E[M_c]}, \qquad \bar{\pi}_{ij} = \frac{E[M_c\pi_{ijc}]}{E[M_c]}, \qquad i,j=1,\ldots,n, \tag{5.1}$$

exist and are finite. These macrocoefficients vary over time. In words, (5.1) can be interpreted as saying that the macrocoefficients are the population versions of weighted-average microcoefficients, with weights proportional to income M_c.

Aggregating the Real-Income Term

The real-income term in (4.5) is

$$\frac{1}{N\bar{M}}\sum_{c=1}^{N} M_c\theta_{ic}\left[d(\log M_c) - \sum_{k=1}^{n} w_{kc}d(\log p_k)\right]$$

$$= \frac{1}{N\bar{M}}\left[\sum_{c=1}^{N} \theta_{ic}\left[dM_c - \sum_{k=1}^{n} q_{kc}dp_k\right]\right]$$

$$= \frac{\bar{\theta}_i}{N\bar{M}}\sum_{c=1}^{N}\left[dM_c - \sum_{k=1}^{n} q_{kc}dp_k\right]$$

$$+ \frac{1}{N\bar{M}}\sum_{c=1}^{N}(\theta_{ic} - \bar{\theta}_i)\left[dM_c - \sum_{k=1}^{n} q_{kc}dp_k\right]. \tag{5.2}$$

The first term on the right-hand side of (5.2) can be further simplified as follows:

$$\frac{\theta_i}{N\bar{M}} \sum_{c=1}^{N} \left[dM_c - \sum_{k=1}^{n} q_{kc} dp_k \right]$$

$$= \bar{\theta}_i \left[\frac{1}{N\bar{M}} \sum_{c=1}^{N} dM_c - \sum_{k=1}^{n} \frac{p_k \bar{q}_k}{\bar{M}} d(\log p_k) \right]$$

$$= \bar{\theta}_i \left[d(\log \bar{M}) - \sum_{k=1}^{n} \bar{w}_k d(\log p_k) \right]$$

$$= \bar{\theta}_i d(\log \bar{Q}),$$

where $d(\log \bar{Q}) = d(\log \bar{M}) - \Sigma_{k=1}^{n} \bar{w}_k d(\log p_k)$ is the change in macro real income.

The second right-hand term of (5.2) is

$$\frac{1}{N\bar{M}} \sum_{c=1}^{N} (\theta_{ic} - \bar{\theta}_i) \left[dM_c - \sum_{k=1}^{n} q_{kc} dp_k \right]$$

$$= \frac{1}{N\bar{M}} \sum_{c=1}^{N} M_c(\theta_{ic} - \bar{\theta}_i) \left[d(\log M_c) - \sum_{k=1}^{n} w_{kc} d(\log p_k) \right]$$

$$= \frac{1}{N\bar{M}} \sum_{c=1}^{N} K_{ic} d(\log Q_c)$$

$$= \frac{1}{N\bar{M}} \sum_{c=1}^{N} K_{ic} V_c$$

$$= Z \text{ (say)}.$$

Therefore the real-income term in the right-hand side of equation (4.5) simplifies to

$$\sum_{c=1}^{N} \frac{M_c}{N\overline{M}} \theta_{ic} \left[d(\log M_c) - \sum_{k=1}^{n} w_{kc} d(\log p_k) \right] = \overline{\theta}_i d(\log \overline{Q}) + Z. \tag{5.3}$$

The Stochastic Limit of Z

Now we evaluate the stochastic limit of Z for sufficiently large N. As $K_{ic}V_c$, c=1,...,N are i.i.d., using Khinchine's theorem, we obtain

$$\frac{1}{N} \sum_{c=1}^{N} K_{ic} V_c = E[K_{ic} V_c] + o_p(1). \tag{5.4}$$

According to our assumption, we have that M_c, c=1,...,N, are identically independently distributed and that $E[M_c]$ is finite. Therefore, from the definition of Z and equations (3.13) and (5.4), we have

$$Z = \frac{E[K_{ic} V_c]}{E[M_c]} + o_p(1). \tag{5.5}$$

We also have $E[K_{ic}] = E[M_c \theta_{ic}] - E[M_c \overline{\theta}_i] = E[M_c]\overline{\theta}_i - \overline{\theta}_i E[M_c] = 0$, where the second step uses equation (5.1). Thus (5.5) can be simplified to

$$Z = \frac{\operatorname{cov}[K_{ic}, V_c]}{E[M_c]} + o_p(1). \tag{5.6}$$

Aggregating the Price Term

The price term on the right-hand side of equation (4.5) is

$$\sum_{c=1}^{N}\sum_{j=1}^{n}\frac{M_c}{N\overline{M}}\pi_{ijc}d(\log p_j) = \frac{1}{\overline{M}}\sum_{j=1}^{n}\left[\frac{1}{N}\sum_{c=1}^{N} M_c\pi_{ijc}\right]d(\log p_j)$$

$$= \frac{1}{E[M_c]}\sum_{j=1}^{n} E[M_c]\,\overline{\pi}_{ij}d(\log p_j) + o_p(1)$$

$$= \sum_{j=1}^{n}\overline{\pi}_{ij}d(\log p_j) + o_p(1), \tag{5.7}$$

where we have used equations (3.13), (5.1) and the relation

$$\frac{1}{N}\sum_{c=1}^{N} M_c\pi_{ijc} = E[M_c\pi_{ijc}] + o_p(1),$$

which is implied by Khinchine's theorem.

The Final Form of the Macro Demand Model

Using equations (4.6), (5.3), (5.6) and (5.7), we can simplify equation (4.5) to

$$\overline{w}_i d(\log \overline{q}_i) = \overline{\theta}_i d(\log \overline{Q}) + \sum_{j=1}^{n}\overline{\pi}_{ij}d(\log p_j) + \frac{\mathrm{cov}[K_{ic},V_c]}{E[M_c]} + o_p(1). \tag{5.8}$$

By Schwartz' inequality we have

$$\mathrm{cov}[K_{ic},V_c] \leq \left[\mathrm{var}[K_{ic}]\,\mathrm{var}[V_c]\right]^{\frac{1}{2}}.$$

For a developed economy, the variability that induces randomness into (K_{ic},V_c) is likely to be small relative to $E[M_c]$. Thus we would expect $(\mathrm{var}[K_{ic}]\,\mathrm{var}[V_c])^{\frac{1}{2}} \ll E[M_c]$. In other words, we would expect $(\mathrm{var}[K_{ic}]\,\mathrm{var}[V_c])^{\frac{1}{2}}/E[M_c]$ to be negligibly small so that the limit of

$\text{cov}[K_{ic}, V_c]/E[M_c]$ is zero as N tends to infinity. Therefore, for sufficiently large N, we write the final form of the macro relation (5.8) as

$$\bar{w}_i d(\log \bar{q}_i) = \bar{\theta}_i d(\log \bar{Q}) + \sum_{j=1}^{n} \bar{\pi}_{ij} d(\log p_j), \tag{5.9}$$

where we have also used $\text{plim}_{N\to\infty} o_p(1) = 0$. Equation (5.9) is the macro demand equation (4.7).

10.6 The Aggregation Bias of the Slutsky Coefficients

In Section 10.5, we argued that $\lim_{N\to\infty}\{\text{cov}[K_{ic}, V_c]/E[M_c]\} = 0$. In this section we shall analyse the behaviour of this ratio from another perspective. As

$$V_c = d(\log Q_c) = d(\log M_c) - \sum_{j=1}^{n} w_{jc} d(\log p_j),$$

we write this ratio as

$$\frac{\text{cov}[K_{ic}, V_c]}{E[M_c]} = a_i - b_i, \tag{6.1}$$

where

$$a_i = \frac{\text{cov}[K_{ic}, d(\log M_c)]}{E[M_c]} \quad \text{and} \quad b_i = \frac{\text{cov}\left[K_{ic}, \sum_{j=1}^{n} w_{jc} d(\log p_j)\right]}{E[M_c]}. \tag{6.2}$$

We can also write

$$a_i = \rho_i \frac{\left[\text{var}[K_{ic}]\ \text{var}[d(\log M_c)]\right]^{\frac{1}{2}}}{E[M_c]},$$

where ρ_i is the correlation coefficient between K_{ic} and $d(\log M_c)$. As $K_{ic} = M_c(\theta_{ic} - \bar{\theta}_i)$ and $E[K_{ic}] = 0$, we have

$$\text{var}[K_{ic}] = E[M_c^2(\theta_{ic} - \bar{\theta}_i)^2].$$

There are three possibilities under which a_i becomes negligible. One possibility is that the *i-th* marginal share of each consumer c, θ_{ic}, is close to the average marginal share $\bar{\theta}_i$. Then $\text{var}[K_{ic}] \approx 0$ and $a_i \approx 0$. The second is when all incomes change proportionately, $\text{var}[d(\log M_c)] \approx 0$, which also implies that $a_i \approx 0$. The last possibility holds under the following assumption. Suppose that at each time point $d(\log M_c)$ is stochastically independent of logarithmic income $\log M_c$ and that $E[(\log M_c)^2]$ is finite. As $K_{ic} = M_c(\theta_{ic} - \bar{\theta}_i)$, under this assumption, we conclude that K_{ic} is stochastically independent of $d(\log M_c)$. This implies that ρ_i equals zero so that a_i is uniformly zero at any time point (Barnett, 1981). As Barnett (1979a) argues, in any of these three cases, the term a_i will typically be small.

Now let us consider the term b_i of equation (6.2). If ρ_{ij} denotes the correlation coefficient between K_{ic} and w_{jc}, then we can write

$$b_i = \sum_{j=1}^{n} \rho_{ij} \frac{\left[\text{var}[K_{ic}]\ \text{var}[w_{jc}]\right]^{\frac{1}{2}}}{E[M_c]} d(\log p_j). \tag{6.3}$$

Using (6.1) and (6.3), and noting the facts that a_i is small and $\text{plim}_{N\to\infty} o_p(1) = 0$, we can write (5.8) as

$$\bar{w}_i d(\log \bar{q}_i) = \bar{\theta}_i d(\log \bar{Q}) + \sum_{j=1}^{n} (\bar{\pi}_{ij} - c_{ij}) d(\log p_j), \tag{6.4}$$

where

$$c_{ij} = \rho_{ij} \frac{\left[\text{var}[K_{ic}] \ \text{var}[w_{jc}]\right]^{\frac{1}{2}}}{E[M_c]}.$$

Barnett (1979a) refers to this c_{ij} as the *asymptotic aggregation bias* of the macrocoefficient $\bar{\pi}_{ij}$. We can see the meaning of this terminology if we compare equation (5.9) with (6.4). Even though the macro Slutsky coefficients, $\bar{\pi}_{ij}$, are symmetric (we shall prove this in Section 10.9), the coefficients of the prices in equation (6.4), $\bar{\pi}_{ij} - c_{ij}$, are not symmetric.

Henceforth, we shall proceed on the basis that c_{ij} is negligibly small and thus use equation (5.9) rather than (6.4). In other words, we shall accept the argument described in the last paragraph of Section 10.5 that this asymptotic bias can be safely neglected.

10.7 Demand Equations in Relative Prices

In this and the following three sections, we consider the demand equations in relative prices. The material of these sections are from Selvanathan (1991).

The relative price version of the differential demand equation for good i and consumer c can be written as [see equation (12.9) of Chapter 1]

$$w_{ic}d(\log q_{ic}) = \theta_{ic}d(\log Q_c) + \sum_{j=1}^{n} \nu_{ijc}\left[d(\log p_j) - \sum_{\ell=1}^{n} \theta_{\ell c}d(\log p_\ell)\right], \qquad (7.1)$$

where w_{ic}, q_{ic}, p_i, M_c, θ_{ic} and $d(\log Q_c)$ are as before (see below equation (4.1))and $\nu_{ijc} = \lambda p_i u_c^{ij} p_j/M_c$ is the (i,j)-*th* price coefficient, with λ the marginal utility of income and u_c^{ij} the (i,j)-*th* element of the inverse of the Hessian of the utility function $U_c = [\partial^2 u_c/\partial q_{ic}\partial q_{jc}]$ and

$u_c(q_c) = u(q_c, s_c)$, where $\mathbf{q}_c = [q_{ic}]$ and $\mathbf{s}_c$ is a finite dimensional vector of taste determining factors experienced by consumer c which is likely to vary over consumers. Therefore, demand functions $\mathbf{q}_c$ and the *microcoefficients* θ_{ic} and ν_{ijc} of the micro demand equation (7.1) are functions of income M_c, price vector $\mathbf{p}$ and taste vector $\mathbf{s}_c$. As before, we assume that M_c, c=1,...,N and $\mathbf{s}_c$, c=1,...,N are identically independently distributed. Consequently, we can consider the microcoefficients of equation (7.1) as random coefficients. These coefficients satisfy

$$\sum_{i=1}^{n} \theta_{ic} = 1, \quad \sum_{j=1}^{n} \nu_{ijc} = \phi_c \theta_{ic}, \qquad i=1,\ldots,n, \; c=1,\ldots,N. \tag{7.2}$$

where $\phi_c = [\partial(\log \lambda_c)/\partial(\log M_c)]^{-1}$ is the reciprocal of the income elasticity of the marginal utility of income, the "income flexibility", while the matrix $[\nu_{ijc}]$ is symmetric negative definite for each c.

As before we define the per capita variables which we shall refer to as the *macrovariables*

$$\bar{q}_i = \frac{1}{N}\sum_{c=1}^{N} q_{ic}, \quad \bar{M} = \frac{1}{N}\sum_{c=1}^{N} M_c = \sum_{i=1}^{n} p_i \bar{q}_i, \quad \bar{w}_i = \frac{p_i \bar{q}_i}{\bar{M}}, \quad i=1,\ldots,n. \tag{7.3}$$

Our objective is to develop a *macro demand equation* in terms of macro variables and macrocoefficients which is analogous to the micro demand equation (7.1).

We define the *macrocoefficients* as

$$\bar{\theta}_i = \frac{E[M_c \theta_{ic}]}{E[M_c]}, \quad \bar{\nu}_{ij} = \frac{E[M_c \nu_{ijc}]}{E[M_c]}, \; i,j=1,\ldots,n, \quad \bar{\phi} = \frac{E[M_c \phi_c]}{E[M_c]}. \tag{7.4}$$

The macrocoefficients $\bar{\theta}_i$, $\bar{\nu}_{ij}$ and $\bar{\phi}$ are population versions of weighted average microcoefficients, with weights proportional to corresponding incomes. As before, we define $K_{ic} = M_c(\theta_{ic} - \bar{\theta}_i)$ and $V_c = d(\log Q_c) = d(\log M_c) - \Sigma_{j=1}^{n} w_{jc} d(\log p_j)$. We assume that the moments $E[M_c]$, $E[M_c\theta_{ic}]$, $E[M_c\nu_{ijc}]$, $E[M_c\phi_c]$, $E[K_{ic}V_c]$, $E[K_{ic}\nu_{ijc}]$ and $E[K_{ic}\phi_c]$ exist and are finite.

10.8 Derivation of the Relative Price Version of the Macro Demand Model

To obtain the macro demand equation we multiply both sides of (7.1) by $M_c/N\bar{M}$ and sum over c=1,...,N to yield

$$\sum_{c=1}^{N} \frac{M_c}{N\bar{M}} w_{ic} d(\log q_{ic})$$

$$= \sum_{c=1}^{N} \frac{M_c}{N\bar{M}} \theta_{ic} d(\log Q_c) + \frac{1}{\bar{M}} \sum_{j=1}^{n} \left[\frac{1}{N} \sum_{c=1}^{N} M_c \nu_{ijc} \right] d(\log p_j)$$

$$- \frac{1}{\bar{M}} \sum_{j=1}^{n} \sum_{\ell=1}^{n} \frac{1}{N} \sum_{c=1}^{N} \nu_{ijc} \theta_{\ell c} M_c d(\log p_\ell). \tag{8.1}$$

We have shown in Section 10.5 that the left-hand term of equation (8.1) can be simplified to $\bar{w}_i d(\log \bar{q}_i)$, which is the macro analogue of the left-hand term of (7.1). Under the above assumption, as before we employ Khinchine and Slutsky theorems to show that the real income term on the right-hand side of equation (8.1) can be simplified to $\bar{\theta}_i d(\log \bar{Q}) + \mathrm{Cov}[K_{ic}, V_c]/E[M_c] + o_p(1)$, where $d(\log \bar{Q}) = d(\log \bar{M}) - \Sigma_{\tau=1}^{n} \bar{w}_\tau d(\log p_\tau)$ is the change in macro real income and $o_p(1)$ is a random variable that converges in probability to zero as N tends to infinity.

Applying Khinchine's theorem gives

$$\bar{M} = E[M_c] + o_p(1) \quad \text{and} \quad \frac{1}{N}\sum_{c=1}^{N} M_c \nu_{ijc} = E[M_c \nu_{ijc}] + o_p(1),$$

Assuming $E[M_c] > 0$, applying Slutsky's theorem, we get

$$\frac{1}{\bar{M}} = \frac{1}{E[M_c]} + o_p(1).$$

From the above two results and equation (7.4), we obtain

$$\frac{1}{\bar{M}}\left[\frac{1}{N}\sum_{c=1}^{N} M_c \nu_{ijc}\right] = \bar{\nu}_{ij} + o_p(1). \tag{8.2}$$

Using equation (8.2), the second term on the right-hand side of (8.1) can be simplified as

$$\frac{1}{\bar{M}}\sum_{j=1}^{n}\left[\frac{1}{N}\sum_{c=1}^{N} M_c \nu_{ijc}\right] d(\log p_j) = \sum_{j=1}^{n} \bar{\nu}_{ij} d(\log p_j) + o_p(1). \tag{8.3}$$

We write the third right-hand term of (8.1) as

$$\frac{1}{\bar{M}}\sum_{j=1}^{n}\sum_{\ell=1}^{n}\frac{1}{N}\sum_{c=1}^{N} \nu_{ijc}\theta_{\ell c} M_c d(\log p_\ell)$$

$$= \frac{1}{\bar{M}}\sum_{j=1}^{n}\sum_{\ell=1}^{n}\left[\frac{1}{N}\sum_{c=1}^{N} M_c \nu_{ijc}\right]\bar{\theta}_\ell d(\log p_\ell)$$

$$+ \frac{1}{\bar{M}}\sum_{j=1}^{n}\sum_{\ell=1}^{n}\left[\frac{1}{N}\sum_{c=1}^{N} M_c(\theta_{\ell c} - \bar{\theta}_\ell)\nu_{ijc}\right] d(\log p_\ell). \tag{8.4}$$

Using (8.2), the first term on the right-hand side of equation (8.4) becomes

$$\frac{1}{\bar{M}} \sum_{j=1}^{n} \sum_{\ell=1}^{n} \left[\frac{1}{N} \sum_{c=1}^{N} M_c \nu_{ijc} \right] \bar{\theta}_\ell d(\log p_\ell)$$

$$= \sum_{j=1}^{n} \bar{\nu}_{ij} \sum_{\ell=1}^{n} \bar{\theta}_\ell d(\log p_\ell) + o_p(1). \tag{8.5}$$

As $K_{\ell c} = M_c(\theta_{\ell c} - \bar{\theta}_\ell)$ and using (7.4) we obtain $E[K_{\ell c}] = 0$. Thus, the second term on the right-hand side of (8.4) can be simplified to

$$\frac{1}{\bar{M}} \sum_{j=1}^{n} \sum_{\ell=1}^{n} \left[\frac{1}{N} \sum_{c=1}^{N} K_{\ell c} \nu_{ijc} \right] d(\log p_\ell)$$

$$= \sum_{j=1}^{n} \sum_{\ell=1}^{n} \frac{\operatorname{cov}[K_{\ell c}, \nu_{ijc}]}{E[M_c]} d(\log p_\ell) + o_p(1), \tag{8.6}$$

where we have again used Khinchine's theorem to obtain $(1/N) \sum_{c=1}^{N} K_{\ell c} \nu_{ijc} = E[K_{\ell c} \nu_{ijc}] + o_p(1)$ and the result that $1/\bar{M} = 1/E[M_c] + o_p(1)$. Substituting equations (8.5) and (8.6) in (8.4) we obtain

$$\frac{1}{\bar{M}} \sum_{j=1}^{n} \sum_{\ell=1}^{n} \frac{1}{N} \sum_{c=1}^{N} \nu_{ijc} \theta_{\ell c} M_c d(\log p_\ell)$$

$$= \sum_{j=1}^{n} \bar{\nu}_{ij} \sum_{\ell=1}^{n} \bar{\theta}_\ell d(\log p_\ell)$$

$$+ \sum_{j=1}^{n} \sum_{\ell=1}^{n} \frac{\operatorname{cov}[K_{\ell c}, \nu_{ijc}]}{E[M_c]} d(\log p_\ell) + o_p(1). \tag{8.7}$$

Using the discussion below equation (8.1) and equations (8.3) and (8.7), equation (8.1) can now be simplified as

$$\bar{w}_i d(\log \bar{q}_i) = \bar{\theta}_i d(\log \bar{Q}) + \sum_{j=1}^{n} \bar{\nu}_{ij} \left[d(\log p_j) - \sum_{\ell=1}^{n} \bar{\theta}_\ell d(\log p_\ell) \right] + Z_i, \qquad i=1,\dots,n, \tag{8.8}$$

where

$$Z_i = \frac{\mathrm{cov}[K_{ic}, V_c]}{E[M_c]} - \sum_{j=1}^{n} \sum_{\ell=1}^{n} \frac{\mathrm{cov}[K_{\ell c}, \nu_{ijc}]}{E[M_c]} d(\log p_\ell) + o_p(1).$$

Equation (8.8) is the macro analogue of (7.1), except the last term. In Section 10.9, we look at the size of the remainder term Z_i.

In applications where N is typically very large we can delete the $o_p(1)$ term from Z_i. Using $V_c = d(\log M_c) - \Sigma_{j=1}^{n} w_{jc}\, d(\log p_j)$, we can write the remainder Z_i in the form,

$$Z_i = a_i - b_i + c_i - d_i, \tag{8.9}$$

where

$$a_i = \frac{1}{E[M_c]} \mathrm{Cov}[K_{ic}, d(\log M_c)];$$

$$b_i = \sum_{j=1}^{n} \frac{1}{E[M_c]} \mathrm{Cov}[K_{ic}, w_{jc}]\, d(\log p_j);$$

$$c_i = \sum_{j=1}^{n} \frac{1}{E[M_c]} \mathrm{Cov}[K_{ic}, w_{jc}] \left[\sum_{\ell=1}^{n} \bar{\theta}_\ell d(\log p_\ell) \right];$$

and

$$d_i = \sum_{\ell=1}^{n} \eta_{i\ell}\, d(\log p_\ell)$$

with

$$\eta_{i\ell} = \sum_{j=1}^{n} \frac{1}{E[M_c]} \mathrm{Cov}[K_{\ell c}, \nu_{ijc}] + \bar{\theta}_\ell \sum_{j=1}^{n} \frac{1}{E[M_c]} \mathrm{Cov}[K_{ic}, w_{jc}].$$

It is quite clear that the terms b_i and c_i have the potential for confounding with the other price terms in (8.8).

Now let us look the two non-random terms a_i and d_i. The following are three possible scenarios. (i) Both terms are typically small. We discuss this scenario in Section 10.9. (ii) The term $(a_i - d_i)$ can be approximated by a non-zero constant. This is plausible, as it is common practice to use an intercept term in the estimation of the demand system. (iii) The term $(a_i - d_i)$ can be written in the form

$$a_i - d_i = x_{oi} + x_{1i} d(\log \bar{Q}) + \sum_{j=1}^{n} x_{2ij} \left[d(\log p_j) - \sum_{\ell=1}^{n} \bar{\theta}_\ell d(\log p_\ell) \right],$$

where the x values are constants. Thus $(a_i - d_i)$ can be confounded with the other terms in (8.8). However, we believe that a_i and d_i are typically small.

Now we shall confound the terms b_i and c_i into the price term of (8.8). We define

$$e_{ij} = \frac{1}{E[M_c]} \mathrm{Cov}[K_{ic}, w_{jc}].$$

Substituting the expressions of b_i and c_i in equation (8.9) into equation (8.8), with the remainder term $(a_i - d_i)$ dropped, we obtain

$$\bar{w}_i d(\log \bar{q}_i) = \bar{\theta}_i d(\log \bar{Q}) + \sum_{j=1}^{n} (\bar{\nu}_{ij} - e_{ij}) \left[d(\log p_j) - \sum_{\ell=1}^{n} \bar{\theta}_\ell d(\log p_\ell) \right],$$

$$i=1,\ldots,n. \tag{8.10}$$

Hence e_{ij} can be considered as the aggregation bias in the (i,j)-*th* relative price coefficient $\bar{\nu}_{ij}$. This aggregation bias e_{ij} will typically be zero for the reasons outlined in Barnett (1979a). Even though the macro relative price coefficients, $\bar{\nu}_{ij}$, are symmetric, the coefficients of the relative price in equation (8.10), $\bar{\nu}_{ij} - e_{ij}$, are not symmetric.

10.9 The Remainder Terms

In this section first we shall consider the remainder terms a_i and d_i in equation (8.9) and discuss the conditions under which these terms become negligible. We then consider the overall remainder term Z_i in (8.8).

Since $E[K_{ic}] = 0$, we have

$$a_i = \frac{1}{E[M_c]} \rho_{1i} \{\mathrm{var}[K_{ic}]\ \mathrm{var}[d(\log M_c)]\}^{\frac{1}{2}}$$

and

$$d_i = \sum_{\ell=1}^{n} \sum_{j=1}^{n} \frac{1}{E[M_c]} \left[\rho_{2ij\ell} \{\mathrm{var}[K_{\ell c}]\ \mathrm{var}[\nu_{ijc}]\}^{\frac{1}{2}} \right.$$

$$\left. + \bar{\theta}_\ell \rho_{3ij} \{\mathrm{var}[K_{ic}]\ \mathrm{var}[w_{jc}]\}^{\frac{1}{2}} \right] d(\log p_\ell)$$

where ρ_{1i} is the correlation between K_{ic} and $d(\log M_c)$; $\rho_{2ij\ell}$ is the correlation between $K_{\ell c}$ and ν_{ijc}; and ρ_{3ij} is the correlation between K_{ic} and w_{jc}. Obviously, when every marginal share θ_{ic} is equal to $\bar{\theta}_i$ then

$K_{ic} = 0$. Hence a_i and d_i are exactly zero. The other possibility that a_i and d_i are zero is that $\rho_{1i} = 0$; $\rho_{2ij\ell} = 0$ for every (j,ℓ) and $\rho_{3ij} = 0$ for every j. However, in general, this will not be the case. By Schwartz' inequality we have cov $[K_{ic}, d(\log M_c)]$, $\mathrm{cov}[K_{\ell c}, \nu_{ijc}]$ and $\mathrm{cov}[K_{ic}, w_{jc}]$ are bounded by $[\mathrm{var}(K_{ic})\ \mathrm{var}[d(\log M_c)]^{\frac{1}{2}}$, $[\mathrm{var}(K_{\ell c})\ \mathrm{var}(\nu_{ijc})]^{\frac{1}{2}}$ and $[\mathrm{var}(K_{ic})\ \mathrm{var}(w_{jc})]^{\frac{1}{2}}$, respectively. For a developed economy we would expect the variability that induces randomness into $(K_{ic}, d(\log M_c))$, $(K_{\ell c}, \nu_{ijc})$ and (K_{ic}, w_{jc}) to be small relative to $E[M_c]$. Hence the terms a_i and d_i will typically be small.

Considering the overall remainder term Z_i given by (8.8) in the form,

$$Z_i = \frac{1}{E[M_c]} \left[\tau_i \{\mathrm{var}[K_{ic}]\ \mathrm{var}[V_c]\}^{\frac{1}{2}} \right.$$

$$\left. - \sum_{j=1}^{n} \sum_{\ell=1}^{n} \rho_{2ij\ell} \{\mathrm{var}[K_{\ell c}]\ \mathrm{var}[\nu_{ijc}]\}^{\frac{1}{2}} d(\log p_\ell) \right]$$

where τ_i is the correlation between K_{ic} and V_c. Following the same arguments as above, we can show that Z_i will also typically be small.

10.10 Properties of the Macrocoefficients

Now we shall consider the properties of the macrocoefficients $\bar{\theta}_i$, $\bar{\pi}_{ij}$, $\bar{\nu}_{ij}$ and $\bar{\phi}$.

Marginal Shares

If we sum both sides of the equation

$$\bar{\theta}_i = \frac{E[M_c \theta_{ic}]}{E[M_c]}$$

over i=1,...,n, we get

$$\sum_{i=1}^{n} \bar{\theta}_i = \sum_{i=1}^{n} \frac{E[M_c \theta_{ic}]}{E[M_c]}. \tag{10.1}$$

The micro marginal shares θ_{ic} satisfy

$$\sum_{i=1}^{n} \theta_{ic} = 1.$$

If we multiply both sides of the above equation by M_c and divide by $E[M_c]$, we get

$$\sum_{i=1}^{n} \frac{M_c \theta_{ic}}{E[M_c]} = \frac{M_c}{E[M_c]}. \tag{10.2}$$

Taking the mathematical expectation of both sides of (10.2) and using (10.1) gives

$$\sum_{i=1}^{n} \bar{\theta}_i = 1, \tag{10.3}$$

which is the macro version of (10.2).

Slutsky Coefficients

The symmetry property of $\bar{\pi}_{ij}$ is obvious from equation (5.1) and the symmetry of the π_{ijc}'s. Summing both sides of the equation

$$\bar{\pi}_{ij} = \frac{E[M_c \pi_{ijc}]}{E[M_c]}$$

over j=1,...,n, we get

$$\sum_{j=1}^{n} \bar{\pi}_{ij} = \sum_{j=1}^{n} \frac{E[M_c \pi_{ijc}]}{E[M_c]}. \tag{10.4}$$

The micro Slutsky coefficients satisfy demand homogeneity

$$\sum_{j=1}^{n} \pi_{ijc} = 0.$$

If we multiply both sides of the above equation by M_c and divide by $E[M_c]$, we obtain

$$\sum_{j=1}^{n} \frac{M_c \pi_{ijc}}{E[M_c]} = 0. \tag{10.5}$$

Taking the mathematical expectation of both sides of (10.5) and using (10.4) we get

$$\sum_{j=1}^{n} \bar{\pi}_{ij} = 0, \tag{10.6}$$

which is the micro version of (4.3).

To prove that $[\bar{\pi}_{ij}]$ is negative semidefinite with rank n-1, consider the quadratic form

$$\sum_{i=1}^{n} \sum_{j=1}^{n} x_i \bar{\pi}_{ij} x_j = \sum_{i=1}^{n} \sum_{j=1}^{n} x_i \frac{E[M_c \pi_{ijc}]}{E[M_c]} x_j \tag{10.7}$$

$$= \frac{1}{E[M_c]} \left[E\left[M_c \sum_{i=1}^{n} \sum_{j=1}^{n} x_i \pi_{ijc} x_j\right]\right] \leq 0,$$

where we have used the fact that $[\pi_{ijc}]$ is negative semidefinite with rank n-1. Thus the macro Slutsky matrix $[\bar{\pi}_{ij}]$ is also negative semidefinite with rank n-1. Equation (10.7) is the analogue of the corresponding condition on the microparameters.

Price Coefficients

Taking the sum of both sides of the equation

$$\bar{\nu}_{ij} = \frac{E[M_c \nu_{ijc}]}{E[M_c]}$$

over j=1,...,n yields

$$\sum_{j=1}^{n} \bar{\nu}_{ij} = \sum_{j=1}^{n} \frac{E[M_c \nu_{ijc}]}{E[M_c]}. \tag{10.8}$$

The micro price coefficients satisfy the relation

$$\sum_{j=1}^{n} \nu_{ijc} = \phi_c \theta_{ic}.$$

Multiplying both sides of the above equation by M_c and dividing by $E[M_c]$ yield

$$\sum_{j=1}^{n} \frac{\nu_{ijc} M_c}{E[M_c]} = \frac{\phi_c M_c \theta_{ic}}{E[M_c]}. \tag{10.9}$$

Taking mathematical expectation of both sides of the above equation, use the property $\phi_c M_c \theta_{ic} = \phi_c M_c \bar{\theta}_i + \phi_c K_{ic}$, $E[K_{ic}] = 0$ and equation (10.8) we obtain

$$\sum_{j=1}^{n} \bar{\nu}_{ij} = \bar{\phi}\, \bar{\theta}_i + \alpha_i, \tag{10.10}$$

where

$$\alpha_i = \frac{\mathrm{Cov}[K_{ic}, \phi_c]}{E[M_c]}.$$

Equation (10.10) is the macro versions of the equation in (7.2), except the last term of (10.10). To analyse the size of the remainder term α_i, we write the above expression in the form

$$\alpha_i = \frac{1}{E[M_c]} \rho_{4i} \{\mathrm{var}[K_{ic}]\ \mathrm{var}[\phi_c]\}^{\frac{1}{2}},$$

where ρ_{4i} is the correlation between K_{ic} and ϕ_c. Obviously, when every marginal share θ_{ic} is equal to $\bar{\theta}_i$ then $K_{ic} = 0$. Hence α_i is exactly zero. The other possibility that α_i equals zero is that $\rho_{4i} = 0$. However, in general, this will not be the case. Following the same arguments as in the last section, using Schwartz' inequality we can show that the term α_i will typically be small.

Now we shall show that the macro price coefficient matrix $[\bar{\nu}_{ij}]$ is symmetric negative definite. As the micro price coefficients ν_{ijc}'s are symmetric, from the definition of $\bar{\nu}_{ij}$, it follows that the $\bar{\nu}_{ij}$'s are also symmetric. To prove negative definiteness, consider the quadratic form

$$\sum_{i=1}^{n} \sum_{j=1}^{n} x_i \bar{\nu}_{ij} x_j = \frac{1}{E[M_c]} \sum_{i=1}^{n} \sum_{j=1}^{n} x_i E[M_c \nu_{ijc}] x_j$$

$$= \frac{1}{E[M_c]} E\left[M_c \sum_{i=1}^{n} \sum_{j=1}^{n} x_i \nu_{ijc} x_j\right] < 0,$$

where we have used the fact that the matrices $[\nu_{ijc}]$ are negative definite for every c. Therefore the matrix $[\bar{\nu}_{ij}]$ is symmetric negative definite.

References

Barnett, W.A. (1979a). 'Theoretical Foundations for the Rotterdam Model,' *The Review of Economic Studies* 46: 109-130.

Barnett, W.A. (1979b). 'The Joint Allocation of Leisure and Goods Expenditure,' *Econometrica* 47(3): 539-563.

Barnett, W.A. (1981). *Consumer Demand and Labour Supply*. Amsterdam: North-Holland Publishing Company.

Christensen, L.R., D.W. Jorgenson and L.J. Lau (1973). 'Transcendental Logarithmic Production Frontiers,' *Review of Economics and Statistics* 55: 28-45.

Deaton, A.S. and J. Muellbauer (1980). 'An Almost Ideal Demand System,' *American Economic Review* 70: 312-326.

Diewert, W.E. (1974). 'The Application of Duality Theory,' in *Frontiers of Quantitative Economics*, Vol.2, M. Intriligator and D.A. Kendric (eds). Amsterdam: North Holland.

Mountain, D.C. (1988). 'The Rotterdam Model: An Approximation in Variable Space,' *Econometrica* 56(2): 477-484.

Selvanathan, E.A. (1987). *Explorations in Consumer Demand.* Ph.D. Thesis, Murdoch University.

Selvanathan, E.A. (1991). 'Further Results on Aggregation of Differential Demand System.' *The Review of Economic Studies* 58, 799-805.

Shafer, W. and H. Sonnenschein (1982). 'Market Demand and Excess Demand Functions,' in K.J. Arrow and M.D. Intriligator (eds.), *Handbook of Mathematical Economics*, Vol.II, Amsterdam: North-Holland Publishing Company.

Sonnenschein, H. (1973). 'The Utility Hypothesis and Market Demand Theory,' *Western Economic Journal* 11: 404-410.

Stoker, T.M. (1993). 'Empirical Approaches to the Problem of Aggregation Over Individuals,' *Journal of Economic Literature* 31: 1827-1874.

Theil, H. (1971). *Principles of Econometrics*. New York: John Wiley and Sons.

Theil, H. (1975/76). *Theory and Measurement of Consumer Demand*. Two volumes. Amsterdam: North Holland.

Index

MIX
Papier aus verantwortungsvollen Quellen
Paper from responsible sources
FSC® C105338

If you have any concerns about our products,
you can contact us on
ProductSafety@springernature.com

In case Publisher is established outside the EU,
the EU authorized representative is:
Springer Nature Customer Service Center GmbH
Europaplatz 3, 69115 Heidelberg, Germany

Printed by Libri Plureos GmbH
in Hamburg, Germany